Caretakers of Our Common House

Caretakers of Our Common House

Women's Development in Communities of Faith

Carol Lakey Hess

Abingdon Press
Nashville

CARETAKERS OF OUR COMMON HOUSE:
WOMEN'S DEVELOPMENT IN COMMUNITIES OF FAITH

Copyright © 1997 by Abingdon Press

Library of Congress Cataloging-in-Publication Data

Hess, Carol Lakey, 1957-
    Caretakers of our common house : women's development in communities of faith / Carol Lakey Hess.
    p. cm.
    Includes bibliographical references and index.
    ISBN 0-687-00963-4 (pbk. : alk. paper)
    1. Women in Christianity. 2. Women—Socialization. I. Title.
BV639.W7H47   1997
270.8'29'082—dc21   97-29450
                                                     CIP

Unless otherwise noted, Scripture quotations are from the New Revised Standard Version Bible. Copyright 1989 by the Division of Christian Education of the National Council of the Churches of Christ in the USA. Used by permission.

Scripture quotations noted NIV are taken from the *Holy Bible, New International Version.* Copyright © *1973, 1978, 1984* International Bible Society. Used by permission of Zondervan Bible Publishers. All rights reserved.

Scripture quotations noted NEB are from *The New English Bible.* © The Delegates of the Oxford University Press and The Syndics of the Cambridge University Press 1961, 1970. Reprinted by permission.

Poem by Rosemary Catalano Mitchell and Gail Anderson Ricciuti, *Birthings and Blessings: Liberating Worship Services for the Inclusive Church* (New York: The Crossroad Publishing Co., 1991) adapted from "The Valor of Vashti" from *Eve and After* by Thomas John Carlisle (Grand Rapids, Mich.: Eerdmans, 1984). Used by permission.

Excerpts from COLD SASSY TREE. Copyright © 1984 by Olive Ann Burns. Reprinted by permission of Ticknor & Fields/Houghton Mifflin Co. All rights reserved.

Selected lines from "Creatio Ex Nihilo" by Kathleen O. Reed used by permission of the author.

To Ernie
my love

97 98 99 00 01 02 03 04 05 06—10 9 8 7 6 5 4 3 2 1

MANUFACTURED IN THE UNITED STATES OF AMERICA

Contents

Acknowledgments

When my older son, Nathan, was a young child, he often asked penetrating questions (he still does, come to think of it). After learning that his ancestors had suffered a great deal, he asked, "Mom, why doesn't God make the world the way it should be?" We mused together on this for a while. I didn't have much of an answer, and I still don't. But, I did say to him that God is with us. Then he offered, "Maybe sometimes God uses us ordinary people to help the world." Soon after that conversation, Nathan sent half of a rather generous birthday check to an organization that feeds hungry children. My wonderful son hasn't stopped raising questions and posing visions, and he continues to take his own role in the future of our world seriously.

In many ways, this book is part of my response to Nathan's question. I don't think the world is the way it should be with regard to a lot of things, especially its treatment of girls and women. But I do think God is with me and with us in the prophetic cry, and I think God is calling us to work to renew relationships between women and men. This book is one ordinary woman's attempt to make a difference. A few children were fed for many days with Nathan's check; I hope a few children and adults will be fed by this book. I begin these acknowledgments thanking my firstborn for the way in which he has, for fifteen years, raised good questions and made faithful responses, which have taught me.

God has gifted me with many people who are not only behind this book in one way or another but who have also made this world a better place.

There are numerous wise women who have encouraged, prodded, taught, and influenced me over the years. The following top the list. My teachers Freda Gardner and Katharine Doob Sakenfeld have taught me much, yet treat me as a peer. Our sage in the office, Kay Vogen, always gives the best advice but never imposes it unsolicited. Longtime friends Doris Weatherby and Deborah Vermaat continue to amaze me with their capacity to understand and respond to the particularities of life. My colleagues and prayer partners Karla Endicott, Nora Tubbs Tisdale, and Janet Weathers have sustained me in mind, spirit, and body; their ideas, their prayers, and their sharing of bread have been a godsend. My colleague down the hall, Elsie McKee, has encouraged me at key moments during the making of this book.

In addition to the above named, other colleagues from near and far have been willing to engage the ideas and passions of this book from its beginnings. Rick Osmer and Jim Loder encouraged me at many points and always gave rapid feedback to pieces I asked them to read. Maria Harris and Thomas Groome read and responded to an earlier work of mine in ways that led to the birth of this book; the Lilly Endowment made this possible. Speaking of Lilly, the thinking of my former teacher, Craig Dykstra, continues to impact me very deeply. I thank my colleague Daniel Migliore, who is a liberating theologian in word and deed, and with whom I had a wonderful time teaching a course called "Man and Woman in Theological Perspective," which contributed to this book. Those who were doctoral students with me remain valued friends and coveted conversation partners: Frank Rogers, Jr., Don Richter, and Elizabeth Frykberg. Mario A. Camposeco makes my work possible in so many ways and graciously tolerates my piles of books and papers. Dana Wright and Leanne Simmons have provided research assistance; I thank them for their diligence in digging up resources and for their thoughtful and expert engagement with the ideas of this book. I'm particularly grateful for the fascinating discussions (and contributions to this book arising out of them) Leanne Simmons and I have had concerning theology and eating disorders.

There are extended family members who have been important to this work. My mother, Thea Schlösser Lakey, has had a tough lot in life; yet she kept going when many people would have given up. My sister, "Aims" (Amy Lakey Henderson), has unwavering confidence in my abilities and forgives me for much. My sister-in-law, Janet Hess, listened to me and pulled for me during difficult periods in the writing of this book. My mother-in-law, June Hess, sent me numerous articles that informed and enlivened this book; my father-in-law, Carl Hess, spent good times with my children, the most memorable of which was the ten hours (yes, ten) he devoted to turning over rocks and logs (not a one went unturned) on a hike with his newt- and snake-hunting grandson, Paul. (I do not, however, thank him for the successful outcome of that hunt.) Although she died before I met her, I feel that I know and owe an immense debt of gratitude to Marie (Hess) Sorenson for the wonderful impact she had on her grandson, Ernie.

And now, last but hardly least, I thank my immediate family. My spunky, sassy, sensitive, and ever-searching children, Nathan, Marie, and Paul, are my three favorite theologians. I have learned more about God from them than from anyone else. They are relentless pursuers of justice in our household, and they dare to go theologically where angels fear to tread. I have also learned a lot about God's creatures from my kids; our dog, birds, and menagerie of snakes and lizards and assorted other reptiles have taken me where I never on my own would have gone. (I am trusting that this journey is part of God's good intentions for me.) My sharpest critics (they are usually right), my kids are also my greatest supporters.

Those who are familiar with my life know that no dedication can do justice to the contribution my husband, Ernie, has made to my work and life. Although I like to kid around and say that I 'liberated' him by nudging him into the world of caring for children and home, he entered this world willingly and wholeheartedly. He is a pro-feminist husband and father, working hard for a world of equal opportunity for girls and women. Ernie and I are joint caretakers in our common house. Our twenty years of loving, studying, arguing, supporting, working, dreaming, and following God together have sometimes been hard work (especially for him, I'm sure) but always a blessing. To my best friend, cherished colleague, everblazing flame, and life-partner, I dedicate this book.

Introduction

"When the king was merry with wine, he commanded [his officials] to bring Queen Vashti before the king, wearing the royal crown, in order to show the peoples and the officials her beauty; for she was fair to behold. But Queen Vashti refused to come at the king's command conveyed by the eunuchs. At this the king was enraged, and his anger burned within him."
—Esther 1:10-12

"Vashti said no. This is the entirety of her direct portrayal, yet her character is an intriguing one. It is drawn in silhouette by the contrast between her 'no' and what it negates."
—Michael V. Fox[1]

"God's power and glory are present in our human condition no matter what the dimension of our suffering, because in Christ's suffering God has chosen to stand with us. Yet when we look to see this power and glory in human life, it shines through most clearly in those whose lives are confronting the suffering by saying no to dehumanizing power."
—Letty Russell[2]

J ust recently my father-in-law, my husband, and I were discussing something, and my father-in-law told me to 'sit there and look pretty.' I was very offended by this remark but didn't say anything."[3]

This comment, which a student in one of my courses found in a woman's magazine, was made by a young woman. Immediately, I thought of Vashti when the student showed the quote to me. The young woman who was told to "sit there and look pretty," unlike Vashti, let the offense go by without resistance. Does it have to be that way, I wonder? Are women fated to not only "sit there and look pretty," but also to sit there and take offensive commands? This is one of the questions I am pursuing in this book. It is not an impartial quest, however. My daughter is in my mind as I write this book. She is now twelve, poised at that "perilous divide" between being a girl and being a woman.[4] I watch cautiously to see how she is being socialized. I celebrate the opportunities she has as a girl that I didn't have, while at the same time I worry about a culture that reacts against the strides my generation has made. She can play on sports teams and her teachers affirm her for her math abilities; it hasn't occurred to her to hide her intelligence in a mixed gender setting. And yet, she is continually bombarded as never before with negative and demeaning images of girls and women. North American culture is described by Mary Pipher as "a girl-destroying place," a place that "causes girls to abandon their true selves and take up false selves."[5] Our culture tends to train girls to "sit there and look pretty" and frequently either ignores or chastises those who want to use their minds in meaningful ways. According to Susan Faludi, the cultural "backlash" against the "handful of small and hard-won victories that the feminist movement did manage to win for women"[6] threatens to make my daughter's future perhaps less hopeful than my own. Will my wonderfully strong-willed daughter fight for her true self and refuse to accept the command to "sit there and look pretty"? Or will the "will" I so admire and fiercely nurture give way to a false self? What sources of support will she have in her development? *Can caring families and communities of faith, specifically the church, make a difference in the outcome of my daughter's development and in the development of other girls and women?*[7]

I believe the answer to this latter question is a resounding "yes." Yes, families and the church can make a difference in the development of girls and women. And, yes, that difference can be in the direction of supporting the development of our daughters'—and even our sisters' and our mothers'—selves. The positive role of the church is not, however, inevitable. The church has, to understate it, a checkered history with regard to girls and women; though Jewish and Christian history is laced with protest against misogyny, these are "thin traditions," which often have been repressed. Churches are too often girl-denying institutions. This is changing, but it is far from transformed; backlash looms ominously on the horizon of church as well.

It is not, however, flagrant misogyny that is the biggest threat to my daughter's future. My concern in this book is not primarily those churches that continue to explicitly promote the subordination of women. I certainly tackle explicit sexism in this book; but girls like my daughter will be more influenced by churches that subtly hinder the development of the self in girls and women. It is implicit and unrecognized "girl-denying" that threatens the future of girls reared in mainline churches.

Beginning with Valerie Saiving's landmark essay in 1960, feminist theologians have pointed out that a male bias in theology can inadvertently (it is sometimes intentional) hinder women's growth. I return to that argument in chapter 1, paying particular attention to critiques leveled against the theology of Reinhold Niebuhr, which emphasizes self-sacrifice. While the theological case against male-biased theology has been made a number of times, it has not been sufficiently directed toward life in communities of faith. I specifically attend to the way in which theologies of self-sacrifice—which are pervasive in many churches that proclaim women's equality—thwart both spiritual and psychological self-development by subverting necessary self-assertion. This critique of male-bias is supported both by recovering neglected strands of the Reformed tradition and reconstructing narrowly conceived elements.

In chapters 2 and 3, I look at different perspectives on cognitive and moral development, attending to the interplay between theology and human development. In chapter 2, engaging the work of Robert Kegan, I look at the way in which a theology of self-sacrifice could hinder the move toward self-differentiation and cognitive autonomy. This is not simply a cognitive issue, however; it is also a spiritual one. As I argue, in order for the kind of "spiritual awakening" that enables women to critically reflect on the reality of sexism, an element of autonomy is needed. Yet, I do not pose autonomy and independence as the primary modes of self-development; I understand the importance of caring and connection. Thus, in chapter 3 I look at the "self-in-relation." In this chapter, I build on Carol Gilligan's description of mature caring that avoids self-abnegation while preserving relationality, reinforcing certain features of Gilligan's work that are surprisingly underemphasized in popular usages of her argument. Further, returning to issues raised in chapter 1, I suggest that a comprehensive understanding of caring includes empathetic caring, conversational caring, and prophetic caring.

Chapter 4, building on themes raised in chapter 3, looks at the nurture of girls' "true selves" in families and communities. Specific attention is given to the dangerous, but significant, "prophetic voice" expressed by girls in the form of eating disorders. This chapter is highly personal; it weaves my own experience with eating disorders into a discussion of the research. The importance of relationships in a diverse community will be further pursued in chapter 5, where I look at the varieties of ways women negotiate life choices. Building on the Genesis tale of Leah and Rachel, who "wrestled mightily" with one another, I look at the way in which women of difference face tensions but can work together to promote varieties of self-development.

Chapter 6 introduces "conversational education" as a means for promoting the development of women in communities of faith. Conversational education, informed by Gilligan's description of genuine relationships that include both self and other, is characterized by what I call "hard dialogue and deep connections." Avoiding the twin dangers of hostile argumentation and surface agreement, both of which are particularly inimical to the education of women, conversational education promotes dissent and differentness in a context of hospitality and community. Chapter 7 turns to leadership, drawing on the story of Deborah in Judges 4 and 5. Deborah—Woman of Fire, Mother of Israel, Wise-Woman Judge—inspires a vision of caretaking that is passionate, empathetic, and wise.

Throughout this book I weave into the discussion various biblical narratives and women's stories. I do this not simply to illustrate my points. I do it to recover liberating texts, remember silenced texts, and offer alternative perspectives on texts that have been interpreted in ways harmful to women. These narratives are central to the purposes of this book. It is my hope that the incorporation of forgotten texts and reinterpretation of harmful texts will affect the shape of preaching and teaching in communities of faith.

One cautionary word before I embark on this "conversation" about "women's" development. Writing about "women" is a tricky task. Women, like all other groups, are irreducibly diverse. Different women face different opportunities for and different barriers to development. In fact, it is almost impossible for me to locate my own position as a woman. I have, on different occasions, been referred to as a WASP and as a woman of color. As an adult, I have mostly enjoyed the privileges of a WASP; but my heritage is only part "Anglo-Saxon." Yes, I am a white North American Protestant woman. But, I am also a daughter of the Holocaust: my Jewish mother is the sole survivor of her immediate family. I am a more distant granddaughter of the Trail of Tears: my great-grandmother on my father's side was full Cherokee. My parents bore, and passed on, both deep scars from their pain-filled legacies and some skills for survival in a hostile world. But, these skills are mixed. My mother, who fled to and found refuge in the United States, experiences this country as a haven from terror; she taught me to assimilate. My father, whose Cherokee ancestors were indigenous to this country, seethes from anger at the near genocide of his grandmother's people; he taught me to be suspicious. I grew up poor—at times impoverished, even homeless—but I have had a good education, spurred by the backbreaking efforts of my mother to locate our family in places with good schools and funded by government aid and generous scholarships that enabled me to pursue higher education. Though this country failed to see the humanity of my Cherokee ancestors and responded too late to the Holocaust to save my grandparents and uncles, it has been good to me. And yet, half Jew and eighth Cherokee that I am, I know I carry the membership card to the American success club—though of mixed lineage, to all observers I am "anglo." To a great degree, and to my increasing sadness, I have forgotten my heritage and assimilated to the dominant culture; and yet, in other ways, I continually uncover both "red roots" of my identity [8] and feel solidarity with those who wore "yellow stars."[9] Thus, I cannot say that I am a white, rather privileged, middle-class American woman (though that is the way I now live), and neither can I say that I am lower-middle-class outsider-American woman (though that is an indelible aspect of my identity). Yes, women are irreducibly diverse; sometimes that diversity resides in a single person. I have woven the stories of many types of women into this book, and I hope the tapestry is rich enough to connect with the experiences of many different women.[10]

A Feminist Work in Practical Theology: an Interdisciplinary Conversation

Even as my identity is a "converstion" among traditions and experiences, so is this book. The methodology is **practical-theological**; I integrate *theology and biblical studies, the human sciences, life realities* and experience, and the *practices of the church*. All of these partners mutually illumine and critique one another in the work of practical theology.[11] The aim of practical theology—discerning God's call (Holy Spirit to human spirit) for just and righteous life together in this world and in particular concrete communities of faith—makes 'theology' a privileged partner in this interdisciplinary conversation. Thus, chapter 1 is a theological exploration of sin, grace, and selfhood, which orients the rest of the book; what unfolds might be termed "anthropology in theological perspective."[12] The privileged position of theology in the work of practical theology, however, means that practical theologians are obligated to listen *more* carefully, not less, to the other partners in the conversation. My Reformed interest in human selfhood and the empowerment of the human spirit—and the attendant doctrines of sin and grace—is foundational; yet studies of the developmental needs of adolescent girls and young women and the experiences of women in communities of faith illumine, and in places correct, my inherited understanding and articulation of the doctrines of human sin and grace.

This work in practical theology is unabashedly **feminist**. It names the flourishing of women and men together as a theological vision; it uses femi-

nist theories of the self to hold theology, psychology, and pedagogy accountable to women's growth; it draws on women's experience in life and in communities of faith as a theoretical resource; it learns from and seeks to impact
the practices of the church so that they become more faithful to human community in its fullness; and it consciously involves the location of the
researcher as a part of the inquiry.[13]

My joint commitment to the Reformed tradition and feminism determines
the dominant themes in this book. Breaking the hold of idols (especially the
idols of narrow images for God and stereotyped ideals for women and men),
facing the reality of sin and partiality of vision (particularly the partiality of doctrines and visions shaped without the input of the voices of women and others),
claiming the importance of the priesthood of all believers (including female
believers), maintaining both an appreciaton for and a critical perspective on and
bold reassessment of tradition, and holding open the possibility for individ-
ual/minority prophetic cries in the midst of a dominant persuasion ("Here I
stand, so help me God!") are cherished legacies of both Reformed theology and
feminism, and these legacies drive, ground, and permeate this book.

I have brought a number of disciplines into this discussion of women's
development, and I hope to engage appreciative and critical conversation
partners from those areas. While my most specific aim is to provide a
resource that will influence the training and education of future leaders in
seminaries and communities of faith, I would be pleased to see this book
make a wider contribution to the cultural climate for women's development.
Let me also note here that I am not disinterested in male developmental
issues. As the mother of two sons, the wife of one husband, the sister of one
brother, and the colleague of many men, I am worried about their future, and
I care about what happens to boys and men as well. Along with bell hooks, I
believe that men are women's "comrades in the struggle" for a just world.[14]
Although I have given clues to some of my key concerns regarding boys and
men, a full address of these issues will come in another book. This book calls
us in families and communities of faith to say "no" to the dehumanization of
girls and women and "yes" to their development.

SAYING "NO" TO DEHUMANIZATION AND "YES" TO DEVELOPMENT

In the first chapter of the biblical book of Esther, Queen Vashti is punished for asserting herself before the king.[15] In an effort to thwart further
occasions for—and wider participation in—female brazenness, the king

and his courtiers set in motion a royal decree that ensures that every man will be "master in his own house" (Esther 1:22). Vashti is deposed, the decree is heralded, and the potential for female independence and development seems securely quashed.

The title of this book, *Caretakers of Our Common House,* is a play on and reimagining of the Vashti tragedy. Vashti's story itself is symbolic of the struggles that women experience as they seek to assert themselves in contexts where they are expected to submit to and care only about others. However, women seek neither to simply reverse the reigning paradigm (and become "masters" in their own houses) nor to narrow the paradigm (and care only about "their own" house). Women are seeking to be caretakers of themselves, of others, and of communities of faith in ways that support both their individual development as well as their potential for caring leadership. This book argues for an educational process in communities of faith that nurtures women toward being caretakers of their own house (self) and of our common house (the community of faith).

I will begin this book by retelling Vashti's story. I do this for two reasons. One, the story has been seriously neglected in Christian communities. When the stories of women are told, it is usually the stories of women who have been submissive and nurturing toward others. Strong and assertive women are not typically evoked. Two, the text itself, read in light of gender issues, beckons us to pay closer attention to its women; indeed, the storyteller leaves us hints that he (or perhaps "she") thinks Vashti and Esther are important heroines. These hints, however, have been virtually neglected until recent times.

While I resonate deeply with Vashti, it is important for me to anticipate chapter 5 and note that she is not the only heroine for girls and women. Her story is an important memory, and it is one that I am boldly retrieving. Yet, Vashti is surrounded by a community of other sisters, of whom Esther is not the least, who took different paths. One of the most important points this book will make is that women of different personalities, decision-making strategies, and life vocations should all be nurtured in communities of faith. Vashti's story is a story we all need to hear; Vashti's "no" is an option of which all should be aware. Not everyone will follow Vashti's example, and not everyone should. But everyone must know that she is a part of our tradition, and not an insignificant part.

Vashti: A Pioneer for Women's Rights

In many ways, Vashti is an unlikely heroine to choose to frame a book on women's development.[16] Mentioned briefly in the story of *Esther,* her claim to fame is that she refused to be paraded in front of a group of men and faded ignobly from the dramatic narrative. She is replaced in the king's harem by Esther, who takes center stage as the heroine of the tale. In the annual enactment of this story during the Jewish festival of Purim, young girls abjure from playing Vashti and yearn to play Esther. The audience may even "boo" Vashti's entrance, identifying her as a rebellious and undesirable creature. However, even the anger fades quickly and Vashti is soon sidelined and forgotten.

Yet, Vashti actually plays a key role in the story of Esther and in the history of women. The unlikeliness that a queen would exhibit such courage as to go against the king's command (even an unreasonable one) is one argument given as evidence against the historicity of this story.[17] Vashti is frequently dismissed as a literary device for paving the way for Esther's entrance into the drama.[18] Yet the narrative itself, and current interpretations of its meaning, allow us to let the spotlight linger on Vashti long enough to see in her an important character. Whether or not she actually was a historical personage, she is a figure in world history; and she is a foremother to those who have made—or will make—history against the tide of cultural role expectations. But few know of her heroic legacy.

Though we know little about this woman, we do know some things about the setting in which we find her. It is generally assumed that the character and reign of Ahasuerus is based on the historical Xerxes I. We can infer from historical sources, as well as from the description of the young women in this story, that one such as Vashti would have been groomed for submission to male authority, obeisance to the king, obedience to the law, training in feminine grace and appeal, and perhaps intensive beauty treatments. There were exceptions to this. Fifth-century B.C.E. historian Herodotus, who wrote an engaging history of Persia, relates how Artemisia, upon her husband's death, served in a military expedition against the Greeks with "manliness."[19] In fact, tales of her exploits were used by the king to humiliate his "womanly" men into greater bravery. Artemisia earned respect for her cunning, and she was even sought out to give advice to Xerxes. The irony passing right by this ancient historian, Herodotus dispassionately reports that on one occasion, when Xerxes is pleased with Artemisia's counsel, he sends her off to take care of his bastard children as a reward! Even "manly" women could not escape their designated roles.

Under Xerxes' rule, crossing the king could at times lead to unexpected clemency; however, the general expectation was that even mere disagreement with the king would be "the end" of a person. When one of Xerxes' loyal subjects asked that the eldest of his five sons be spared from battle so that one might live to carry on the family responsibilities, Herodotus reports that the enraged king not only refused his request but cut the son in two and set a half on each side of the road as trail markers for the army to march through. As if to spoof his own nature, the impulsive king is reputed to have lashed and fettered the stormy *sea* as punishment for "wronging" him. In such an empire, young maidens could be rounded up for the king's harem, young boys would be conscripted into service as eunuchs, and children of nobility were on occasion buried alive as a sacrifice to the gods. Such is the historical backdrop into which the tale of Vashti is spun.

The story of *Esther* opens with King Ahasuerus hosting a long (180 days) and opulent house party. For the final (week-long) feast, "drinking was by flagons, without restraint; for the king had given orders to all the officials of his palace to do as each desired." This lavish feast (literally "drinking bout") apparently was for men only, as Queen Vashti gave a separate, sparely described banquet for the women. The implied reason for the king's six-month extravaganza is so the monarch could "display the great wealth of his kingdom and the splendor and pomp of his majesty." Just when he has seemingly saturated his audience with his displays, he announces, so to speak, that they "ain't seen nothin' yet." As a climax to this exhibition, Ahasuerus, "merry with wine," plans to show off *the* "crown" of his possessions. His beautiful wife, Queen Vashti, is ordered to appear *with* crown.

Incredibly, Vashti refuses to come at the king's command. Though the author gives no explanation for Vashti's momentous defiance, its setting in the midst of a drunken court, which at that point was occupied only by men, suggests personal reserve and integrity to be the motives.[20] It may also be possible that this woman, though groomed for compliance, is simply exerting her will.[21] However, given the inviolability of the command of the king (a recurring theme in the story), it is questionable that Vashti would risk her life on a whim. Whether out of modesty or whim, the queen imposes a restraint on the king—whose will is tantamount to law.

Such brazenness from the queen stirs up a furor in the court. Burning with anger at this defiance, Ahasuerus consults his legal counselors for a course of action. The king's adviser, afraid that other wives will follow suit, recommends that Vashti be deposed as queen. In a twist on Vashti's own intentions, she is ordered "never again to come before King Ahasuerus." Her royal position is to be given to one "better than she" (in other words, more obedient). To quell any further rebellion, a law is to be set in motion that declares every man should be master in his own house, and every woman should honor and obey her husband. The full panoply of Persian law, administration, and communications systems is deployed in a frantic effort to restore and ensure order in the kingdom.

However, there is a hint that the exertion of power is not full consolation for a now lonely king. Though he appears to have second thoughts about the harsh edict he imposed on Vashti,[22] the immutability of the law binds the autocrat to his own decree. To forestall further regret, the king's servants suggest that all the young virgins in the kingdom be gathered to the palace to vie for Vashti's vacated place in the harem. The girls are so gathered, and among them is Esther, a young Jewess who keeps her heritage a secret. Each girl receives twelve months of cosmetic and perfume treatment, which leads up to an all-determining night spent in the king's bed. Only those who delight the king are invited back. Esther finds favor with the king, and he sets the royal crown on her head, making her queen "instead of Vashti." A good excuse for celebration, the king gives another lavish banquet in Esther's honor. Vashti is now completely out of the picture. The drama moves on and weaves around an evil plot against the Jews, pitting Esther and her cousin Mordecai against the king's chief vizier, Haman.

Some interpreters identify Vashti's plunge into oblivion as a thinly veiled warning to brazen women. *Esther* may reflect a period of social turmoil when upper-class Israelite women were beginning to chafe at traditional societal expectations and constraints. "If this hypothesis is true," posits Alice Laffey, then "the details of this 'fiction' are meant to be didactic: do not mess with the system, or you too will be rejected."[23] The joining of Vashti's downfall with Esther's triumph through compliance is seen as an attempt to reinforce stereotypic feminine behavior. This interpretation may explain how the story has functioned in tradition. Though a considerable number of ancient rabbis were sympathetic to Vashti, others called the recalcitrant queen "wicked Vashti";[24] Martin Luther advised husbands to rebuke disobedient wives and to follow Ahasuerus's example if their wives resisted: "If she still refuses, get rid of her; take an Esther and let Vashti go, as King Ahasuerus did."[25] There are some literary features of the text that support an alternate reading of the *author's intention*. I believe that for the author Vashti was a heroine and not a villain; following Michael V. Fox, I wish to argue that in supporting Vashti we need not read "*against* the text." Though the author masterfully exposes the prevailing standard for female subordination, she or he does not condone them.

In the introductory narrative, told for comedic effect, the king is portrayed as a partier and boaster, having to rely on and exert external power.[26] Vashti, on the other hand, appears as proudly dignified, upheld by inner valor. While Ahasuerus can dispatch a law to force homage, the necessity of such a desperate measure reveals his personal ineffectiveness. Vashti has no strings to pull and no power brokers to defend her, and yet she earns silent honor. To be sure, Vashti suffers the consequences of refusing to ingratiate the men, but it is the latter's foolishness that is put into relief in the story. The author's expansive and farcical account of the king's excessive behavior stands in striking contrast with the sparse and serious reporting of the queen's resolute deportment. Michael V. Fox goes so far as to state that the author portrays the king as a "buffoon," "weak-willed, fickle, and self-centered."[27] He and his advisers are "a twittery, silly-headed, cowardly lot who need to hide behind a law to reinforce their status in their homes."[28] The author is making a crucial point here: outward success is not equal to inner worth. The king's elaborate palace and supreme power are facades; Vashti is the truly regal one. This implicit message was perhaps some solace to the majority of people in western Asia, whose dire poverty was mocked by such royal extravagance.

Even if he is sympathetic, the author does not romanticize Vashti's actions.[29] "The girl who pleases the king" was put in her stead, and Vashti was put in her place, so to speak. She broke out of the pattern expected of women, and she paid a great cost for doing it. But this does not necessarily imply that the author condemns Vashti's actions. In fact, the story line develops so that what Vashti sows, Esther reaps. Vashti's cause does not die with her banishment, it merely goes *sub rosa*. Though she could not fully blaze the trail, she enabled her successor, Esther, to have a foothold.[30]

In fact, Esther is no less rebellious. Vashti would not come forth when summoned; as the story unfolds, Esther comes to the king *without* summons.[31] Upon discovering that Ahasuerus, instigated by Haman, has sanctioned a pogrom (organized massacre) against all Jews, Esther risks her life to convince the king to rescind his murderous edict. Though entering the king's presence without a summons is punishable by death, retractable only if the monarch extends his scepter and welcomes the visitor, Esther takes the chance. Bedecked in her royal robes, the beautiful queen humbly seeks audience with the king; unpredictably, she is received. She dazzles and pleases Ahasuerus and Haman through a series of banquets. While the royal guard is lowered, this seemingly subservient queen persuades her husband to pronounce a counter-edict that implicates Haman and offsets the danger to the Jews. First Vashti would not lend her beauty to satisfy the king's boastful whims, and subsequently Esther uses her beauty to overturn his capricious laws. A woman's right to possess her own beauty has finally been vindicated.

The novella as a whole is replete with such "reversals of expectation," including episodes in which "the villain suffers the fate of his intended victim."[32] After Vashti's martyrdom, it is as if her spirit is resurrected; insubordinates gain full reign. Mordecai, who refuses to bow down to the imperious Haman, affronts the man in a way that is parallel to Vashti's provocation of Ahasuerus. As Vashti is deposed and women in general ordered to submit to their husbands, Mordecai is sentenced to be hanged and Jews in general massacred. However, as the Hebrew text announces, this time "the opposite happened."[33] Interestingly, while in Vashti's case, there is no male defender to come to her rescue, in Mordecai's case, the female champion Esther brings deliverance.[34] The villain Haman receives a twist on the elevation he sought. He is literally hoisted on his own petard as the gallows he erected for his victim are employed for his own death.

Though at the end of the tale the surviving males (Ahasuerus and Mordecai) are paid token tribute, they are completely upstaged in the story line by the women protagonists. The first scene of the drama portrays the ruler's desperate attempt to assure that the queen listen to the king; the climax of the story has the king taking orders from the queen. The cracks in the facade of male dominance, despite attempts to seal them up, now run all the way to the foundation of the court. As Fox states: "The king and his nobility are the butt of some rather broad irony. The world ruler banishes a wife he cannot control, only to take on later a new one who controls him completely." In a world where the deadliest insult was to call a man worse than a woman,[35] the author leaves open the possibility that women are wiser than men. Indeed, some commentators have conjectured that Vashti's name is a derivative of the Avestan word *vahista*, which means "the best."

As Katheryn Pfisterer Darr notes, it turns out that Esther, as well as Vashti, is "more than just a pretty face."[36] These two women, through bravery and wit, together drive the course of events in this tragicomedy. It is commonly assumed that the story of Esther is a study in realism. *Esther* communicates to its readers that human agency is necessary in life; the surprising lack of reference to God implies that even those who are the people of God cannot passively wait for divine intervention in this dangerous world.[37] It is noticed less that the story suggests that this is true for women as well as men. The tale as a whole announces that women are not just *created by* history, but they also are *creators of* history. Commentators who consider the teller of this story to be a "proto-feminist" have some basis for such a claim, especially given the context in which it was written.

Though deposed in the narrative, Vashti is rising to importance in women's history. Some early commentators on this defiant queen were so indignant at her lack of compliance that they deemed her "the wicked queen" and concocted for her a villainous pedigree of deeds and relations. Others, more sympathetic to her cause, considered her tactics unrealistic and foolish. However, contemporary feminists laud Vashti's "damn the consequences" heroism in openly defying authority and find in her forthright activism a model superior to Esther's stereotypic use of feminine wiles. Artist and writer Marjory Zoet Bankson celebrates that Vashti's "reckless strength," though it is costly, "meets a longing" in herself to refuse violation and exploitation.[38]

We need not pit Vashti and Esther against one another. Those who seek to shape the course of history are not of one mold. Vashti, though clearly cooperative on many matters (such as being a beautiful and gracious hostess for the women's banquet), comes to a point of uncompromising insistence on what she sees as right. Esther, after a history of compliance, continues to work within the status quo. Yet, despite her careful use of sexual tactics, Esther too reaches a point where she throws role expectations to the wind. Though she was successful, that success was not predictable. She makes her decision to go to the king, knowing full well that she may die for choosing to make an unsolicited visit (4:11).

Because Vashti's actions are not personally triumphal, her story is either misinterpreted as a warning or ignored altogether. Certainly there is a realism to Vashti's harsh fate that we cannot deny, and many women will justifiably prefer more tempered approaches to promoting change.[39] Nevertheless, Vashti's "failure" does not gainsay her efforts. As Esther's triumph is indebted to her forerunner, so have others gained from the likes of Vashti. Vashti not only stands *with* those who are condemned for their costly steps, but she also walks *before* those who have succeeded in making positive strides. She and those like her are pioneers, and we do well to uncover the traces of their trail. For it has made many of our paths a little easier. Renita Weems comments that, "If the truth be told, we today are who we are—if we are anybody—because some woman, somewhere, stooped down long enough that we might climb on her back and ride piggyback into the future. Ask Queen Esther."[40] One is reminded of these words attributed to Jesus: "Others have done the hard work, and you have reaped the benefits of their labor" (John 4:38 NIV).[41]

Surely, the hard work is not all done, and women still struggle to possess their own feelings, opinions, and bodies. Recently, "A Report on the Realities, Concerns, Expectations and Barriers Experienced by Adolescent

Women in Canada" was published. Entitled *A Cappella*, the study indicated how hard it is for young women to forge independent identities in today's world. To sing *a cappella* is to "carry a tune without instrumental accompaniment. It's a high risk musical style; it's much easier to lose pitch when the orchestra isn't providing a familiar melody." Furthermore, without "a strong rhythm section" to keep one's voice on track, a singer can lose her way. Vashti sang *a cappella*; she had no accompaniment to carry and support her voice, and the tune to which she sang was perilously unfamiliar. Like the young women in Canada, Vashti's "song [was] not heard" and risks being muted altogether. Her inclusion in this book lets us hear her song; it also lets girls know that they are not alone. The melody is both sad and triumphant—for you see, it was in her refusal to parade her beauty that Vashti's regal beauty was displayed for all the world to see:

> Queen Vashti lost her crown but not her head.
> Xerxes had power to vacate her throne
> but not the knack to make her hate herself
> or denigrate her beautiful integrity.
> He could not terminate her majesty.[42]

Echoing the words of Mary Gendler, "I propose that Vashti be reinstated on the throne along with her sister Esther, together to rule and guide the psyches and actions of women."[43] AND to shape the imaginations of young girls.

Writing "Vashti and Esther" Foreword: Caretakers of Our Common House

Alicia Ostriker, in considering the book of Esther, remarks: "I am not ready to wonder if Vashti and Esther could be secret allies, ridicule of the king joined to manipulation of the king. Sleek small moles under the ground of tyranny, grain by grain overturning the world."[44] Though she herself may not be ready for such a wonder, I myself am moved toward a midrash in this direction of "secret allies." In fact, the gaps and silences in the story leave room for such possibility.[45] I would like to plunge into these gaps and make midrash with this story. There is a long tradition in Judaism of "making midrash," playing with and wrestling with the biblical text to discover meaning between the lines and in the silent gaps.[46] The point of midrash is/was not to recover past meaning but to imagine and to celebrate present relevance. "Assuming the infinite meaningfulness of biblical texts, the rabbis took passages that were sketchy or troubling and wrote them forward," explains Judith Plaskow.[47] Jewish feminist midrash often asks the question, "What was the woman thinking?" What did Eve think about gaining the knowledge of good and evil? What did Sarah think about Abraham's trip to Moriah? What did Mikal think about being a bridal pawn? The woman's sides of biblical stories are often screaming from the silent gaps. Listening to the cherished biblical narratives, we can, claims Lynn Gottleib, wait for the voices of women "to rise out of the white spaces between the letters in the Torah."[48] Following the very same outline given in the biblical text, let us read between the lines and listen for the story rising from the silent gaps.[49] Perhaps the book of Esther, rather than the "solo" its name suggests, is really a cleverly arranged "duet." Let us play with this possibility; let us make midrash.

Imagine that after being deposed as queen, Vashti is banished from the kingdom. Though it is often assumed that execution followed dethronement, the text leaves open a variety of possibilities. Suppose that a group of women, protesting her fate, whisked her away and hid her on the outskirts of the kingdom.[50]

> She continued to hold banquets, only the fare was extremely simple and spare. Women she never thought she would associate with sat at her table; eventually her own clothes match the tattered garments her visitors don. Some time after her banishment, Vashti has a caller in the night. As she peers out her door in stoic resignation, half expecting the king's executioners, she is startled to see a beautiful woman in exquisite garb facing her. Vashti looks away, remembering both the privilege and the oppression of her former way of life. The pale visitor appears fearful; trembling, she slips into Vashti's quarters before a word has been exchanged. The young woman bows in her presence, and for a brief moment Vashti is back in time, accepting it as a matter of course that the young woman show obeisance. Then, returning with a jolt to the present reality, Vashti stares in surprise—then fear. Who is this that knows her identity. A spy? Then she notices the royal robes—robes like she used to wear. Could it be? Yes, it is the queen, the new queen, the one chosen in her stead.
>
> "Why did you come here? What do you want of me?" Vashti asks, suspicious, curious, and afraid—all at the same time. Her initial inclination is to disdain this woman, but the impulse is fleeting. *Why did this woman bow to me?*
>
> "I am the new queen," says the young woman, with a flush of embarrassment. "Haman told me the story of your demise, as if to warn me against following in your footsteps. The men are so nervous! Hathach, the king's eunuch who speaks to me often, told me that he thought you were wrongly

treated and that he sneaks food to you for your banquets. Ever since hearing your story, I have wanted to speak with you. I begged him to bring me to you, and he has finally relented; I know we may both be punished." The queen diverts her eyes and looks fearfully at the ground. *The young queen is hardly more than a girl*, thinks Vashti as she listens to her trembling visitor.

"Queen Vashti, I cannot do as you did, but I want to learn from the strength that enabled you to do it. You see, I too am in trouble. I am a woman and a Jew—and Ahasuerus is intent on controlling both. He does not know I am a Jew, and, roused by Haman's paranoia, he is about to have my people killed. I learned this from Hathach, who brought this message from my uncle Mordecai. I do not want your sacrifice to be in vain; and I do not want my people to die. What shall I do to serve women and to preserve my people?"

"Ah yes, Haman, whose desire for power will not be tamed," retorted Vashti knowingly—and with unmistakeable anger. "You are brave to come here. If the king finds out, you too could be banished—or worse. I must tell you, that if I were to do everything over, I would do the same thing that I did before. I would stand up and tell the king what I thought."

"Yes, your majesty, I know," replied the young queen with a hint of shame. "But, pray do not be angry, I am indebted to you, but I am not you."

"No, you are not me, and my way is not the only way." Vashti knew that with the survival of her people at stake, the young queen would proceed very cautiously. And for good reason; the king did not react very well to strong-willed women, to say the least. No, another way must be found. "I also have another idea." The wryest smile appeared on Vashti's still regal face. "The king wants beauty and submission . . . give him what he wants. Dress up in your finest! Perfume yourself exquisitely! Prepare a sumptuous banquet! . . ." And the two schemed on into the night, and by early morning they had a plan. "My maids and I will fast for three days, and then I will go to the king, though it is against the law. If I perish, I perish; I must do what I must do," concluded Esther, with a boldness in her voice that was not there earlier in the evening. "I and my community of women will fast as well, and we will be with you in spirit" promised Vashti, "and may the company of your sisters strengthen you."

As Esther rose to depart, she commenced to bow again—but Vashti took her arm and held her erect. "I accept your respect, but I do not wish your abasement. The problem with the king and his men is that they want to be masters in their houses; they want to exert control over others—they fear dissent and independence. We must resist this kind of control, and we must seek a way for people to live together in their houses and kingdom. Some day, perhaps, women will be free—but not to become masters of our own house. The men were afraid that *all* women would seek independence. In a way they shall. Not to lord it over or disregard others, but to live with others in freedom. For our houses belong to all of us."

"You have lost so much," Esther said with emotion.

"Yes, I have lost much, and many think me foolish," replied the former queen. "But, I would have lost *all* if I had given away myself. I have my self, and I have the company of others who respect me. I am sad, but not defeated. Carry on, Esther, what I have started. For the sake of our sisters and daughters. May it be so that one day our houses will not be ruled by masters but tended by caretakers who support the development of girls and women. Esther, do you think someday this will happen? Can we begin to dream of a day when leaders will welcome and raise girls and women so they can be *caretakers of our common house?*"

"Dare we?"

"Yes, we dare. We dare," answered the queen.

Chapter One

Theology and Women

GIVING OUR SELVES AWAY

"*Women constantly confront themselves with questions about giving. Am I giving enough? Can I give enough? Why don't I give enough? . . . They are upset if they feel they are not givers.*"
—Jean Baker Miller[1]

"*I admired and clearly benefited from [my mother's] years of selfless care, yet I also mourned her long before she died; I mourned the self she'd sacrificed to be such a 'good woman.*' "
—Julia Wood[2]

"*The greatest hazard of all, losing the self, can occur very quietly in the world, as if it were nothing at all. No other loss can occur so quietly; any other loss—an arm, a leg, five dollars, a [spouse], etc.—is sure to be noticed.*"
—Søren Kierkegaard[3]

The loss of self is quiet indeed. Had Queen Vashti disregarded her own feelings and submitted to the will of King Ahasuerus, the resulting loss of herself would have occurred ever so quietly. No one would have noticed; she would simply have colluded with the quiet conspiracy that is a matter of course in women's lives. It was a wife's duty to obey her husband's wishes, especially if her husband were the king—even if these wishes were unreasonable. Strikingly, some commentators who agreed with Vashti's inclination still thought she should carry out the wishes of her husband. J. Vernon McGee, a radio evangelist, had this to say about Vashti:

> Although Vashti was perfectly justified in refusing to come [to the king's party], I think she should have thought the situation over in this manner: "I can refuse and I probably ought to refuse. But this is a scandal that will get out and this will hurt my king, my husband. I think the circumstances, I'll go." On that basis, she should have gone to the banquet. She should have obeyed.[4]

Obedience to husband, social convention, and other authorities is often thought more important than woman's obedience to her inner call to integrity. Those who feel the call to integrity but obey the cultural authorities go unnoticed. In fact, the quiet loss of women's selves is far more prevalent than the fuss and fanfare of women's public humiliation. For it is not simply a matter of punishment in the face of assertion that prompts women to give themselves away, it is more subtly a matter of selective reinforcement in the direction of self-denial that causes women to give themselves away. The words of Julia Wood quoted at the start of this chapter reflect her ambivalent response to the eulogy given at her mother's funeral. "She never thought of herself, always took care of others, the most selfless person I've ever known. She really was a good woman."[5] Throughout her book *Who Cares?* Wood laments the quiet way in which her mother, who used to have dreams, gave herself away.

Consider with me the way in which theological teachings in communities of faith, teachings that culminate with eulogies such as that of Wood's mother, nonetheless quietly and without notice yet ever so forcefully, pose a hazard to women's self-development.

Lest we consider the relationship between theology and women's development to be merely an academic issue, I would like to begin with a widely used story that bears an important theological message—*The Giving Tree* by Shel Silverstein.[6] This is a modern parable of sin and grace that is frequently used as a theological lesson. It is a widely read story; though it is used with all age-groups, it has a particularly unwaning popularity as a children's sermon.

The Giving Tree is a charming narrative that is often used as an allegory of the beauty of self-sacrifice. The story begins with a touching description of a somewhat mutual relationship between a lush flourishing apple tree and an energetic little boy. The two play together and form a close bond; the boy gives company to the tree and the tree gives shade, recreation (branches to climb and swing on), and food (ripe apples) to the boy. Alas, the boy grows up, finds other interests, and abandons the tree in favor of girls, travels, and the world beyond the root-bound, immovable tree. The tree is lonely, and spends her days longing for the boy. The boy repeatedly returns, and each return brings immense joy to the tree—though the boy is increasingly dissatisfied with his life and travels. One after another, the tree offers what she has to meet his increasing demands: first all her apples to sell (giving him money to buy things), then all her branches (giving him material to build a house), and finally her trunk (giving him wood to make a boat so he can sail away). The boy unabashedly takes all her offerings, and each time we are told that this makes the tree happy. After all her self-sacrificial giving, the tree is reduced to a nearly flattened stump. For the first time we are given a hint that all is not well with the pattern of give-and-take; the tree "is happy . . . but not really." The tree is abandoned for ever so long. Then the Boy Wanderer returns one last time. This time the tree is distressed; she has nothing else to offer. "I wish that I could give you something . . . but I have nothing left. I am just an old stump. I am sorry . . . ," she apologizes. As it turns out, the boy, now too old and dissipated to enjoy most of life's amenities, has need for only one thing—a place to rest. The tree, in her immolated state, can at least provide that. And now, giving even this her all, she straightens herself up as best she can so the boy can sit upon her and rest from his wearying life. She is happy again.

Ponder for a moment the story line: boy takes selfishly, tree gives heedless of self. At first glance this may seem to be a pro-female story. The tree, referred to as "she" is the heroine; the boy is a spoiled and restless anti-hero. In fact, in light of many theological formulations, the boy is a dead ringer for sin and the tree is the embodiment of grace. This indirect compliment is, however, potentially harmful to the development of women.

I would like to consider the story of *The Giving Tree* in connection with feminist critiques of the theology of Reinhold Niebuhr. Few thinkers have influenced North American theology as significantly as this theologian. Writing in the middle of our century, he addressed a world afraid of the destructive fascism of World War II. Aware of the incredible creative possibilities human beings possessed, he was also concerned about the sinful distortions of human potential evident in such grand schemes as the Third Reich. Recovering traditional notions of sin and grace, Niebuhr exposed the depth of sin and pointed to the need for grace. His theological anthropology both looked back to key thinkers and themes in our tradition and projected forward a highly influential stream of thought for Christian theology. With the giving tree in mind, I'd like to consider why his thought has raised crucial questions from women.

Niebuhr's anthropology trades on the assumption that "man loves himself inordinately." Driven by the creative yet diabolical combustion of incredible possibility and monumental insecurity, 'his' whole existence is tainted by inordinate self-interest, ideological narrow-mindedness, pride, and will-to-power. Such egotism and will-to-power are the "quintessence of sin" in Christian thought, according to Niebuhr.[7] Furthermore, egotism is shackled in "the prison of self-possession" and can only be freed by being possessed by something beyond itself, the Holy Spirit.[8] Niebuhr recognizes an alternative expression of sin, sensuality or evasion of the self; and we will return to the quite significant insights he had into sensuality. Had this side of his thought been developed as fully as the other side, the problematic consequences of his work would have been alleviated. Unfortunately, Niebuhr's attention to the evasion of the self is overshadowed both in his work and in the appropriations of his work. Sensuality fades into the background, and sin is primarily understood to be "the unwillingness of man to acknowledge his creatureliness and dependence upon God and *his effort to make his own life independent and secure.* . . . It is the vain imagination by which man hides the conditioned, contingent and dependent character of his existence and seeks to give it the appearance of unconditioned reality."[9] Grace addresses the reality of pride; it *shatters* the self, which alleviates self-love and self-interest and renews the capacity for self-sacrificial giving. To reiterate the parallel, the boy in our story is a superb depiction of self-centered sin and the tree in our story is the "embodiment" of grace-imbued self-sacrifice.

As striking as the giving tree/Niebuhr parallel is, ironically, the story line of the tale inadvertently contains its own nemesis and supports some trenchant critiques of Niebuhr's thought. We can agree that the nature of the boy symbolizes and reveals sin; yet, the destiny of the tree subverts its apparent symbolism—the tree's extreme immolation causes us to question the book's very message. The giving tree is a graphic illustration of where giving "heedless of the self" (Niebuhr) can lead. In fact, a young child is the first one who brought this to my attention. After being read the story once and asked at a later time if he wished to hear this story again, he promptly tossed the book aside and remarked "No, I don't like that story. The tree is ruined, and that's not a good thing." Indeed, that is not a good thing—either in the story or in the theologies that parallel its message.

Judith Plaskow, building on the pioneering essay of Valerie Saiving, contends that Niebuhr offers a limited description of human sin.[10] A representation of sin as self-assertion, self-centeredness, and pride speaks out of and to the experience of *powerful men*, she avers. Women are better indicted for such things as lack of self, self-abnegation, and irresponsibility. When sin as pride is generalized, self-abnegation is rendered a virtue and harmfully reinforced. A theology that emphasizes self-sacrifice as the human telos functions to further enervate women's struggle for self-assertion. Such a theology may chasten the little boys, but it will hasten the devastation of the trees. We must honestly ask ourselves: Is stumphood really what God wills for our lives?

I must say that I am in general a Shel Silverstein fan. I loved *The Giving Tree* the first time I read it, and I continue to be moved by the narrative and pictures. However, I am more and more distressed by this story's apparent moral. I think it conveys an extremely dangerous and potentially destructive message. While some have noticed the selfishness of the boy and proceeded to knit their brow at his behavior, this chastisement is always accompanied by holding up the tree as an exemplar. Even when describing this as a parable of sin, not many have identified the *destructiveness* of the tree. Self-immolation is reinforced as noble and posed as inherently rewarding. Nowhere is mutuality suggested as normative. But what troubles me the most is the male/female split in this story. The boy does all the taking and the tree does all the giving—both to extremes.

Though trees are often considered phallic symbols, the *giving* tree is personified as a *she*. One might easily transpose the title into *The Giving She*. Indeed, even before he begins to defoliate and truncate his love interest, the boy carves his initials in her trunk, an indelible reminder that he possesses her—an eerie portend of what is to come. The imagery of the story reinforces the message: boys go out and explore and grasp the world, girls stay planted on the home front providing stability and giving of themselves sacrificially to support the male need to conquer the world. When there is nothing left to give, the female has no value to the male; she is abandoned unless she can resurrect the fragments of her existence for one final offering. Her glory is to be sat upon by a finally satiated male.

Make no mistake, boys and girls who hear this story will learn more than the importance of giving—they will also learn who it is that should give and who it is that will take.

The book is in some ways a mirror of society, which asks women to cut off their heads and forgo intellectual development, cut off their arms and recoil from aggressive and creative grasping of the world, and even cut out their wombs to repudiate their mysterious relation to nature. Women are encouraged to keep looking for what it is they can give, rather than to challenge the very assumption that their giving is de facto beneficial (was the boy truly helped?) and their sole purpose in life. The words of George

Eliot's character in *Daniel Deronda,* "You can never imagine what it is to have a man's genius in you, and yet to suffer the slavery of being a girl,"[11] betrays the dissonance many girls feel when they discover their own genius for male-dominated spheres of life.

"One might expect of theologians that they at least not add to these pressures," charged Valerie Saiving, adding, "one might even expect them to support and encourage the woman who desires to be both a woman and an individual in her own right." However, she concluded, "theology, to the extent that it has defined the human condition on the basis of masculine experience continues to speak of such desires as sin or temptation to sin,"[12] and continues to contribute to the "slavery of being a girl." Rather than demonstrating an "unwillingness . . . to acknowledge [her] creatureliness and dependence upon God" and rather than exerting an *"effort to make [her] own life independent and secure,"* it is precisely the refusal to make her life independent and the acceptance of the dependent character of existence that plague many women. Rather than exercising a "vain imagination," which "hides the conditioned, contingent and dependent character of [her] existence and seeks to give it the appearance of unconditioned reality," woman is more tempted to squelch her imagination and find herself determined by the conditions of her environment. In fact, as many feminist psychologists note, dependency in women is often considered to be the "hallmark of femininity." Harriet Lerner writes of the "de-selfing" that results from cultural pressures on women to conform to the "nurturing imperative" and deny personal assertion. To the extent that women accept the nurturing imperative, "they ensure their own emotional demise." This is "not because attachment and responsiveness to others are inherently damaging (to the contrary), but because the rules allow no room for women to act on their own behalf."[13] The irony, as we shall see in chapter 3, is that such de-selfing not only impairs the self, but it also, in the end, deprives others of true relationality and community.

NOT BEING MASTERS OF OUR OWN BASEMENTS

Because theology has historically been written by men, the sins of pride and self-centeredness have been emphasized. This would not be a bad thing if powerful men were the ones who received and responded to this message. In cases where this has happened, this theology has been a good and redemptive factor in Christian history. As Daphne Hampson puts it, "Christian theology, written by men, has well understood *their* problem. Indeed, these myths and stories about pride, and fall, have been formulated because they correspond to *a* truth."[14] Certainly, in Niebuhr's historical context of world fascism and tyranny, this was a much-needed message. As the daughter of a Holocaust survivor on one side and the great-granddaughter of a Cherokee on the other, I would not want to lose the prophetic cry against pride and imperialism any more than I want to deny the call to courage.[15] Pride, and its attendant corruptions, is surely a problem in our world. Those who carry the privilege of power need a theology that exposes oppression and critiques patterns of dominance.[16] In fact, I'd love to hand King Ahasuerus a copy of Niebuhr's magnum opus; it is as if he had this insecure and powerful king in mind when he stated there is "no level of greatness in which the lash of fear is not at least one strand in the whip of ambition."[17]

Unfortunately, like King David who pointed his finger at Nathan's hypothetical oppressor but missed his own error (II Samuel 12), reproof too often slips right by the perpetrators. Sadly, it is often the already humble who take the message of pride to heart. Women who are raised to be subordinate and submissive end up hearing "You are the woman," and they further quench any temptation to assert themselves or stand up for justice. Niebuhr himself noted that the Reformed emphasis on grace had the ironic consequence that "the saints are tempted to continue to sin that grace may abound, while the sinners toil and sweat to make human relations a little more tolerable and slightly more just."[18]

According to Susan Nelson Dunfee, the tragedy of an overemphasis on pride is two-edged. By "encouraging woman to confess the wrong sin, and by failing to judge her in her actual sin, Christianity has both added to woman's guilt and failed to call her into her full humanity."[19] In a helpful manner, Nelson speaks of "the sin of hiding," which very aptly expresses woman's temptation to withhold herself. Jacquelyn Grant, writing to African American women who have taken on the greatest burden of service in our society, speaks even more boldly of "the sin of servanthood" and calls for "the deliverance of discipleship." "A language needs to be adopted or emphasized that challenges the servant mentality of oppressed peoples and the oppressive mentality of oppressors," she insists.[20]

I would like to state it a different way: many women, due to socialized patterns of subordination, are tempted to *give themselves away*. "Self-possession" is precisely what women need, not the prison from which they should escape. As we shall examine in the next chapter, the promotion of self-sacrifice occurs for women before there is a self to give away. While the "sin" of giving themselves away is not fully women's own fault, and giving itself is not to be condemned, perpetual self-giving does not further the humanity of women and men in their lives together. If Silverstein's parable is any indication, we end up with alienated, dissatisfied men and lonely, diminished women.

Ted Peters, revisiting the theme of "original sin," comments that "as soon as we arrive, fresh from our mother's womb, we are issued the invitation to join the party of concupiscence, aggression, injustice, and violence. The pot of the world's misery is already filled with sin and its fruit, the suffering of innocent victims. And we ourselves will add still more. This is the given."[21] What Peters does not tell us is that, as with the banquets in the palace of Ahasuerus, there are two parties going on. Some of us are issued the invitation to join the party serving pride-stew with the ingredients of aggression, injustice, and violence; others of us will be served from the pot of submissiveness-stew, chock-full of underdevelopment, passivity, and depression.[22] This too is a given, and it is one that needs to inform our theological reflection and teaching in communities of faith.

It is important for me to stress that I am not seeking to exonerate women from sin. Quite the contrary. Along with Plaskow, Saiving, and Dunfee, I wish to *make the theological weight of irresponsibility more visible to women*. While we must be careful not to blame the victim, we must also be careful not to reinforce the victim by calling what is harmful a virtue. Sara Ruddick minces no words when she writes of "the perversion of value" that arises when reality is sentimentalized and women's temptations "are redescribed so that defects emerge as virtues."[23] Giving up oneself—sometimes even in service to another—can be an act of sin if it is passive, splits community into those who care and those who assert, and fails to hold other people accountable for their actions. In fact, this is increasingly recognized in the addiction literature where both addiction and codependence—inadvertent nurturing of the addiction through caregiving—are being analyzed.[24] The reality of sin, as far as I am concerned, is not in dispute. It exists, it is pervasive, and all—men and women—are guilty of it.

Yes, sin is a given. *What* constitutes sin, however, is under contention. Pride is not always a sin, and self-sacrifice sometimes is. Conversely, as Elisabeth Cady Stanton was fond of saying, sometimes "self-development is a higher duty than self-sacrifice."[25] We need to recognize the complexity of sin and, most important, we need to acknowledge the way in which the pride of the powerful depends upon and is fueled by the self-sacrifice of others. We will never overcome pride simply by denouncing the proud; we must also empower those who would be victims—or inadvertent accomplices—of selfish pride.

Niebuhr was deeply indebted to Søren Kierkegaard in developing his understanding of human nature. Due to the historical situation, he attended more fully to Kierkegaard's exposure of pride than he did to the equally important theme of self-evasion. The latter theme, self-evasion, is actually the more dominant theme in Kierkegaard's work, *The Sickness Unto Death*. Far from presuming the egocentricity of the self, in that work Kierkegaard did not even believe most people were selves. For Kierkegaard, human sin was not so much a result of inflated and self-possessing egocentrism, but rather a consequence of a person's refusal to become a self, i.e., self-abdication. He viewed despair over becoming a self as the common human condition, and he emphasized the importance of the self *choosing and becoming a self,* contending that "the self has the task of becoming itself in freedom" and choosing itself before God.

That is not to say that Kierkegaard did not acknowledge the self-aggrandizement and egocentrism known as pride. For Kierkegaard there were three manifestations of human despair over becoming a self: (1) "spiritlessness," the failure to realize one's possibility; (2) "weakness," the move to escape from one's self; and (3) "defiance," the attempt to affirm and master oneself by denying dependence upon God.[26] These represent levels of consciousness, ranging from the first one being nearly unconscious and lacking in self-knowledge to the third level being hyperconscious, yet in a self-deceptive manner. All three of these conditions are despairing ones, because they do not represent the self's proper condition before God and the proper balance of finitude and infinitude, necessity and possibility. As Niebuhr so poignantly said: "man is a child of nature, subject to its vicissitudes, compelled by its necessities, driven by its impulses . . . man is a spirit who stands outside of nature, life, himself, his reason and the world."[27] The "spiritless" one submits to nature; the "weak" one remains within the social conventions and necessities of life; the "defiant" one defies nature and necessity and seeks to transcend the world as given. Spiritless and weak persons deny their possibilities, they accept their lot and frequently give over their lives to the rule of others; defiant persons ignore their finitude, seeking always to transcend limits and control others.

Because the "spiritless" and "weak" persons succumb to their external conditions, they do not imagine possibilities and nurture their own creativity. In fact, their lives seemed too trivial and spiritless to Kierkegaard to even be called sinful in any substantive sense of the word. Kierkegaard eloquently exposed the risk-avoiding, sedated existence of weakness. "Not to venture is prudent. And yet, precisely by not venturing it is so terribly easy to lose what would be hard to lose, however much one lost by risking, and in any case never this way, so easily, so completely, as if it were nothing at all—namely, oneself."[28]

The defiant person, on the other hand, ignores finitude and seeks to master life. This one, in defiance of limitations, grasps at possibility. While this expansive self seeks and accomplishes great things, eventually this self flounders in possibility until exhausted. "The instant something appears to be possible, a new possibility appears, and finally these phantasmagoria follow one another in such rapid succession that it seems as if everything were possible, and this is exactly the final moment, the point at which the individual himself becomes a mirage."[29] Thus, in either case, the self as self is lost to genuine self-consciousness.

Interestingly, Kierkegaard thought weakness was the "feminine" form of despair while defiance was the "masculine" form. Woman, according to Kierkegaard, was by very nature devoted to others, and thus tended to lose herself in the other. Rather than will to be her own self, woman "abandons herself, throws her self into that to which she devotes herself." Thus, "her despair is: not to will to be oneself."[30] She accepts such devotion as a matter of course, does not question the convention that promotes it, and refuses to consider the possibility and eternity of that which she can be. She submits to external masters and denies her internal power to create.

Man, in contrast, wants to be master of himself, and he recognizes no power over himself. He is all possibility and no limit; he wants to enjoy the total satisfaction of making himself into himself. However, as the woman denies her creative potential, the man obscures his limit, tries to neutralize external forces that get in his way. He tries as long as he can to hide the reality that he "is always building only castles in the air, is only shadow-boxing."[31] Holding out as long as he can, the defiant man may ultimately succumb to "demonic despair," which wallows in misery and denies all goodness. Dostoevsky, in his haunting novel *The Possessed*, describes such a person whose desire for absolute freedom leads to nihilism. "Every man who desires to attain total freedom must be bold enough to put an end to his life. . . . This is the ultimate limit of freedom; this is all; there is nothing beyond this. Whoever dares to commit suicide becomes God. Everyone can do this and so bring the existence of God to an end, and then there will be absolutely nothing."[32]

While women and men tended to fall into the "feminine" and "masculine" forms of despair accordingly, the lines were not rigidly drawn by Kierkegaard. In fact, he seems to presume that "the majority of people," men as well as women, live subconscious existences. Kierkegaard uses the imagery of a house to make this point. "Now if what it means to be a human being is compared with such a house [a house with a basement, first floor, and second floor], then all too regrettably the sad and ludicrous truth about the majority of people is that in their own house they prefer to live in the basement."[33] On the other side, he spoke of "Christian heroism—a rarity, to be sure," as venturing "wholly to become oneself, an individual human being, this specific individual human being, alone before God."[34]

Clearly these are stereotypic categories that reduce the complexity of male and female experience. "Woman" comes across as a vacuous drone; "man" is rendered active and virile, even if deluded. Though both are in despair, Kierkegaard names womanly despair as more debased (less conscious) than male despair. We must ask, with the tree and the boy fresh in our memories, if the boy really lives at a higher level than the tree; his "self" mastery seems utterly oblivious—the tree, at least, is still somewhat in touch with her feelings. In fact, I do not think defiance is a higher stage of consciousness per se. The "weak" persons are more conscious of the external expectations of others; the "defiant" persons are more conscious of their own dreams and aspirations. As I will develop in the next two chapters, the "self" is always a "self-in-relation," which requires both an awakened, self-authoring confidence, and an empathetic, caring capacity for conversational relationships. "Weak" persons require self-authoring differentiation; "defiant" persons require caring connections. Neither weak nor defiant persons are *critically* conscious, that is, capable of questioning and examining that which drives them.

My purpose is not to adopt Kierkegaard's scheme. It is rather to recover the striking way in which this nineteenth-century Dane perceived important nuances in the types of sin present in Christendom. Kierkegaard is perceptive in naming self-abnegation as well as self-aggrandizement as despair leading to sin. While there are disturbing signs that Kierkegaard did not want to disrupt the devoted nature of women,[35] he exposed societal pressures that are very real. Giving up oneself is no more faithful to God than seeking to master oneself. "Sin is: before God in despair not to will to be oneself, or before God in despair to will to be oneself."[36] For Kierkegaard, the self must be grounded in God alone; that means that the self must not be lost in the crowd of convention or give up its spirit to that which is a "matter-of-course" that results in the spirit being "secured against becoming aware."[37] Becoming aware, living an examined life, is an important result of knowing oneself to be grounded in God.

It is essential, for the healthy development of women, that this important insight into sin as self-abnegation not become overshadowed by sin as self-centeredness. If women are to become caretakers in our common house, we must transform those teachings that inadvertently press women into the basement. The effect of grace is precisely to move people out of that basement into the fullness of household life. I would like to look next at a set of spiritual disciplines that may inadvertently hold women in the basements of their communities of faith.

Theology, Gender, and Spirituality

Theologically driven censures on pride have had a profound impact on Christian spiritual disciplines, those practices that a community employs to shape the human spirit toward God and others. A strong emphasis on humility, obedience, and submission of the will is prevalent in many classic formulations of spiritual disciplines. A recent surge of interest in spirituality has led to a recovery of these disciplines; St. Benedict's teachings on humility and obedience are particularly popular. This is unfortunate, especially for women. Rather than being used within the complex context for which they were created, portions are retrieved and mass-marketed in reduced and simplistic ways. In a recent compilation of spiritual classics, Benedict's ladder to humility is reproduced. In this material, St. Benedict warns that "every exaltation of ourselves is a kind of pride," and that the way of ascending the "ladder of humility" is to remove traces of pride.[38] Viewing these disciplines through the lenses of women's development raises serious concerns about their universal helpfulness.

THE CALL TO ASCEND THE LADDER OF HUMILITY

Humility involves the recognition that "everyone who exalts himself shall be humbled; and he that humbles himself shall be exalted." The steps to humility are:

1. Reverence for God: "Again, the Scriptures say, 'There are ways that seem right to us, but in the end will lead us to ruin.'"
2. Rejecting our own will and desires and, instead, doing God's will.
3. Obedience to Others: "we submit ourselves to another in all obedience";
4. Enduring Affliction: "enduring with patience the injuries and afflictions we face. . . . Those who have faith must bear every disagreeable thing for the Lord";

42

5. Confession: "keep no secrets from the one to whom we confess. We must humbly confess all our evil thoughts and all our evil actions."
6. Contentment: "be content in all things . . . mindful of our own lowliness";
7. Self-Reproach: "we declare with our tongue and believ[ing] in our inmost soul that we are the lowliest and vilest of all";
8. Obeying the common rule: "we do this by doing nothing except what is sanctioned by the rule and example of elders."
9. Silence: "to withhold our tongue from speaking, keeping silence until we are asked";
10. Seriousness: "when we are not easily provoked to laughter."
11. Simple Speech: "we are to speak gently and not with a loud voice."
12. Humble in Appearance: "Our attitude should be that of the publican in the Gospel who said, with his eyes fixed on the ground, 'Lord, I am a sinner and I am not worthy to lift my eyes up to heaven.' "

Humility as a Way of Life: "we shall arrive at that love of God which, being perfect, casts out all fear."[39]

Humility, which is often seen as the foundation of spirituality, is understood to be the antidote to the vices of anger, ambition (seeking to control one's life), and pride. Rather than express anger at another, the spiritual person is to seek the wrong in oneself; rather than control one's life, the spiritual person is to patiently endure its suffering; rather than assert autonomy in relation to one's spiritual leaders, the spiritual person is to obey and submit. The outcome of humility is frequently named as "apatheia," a stoic term referring to the ability to distance oneself from one's passions, egocentric compulsions, and striving needs.[40] The one with "apatheia" possesses an internal calm—even insularity—which remains undisturbed in the face of external vicissitudes.

There is much to be gained from a humility-based spirituality. Particularly, for those who are exalted and powerful, these exercises provide an important balance. Humility brings the mighty down from their lofty heights. Moreover, a capacity to distance oneself from one's passions and desires can be important in difficult circumstances. These virtues, and the exercises that promote them, however, are problematic when reduced to self-denial.[41] For those whose voices are suppressed, these exercises—especially when extracted from community life—can lead to damaging intensification of suppression. The needed assertion of the already lowly may be thwarted and necessary voices silenced.[42] If anger, control, and pride are denounced, then prophetic anger and rebellion against evil are precluded. When a bald understanding of obedience is promoted, this removes personal and social responsibility and produces a shallow discipleship. In her convincing critique of authoritarian religious life, Dorothy Soelle contends that an "obedience that is blind to objective concerns and to the world, that merely listens to what it is told, has *divested itself of all responsibility* for what is commanded."[43]

That is not to say that humility and reverence for God are unimportant. To the contrary, I believe these are central to women's spirituality. Humility and reverence for God cannot be reduced to self-abnegation and self-surrender. As Roberta Bondi has pointed out, for the monastic teachers humility was based on the understanding that the worth of each person comes from God.[44] Because of this, genuinely humble persons can be both confident of their own worth and open to and receptive to the value of others. This is empowering as well as subduing. In fact, the impulse of humility is often assertiveness. When God is understood to be the center of one's identity, the courage to assert oneself on behalf of justice is inspired. Soelle goes so far as to say that "obedience works for death and resistance for life."[45] These exercises, unfortunately, can reinforce an obedience that works for death and can obscure the kind of resistance that works for life. This leads to a spiritual problem that I call "prophetic torpor."

THE DEADLY SIN OF PROPHETIC TORPOR

One of the traditional "seven deadly sins" was "acedia." *Acedia* is variously translated as apathy, indifference, or sadness,[46] and it is sometimes referred to as "spiritual torpor" or "spiritual lassitude." Acedia connotes a lack of interest in life, and it brings a lack of concern or feeling for distressing situations. It is to be *dispirited*, empty of passion and feeling. In severe forms, acedia "believes in nothing, cares for nothing, seeks to know nothing, interferes with nothing, enjoys nothing, hates nothing, finds purpose in nothing, lives for nothing, and remains alive because there is nothing for which it will die."[47] Thomas Aquinas associated acedia with voluntary respect for the knowledge of and ignorance of God.

I believe that we are shaping women toward a particular form of acedia. Borrowing from the idea, I wish to also rename it. I want to speak of "prophetic torpor," or the diminished capacity to care about and respond to injustice. It involves either an ignorance of suffering or a misguided decision to acquiesce to suffering. By naming the sin of "prophetic torpor," I am reclaiming and modifying another strand in Christian tradition.

While the term "prophetic torpor" is, well ugly, I use it because I wish to make connection with the tradition of vices and name this as one of them. Prophetic torpor, as opposed to spiritual torpor, is inadvertently shaped by the theological tradition we are examining. An overemphasis on self-abnegation blunts the person's prophetic and dissenting voice. In fact, many who are suffering from what I am calling prophetic torpor are very spiritually disciplined according to the kind of spiritual disciplines delineated above. While there is surely a kind of ignorance operating in prophetic torpor, it is an ignorance based on a faulty spirituality rather than on spiritual lassitude. And, while it may seem as if a tradition emphasizing self-abnegation cannot be said to diminish a person's capacity to care about others, I believe it can and does.

When we anathematize resistance, self-love, and assertiveness, we ironically diminish the capacity of individuals and communities to care deeply about the world and others in it; in short, we shape prophetic torpor.[48] Anger, sorrow, and compassion are inextricably tied; it is often sorrow and compassion that lead to anger. When we remove anger, we quell its companions. Don Capps, correlating the sin of acedia with the virtue of care, contends that care is the antidote to acedia. "What challenges our apathy and indifference is the awareness that God cares for the world, and thus we are obliged and privileged to care for it too. This means allowing our understanding of God's care for the world to inform our own intentions and acts."[49]

We shall see in the next chapter how the socialized understanding of female goodness can limit a woman's understanding of care. Women show a "reluctance to judge" that impedes their taking a stand, particularly when it comes to public concerns.[50] While abjuring from judgment may seem to be a caring attitude, it prevents significant participation in societal caretaking. It reduces caring to congeniality and tolerance and robs compassion of its fight for justice. This is certainly not the kind of care that we associate with the household of God.

God's care must not be flattened so that it becomes surface niceness or self-effacement. *Care* must be understood as God's concern for human wholeness and widespread justice. The kind of pseudo-care that is often fostered leads to indifference. If care means never rocking the boat or never asserting oneself, then it is listless, lifeless, and faulty. Vernon McGee, in the illustration in the early pages of this chapter, provides exemplary training for pseudo-care and prophetic lassitude. He contends that Vashti, even when she notices a genuine wrong, should suppress her protest and submit to her husband. Those who are trained to value submission over voice and to endure patient suffering over prophetic assertion are at a high risk for prophetic torpor. Of course, the most efficient way to produce prophetic lassitude is to train people not to notice oppression at all. This is why slave masters used to read to their slaves only the portions of the Bible that commanded obedience and promised a reward in the afterlife for those who accepted their lot without complaint. That is why so few women have had their imaginations shaped by the stories of strong women in the Bible, women such as Deborah (Judges 4).[51] Too many communities have carefully sought to nurture prophetic lassitude.

Prophetic torpor and its corresponding expressions of indifference and apathy are not always the results of evil intentions. Sometimes, they are inadvertent consequences of good, though misguided, intentions. In many cases prophetic torpor emerges out of a genuine commitment to community life. Many of us hope for peaceful and comfortable community experiences. This may, however, lead to a fear of conflict. The feeling that if one dissents or cries out against convention, one disrupts communal life often diminishes one's tendency to notice community dynamics. Thus, concern for community could discourage prophetic voice. It is important for participants in communities of faith to understand that a "covenant of courtesy" that precludes dissension and conflict is not conducive to genuine life together. This is a surface understanding of community—though it is very prevalent. In the end, this "covenant of courtesy" kills community life. There is a sense in which prophetic torpor is truly a "deadly sin," in its subtle destruction of community honesty. If one is afraid to challenge convention, disagree with others, open up conflict, one has in essence given up on community. Community only results when there are genuine relationships that probe life's issues deeply and honestly. To truly create a household of faith, to truly be a caretaker in a community of faith, is to encourage vigorous communication. When such communication is obstructed because of false courtesy, then distrust, indirect manipulation, and ultimately schisms occur. Rather than "communities of pretense," churches ought to be a "place where [people] are free to tell the truth," and yet this is so often not the case. Christians who retreat from honesty out of fear of offense are removing this central characteristic of faith community life.[52] Honest communication that invites prophetic dissent does not promote individualism, it rather contributes to healthy household life. This will be a major theme in later chapters of this book.

Probing even farther, another key contributor to prophetic torpor is a belief in and commitment to a particular understanding of "the order" of things. While order is not to be eschewed, articulations of natural order are to be held in suspicion. Our task is not simply to find our place in the order of things as they are, our task is sometimes to seek transformation of that order.[53] This requires, according to Soelle, "spontaneity." Persons with freedom and spontaneity do not take for granted a given order; they are not afraid to ponder and question a given order. Such persons celebrate order when it is life-giving and seek to change an order when it is death-dealing. It is important to nurture people in communities of faith so that when they look at the constellations in the sky at night, so to speak, they are aware that it is we who are doing the constellating, not the stars or the heavens. And they are not afraid to pose a different constellation when a standard construction privileges only certain orbs and screens out huge collections of other stars.[54]

Consider for a moment Rosa Parks, who refused to abide by "the order" of society that required her to give up her seat on a bus to a white person; she initiated the bus boycott that played such an important role in the Civil Rights Movement. Consider also Betty Friedan who resisted the cultural "order" that defined femininity; she is attributed with setting off the second wave of feminism. These women "changed the laws of history" by asserting them*selves.* They were prophets calling their culture to "say no" to dehumanization. Though their courage was celebrated by many, they were (and are) far from universally applauded. It would have been easy to lose their selves quietly: acquiesce on the bus, submit in the home. And yet, not only would they have lost themselves, but history would have lost also. Asserting their voices did not merely preserve their selfhood, it also set justice in motion. Their prophetic cries were (and still are) needed; the loss of those cries would have been tragic. In fact, it is a fight for survival for those who wish to follow them. When women, and others, give themselves away, the community loses as well. When faithfulness to the self is silenced, the community's hope for social justice is diminished; when faithfulness to the self is encouraged, the community's hope for justice is enhanced.

PROPHETIC VIGOR

Rather than a spirituality that encourages prophetic torpor, I propose that we nurture a vital spirituality characterized by prophetic vigor. Such a spirituality, I believe, finds expression in two ways: hope in God's redemptive will and conscious anger at the present condition of injustice. Spirituality is much more than a call to humility. In its deepest sense, spirituality is a call from Holy Spirit to human spirit. It is a call to become a self, a call to celebrate that selfhood, and a call to participate in and be shaped in relation to a community with others who are becoming alongside and in relation to oneself. I define *spirituality* most fundamentally as the practice of remembering, and at times rediscovering, our center in God; this leads us to both prophetic vigor and prophetic humility as we seek to follow a God who loves and seeks to bring about justice, peace, righteousness.

Vigorous spirituality welcomes both anger and weeping into the spiritual life. Unfortunately, "anger" is also often named as one of the deadly sins. This is unfortunate because the denial of anger can contribute to apathy and lassitude. Anger, no doubt, can be expressed in sinful and destructive ways; the consequences of passionate anger can be deadly. And yet, to name anger itself as a sin is to deny the important place of "righteous anger" in the spiritual life—especially women's spiritual lives.[55] Theological injunctions against anger per se contribute to prophetic torpor—and in many cases cause it. We will return to the issue of women and anger in the next chapter, but it is important to note here that a negative view of anger is spiritually impoverishing, dispiriting. It is anger over injustice that motivates the spiritual person to social transformation. Anger tells us that something has to change. As Beverly Harrison states, "We must never lose touch with the fact that all serious human moral activity, especially action for social change, takes its bearings from the rising power of human anger. Such anger is a signal that change is called for, that *transformation in relation* is required." This is where apatheia, obedience, and humility require nuance. We must not be content with injustice, we must not be obedient to unjust demands, and we must not retreat timidly from unjust persons. When we quench anger, we kill the capacity to recognize and fight such injustice. It is especially important that the virtue of patience and the capacity to "wait on God" for the divine will to come to pass not be translated into passivity. Elisabeth Schüssler Fiorenza envisions a communal spirituality that "calls us to gather together the *ekklesia of women* who, in the angry power of the Spirit, are sent forth to feed, heal, and liberate our own people who are women."[56]

Along with anger, weeping should be invited. We should be encouraged to weep for the suffering in this world, and it should be a weeping that moves us to action. As Hildegaard of Bingen proclaims of God: "I call forth tears, the aroma of holy work. I am the yearning for good."[57] Tears and the yearning for good go together, and both are holy work. Tears and anger need to be welcome in order for the kind of awakening both

Kierkegaard and Christ promote. Fear of tears and suppression of anger prevent awakening and block the power of the Spirit to resist death; fear of tears and suppression of anger block the power of the Spirit to sustain and renew life. In a poem poignantly titled "S M," Alice Walker writes:

> I tell you, Chickadee
> I am afraid of people
> who cannot cry
> Tears left unshed
> turn to poison
> in the ducts
> Ask the next soldier you see
> enjoying a massacre
> if this is not so.
>
> People who do not cry
> are victims
> of soul mutilation
> paid for in Marlboros
> and trucks.
>
> *Resist.*
>
> Violence does not work
> except for the man
> who pays your salary
> Who knows
> if you could still weep
> you would not take the job.[58]

The apostle Paul, when celebrating the presence of the Spirit of God in Romans 8, noted that this presence in us is accompanied by a groaning for the renewal of creation. With hope in a God who took on suffering in human flesh, let us allow our tears, our anger, and our groans to express our compassion for those suffering the present state of things. When we allow this kind of passionate judgment on injustice, we also invite voluntary suffering on the behalf of others. As Kierkegaard understood it, Christian faith entails suffering, but it is a suffering that results because one chooses to stand firm in a faith that doesn't pander to convention and to the powerful.[59] This is to be contrasted with imposed suffering or passive submission to an oppressive status quo. When one chooses to marginalize oneself and assertively suffer with the powerless, one is taking a firm stand against injustice. The purpose of this stance is to oppose, denounce, and vigorously resist suffering—not to passively accept suffering or, God forbid, glorify it as virtue-producing. We must avoid both the "cult of suffering," and "apathy"; the former accepts and even seeks suffering while the latter becomes desensitized to it and avoids it. Both perpetuate injustice.[60] Along with bell hooks, "I make a definite distinction between that marginality which is imposed by oppressive structures and that marginality one chooses as a site of resistance—as location of radical openness and possibility."[61]

THE NATURE AND DESTINY OF POWERFUL WOMEN AND OPPRESSED MEN

This discussion of theology and gender, pointing to different sinful propensities in men and women, no doubt leaves some unanswered questions. Can we put all men and women into either pride or self-abnegation categories? Can men be self-abnegating? Can women be puffed up with pride, self-centeredness, and the taint of self-interest? Can women be oppressive masters? We will return to these questions from time to time, but I would like to begin addressing them here.

Clearly, the "add woman and stir" solution to male-biased theology is untenable; women's experience does not readily fit the portrayal of human nature that is based on male experience. However, in spite of an undeniable differential between powerful men and self-abdicating women, a "separate woman and stir separately" resolution would be oversimplified. The gender/sin/grace correlations (male/pride/self-sacrifice; female/sensuality/self-development) do not fit all men and women. While concurring that women and men have different tendencies that render pride and sensuality *gender-related*, these tendencies are complex and we would overgeneralize to say they are *gender-specific*.[62]

Questions arise about the possibility of men who are self-abdicating. Sartre's famous injunction—Are you a man or a mouse?—exposes that not all men need to be taken to task for excessive self-assertion. In fact, feminists are not the first ones to point to Niebuhr's overemphasis on pride. Humanistic psychologists, Marxist thinkers, and process theologians took him to task for ignoring the role of self-actualization and the plight of the weak. In the mid-fifties, in an essay entitled, "Reinhold Niebuhr's Doctrine of Man," William John Wolf suggested that Niebuhr more fully develop an account of "some human perversities quite inadequately explained by 'pride' which . . . [Niebuhr really makes] the basic form of sin." Wolf remarked that some men need to be encouraged to have more pride (in his words, "be the man"!) and live up to the responsibilities of creaturehood. Wolf writes:

> Niebuhr's categories fail adequately to account for the sins of the weak man as they do so forcefully for those of the strong man. This failure to be the man needs to be included in the Niebuhrian topography of sin. It is surely as common as our strategies of pride, and perhaps just as serious in God's eyes as the latter, because into this vacuum of weak irresponsibility and irresolution move the strong men of pride to bedevil our history.[63]

This is striking not only because it presents the problem so poignantly, but also because it recognizes it as (indeed probably identifies it with) an alternative *male* predicament. Furthermore, this analysis points to the insidious *connection* between the *two forms of sin*. To collapse sin into one side (pride) of human activity and virtue into the other (self-sacrifice) is to miss the important relationality in life. Neither sin nor virtue stands alone as an isolated phenomenon; they are both defined, vis-à-vis relationships. Self sacrifice for the sake of self-sacrifice can actually become a very individualistic and even self-centered activity. Pride or self-assertion for the sake of the other can be a very loving and liberating activity. Self-sacrifice can actually stunt the growth of the one who is receiving all the sacrifice, and self-assertion from the other can promote the growth of the one who is refused the temptation of "bedeviling" his (or, as we shall see, her) own, or another's, history. Powerful men are Niebuhr's real target, and many men do not have the power he describes.[64] And thus, many men may need to be encouraged toward self-assertion rather than toward self-abdication. It must be noted, however, that less powerful men are still in positions of power over women due to the larger social structure that subordinates women to men. Even if they do not have the kind of power that fuels egocentricity, they may still face gender socialization patterns that promote their "will to power" over others (including women).

Similarly, questions arise about women and pride. Can women be prideful? Can women be oppressors? Obviously, history and experience tell us the answer to these question must be yes. The sin of pride does not reside in the "Y" chromosome; it is socially constructed.[65] There are some women who would benefit from reading Niebuhr's anthropology. Women are capable of being power hungry, self-centered, and unjust. This happens as women enter patriarchally structured spheres and adapt to the prevalent cultural patterns. It also happens when women exert their social, racial, and economic status over those with less status. For example, in the biblical story of the tortured relationship between Abraham, Sarah, and Hagar (Genesis 16–21), we read of Abraham's patriarchal authority, but we must also notice Sarah lording it over Hagar. Abraham uses his wife as a pawn to spare his own life, and Sarah uses her maid as a pawn to assure her future. In relation to Hagar, Sarah is proud and self-absorbed.[66] Her concern for herself and her child becomes inordinate, leading to cruelty and injustice toward the woman and child less powerful than she.

While particular persons lean toward either pride or self-abnegation, it is often the case that power dynamics of a relationship influence a person's posture. That is, pride and self-abnegation have a relational quality. White privileged women, trained to defer to white men, often perpetrate injustice against women of color, lesbian women, and women of lower socioeconomic status. While sometimes this is intentional, as in white women who mistreated slaves and servants and who continue to dehumanize domestic workers, at other times this is unintentional, as when early feminists mistakenly thought they could speak for all women. White privileged women, when in relationship to less-privileged women, sit in the seat of greater social power. In such relationships, we need a good dose of humility and silence. As Audre Lorde laments in an open letter to Mary Daly, "The history of white women who are unable to hear Black women's words, or to maintain dialogue with us, is long and discouraging."[67] The painful history of our role as oppressors must be confronted, confessed, and transformed. This can only happen if we listen, hear, and really seek to learn from other women whose voices we are inclined either to dismiss or to screen for what legitimates our own framework.[68]

My point is not to draw rigid gender lines in theological reflection. While women and men may face different tendencies, the power relations between persons may be as important in determining one's sinful temptations as one's gender training. The implication of this chapter is not that we round up all men and preach to them about the dangers of pride and round up all women and preach to them about the dangers of self-abdication. It is rather that we balance our teachings to expose both pride and sensuality, both selfishness and harmful selflessness. In fact, we would do well to point out the way in which power influences our practices in one direction or another.

Taking Our Selves Back and Building up Community

In this chapter I have argued that a theological censuring of pride and celebration of self-sacrifice can lead to the underdevelopment of women's spiritual self due to the social convention that already promotes women's self-abnegation. This not only hinders women's development and participation in communities of faith, but it also diminishes community life. Thus, the problem of self-abdication is not simply a personal "sin" that needs to be named, but also a key contributor to communal dysfunctions (a theme more fully developed in chapter 3). When pride and self-assertion are frowned upon, prophetic voices are quelled. In the end the "loss of self" that is promoted in communities is also a loss of genuine community. Persons, both women and men, are selves in relation to others; thus, when some are compelled to "give themselves away," genuine community life is also given away.

If discussions of sin and grace were going on in sequestered ivory towers with little effect on the world, this discussion would not be so urgent. By beginning with *The Giving Tree* and exploring the popularized versions of spiritual disciplines, I alert leaders to the fact that male-biased theological formulations of sin and grace are influential and pervasive in community life. Teachings, narratives, and practices in our communities are a potential hindrance to appropriate self-development of women. By reinforcing women's concern for giving, many of our teachings promote women to both give *of* themselves and to give *away* their selves—their responsible and assertive identities.

Women, and others whose selves are in "hiding," need to claim their selves before God; leaders of women need to proclaim this side of the gospel news and promote the development of women's selves. In arguing for the importance of self-development, I do not claim that the Christian virtue of self-sacrifice is to be categorically denounced—or that women's capacity for caring and relationality is to be suppressed. In fact, I uphold relationships as an important aspect of human, including women's, identity. In the next two chapters, drawing on the insights of developmental psychologists Robert Kegan and Carol Gilligan, we will look at the importance of relationships for self-identity in women. In reclaiming relationality, we will further examine the way in which self-abnegation not only thwarts the development of the self but also prevents the emergence of genuine relationships.

In her book *Between Mothers and Sons: The Making of Vital and Loving Men*, Evelyn S. Bassoff also pays critical attention to *The Giving Tree*. She gives the story a more Freudian interpretation, finding in it a symbolic depiction of the relation between mother and son. Drawing on the ancient association of trees with the life-giving power of the mother, Bassoff identifies the giving tree as mother. Rather than life-giving, Bassoff sees in the tree a mother who will not let her child grow. By indulging her son and truncating her own life, the mother/tree stunts both her son's growth and her own. Backing her discussion with the work of Jungian analyst M. Esther Harding, Bassoff reminds us of the mother's responsibility to keep growing and to allow for the growth of the other. It is the mother's task to accept "the necessary maternal transformation," which requires her to relinquish "her position of superiority as *giver* in order that the son can be released from his demeaning position of *taker*."[69]

Whether the tree symbolizes an overindulgent mother or an under-assertive mate or friend, the way in which self-destructiveness also becomes debilitating to the "other" is evident. In order to allow "takers" to grow, friends, mates, and mothers will need to put themselves back into the relationship. When women are encouraged to take themselves back, so to speak, communities will be the better for it.

Chapter Two

The Dance of Human Development

IN CELEBRATION OF "SHEILA"

The courage to leave the place whose language you learned
as early as your own, whose customs, however
dangerous or demeaning, bind you like a halter
you have learned to pull inside, to move your load;
the land fertile with the blood spilled on it;
the roads mapped and annotated for survival.

We honor those who let go of every-
thing but freedom, who ran, who revolted, who fought,
who became other by saving themselves.
    —Marge Piercy [1]

   "Until we can understand the assumptions in which we are drenched we cannot
know ourselves."
    —Adrienne Rich [2]

DEVELOPMENT FOR EMPOWERMENT: WELCOMING WOMEN AS PARTNERS

*I*n the previous chapter I argued that theologies that promote self-sacrifice and censor self-assertion can inhibit the growth of women; in this chapter I will look at the way in which the theological constraints on women described in the last chapter interact with the process of psychological and cognitive development for women.

This powerful combination of forces can "bind [women] like a halter," to use Piercy's words. This does not have to happen. Communities of faith can foster women's growth from pliancy to power.

In this chapter and the next, I will put Reinhold Niebuhr's thought into conversation with theories of human development. Niebuhr wouldn't have minded such a conversation, for he himself noted in the preface to the Scribner Library edition of *The Nature and Destiny of Man* that his reading of developmental psychologist Erik Erikson both confirmed much of his thought but also "would have prompted some changes in my statement of the reality." I will continue to indicate where I would like to see "some changes" in Niebuhr's thesis; I will also, however, express some contributions that he makes to our understanding of human development in general and women's development specifically. I believe that in naming the sins of pride and sensuality, Niebuhr identified important temptations that are developmentally significant. Furthermore, Niebuhr's call for "self-sacrifice" and even the "shattering of the self," can be recovered, but in a surprising manner.

I will carry on this conversation between theology and human development by considering Niebuhr in relation to contemporary developmental theorist Robert Kegan. Kegan was inspired by the genius of Jean Piaget, whose pioneer work on the evolution of human thinking (cognitive development) still forms the basis for much that is done on cognitive and moral development. The limitations of Piagetian theory have not gone unnoticed, however, particularly by feminist scholars and researchers. As Piaget is the forefather of "classic" developmental theory, Carol Gilligan might be named the "foremother" of feminist critique and revision of the reigning paradigm. In her first major work, *In a Different Voice*, Gilligan not only exposed the way in which original research into human development was done looking solely at males, but also reframed developmental theory in light of women's experience. Gilligan questioned the way in which human development theory was constructed to favor autonomy, independence, and the capacity for impartial abstract moral reflection. Women, according to Gilligan, are more likely to make meaning in light of relationships, connectedness, and a capacity for caring for the concrete needs of others. Thus, women appeared to be less mature in studies of cognitive and moral development based on the classic paradigm.[3] In chapter 3, I will turn to Carol Gilligan's groundbreaking work, which places relationality rather than autonomy at the center of human development.[4]

It might seem odd to probe into women's development by looking at Kegan's work first. If Kegan builds on the classic Piagetian paradigm of cognitive development, and Carol Gilligan has exposed its male-bias, why start with Kegan? Wouldn't it make more sense to begin with Gilligan?

I begin with Kegan for three reasons. First, Kegan is conscious of and sensitive to feminist concerns. As we will see shortly, his formulation of Piagetian theory recognizes the human need for separation *and* connection. In fact, this is probably one of the reasons why Kegan muses that although his theory grows out of Piaget's groundwork, he is still "left with the slightly uncomfortable feeling that the father of the creation might not recognize the child as his own."[5] Furthermore, Kegan is conscious of potential male-bias in the construction of theory. In his latest work he contends that we must "resist our tendencies to privilege what is familiar [i.e., male experience] and judge critically [i.e., female experience] what is different." He warns:

> Any time a theory is normative, and suggests that something is more grown, more mature, more developed than something else, we had all better check to see if the distinction rests on arbitrary grounds that consciously or unconsciously unfairly advantage some people (such as those who create the theory and people like them) whose own preferences are being depicted as superior. We had all better check whether what may even appear to be an "objective" theory is not in reality a tool or captive of a "ruling" group (such as white people, men, Westerners) who use the theory to preserve their advantaged position.[6]

Second, classic developmental theory is not simply an objective description of the ways people think, it is also a value laden theory that reveals deeply embedded norms of our culture. To ignore classic cognitive developmental theory because it is male-biased would not serve women. Women are thrown into this culture, and to refuse to give them the "street smarts" they need to be aware of this culture is not helpful. Kegan argues that the demands of life in the modern world require the kind of cognitive maturity that developmental theory has identified. This doesn't mean we need to accept the norms and biases of this culture; but it does mean that we should help women to be aware of them and to negotiate a world that reflects these values. We need to understand the paradigm and raise consciousness about the ways in which women are disadvantaged in meeting the standards of this paradigm, while at the same time raising critical issues about the value of the paradigm. Women are being socialized in a way that disadvantages their cognitive development, and this should be remedied. While we need not celebrate the cultural norm that overemphasizes autonomy, independence, and abstract reflection, we ought not to use our critique of this norm as an additional force against the necessary self-differentiation of women.

This leads to my third reason for beginning with Kegan. The capacity for autonomy is not inimical to women's development. Feminists such as Carol Christ have pointed to the importance of "awakening" in women's movement to self-affirmation.[7] Awakening involves the ability to stand apart from one's cultural prescriptions for femininity and women's place. While awakening leads women into a community of women-affirming persons rather than into isolation, it still requires the kind of cognitive strength that presupposes an independence of spirit and voice, which is the hallmark of Piagetian developmental theory. "The courage to leave the place whose language you have learned" is important for women as well as men. While I will not celebrate autonomy per se, I will argue that in order for women to be selves-in-relation to other persons, they must be encouraged to be selves. In order to be selves, women must have the capacity to reflect critically on the cultural assumptions in which they are "drenched." And yet, North American culture tends to nurture women toward underdeveloped selfhood and men toward hyperdeveloped selfhood—in ways that distort both connectedness and separateness. By promoting the underdevelopment of self in women and the overdevelopment of self in men, we are promoting expressions of sin that prevent women and men from developing toward genuine relationality that requires mature interdependence. This not only influences the selfhood of women and men, but also distorts community life.

THE "DANCE OF HUMAN DEVELOPMENT": SEPARATING AND CONNECTING

In his important work *The Evolving Self*, Robert Kegan images human development as a lifelong "dance" between our dual longings for *inclusion* and *independence*.[8] The former is a "yearning to be included, to be a part of, close to, joined with, to be held, admitted, accompanied," and the latter is a "yearning to be independent or autonomous, to experience one's distinctness, the self-chosenness of one's directions, one's individual integrity."[9] While a person is always negotiating a path between inclusion and independence, it may be that some persons (more often women) experience connection as the base from which agency is formed while others make the experience of independence (more often men) the base from which connections are formed.[10] If healthy development takes place, the self achieves increasing "differentiation," the ability to know one's uniqueness, *and* increasing "relationality," the ability to be genuinely connected to others.

As "personal authority" grows so does attentiveness to the differentness of others. Differentiation means "continuing to hold onto one's precious connections and loyalties while refashioning one's relationship to them so that one *makes them up* rather than *gets made up* by them."[11] Thus, according to Kegan, differentiation does not bring disconnectedness; it rather enables genuine connection. The less differentiated one is from others, the less one is able to truly appreciate the differentness and otherness of those with whom one is in relation. The highest expression of human maturity, in Kegan's understanding, is "inter-individuality." Inter-individuality is to be distinguished from dependency, which signals a lack of self, and independence, which points to alienation from others. When persons are able to respect the distinctiveness of self and others while also remaining in mutual relationships with others, then they are psychologically mature.

On the way to this mature interdependence, the human self goes through a number of stages. We will focus in this chapter on the last three levels of human development in Kegan's scheme. It is important to briefly sketch the whole, however. The human "self" begins in a state of oneness (or fusion) with its mothering figure. While the mothering figure is aware that this needy infant is a separate being, from the infant's "perspective," self and other are merged. The infant experiences the mothering person as warmth, food, and comfort rather than as another being. Thus, Kegan calls this phase of selfhood the "**incorporative**" self. A very fragmentary sense of self begins to emerge as the young child recognizes that there are objects separate from himself, but he experiences those objects in light of his own perceptions. This stage is egocentric in the sense that the child cannot distinguish between her own perspective and reality; she thinks she caused the world to go dark by closing her eyes. Because the child at this stage is subject to and cannot stand back from his impulses, this is dubbed the "**impulsive**" form of self by Kegan. In middle childhood, the beginnings of the self emerge when the child recognizes that she has needs, interests, and wishes for which she must work to be met. In fact, because the child's needs and interests are near synonymous with the self at this phase of life, Kegan aptly names this the "**imperial**" stage of selfhood. Though not yet able to understand and empathize with another person, the imperial self is able to cut deals with others that yield an equal exchange of services. In the teenage years and on into adulthood, the self develops the capacity for interpersonal relationships; it defines itself by the expectations of its family and group (the "**interpersonal**" form of self). While many persons plateau at this stage of development, the next movement is into self-authorship, which brings the capacity to stand back or even apart from one's relationships (the "**institutional**" form of self). This is the first evidence of a fully chosen self, and it generally expresses its identity in terms of an ideological orientation. If a person reaches full maturity, she or he reaches the "**inter-individual**" form of selfhood, characterized by the capacity to know oneself and to appreciate others in genuine interdependence and mutuality.

The most important factor in determining a person's growth for maturity, in Kegan's view, is the "holding environment." The term was coined by D. W. Winnicott in reference to the maternal environment that positively mirrors the infant's "self" (rather than projects its own self onto the infant) and responds to the infant's needs. At each phase of life, the person is highly dependent upon his or her social and cultural environments. These environments begin with the "mothering person" and then extend into family, school, peer groups, partnering relations, professional arenas, and genuinely intimate relations. Ideally, these environments are able to support the person where they are (hold on), challenge the person to move beyond where they are (let go), and remain in relation with the person when they change (stay put). In reality, these environments often either fail to support the person as they are ("let go" too soon) or work to keep the person from growing into something different ("hold on" too tightly). Furthermore, all too many environments reject a person who has grown in a disapproved way, thus failing to stay put for the reintegration of the new self into the former self.

Women face the peril of all these failures. Some theorists are particularly concerned that women are being let go of too soon or held on to too loosely. This occurs when women enter male-dominated spheres of life (which are often institutionally oriented) and are expected to reflect the fierce kind of independence and autonomy for which men have been trained, without any affirmation for the kinds of interpersonal qualities for which women have been trained. This is an important problem, and we will not neglect it. I believe that the most prevalent problem for women, however, is that their environments hold on too tightly to conventional understandings of womanhood and refuse to stay put when women grow into differentiated selves.

In supporting women's movement toward greater independence, I do not denigrate relationality. I wish to avoid two pitfalls that occur in theories of women's development. On the one side is the error of making male development the standard, thereby devaluing and even pathologizing women's patterns of relationality. Women are therefore seen either as beings in need of remedial work so as to reach male standards, or as deviants who follow a different (and thereby lesser) pattern. Women's experience is discounted and devalued when this direction is taken. On the other side is the error of making women's relationality definitive of women's being, and thereby reinforcing gender patterns that exist. Relationality is affirmed and held in high honor, and women's experience is deemed as valuable and even superior. In the former case, male norms are accepted uncritically as universally good and women are expected to meet them; in the second case, female relationality is uncritically accepted and the responsibilities of caring for humanity are once again assigned to women. A degree of autonomy and self-authoring is essential for genuine relationality; in supporting women's development we need to press for a deep understanding of relationship that does not perpetuate the oppressive burdens put on women to give their selves away in the name of female goodness. This means that we need to confront the way in which cultural expectations for women work to hold them tightly in the interpersonal phase of cognitive development.

The Interpersonal Self and the "Good Woman"

The interpersonal orientation, as its name suggests, is characterized by the self's deep connection to others. The interpersonal self is, in fact, inseparable from—in technical terms, "embedded in"—its close relationships. Being embedded in personal relationships, the interpersonal self's reality is a priori a shared reality. The self that previously overidentified with its own needs and desires gives way to a self that is able to understand and address the needs and desires of others. The strength of this way of making meaning is the willingness and ability to meet mutual expectations. The person at this stage is often able to intuit needs and expectations and will try to meet needs even before they are expressed. Relationships are central to life, and reality is defined by the important connections in one's life. For teenagers in this stage, peer and family relationships are paramount; for young adults, marriage and life partners are most significant.

Men and women can reflect this phase of life in quite disparate ways because they meet different social expectations. Interpersonally oriented women are pressed to meet social expectations for femininity: submissiveness, passivity, and dependence. Interpersonally oriented men are often shaped by social expectations for bravado and self-assertion; what looks like independence, however, is conformity to conventional understandings of masculinity.[12]

In her national best-seller *Dead Man Walking*, Sister Helen Prejean introduces us to death row inmate Robert Willie, a man who swaggers with bravado and smirks with defiance. Willie, a man involved in the rape and murder of a young woman, projects an image of utter self-reliance. This is far from the reality. Many of his criminal acts were done in compliance with his peers. When he tells Sister Prejean that he was once part of the Aryan Brotherhood, his interpersonal orientation is exposed. "A dude I had met in Terre Haute had sent a letter of recommendation for me to the brotherhood before I got to Marion [prison], and when I got there, as soon as I arrived, they took me in, gave me cigarettes, drugs, the shirt off their backs. Everything they had they was willing to share," he explained. "That was the best part of it, the sharing. You belonged, man. Once I got hold of a hundred Valiums and I shared them with the brothers. And when the other brothers got stuff, they shared with me. It was one for all and all for one. Once you're in the brotherhood, it's for life—you can't get out until death." Sister Prejean asked what would have happened if he had decided not to share his drug booty. "They would've killed me," he replied. When she remarks with intended sarcasm, "cozy family," he responds with seriousness, "It was. It really was."[13] Willie is clearly an interpersonally related man, highly susceptible to the group to which he belongs. While he is expected to project defiance toward the establishment and exercise domination over women, he is also fully subject to the authority of his group.

In this conventional and conformist stage of life, beliefs are tacitly held since they depend as much upon who one is related to as what one decides. In fact, the interpersonal self is a composite of shared realities; there is no coherent center that organizes the different relationships. There *is* no self independent of the context of other people; "the other is required to bring the self into being."[14] Beliefs may shift dramatically with changes in interpersonal contexts; the desire to belong can, as with Willie, make even a neo-Nazi group seem appealing. Furthermore, at this stage, any belief or choice that threatens the loss of one's relationships (which are confused with the self) threatens the loss of the self per se. Technically, we might say that the interpersonal "self" is not yet really defined. The self is not yet a chosen self; in psychological lingo, this self still lacks internal coherence, self-authorship, and the capacity for distanced self-reflection.[15] While extremely adept at meeting the expectations of the other, the interpersonal self does not have the ability to review and reflect upon its relationships.

Because the boundary between self and other is extremely permeable, there is what Sharon Parks described as the "tyranny of the they." The source of personal regulation is "outside" the self and in the surrounding significant environment. Being defined by their relationships, persons at this phase of life are highly vulnerable to the viewpoints of their significant others, who shape their identity and determine their self-esteem. This "tyranny" can be experienced as voices variously commanding, reinforcing, or disapproving of one's behavior. Women in particular are vulnerable to the tyranny of they, since serving "the they" is frequently "the basic principle in women's lives."[16]

In her recent work *Who Cares? Women, Care, and Culture*, Julia Wood argues that women are highly susceptible to what she calls "motivational displacement." A woman groomed for caring can easily displace her own interests and motives in life and come to believe that the interests and motives of those for whom she cares are her own. She loses the capacity to own and name her own interests, and she replaces her own motives with the needs and interests of others. Wood further contends that the continual displacing of her own impulses, goals, and aspirations can lead to a woman's "compromised or undeveloped autonomy."[17] Years of convincing herself that *their* interests are *my* interests cause a woman to silence her own needs and interests in order to focus on those of others. While this is an important skill for all people to exercise at critical moments, when a person loses or never develops the capacity to name her own impulses, goals, needs, and aspirations, it obstructs self development.

Sophie Tolstoy (wife of Russian novelist Leo Tolstoy) wrestled with her desire to use her intellectual powers and her desire to conform to the kind of wife that she was expected to be. In 1865 she wrote in her diary:

> [Lyova] said that youth meant the capacity to say: "I can accomplish everything." As for me, I both *can* and *want* to do everything, but after a while I begin to realize there is nothing to want, and that I can't do anything beyond eating, drinking, sleeping, nursing the children, and caring for them and my husband. After all, this *is* happiness, yet why do I grow sad and weep, as I did yesterday?[18]

The dependency of the interpersonal self on others can be exploited. The interpersonal self, particularly the female interpersonal self, will sometimes give up dreams, safety, and health for attachment. The lyrics of popular songs are replete with such self-abnegation. Carole King, in the 1970s, crooned: "Where you lead, I will follow; anywhere that you tell me to. . . . I always wanted a real house with flowers on the window sill, but if you want to live in New York City, honey you know I will." Things have not changed. Tracy Chapman, in the 1990s, sang: "The things we won't do for love; I'd climb a mountain if I had to, risk my life if I could have you, you, you."

The self who so sacrificially gives itself for others can become a victim of domineering personalities and a prime candidate for what Anne Wilson Shaef calls "relationship addictions." Relationship addiction refers to the unhealthy way in which relationships can become the source of validity, meaning, and security to such an extent that they are held on to at any cost. The person suffering from this addiction perceives that they will be "nothing" without a key relationship—typically for a woman this means a man is necessary for validity, meaning, and security of self-esteem.[19] Anger and self-assertion are avoided when relationships become all-defining, for expressing anger or needs risks losing the relationships that make up one's very being.

The interpersonal phase of life is an important one in human development; it marks a person's capacity to listen to and comply with the expectations of his or her group. These abilities prepare the way for later interdependence. In terms of cognitive development, however, the interpersonal orientation is not fully mature. And, as the above discussion exposes, the accomplishments of the interpersonal self are joined with limitations and serious dangers. When the interpersonally oriented person remains dependent and continues to be drenched in the tacit structures of its world, she or he is, ironically, vulnerable to a particular expression of "self-centeredness."

"SELF-CENTEREDNESS" AND THE SLUMBERING OF THE INTERPERSONAL SELF

Human development is often described as a continual process of the centering, decentering, and recentering of the self. At each phase of life, the person achieves a stable balance that is adequate for a period of time; growth occurs when the stable center gives way to a new balance. We can understand "self-centeredness," then, as the self's attempt to sustain and secure its present way of being. Unhealthy "self-centeredness" occurs when the self stabilizes and resists growth indefinitely.

The interpersonal self, as all developmental balances, is a "centered" self that is tempted to remain in its present state of being. This self is centered in its relationships and assimilates reality in terms of those relationships. "Self-centeredness" at this stage is, therefore, relational. If prolonged or distorted, this form of self-centeredness works against the emergence of a coherent and chosen self. It is only with the move to the next phase, which Kegan calls the institutional, that the person can stand outside of their relationships and look at them critically.

It is helpful here to return to the discussion of sin from chapter 1. While caring deeply about one's close relationships and making meaning in light of interpersonal expectations in itself is not sin, the interpersonally orientated person is particularly vulnerable to the "sin of sensuality" as Niebuhr describes it. Sensuality, the expression of sin that Niebuhr named but underemphasized, is characterized by a denial of freedom and a loss of the self in some mutable good. A person falls into sensuality when seeking to escape from the unlimited possibilities of freedom and the perils and responsibilities of self-determination. Sensuality is an escape from self. The self, "finding itself to be inadequate as the centre of its existence, seeks for another god amidst the various forces, processes and impulses of nature over which it ostensibly presides."[20] The result of this flight from self is a subconscious existence, an existence that is not critically aware of its surroundings. Such a person is susceptible to escaping responsibility and self-authorship by finding a god in a person or persons outside the self and deferring difficult decisions to the other. Faced with life's insecurities, the interpersonal self finds its security in others. Niebuhr speaks of the self that "slumbers" in its tacit and uncritical appropriation of the world around it.[21]

According to Valerie Saiving, women are typically encouraged to surrender self-identity "and to be included in another's 'power of being.' "[22] For Saiving, this surrender of identity is more accurately woman's *sin* than it is her virtue, and it is a far cry from the pride of man.

> The temptations of woman *as woman* . . . have a quality which can never be encompassed by such terms as "pride" and "will-to-power." They are better suggested by such items as triviality, distractibility, and diffuseness; lack of an organizing center or focus; *dependence on others for one's self definition*; tolerance at the expense of standards of excellence; inability to respect the boundaries of privacy; sentimentality, gossipy sociability, and mistrust of reason—in short, *underdevelopment or negation of the self.*[23]

Developmentally speaking, the interpersonally oriented self must yield to the emerging institutional orientation. It must give up—sacrifice—its immersion in its relationships and take responsibility for its choices and self-authorship. Traditional forms of spirituality and piety, which over-emphasize self-denial, conspire with social pressures to thwart this move-ment. The prophetic torpor that we described in chapter 1 contributes to the "overholding" of women in the interpersonal phase of life. For women at the growing edge of this stage, theological teachings that emphasize empowerment, self-development, and assertive judgment are needed. Teachings that exclusively focus on self-sacrifice and nonassertiveness will obstruct the development of women in transition—or force these women out of the church in legitimate *self*-preservation.

Recall that Niebuhr claimed that "the self in this state of preoccupation with itself" must be "broken," "shattered," and "crucified." I have stated that this has been harmful to women who are neither self-occupied nor in need of breaking. Now I would like to revisit this language of Niebuhr's and argue that we can support a kind of "shattering" of the interpersonal self through the "empowering" of a responsible self.

SELF-SACRIFICE FOR THE INTERPERSONAL SELF: KILLING THE "ANGEL IN THE HOUSE"

The evolution of the self, at any stage of development, according to Kegan (and Piaget) entails both the loss of the self that was (decentering) and the emergence of a new form of selfhood (recentering). In terms not unlike Niebuhr's "shattering of the self," Kegan describes an often painful and emotionally charged process of destabilization and transition. The self truly *dies* to the self that was, and the new self that emerges is a kind of rebirth. The psychological processes of decentering and recentering are analogous to (though not the same as) the theological experience of death and resurrection. In fact, Kegan even claims that these transitions are of ultimate proportions. When the "dying" of the self results in a pos-itive "rebirth," a person develops hope in the transformational potential of life.

Although to insist on traditional forms of self-sacrifice at this stage is to reinforce the underdevelopment of the self, the notion of self-sacrifice need not be completely discarded. We can responsibly promote "self-sacrifice" if we understand the term to mean the willingness of the self to grow beyond its present constitution. The sacrifice that the self at this stage may need to make is what Paul Ramsey called "the sacrifice of the sacrifice," the willingness to forgo self-renunciation in the name of edifi-cation.[24] We can recover the language of self-sacrifice, but we cannot reduce its meaning to self-abnegation. Women who are interpersonally oriented legitimately practice self-sacrifice by giving up self-abnegation and taking on the responsibility to assert their voices. Self-abnegation is in fact at this stage the equivalent to self-centeredness. The challenge—both theological and psychological—to the person with this psychological orientation is the challenge of self-responsibility. This does not mean that all forms of traditional self-giving and self-sacrifice are illegitimate; it does mean that self-abnegating self-sacrifice may be more an expression of "self-centered" existence than a yielding of the "self."

There is gospel support for this. If we look at the portrayals of women in the resurrection narratives, we see that they are tempted to hold on to a former way of understanding Jesus. The message of Jesus to Magdalene at the end of the gospel of John seems to be: "Where you seek permanence, there is only death. Where you are changed, there is life." Mary can no longer cling and hold on to a faith that was just emerging, she was being called to grow and mature.[25] Thus, even as Mary experienced the death and resurrection of Christ, she also experienced a dying and raising in her faith and life.

In a very moving statement, Virginia Woolf wrote about having to kill the "Angel in the House," in order to give birth to a self that was emerging:

> It was she who used to come between me and my paper when I was writing reviews. It was she who bothered me and wasted my time and so tormented me that at last I killed her. You who come of a younger and happier generation may not have heard of her—you may not know what I mean by the Angel in the House. I will describe her as shortly as I can. She was intensely sympathetic. She was immensely charming. She was utterly unselfish. She excelled in the difficult arts of family life. She sacrificed herself daily. If there was chicken, she took the leg; if there was a draft, she sat in it—in short she was so constituted that she never had a mind or a wish of her own, but preferred to sympathize always with the minds and wishes of others. . . . I turned upon her and caught her by the throat. I did my best to kill her. My excuse, if I were to be had up in a court of law, would be that I acted in self-defense. Had I not killed her she would have killed me.[26]

"[The Angel in the House] was so constituted that she never had a mind or a wish of her own, but preferred to sympathize always with the minds and wishes of others." Though she did not name it this way, Virginia Woolf faced the decentering of her interpersonal self. In order to save the life of the self she was becoming, Woolf needed to "sacrifice" (kill) the self that used to be. What Woolf does not say, and probably did not realize, is that killing this angel not only led to her own self-development but also led to the development of those who were too accustomed to always having their needs met, always eating the choice pieces of chicken, and always being put first. This was not simply self-defense, but also a defense of the growth of others.

Women who are "overheld" in the interpersonal orientation are encouraged to be so constituted that they never have a mind or a wish of their own, but prefer to sympathize always with the minds and wishes of others. *Indeed, what should be a phase in life becomes the definition of womanhood.* The "organizing center or focus" yearned for by Saiving, is the sine qua non of the next phase of development. It is discouraged in women because their cues are supposed to come from the needs of those around them. We shall explore the dangerous consequences this has on teenage girls in chapter 4. Here it is important to recognize that this holding back of women from movement into self-regulated identity is promoting a type of "self-centeredness" that prevents growth. This is accomplished by fusing cultural femininity and a distorted understanding of Christian virtue together to produce a sanctified underdeveloped self.

THE INSTITUTIONAL SELF: MASTERING ITS OWN HOUSE

As opposed to Woolf's "angel," the institutionally oriented self has a mind of her own, and she prefers to use her own mind rather than to cater to the whims of others. This does not mean that she neglects others; rather she is no longer defined by others. While the interpersonally oriented self *is* its relationships, the institutional self *has* relationships. All experiences and relationships are now mediated by the "self-system" or ideology that gives the person identity and individuality. The institutionally oriented self, at least psychologically if not in other arenas of life, is to a large degree "master of her own house." Kegan describes the institutional self as "a form or system" and names its strengths as "its capacity for self-regulation, its capacity to sustain itself, to parent itself, to name itself—its autonomy."[27] No longer reliant on external sources of authority and able to gain critical distance from its previous assumptive value system, this self-negotiation is more of a conscious and deliberate choice. "Stage 4's ["institutional"] delicate balance is that in self-government it has rescued the 'self' from its captivity by shared realities."[28] While in the former stage of life a person knows she or he has feelings, thoughts, and experiences, in this stage the person knows that she or he is "author, maker, critiquer, and remaker" of those feelings, thoughts, and experiences.[29] She feels comfortable creating and initiating her own work, sharing and following her own visions, and taking responsibility for her life. This is a momentous gain for one who has only been able to hear herself or himself in relation to the voice of others.

The self-mastery of this phase of life is either expressed by confidence in one's inner voice or by the adoption of a self-chosen ideology.

THE INSTITUTIONAL SELF: INNER VOICE AND IDEOLOGY

In this chapter and the next three, I will repeatedly argue for the importance of "voice" in the lives of women. Having confidence in one's "voice" and knowing that one's voice will be listened to are critical to healthy participation in a community. In employing the "megametaphor" of voice, a term much bandied about these days, I mean more than simply the ability to express oneself. *Voice* means having the ability to express oneself *and* the right to be heard; it means knowing one's mind and will *and* trusting that one can express oneself in one's community. Voice is one's feeling of "presence, power, participation, protest, and identity."[30] When one knows one's voice will be heeded and taken seriously, one is a true participant in a community.

Gaining confidence in one's voice is to be distinguished from following intuition. Intuition, or one's "gut level," pre-reflective feeling about matters, is sometimes identified as "women's way" of understanding. For those who disrespect women, intuition is then dismissed; for those who value women, intuition is celebrated. We need to be cautious about both reactions to intuition. Women's confidence in their own capacity to think critically, make decisions, voice an opinion, name their own experience, and stake a claim in community life is very important; women's pre-reflective thoughts and feelings are not to be uncritically acclaimed, however.

Christie Cozad Neuger has warned that "what is often called intuitive has been deeply distorted by internalized patriarchal biases and externalized reinforcement for following through with those biases."[31] Pre-reflective ways of thinking, while sometimes helpful, can also be deeply embedded with patriarchal (and women-demeaning) assumptions. Many persons who are subordinated in society internalize dominant beliefs about these assumptions, especially if they do not have a place of refuge that offers an alternative worldview. Dana Jack, in her work on women's depression, has found that internalized images of the "good woman" who sacrifices herself are so strong that women are reluctant to challenge the images even when their experience tells them the model of goodness is harmful.[32]

In order to combat the low self-esteem that is a consequence of oppressive views, we need to free people to be "counterintuitive," to think thoughts that go against the assumptions of the prevailing worldview. While intuition can sometimes be a source of wisdom, intuitive thoughts and feelings must first surface for reflection. And people who rely on their intuition need also to be open to exploring the sources of its knowledge. Inner voice, as I am using it here, is not the same as intuition. Inner voice requires a critically aware engagement with the world, and it includes the freedom and the confidence to think counterintuitively.

Counterintuitive thinking, it is important to stress, is not antitraditional thinking. Many women and men in culturally oppressed groups have legitimately challenged the modern repudiation of tradition, and they argue that a valuing and reclaiming of the richness of culture and tradition are needed in our world today. They point out that the modern emphasis on critical reflection and self-chosen ideology renders people suspicious and ashamed of their cultural and religious traditions. It may seem as if my use of Kegan plays right into the hands of the modern repression of tradition and culture. Admittedly, promoting self-authoring identity unavoidably makes people strangers to their surroundings, but it also provides a tool for reclaiming one's cultural heritage. Culturally marginalized persons often suffer from an internalized negation of their culture; reclaiming their cultural identity requires the tools for reflecting critically on the dominant culture. The capacity for counterintuitive thinking actually enables culturally marginalized persons to raise suspicions toward dominant viewpoints (especially those that denigrate their own person and culture) and to choose positively for their cultural identity.

From the perspective of dominance, fostering the voices of others takes commitment and openness. Frequently those who gain voice after having been oppressed or marginalized wish to rename themselves and their experiences that were named for them by oppressive structures. This attempt to claim power is not always well received. In fact, denying another's voice is an effective way to disempower another. One feminist pastor, chastised for using inclusive language for humanity instead of the generic "men," reports that she was forced to make a choice between loyalty to her church and exercise of voice—squelching her voice was made a requisite for keeping her job. "The session said they might consider letting me stay *if* I would promise never to use inclusive language again in worship. I said that I couldn't do that without betraying my faith or compromising my personal integrity."[33]

Sheila Larson, who was interviewed by Robert Bellah and associates and included in their book *Habits of the Heart*, is perhaps the most famous woman who has gained confidence in her inner voice. Having "liberat[ed] herself from an oppressively conformist early family life," Sheila now hears God through her own internal voice.[34] She trusts herself, and she listens to the guidings that come from within. She is not fused with God or alienated from others, however. Sheila, a young nurse, describes the basic structure of her faith as: "It's just try to love yourself and be gentle with yourself. You know, I guess, take care of each other. I think He [God] would want us to take care of each other." The two religious experiences that define Sheila's faith are an assurance from God when she underwent surgery and the feeling of having been Christ to a distraught husband and his dying wife in the woman's final hours.

Confidence in one's voice is a momentous gain for women, but our society is often uncomfortable with women who are masters of their own houses. Indeed, Sheila herself has become infamous. Having described her personal faith as "Sheilaism," she has been the whipping girl of many theological and philosophical attacks on individualism. Worried that her loyalty to inner voice leaves open "the logical possibility of over 220 million American religions," her interviewers lament such privatized religion that allegedly answers to no transcendent authority or larger community. William Placher, who sees Sheila as "only the extreme case of a common pattern," uses her faith as the foil for his discussion of biblical notions of Christian community.[35]

It's not surprising that a woman's confidence in her inner voice sets people reeling; what is puzzling, however, is that Sheila is being dismissed as the epitome of an individualist devoid of God. I'm not claiming that Sheila should become an exemplar for religious experience; rather I am trying to expose what has become an inadvertent bashing of women's inner voice. Although Bellah and associates intended to judge her privatism, the subtle message that has been conveyed by the ongoing attack on "Sheilaism" is that women's confidence in their inner voice is the major source of breakdown in North American religious life. Place this alongside the clarion call for a return to "traditional families," and you have a concerted effort to put women back into—or keep them eternally in—their interpersonal place.

Sheila's movement to self-authorship is expressed by confidence in her inner voice and the authoring of her self-system. It can also be the adoption of a specific ideology that enables the transition from the interpersonal to take place. Counter-dominant ideologies have recently become a source of empowerment for many on the margins of society. For those who are not white, male, heterosexual, Christian, economically advantaged or able-bodied, their marginalized status can become a source for personal authority and political engagement. The variety of feminisms have provided supportive holding environments within which maturing women can theorize about their oppression and reflect critically on the externally generated values, ideologies, and loyalties. Kegan, in fact, considers women's movements to sponsor for women "the most dramatic and publicly moving demonstrations of the evolution out of the interpersonal balance in the culture today." Women's movements and feminist ideologies, he notes, offer "the invitation to women to see the very fact of their womanhood as entry to the ideological participation which is essential to the institutional evolutionary balance."[36]

While feminism often provides a woman the means for moving out of the interpersonal into the institutional orientation, the chosen ideology can be of many different types. Ideological forms of mothering, in fact, may serve as a transition for young women moving from interpersonal to institutional forms of meaning making. Committed to the nurture and well-being of her children, a woman may search for and explore various theories of parenting—*and choose* a framework compatible with her inner values. In adopting an ideologically, rather than interpersonally, oriented style of parenting, the young mother is on her way to self-chosen ideals.

This can generate conflict between generations of mothers. An ideological mother may, to the consternation of her foremothers, disregard the kind of interpersonally shared knowledge that used to pass between women.[37] In asserting her ideology with confidence and even rigidly, she will be at times less than gracious toward those who wish to pass on their wisdom and experience in the form of advice. Those sages who are willing to share their wisdom and let it be screened according to the will of the maternal ideologue will get along fine with her and nurture her developmental needs; those who do not understand the developmental needs of this mother and expect to be accepted as the "expert" will feel hurt and demoted, and probably will withdraw in alienation.

This is a sad, and I think frequent, conflict between this generation's women and the women before. The developmental needs are at cross-purposes. The older women, wizened by experience, desire to pass on what they have learned to their younger daughters. The younger women, still early in their sense of identity, need to be confirmed in their own knowing. Several years ago, a series of "Dear Abby" (or Dear Ann, I forget which one!) letters were brought to my attention. The first letter was from a mother-in-law who lamented that her daughter-in-law did not appreciate her, evidenced by the fact that she never sought her counsel on anything. The mother-in-law then exhorted new daughter-in-laws: ask your mother-in-law for advice and share in the knowledge she has gleaned over the years. This provoked responses from daughters-in-law who expressed that they felt unaffirmed. Their advice to new mothers-in-law: show confidence in your daughter-in-law and affirm her confidence in her capabilities and choices!

Both needs are legitimate, but they can easily feel in opposition to one another. Sadly, what starts as two ships crossing in the night can end up as two ships firing missiles at one another in the national news. Perhaps if we leaders could teach the older generations of women the skills of letting go (supporting their daughter's self-chosen styles of parenting) and the younger generations of women the skills of holding on (valuing, even if not always adhering to, the wisdom of their mothers), we would help build a holding environment that supports both continuity and change between the generations. This continuity not only helps bridge the generations of women, it reduces the temptation to destructive self-mastery to which the self-authoring person is susceptible.

The possibilities for ideological forms of mothering point to another important issue concerning women's growth in self. It is easy for those of us who are feminists to want to see women grow into our particular expression of feminism. We must be careful this does not lead us to reinforce interpersonal compliance over personal power. We must avoid the temptation toward prescribing an ideology for another; for when we do this, we inadvertently reinforce regression toward interpersonal identity. To command or pressure a woman toward a particular ideology does not serve her developmental needs. We can offer arguments and reasons, but we must create an environment that is free and not coercive. We will return to leadership strategies in chapter 7; here we need to recognize that supporting the self's confidence is critical for maturity. Our ideologies, helpful though they may be, must be subordinated to the woman's developmental needs. Strict compliance is not the virtue we seek—even compliance to our good cause; we must nurture women to choose for themselves an authentic personal identity.

"GOOD WOMEN" IN TRANSITION:
A HIGH-RISK SITUATION

It is important to reiterate that women in transition from the interpersonal to the institutional phase of development are in a high-risk situation. The danger of being "held tightly" in this stage is far greater for women because the expectations of the "good woman" are very close to the psychological demands of this phase of life. While the journey into selfhood is considered heroic for men, it is considered deviant and unfeminine for women. This means that a woman's femininity is affirmed in terms of womanhood while it disadvantages her in terms of personhood. For the fact of the matter is, while women may be affirmed for being feminine in private spheres, the qualities of feminine are disrespected in public spheres.

Many holding environments and communities simply do not stay put for women here. Kegan quips that "in order to get yourself together, you first have to get yourself apart."[38] The tragedy is that for some, the very real threat is "if you get yourself apart, *we* will no longer be together." That is to say, many "significant others" in women's lives will not stay put for them when they seek to differentiate themselves. It is at this transition between cultural adaptation and self-chosen values that a woman "needs women's support to be able to tolerate the pain and punishment that result from seeing and speaking her truth."[39]

A community of faith can, if it is aware of its role, provide the kind of holding environment that welcomes women as equal partners in the dance of human life and development. Rather than being a place that colludes with our sexist culture, it can be a place that holds on to women in affirmation, appropriately challenges and lets go of women as they grow, and stays put as these supported women celebrate their distinctness and exercise their voice.

This community is not always available. In many cases, the community of which one is a part will not abide the awakening of a woman. The path of awakening may require going in search of a supportive community rather than remaining with the community that seeks to bind one to convention. In order to preserve her emerging self, a woman must sometimes seek another community and another frame of reference that can give her both distance on her past and support for her future. This is a painful, but sometimes unavoidable, choice. If she finds a community with a strong commitment to the empowerment of women, she can make the transition with hope. When there is no place to go to find support, women can face isolation—or worse.

The difficulty posed by this developmental process is tragically narrated in Kate Chopin's story, *The Awakening*. The heroine, Edna Pontellier, was reared to be a traditionally "good" wife and mother. Religion "took a firm hold" on her when she was a "very little girl." Though she always harbored dissonant thoughts, during her early life she kept them at bay.

> Mrs. Pontellier was not a woman given to confidences, a characteristic hitherto contrary to her nature. Even as a child she had lived her own small life all within herself. At a very early period she had apprehended instinctively the dual life—that outward existence that conforms, the inward life that questions.[40]

A few years into wifehood and motherhood, however, she can no longer suppress her hidden self, and begins to question and defy conventional standards of the "good woman." Beginning with overcoming her fear of water, she learns how to swim. This is the beginning of the unleashing of an independent spirit, and convention begins to lose its control over her actions. Her husband's word is no longer effective to guide and order her life. Her erratic behavior grows incomprehensible to those around her, especially Mr. Pontellier. When she slowly eschews the "tacit submissiveness" of the wifely character, he wonders if she is losing her mind. "He could see plainly that she was not herself," writes Chopin. And then, she poignantly adds, "That is, he could not see that she was becoming herself and daily casting aside that fictitious self which we assume like a garment with which to appear before the world."[41]

In an extraordinary conversation with a friend, who is the embodiment of feminine goodness, Edna confides: "I would give up the unessential; I would give my money, I would give my life for my children; but I wouldn't give myself. I can't make it more clear; it's only something which I am beginning to comprehend, which is revealing itself to me." When her companion observes that to give up one's life for another is already the ultimate sacrifice, and that there is nothing more that one can give up, she asserts, "Oh yes they could!" Later she would reflect that her husband and children "were a part of her life. But they need not have thought that they could possess her, body and soul."[42] To offer one's life is the act of an agent; to give oneself to be slowly possessed by the conventions and expectations of society is to give up agency.

"One of these days," she said, "I'm going to pull myself together for a while and think—try to determine what character of a woman I am; for, candidly, I don't know. By all the codes which I am acquainted with, I am a devilishly wicked specimen of the sex. But some way I can't convince myself that I am. I must think about it."

An eccentric musician friend of hers, in what turns out to be a premonition, remarks: "The bird that would soar above the level plain of tradition and prejudice must have strong wings. It is a sad spectacle to see the weaklings bruised, exhausted, fluttering back to earth." Caught between a tradition of self-sacrifice that she cannot fully flout and an independent spirit that is disastrously out of place, Edna feels that the only way she can hold on to herself is to give up her life. She drowns herself in the sea that first gave birth to her self-identity.

SELF-MASTERY AND SELF-CENTEREDNESS IN THE INSTITUTIONAL SELF

In addition to mastering her self, an institutionally oriented woman can take part in movements that call for social transformation. While prophetic voices may emerge at any stage in human development, it is the assertive voice of the institutionally oriented person that is most likely to press for institutional change. In order to faithfully accomplish this cultural transformation, women will have to confront and name the temptations of the institutional self. Though I boldly promote the move to self-authorship, I do not romanticize or uncritically advance this later orientation of the self. Along with Niebuhr, I affirm that "each new development of life . . . presents us with new possibilities of realizing the good in history," while recognizing that "we also face new hazards on each new level . . . [there is] no emancipation from contradictions and ambiguities to which all life in history is subject."[43]

Just as the strength of the interpersonal orientation (the capacity to care about what others think and feel) brings with it a limitation (evasion of the self in relation to others), so too the strength of the institutional comes with a limitation. At their best, ideologically oriented persons can claim their personal authority while respecting and appreciating others whose stances and cultures are different. The temptation toward ideological zeal is, however, always present. The sense of authority that comes with a chosen self can become absolutized and rigid. Rather than respecting difference, the institutional self can seek to eradicate it. The self-mastery that is so important can evolve into the will-to-power that is so dangerous. Regarding this phase of life, Kegan states:

> Its self-naming and self-nourishing converts the world within its reach to operatives on behalf of its personal enterprise. What is experienced from

within the balance as independence and self-regulation might as accurately be seen from beyond the balance as a kind of psychological isolation or masturbation. From within the system this constraint (embeddedness in autonomy) is a matter of vulnerability to whatever threatens self-control.[44]

This system-building self can prefer theory building over concrete practices in particular situations. Favoring abstracted and decontextualized organizations over the particular, this highly skilled thinker can lose touch with the messy, complicated processes of life. It is for this reason that students in my courses, when introduced to developmental theory, frequently express surprise that the institutional orientation is understood to be an advance over the interpersonal orientation. The movement toward abstract reflection can bring a loss of empathetic caring and sensitivity to the needs of real people in real-life situations. In fact, it is the case that certain advances in cognitive development actually jeopardize some moral sensibilities even while they enlarge others. Although a more interpersonally oriented person may readily respond to a human need out of gut-level compassion, the more sophisticated institutionally oriented person can analyze the situation with cool distance and objectivity. The latter may be more "mature" in terms of cognitive ability, but the former seems more human. While an institutionally oriented person may be more likely to raise a prophetic voice against abstract social structures, it is often the interpersonal prophet who tends to the needs of particular, concrete others. A friend of mine who is an elder in a Presbyterian church described the following incident that occurred during a session meeting she had attended:

> One day I was sitting in a meeting, and the topic of discussion turned to a family in need. Several men on the committee discussed the situation, weighing the needs of this family against the fact that our emergency funds were depleted—although other designated funds were still unspent. One man, after this rather dispassionate discussion, said matter-of-factly, "we've dispensed all our emergency funds this month." The implication was that this family's need could not be met according to the budget categories, and thus it was to be rejected. I was stunned by this decision, but I was new and didn't have any confidence in my own opinion. Just as I was about to resign myself to the men's reasoning, a small voice emerged from the rubble of the meeting. Helen, who is generally very timid and shy in demeanor, said with a quiet ferocity: "I just can't believe we aren't going to help this poor family because they don't fit into our budget categories! Those children are hungry, dammit. Take the money from someplace

else." We all looked at her in stunned silence; we didn't know she had it in her to speak up. I think it was such a spontaneous feeling, that she let it out before she had time to squelch herself. By gosh, the businessmen were stopped in their tracks and that family got their help! Even they could see that her indignation was something like the Word of the Lord in our midst!

Kegan puts it well, "the hallmark of the institutional balance—its self-possessiveness—is also its limit."[45] The importance of self-control is so great that the self may defend rigidly against threats to its system. This is especially likely if the self has the power to control its opposition. The powerful institutionally oriented self sees via its system but cannot gain the distance to see it as a provisional perspective that does not have the corner on truth. *The Nature and Destiny of Man*, the story of "the self in [a] state of preoccupation with itself," is primarily the story of the powerful institutional "man" and the institutional society. It is the story of human beings who are centered by their "self-regulating, self-sustaining, self-naming" (Kegan) and who go awry when they bolster their autonomy through controlling others.

Clearly, self-centeredness in this stage is centeredness in a system or ideology, and it brings the ideological taint that Niebuhr so brilliantly exposed. Because one *sees* through the ideology that gives one coherence, one often cannot see *through* the system and contemplate its provisional-ness and relativity. Niebuhr recognized that this happens to the virtuous ideologies as well as the destructive ones, for it is the structure of the orientation, with its embeddedness in institutions and ideologies, that causes it to close its mind.[46] In her well-known discussion on "the banality of evil" Hannah Arendt contends that the masterminds of the Holocaust acted, for the most part, not out of personal self-interest, but out of intense loyalty to their institutions. It was this loyalty that enabled these ideologues to "resist temptation" toward compassion and spontaneous moral impulse.[47] Heinrich Himmler, in a speech to SS leaders, exults in the "moral" discipline shown by his men: "Most of you know what it means to have 100 corpses lying side by side, or 500 or 1000. To have endured this and to have remained decent men in the process—except for exceptions caused by human weakness—this has made us hard as nails. This is a glorious page in our history."[48]

It is not simply heinous ideologies that are subject to the temptations of system rigidity. Here it is instructive to consider a chapter in Erik Erikson's book on Mahatma Gandhi. Erikson was attracted by Gandhi's philosophy of militant nonviolence and his disciplined search for Truth. While in the middle of a book that sensitively details the integrity and genius of this peacemaker, Erikson comes to an impasse. In a "letter" addressed simply to "Mahatmaji," the writer's emotion is almost palpable. Erikson reveals that in studying Gandhi's writing he came "to the point where I felt unable to continue writing *this* book because I seemed to sense the presence of a kind of untruth in the very protestation of truth; of something unclean when all the words spelled out an unreal purity; and above all, of displaced violence where nonviolence was the professed issue."[49] Gandhi's commitment to his objectives rendered him unempathic and cruel at times to the needs of concrete others in his life. Erikson was incensed by Ghandi's domineering and paternalistic relationship to his wife, Kasturba. "I was a cruelly kind husband. I regarded myself as her teacher and so harassed her out of my blind love for her." While promoting the value of the "inner voice," he seems disrespectful and dismissive of Kasturba's voice "for she was educated neither by her parents nor by me at the time when I ought to have done it."

Erikson quotes from Gandhi's description of an event where some boys and girls were put together in order to teach self-restraint. Learning that the boys were behaving improperly to the girls, Gandhi remonstrated the culprits. He further decided that, to offer a warning to all young men, he would give the girls a "mark" of protection. He cut "off their fine long hair," against the protests of the girls and the initial disapproval of the elderly women. "It does not take much to see, Mahjatmaji, that there is some violence in this," reproves Erikson. Erikson notes that if nonviolent respect for others cannot be achieved in ordinary everyday life of mutual relationships, then we will breed violence when we profess nonviolence. Nonviolent respect, however, is difficult to achieve when concrete persons are subordinated to philosophical systems.

In contrast to women, North American men are typically overheld in the institutional orientation. In fact, they may be so pushed toward this stage that their interpersonal experience is shortchanged, leading to either a superficial or an inadequate negotiation of interpersonal reality.[50] Thus "great men" can be insensitive in interpersonal dealings. The fierce reinforcement of women in interpersonal selfhood and men in institutional selfhood leads to exaggerated forms of these stages and deep clefts between both the arenas of masculine/feminine activity and the norms of masculine/feminine behavior. The fact that there is a mutual gain in anxiety reduction for those on either side holds it in place and creates a "mutual protection against growth." Women gain material security and are absolved of certain responsibilities in the work world; men gain emotional support (and perhaps veneration) and are absolved of certain responsibilities in the home.

SELF-SACRIFICE OF THE INSTITUTIONAL SELF

It is the corrupted institutional self that Niebuhr wished to break and shatter. The result of this shattering, produced by a power beyond the self, is "the experience of release from the self" and an experience of release toward others in love that is capable of being heedless of the self. It is the movement from idolatrous ideology toward the finding of security in God. The self-regulating, self-authoring person can become self-centered in an obvious way; it is at this stage of life that "pride" is a genuine problem. The virtues of the former interpersonal self—sensitivity to the needs of others and the capacity to attend to the concrete details of others' lives—can be left behind in the zeal for self-possession and creativity. When this happens, the self needs to be reprimanded to listen to the voices of others, to expand its horizons of knowing and caring, and to give freely without calculating how it might benefit.

At this stage, theological teachings on responsible and chosen self-giving are helpful. It is important to note, however, that such self-giving is *giving on the other side of self-ownership*. While at this stage love can truly be self-*giving*, at the interpersonal stage it runs the risk of being *self*-giving. Appropriate self-giving is voluntary, and it presumes that there is a self that is giving—it is a kenosis that gives of what it has without destroying (or precluding) its fundamental identity (Philippians 2). As Soelle states, "the greater one's realization of selfhood the greater one's ability for true renunciation."[51]

At this point, questions arise. If this phase of life is so vulnerable to pride, why encourage women's development toward it? Greater cognitive sophistication isn't an absolute good, so why promote it? Why not affirm the strengths of the interpersonal phase and raise women's confidence rather than their level of thinking?

The appropriate response to the temptation of the assertive self is not thwarting the development of emerging selves but rather expanding the arena of self-authoring selves and giving those selves the skills for interideological dialogue. Oppression occurs when there is an imbalance between groups who are encouraged to develop and groups who are prevented from developing; alienation occurs when different groups are isolated and incompetent conversationally. If we support self-authoring and dialogue across ideologies, then we decrease the potential for particular persons gaining the lion's share of power and increase the influence groups can have on one another. Power-hungry leaders, in fact, prey on interpersonally oriented persons who can be tempted to succumb to authoritarianism.

DANGER OF BACKLASH: SELF-GIVING AND LEGITIMATE SELF-CARE

Here we must be careful that our teachings on voluntary giving and chosen vulnerability not become harangues against legitimate self-care and self-fulfillment. Women, even when institutionally oriented, still carry the baggage of being socialized into an image of feminine goodness that denigrates self-concern. While aware of the temptations to sin, let us not lose track of the virtues of the institutional self. We must be careful not to quash the self while inviting authentic self-giving; we must continue to affirm the virtue of righteous self-assertion even when encouraging listening and opening; we must leave room for individual expression even while building community together. The backlash against the necessary assertion of individual rights comes very quickly.

Recently, I sat in on a homily given by a vice president in a powerful and well-established religiously affiliated corporation. The VP was addressing his subordinates, most of whom were in low positions of power. The institution was just beginning to be stretched by the voices of women and cultural/ethnic minority persons. In the wake of this empowerment of the formerly "compliant," this powerful man called for Christians to give up their quest for individual rights and to submit their selves to a concern for the common good. Using his own booming voice, he exhorted his listeners to meekness and humility. Lambasting those who were pressing for rights, even backing up his chastisement with the words of Martin Luther King (taken out of context), he adroitly worked to enervate his audience. This sermon may have been an appropriate one for him and others in power to *hear*; but it was an inappropriate one for him to *preach* to the newly empowered. Let me be more direct: it is wrong for those in power to call for the disempowerment of those who are struggling for justice. Bonnie Miller-McLemore observes, with poignant irony, the recent outcry against individualism and selfishness just as oppressed persons are gaining rights:

> Just as women have begun to claim some of the fruits of self-fulfillment and individualization, everyone, from politicians to scholars . . . have decried the dangers of rampant individualism and the decline of commit-

ments to the common good and family values. . . . Heretofore, unbridled, competitive self-interest has been allowed, even encouraged, but primarily on the part of certain privileged men in the public world of work. It has not been allowed other specific groups in our society.[52]

This is not to say that all of the claims of previously oppressed persons are de facto legitimate—or that the lessons learned by the powerful cannot be passed on to the newly empowered. Had that preacher exemplified a chosen disempowerment, his exhortation might have been credible and appropriate. He did not do so; he was, to use an analogy Jesus used, pointing to the splinter in the eye of the other while a log remained in his own. He did not articulate that checks to his own long-held power were just as important as warnings toward the newly empowered. Furthermore, like Ahasuerus in the story of Esther, he was so afraid of what others might do if they gained their rights that he, in effect, aborted the growing movement.

When prophetic torpor is valorized, both sensuality and pride are increased. We see how well-intentioned theology here works against the good of the community. Though he means to benefit the community, the preacher above really entrenches the power of those currently in control. This powerful man enables his own will-to-power to increase as he labels as sin the struggle of the less powerful.

Niebuhr himself recognized this; he stated quite emphatically that "it is not even right to insist that every action of the Christian must conform to *agape*."[53] Sometimes the Christian ego needs to assert itself in the name of love for others.

> Unwillingness or inability to put in one's claim amid the vast system of claims and counter-claims of society means that one's claims will not be considered. A saintly abnegation of interest may encourage the ruthless aggrandizement of the strong and the unscrupulous. . . . Every effort to introduce suffering love as a simple alternative to the complexities and ambiguities of social justice must degenerate into sentimentality.[54]

Niebuhr was insistent that self-sacrifice as an ideal be mediated by a concern for justice and equality in life situations. The ominous reality of tyranny in his era particularly contributed to Niebuhr's realism and his growing disillusionment with his former pacifist stance. Niebuhr came to view most forms of pacifism as idealistic and irresponsible, supporting oppression in the name of avoiding conflict. Spurning the use of the principle of sacrificial love as a screen to avoid necessary conflicts and rebalancing of power, Niebuhr drove his point "home" rather acerbically.

"There are Christian 'idealists' today who speak sentimentally of love as the only way to justice, whose family life might benefit from a more delicate 'balance of power.' "[55] While his realism tended to be overshadowed by his holding up of self-sacrifice as the Christian ideal, Niebuhr's concern for justice (checks on power and distribution of rights) was evident in his ethical writings. In the next chapter I will develop both the justice and the love side of ethics when I put forth an understanding of "prophetic caring," which attends to both sides of Niebuhr.

IDENTITY, VOICE, AND GRACE

This discussion on legitimate self-care brings us back to Sheila. If the problem with individualism is that "the self has become the main form of reality," then Sheila hardly qualifies for becoming the icon of individualism.[56] A woman who ministers to others out of a strong sense of self may be an individual, but she is hardly the epitome of individualism. She is a woman who knows God and herself and ministers to others out of an overflow of grace and positive self-understanding. Rather than condemn Sheila for leaving religious institutions, we ought to ask why it is that a person whose "faith has carried [her] a long way" and motivated her to care for others, does not find these institutions life-giving.[57]

I do not wish to extol individualism, especially if we take it to mean "the freedom to express oneself, against all constraints and conventions."[58] I simply uphold the importance of the individual, especially the female individual. Individuality is not the problem of the institutional orientation; individuality is the achievement. While our theological teachings should warn against the abuse of power and should invite vulnerability, they should not denigrate confidence and self-assertion.

Sheila is a strong individual with confidence in her voice and commitment to her self. Though not embedded in her relationships, she is still highly relational. Her understanding of self is very connected and communal; it is a self-in-relation. Women such as Sheila help us understand individuality and identity in a different manner from that in which they have classically been understood. The linchpin of human development was described by Erik Erikson as a stable and continuous sense of self; this is in contrast to "role diffusion," which indicates that identity is not achieved. For those who have been nurtured in the skills of listening to others, "stability" is not the best way to define identity.[59] Rather, identity might better be understood as a sense of confidence in offering one's voice while also listening to the voices of others. In this definition, identity may shift, not due to identity confusion or to embeddedness in others (as in the interpersonal orientation), but rather due to a sensitivity for context and differing needs in relationship.

While we cannot solve the ambiguities of existence that Niebuhr described, we can correct the problem of gendered patterns that increase temptations toward sensuality (evasion of self) and pride (control of others). We can do this by raising our girls and boys to be selves-in-relation who have confidence in their own authority but who also have a capacity to listen to and take into consideration the authority of others. In order to reduce the temptation to sensuality, we will need to redefine the "good woman" and support female self-assertion; in order to reduce the temptation to pride, we will need to modify our understanding of what it means to "be a man" and nurture male interpersonal abilities. As stated earlier, these sinful gender patterns are "co-dependent" upon one another. The self given to sensuality fuels the self given to power. Let us name both sensuality and pride, and let us repent from our sinful practice of encouraging women and men toward an unholy alliance between these two tendencies.

Furthermore, let us operate with an understanding of authority in our communities that does not deny human agency (and reinforce interpersonal conformity). Authority is too frequently conceptualized to require "that subjects suspend disbelief once a leader's right to rule is established." This misses, according to Kathleen Jones, "the internal connection between authority and caring."[60] Leaders with genuine authority are those who exercise agency and voice, but who also nurture agency and voice in others. A caring leader supports the transition between an interpersonal and an institutional orientation; she enables others to "author" their own views, even as they respect and remain in relation to others. The bird who soars "above the level plain of tradition and prejudice" flutters back to earth not so much because she has weak wings, but rather because we too readily clip her wings just as she is beginning to take off. We will return to an understanding of "caretaking leadership" in chapter 7.[61]

A Vision of Inter-Individuality

Piaget understood the autonomous self capable of abstract reflection to be the culmination of cognitive development. Some who follow him posit an additional stage. Kegan describes "inter-individuality" as full maturity. Inter-individuality is a synthesis between the interpersonal capacity for empathy and the institutional achievement of self-authorship. This results in a fully developed sense of self and others that is interdependent and reciprocal. The inter-individually oriented self gains perspective on her system, recognizes its ambiguities and incompleteness, and is aware of her own role in constructing knowledge. She can celebrate her stance and perspective while remaining self-critical and self-renewing. Although no longer tacitly determined by her relationships, she is deeply aware of the relational and interdependent nature of her existence. Thus, she can no longer draw dualisms between herself and the other; while recognizing difference, she also sees parts of the other in herself.

Kegan recognizes that this is a difficult movement for the institutional self to make. This is partly due to the fact that our society as a whole prizes the institutional self and there are few environments that will support its dethroning. The transition out of institutional identity is akin to the *Dark Night of the Soul* described by John of the Cross. It is the facing of one's rational limits, the breakdown of one's capacity to understand, analyze, and synthesize one's reality. It is appreciating ambiguity, mystery, the paradoxical structure of life and faith. Kegan warns that we cannot expect people to make this move if they have not yet met the demands of selfhood. "Before people can question the assumptions of wholeness, completeness, and the priority of the self, they must first construct a whole, complete, and prior self," Kegan contends.[62]

THE IMPORTANCE OF OUR MOTHERS' HISTORY

I have argued in this chapter that the combined forces of theology and culturally defined "femininity" work to retain women in the interpersonal phase of human development. I name the church's collusion with this as sin, and I urge that communities of faith intentionally become the kind of holding environments that foster and support women's growth from compliance to power. While it is important to foster and support women's development, it is not helpful to despise our own past of self-giving or ridicule the importance our foremothers placed on relationships. When we do so we denounce woman's history. Both the individual woman who is emerging and the community of women who reach toward new understandings of female maturity need to grow with a sense of appreciation for (critical, to be sure) and not simply rejection of woman's history. In Kegan's terms, the self that "was" needs to be integrated into the self that is becoming. When Simone de Beauvior remarked that patience was one of those "'feminine' qualities which have their origin in our oppression but should be preserved after our liberation," she was groping toward a future that was not cut off from the past of "herstory."[63]

Healthy development requires a sense of continuity as well as discontinuity. When the self is in transition, there is a temporary feeling of disintegration. The self that was is no longer viable, but the self that is to be is not yet stable. The person who completely rejects the former self does so at risk to her future. If some degree of positive integration of the past does not follow the momentary disintegration of the ego, movement into the new self can proceed with residual depression. Therefore, I want to make it clear that the emergence of the self involves a "shattering" of the cultural conceptions of femininity but not a "killing" of our mothers.[64] This means, on the one hand, moving beyond where Esther was able to go. Esther took control of her "femininity" for a while (that is, used it to her advantage), but she probably did not have the power to define her womanhood apart from the expectations for femininity. Can we further the task that Esther started—not simply take control of femininity, but redefine what it means?—not simply use "feminine" wiles to attain "feminist" goals, but name for ourselves what it means to be a woman?[65] On the other hand, we need not denigrate our mothers as we do this. Development involves awakening to and renaming femininity while affirming the wisdom of our mothers, reappropriating the value of relationships, and recovering the history of women's courage and assertiveness.

In the next chapter, we will more explicitly seek to "rebuild our mothers' house." We will look at women's growth in relationality, growth that builds on the goodness of the past while also seeking the power of a new future. Although Gilligan and Kegan use different frameworks, they help us develop a similar theme. In order to promote genuine relationships in communities of faith, we need to recognize the importance of self-development as well as concern for others. Though Gilligan is both heralded and denounced for raising the importance of women's relationality, this is really not her major contribution to psychology. Her greatest contribution, largely ignored by fans and critics alike, is her recognition that genuine relationality and caring require attention to self as well as other. Rebuilding on the legacy of our mothers begins when we lay this insight as the foundation for our new house.

Chapter Three

Rebuilding Our Mothers' House

CARETAKING AND BEING IN GENUINE RELATION

What is it that makes LOVE
  so elusive?
One syllable can hardly contain
  all the meaning that it has
There are agape,
    romantic,
      and brotherly
    kinds of love,
but even they don't quite get it
Love means giving,
    but it means receiving too
To sacrifice is to love,
but sometimes the one who stands firm
    loves most of all.
  —George Pasley, "The Hardest Word"

*I*n the last chapter we looked at the potentially harmful connection between theology and self-development. Viewing women's development through the lenses of Robert Kegan's theory of cognitive development, we considered the way in which theologies that tame self-centeredness converge with cultural expectations for femininity to inhibit the emergence of a confident self in women. I suggested that this situation is not only harmful to women, but is also detrimental to community life as a whole. While repudiating individualism, I insisted that confident individuals were essential to healthy communal life.[1] The ongoing subordination of women intensifies the temptations toward the sin of sensuality in women and the sin of pride in men, *both* of which contribute to the will-to-power phenomenon Reinhold Niebuhr condemned.

While Kegan was most helpful in uncovering the barriers to female *selfhood*, he also hinted at the obstacles that are erected against genuine *relationality*. Denial of the selfhood of some leads to the diminishment of the relationships in a community. Carol Gilligan, professor of human development and psychology at the Harvard Graduate School of Education, helps us to see the connection between selfhood and relationality more fully. I would like to follow our consideration of Kegan's theory of the evolving self with Gilligan's understanding of what we might call evolving relationality. In doing so, I am shifting frameworks. Kegan traces cognitive development; Gilligan works with moral development. Gilligan, moreover, opposes her theory to that of Lawrence Kohlberg, who is also indebted to Piaget. And yet, as we shall see, Gilligan's work confirms the conclusion that we reached in the last chapter: it is important to support the development of female selfhood for the purpose of genuine relationality.

FROM GOODNESS TO TRUTH: THE EVOLUTION OF RELATIONSHIPS

According to Lawrence Kohlberg, persons grow in their capacity for "justice reasoning" according to a hierarchy of stages. The attainment of justice marks moral maturity, and it occurs when one achieves the capacity for "impartiality, universalizability, and the effort and willingness to come to agreement or consensus with other human beings in general about what is right."[2] Thus fairness, the negotiation of competing rights, and the ability to put aside one's interests are the primary virtues and cognitive capacities needed. Enmeshment in the particulars of one's life and relationships are judged in the Kohlbergian model to be less mature than distance from and impartiality toward one's concrete surroundings. In assessing moral development, which he and his associates did by posing hypothetical dilemmas to interviewees, Kohlberg thus favors abstract theorizing over narrative style, universalizing reflections (what can be said to be true for the "general" person) over contextual judgments (what can be said to be true for specific persons), and a sense of personal autonomy over relationship orientation. As noted already, women interviewees leaned toward the disfavored side of these poles, and thus were seen as deficient or less mature in their justice reasoning. Tending to be more interested in offering narratives over grand theories, and leaning more toward the needs of particular others over abstract and general others, women were disproportionately deemed "conventional" in their morality.

Uncomfortable with these results, and knowing that the original schemes of cognitive, moral, and psychosocial development were based on studies of males alone, Gilligan wondered what different results and insights would emerge if she constructed a model of moral development based on the study of a female group facing an actual, concrete moral problem. She thus shifted the research pattern of previous studies, which tracked a person's capacity to render impartial judgments regarding hypothetical, abstract moral dilemmas. In collaboration with Mary Belenky, she interviewed a modest-size group of women contemplating abortion. In this study, Gilligan noticed that the themes of care and connection framed women's moral deliberation. "The conflict between self and other constitutes the central moral problem for women," Gilligan wrote.[3]

While relationality was consistently important to women, and their repeated use of the theme could lead one to mistakenly assume that most women were conventionally moral and interpersonally oriented, Gilligan found that gradations of relationship were evident. These gradations, representing deepening views of connection, could be missed as significant in a framework looking selectively for signs of autonomy and impartiality. While not overturning Kohlberg's findings, Gilligan contended that there was another way to assess moral development. Rather than growth in justice reasoning, she noticed growth in one's capacity to care. The women sampled tended to follow a pattern in the development of what Gilligan termed "an ethic of care"; there was a (progressive) move from an orientation to survival (where the *needs of the self* are paramount) to conventional "goodness" (which for women means *caring for others* in self-sacrificing ways) to a concern for truth (which balances the *needs of self and others in relationship*).

In this sequence, an initial focus on caring for the self in order to ensure survival is followed by a transactional phase in which the judgment is criticized as selfish. The criticism signals a new understanding of the connection between self and others which is articulated by the concept of responsibility. The elaboration of this concept of responsibility and its fusion with a maternal morality that seeks to ensure care for the dependent and unequal characterizes the second perspective. At this point, the good is equated with caring for others. However, when only others are legitimized as the recipients of woman's care, the exclusion of herself gives rise to problems in relationships, creating a disequilibrium that initiates the second transition. . . . The third perspective focuses on the dynamics of relationship and dissipates the tension between selfishness and responsibility through a new understanding of the inter-connection between other and self.[4]

According to this framework, the way in which the self functions in relationship to others is central to moral development. The morally mature person balances wisely, without damaging relationships, between caring for the self and caring for others. The morally mature person moves beyond the dualism of survival and goodness and negotiates a more paradoxical path of moral living. "Moral problems can be expressed in terms of accommodating the needs of the self and of others, of balancing competition and cooperation, and of maintaining the social web of relations in which one finds oneself."[5] This third level of moral development is in fact genuine care; for " 'care' isn't simply a matter of being 'the nice girl' or 'the perfect woman'— it's about being responsible to oneself as well as to others."[6] Prior to responsible care, neither the responsible self nor genuine relationality exists. At the second level, morality is conformity to the norm of female goodness, and thus it lacks choice and responsibility. In fact, it is the realization by women that self-sacrificing goodness precludes taking responsibility for one's actions that precipitates moral development beyond goodness. It is only with the third level that the self knows its needs and interests and can separate them from externally imposed ones, and thus at this level the self accepts responsibility for its choices and enters into genuine, mutual relationships with others. Moral maturity in Gilligan's scheme is, however, a realistic rather than idealistic one. Though hard won, truth as she has described it is attainable and livable in concrete communities; it is not a lofty vision.

A WOMAN'S DEVELOPMENTAL CRISIS

Developmental theorists generally concur that moves toward greater maturity are precipitated by moral crises. In the face of an important moral decision, girls can be moved out of survival (first level) into sacrifice for others (the second level) or out of self-sacrifice into mutuality (the third level). Gilligan reveals that the move from the second orientation to the third can be difficult for women to maneuver. The strongly held image of feminine caring, which focuses on self-sacrifice, can cause great difficulties in the move toward mature caring. The move to the third level of caring comes about when a person realizes that living up to the expectations to care for others can become slavish and dissatisfying when mutuality is absent. The conventional image is so strong, however, that it may even stabilize a woman at the second level of care; a "well-socialized girl" would not even enter into the "reflective conflict" that prompts developmental growth to level three.[7] The conflict, alternatively, may actually lead a woman backward. Though some women can become entrenched in rigid self-sacrifice, others, finding the conventional notion of self-sacrifice unacceptable, may "retreat from care" and revert to survival out of disappointment in love relationships.[8] Seeing no adequate alternative other than "deliberate isolation" for protection, the latter group may succumb to "moral nihilism."[9] Women's dilemma, as Gilligan sees it, is that of being "suspended between an ideal of selflessness and the truth of their own agency and needs." Thus a developmental problem is created by the opposition set up between female morality, defined as self-sacrificial caring, and truth, which points to mutual care and reciprocity.[10] Conventional norms of feminine virtue, which hold up selflessness as a moral ideal, conflict with the truth about relationality that a woman eventually begins to know from her actual experiences of connection.

RELATIONSHIP AUTHENTICITY: INCLUDING SELF AND OTHER

Care, a notion central to the moral voice Gilligan discerned, is typically understood as not hurting others, having compassion on others, or tending to the needs of others. While Gilligan clearly hears these aspects of care, she finds deeper tones as well. Care is not simply tending to others but nurturing *relationships* with others. Mature caring involves a deep commitment to a mutual relationship. As Joan Tronto sums it, care is "a commitment to maintaining and fostering the relationship in which one is woven."[11] There is an important difference here, and one that we must not overlook. Caring for another person, regardless of self, is either a parent/child or slave/master kind of relationship. At its best, the one caring is a benevolent parent, at its worst it is an exploited servant. Caring for a relationship, however, is a mutual, reciprocal type of caring. It attends to another person, but it also holds another person accountable. The tragedy of the "Giving Tree" (chapter 1) is not simply that she lost herself but that she also lost her relationship to the boy. Their connection began as a beautiful give-and-take relationship, and then it degenerated into exploitation. As she grew more and more self-sacrificing, he grew more and more selfish, and their relationship became empty. Thus, in their old age, all that they have left to unite them is their joint disillusionment. The picture of the decrepit old man sitting on an old stump is not a joyous reunion. Their partnership, rather than celebrating the integrity of a mature relationship, projects the despair of an infantile regression.

A "self-in-relation" is neither "self" nor "in relation" if there is no "relationship-authenticity," which involves differentiation as well as connection.[12] Both connection *and* separation, affirmation and challenge, are essential not only for women's survival in the world but for women's flourishing and development. Furthermore, connection and relationality only occur if there are differentiated persons to relate to one another. We are only in relation when we have shared our voice and presented our differences. As Gilligan notes, "making connections with others by excluding oneself is a strategy destined to fail," for "relationship implies the presence of both self and other."[13] A relational world is a world where there are disagreements; it is sometimes hurtful and painful. In fact, conflict often emerges from the strength of a relationship, for it signals that two people have probed deeply enough to find out where they are different.

Sometimes, as the poem at the beginning of this chapter states, "standing firm" is the greatest love of all. Relationality does not mean "giving ourselves away," and in fact it may mean "taking ourselves back"; relationality at its best involves give-and-take, speaking and listening, asserting and surrendering, holding accountable and forgiving. An authentic genuine relationship, and genuine community life, require capacities for both self-assertion and self-giving. One of the ironic consequences of self-abnegation is that it contributes to loss of relationship. Denying one's self in relation to another eventually leads to an unauthentic relationship.

TRANSFORMING LEMONS INTO CHOCOLATE: REREADING GILLIGAN

Summaries of Gilligan often emphasize her celebration and recovery of women's experience. Her work is summoned to support the importance of care and connection for moral development. A less-reported but even more important aspect of Gilligan's work is her insistence that *conventional understandings of care as self-giving need to be corrected by a genuine relationality that includes self as well as other in the ethical deliberation.* Although Gilligan's work surely "trumpets aspects of women's experience found defective, deficient, or undervalued by the broader culture [namely, caring for particular others]," she also sounds a clarion call for critical assessment of women's experience, which has been shaped by a patriarchal insistence on female self-sacrificial caring. A number of Gilligan's critics charge that she does not explore the psychological limitations of the "female" voice that she identifies; I think these particular charges are inaccurate. Linda Kerber is one who has argued against the "romantic oversimplification of caring and of women's experience" toward which she fears Gilligan leans.[14] Kerber notes that Gilligan does an admirable job of recovering and revaluing those aspects of life that have been important to women. While granting that women have done a good job with the opportunities open to them, she wants to avoid cementing the association between women and nurturing, and she seeks to broaden the scope of opportunities for women beyond domestic spheres. She fears that Gilligan's announcement of the "different voice" of women reinscribes women's destiny as nurturers. "Gilligan describes how women make lemonade out of the lemons [women] have inherited. She does not tell how to transform the lemons into chocolate," Kerber accuses.

I certainly agree with Kerber's concern that we avoid cementing any association between women and nurturing.[15] I read Gilligan's work, from the very beginning, as negotiating a complex path between recovery of women's concern for care and critique of the way in which care has been distorted. Her recent collaboration with Lyn Mikel Brown, which reports their intensive study of a girls school, gives a far from idealized vision of female connection and warns us loudly that the forms of connection into which women are being socialized are fraught with destructiveness.[16] Rather than a celebration of traditional femininity, Gilligan offers a trenchant critique of the cultural identification of caring with women's self-sacrifice. Clearly, Gilligan is not promoting caring as "goodness," but rather is arguing that goodness must mature into truth of relationship. By arguing for self-inclusion in women's caring, she challenges the conventional understanding of feminine goodness by "severing the link between care and self-sacrifice."[17] She is further implying that "goodness" itself is ill-conceived in that it is too closely aligned with women's caring for men. Thus, not only would she like to see women's growth into truth, but she would like to see both women and men caring for others. If this occurs, the imbalance in favor of caring for others that occurs in this second level of moral development will be experienced by men as well as women and the distortions of goodness will be alleviated.

Gilligan does not always state her case clearly, and although I am more willing than she is to directly name the damaging aspects of women's caring, I think Kerber's complaint is unfair. Transforming lemons into chocolate is precisely where Gilligan's work (read thoroughly) takes us. Gilligan does not compel women to become as "good" as we can be; she calls us toward "truth." You cannot get to truth by squeezing goodness for all it's worth; you only get to truth by transforming goodness into genuine relationality. Unfortunately, both culture and church are handing women lemons, and they make this transformation very difficult.

Women who are shaped by a "self-assertion is sin" theology will face an additional obstacle in moral development. Being told that caring for the self is sinful and that the capacity to set aside the needs of the self is the utmost in spiritual maturity, the move toward truth can be obstructed. Theology may prevent women from knowing the truth that shall set them free. Here we return again to Niebuhr, who envisioned self-sacrifice to be the God-given grace of the Christian life, and who inadvertently put lemons where chocolate should be.

FROM TRUTH TO GOODNESS AND BACK: RECONSTRUCTING NIEBUHR

Because of the problem of inordinate self-interest, Niebuhr was suspicious of notions of mutuality and reciprocity. Ever afraid that mutuality would dissolve into calculated reciprocity, he elevated self-sacrifice as the norm and aspiration. "The self cannot achieve relations of mutual and reciprocal affection with others if its actions are dominated by the fear that they may not be reciprocated," he warned. "Mutuality is not a possible achievement if it is made the intention and goal of any action."[18] Although Niebuhr believed that nations should function according to justice and equality, he felt this was a concession to human sin rather than an expression of genuine truth. Self-sacrificial love, patterned after Jesus, was the highest form of behavior, and it transcended "historical harmonies" aimed toward mutuality and justice. "Sinful egoism," he insisted, "makes all historical harmonies of interest partial and incomplete; and a life which accepts the harmonies as final is bound to introduce sinful self-assertion into the ethical norm."[19] Niebuhr claimed that self-sacrificial love was more nearly approached in intimate relationships than in public life (where the lesser norm of justice was more appropriate). The fact that women bear children, which Niebuhr considered to put a restraint on their "various potentialities of character not related to the vocation of motherhood," inadvertently renders women the specialists in self-sacrificial love.[20]

By elevating self-sacrifice in Christian ethics and demoting mutuality and justice to the status of concessions, Niebuhr's anthropology obscures the roles of self-concern and self-regard in the Christian life. This means that, if viewed in light of Gilligan's developmental scheme, Niebuhr's thought inverts the movement: mutuality is considered the lesser form that must give way to self-sacrifice. Rendering self-sacrifice as superior to mutuality, this theological formulation stabilizes women in "goodness" and prevents the movement toward "truth."

Don Browning argues that Niebuhr's fear of inordinate self-concern overwhelms his recognition that there is a place for ordinate self-concern. Knowing only the powerful male experience, he was convinced that people had already mastered taking care of themselves. Browning, building on the work of Louis Janssens, offers a reconstruction of Niebuhr that understands mutuality and equal regard, rather than self-sacrifice, to be at the center of Christian love. Equal regard, when properly understood, contains within it self-regard. As Janssens maintains, "one is to have equal regard for self and for others, since the reasons for valuing the self are identical with those for valuing others, namely that everyone is a human being."[21] Valuing oneself as well as the other is part of the ethics of mutuality. Ideally, my self-regard should count for no less and no more than my regard for the other. While for some, it is the case that, as Niebuhr argues, "under the pressure of sin [defined here as pride] mutuality as equal regard is always sliding into calculating reciprocity," for others, I must add, it is the case that under the pressure of sin (defined here as sensuality) mutuality as equal regard is always sliding into *unthinking giving*. We must avoid, says Janssens, the temptation "of advancing the corrupted form of mutuality as its only definition"; I add that we must also avoid the temptation of advancing the *un*corrupted form of self-sacrifice as its only manifestation.[22]

For Janssens, self-sacrifice is *not* the goal and norm of the Christian life. Rather mutuality and equal regard constitute both the essence of love and the ethical vision for community life. Self-sacrifice, though not the quintessence of love, does, however, have a place in community life. It "is the extra mile" we must travel to help bring a situation of conflict and disharmony into mutuality again. The goal is mutual, respectful, and reciprocal relationships between persons, men and women. The "extra mile" moments are gracious; they are, however, catalysts for reviving a relationship and not the inherent pattern of a relationship.

Browning offers us a helpful reconstruction of Niebuhr. He elevates mutuality as the vision of Christian community while preserving a role for the kind of self-sacrifice that has always been a part of the Christian tradition. It is important, even with this corrective, that we not implicitly convey the message that women are always the "peacemakers" who take it upon themselves to insert the self-sacrifice into a fallen relationship. In some instances, the very thing that a fallen relationship might need is an assertion of personal worth on the part of a repeatedly wronged party— the justified refusal to go "the extra mile."

Self-sacrifice can be a helpful move in the midst of a broken relationship, and both women and men will at times be called upon to exercise it. This is the part of caring that is compassionate, and I call it "empathic caring." I am arguing, however, that genuine caring is more than compassionate and self-sacrificing. Genuine caring has three aspects to it, of which compassion is only one. *I propose that genuine caring includes: empathic caring, conversational caring, and prophetic caring.* Empathic caring is the kind of caring that understands others and goes the extra mile for others. Conversational caring is dialogical engagement in the deepest sense: the give-and-take of reciprocal mutuality. It is touching and being touched by another. Prophetic caring involves caring about another enough to confront and challenge them. I will develop each of these in turn, paying special attention to some of the critical issues that arise from the expressions of each form of caring.

It is important to reiterate that my emphasis in developing an understanding of caring is on the relationship between persons who care for one another and not simply on the caring of one person on behalf of another. When we care, in the deepest sense, we cultivate a relationship. Certainly persons are cared for in that relationship, but they are cared for in a way that supports healthy relationality rather than the asymmetrical flourishing of one party. Caring for relationships, in the end, is caring for the persons in those relationships. For we are created to be in relation and we come to self-understanding in the context of relationships; when we forget the importance of genuine relationality, we neglect the persons as well.

EMPATHIC CARING: CARING WITH COMPASSION

"To care for another person, in the most significant sense, is to help him [or her] grow and actualize himself [or herself]," wrote Milton Mayeroff in the 1965 International Philosophical quarterly.[23] Caring for another is most often understood as nurturing and supporting another's actualization. While I am arguing that understanding and supporting another person is not all there is to caring, it is still a part of caring. It is the empathic, or compassionate, side of caring.

Empathy refers to a person's ability and motivation to perceive, understand, and respond to another's cues. While empathy is often described as the experience of walking in another's shoes or looking through another's eyes, these descriptions are somewhat naive. No one can truly be in another person's situation; the line between self and other is always there. It is when we think we are seeing through another's eyes that we rob them of their integrity. Empathy is more accurately the capacity to understand and accept the similarities and differences of another. Nel Noddings, who has done significant work on education and care, uses the concept of "engrossment" to describe the empathic side of caring. To engross oneself in another is to focus one's attention fully on the other. "It is as though his eyes and mine have combined to look at the scene he describes. I know that I would have behaved differently in the situation, but this is in itself a matter of indifference. I feel what he says he felt. I have been invaded by this other."[24] The person with empathy, who is capable of engrossment, has the flexibility and the openness to listen to and be present for another and the willingness to respond appropriately and specifically to another. At its best, empathy identifies the good, understands the bad, deciphers the suffering, and intuits the needs of another.

Empathy involves a degree of emptying oneself and opening oneself to vulnerability and change. Rather than telling another who they should be, the empathetic person listens to who the other says she is; rather than judging another for not matching previously determined norms, the empathetic person grants integrity to the differentness of another; rather than seeking to convert another to one's viewpoint, the empathetic person seeks to learn and is willing herself to be changed by the encounter. This can occur on a number of levels, spanning the spectrum from simple compassion all the way to intense self-emptying.

EMPATHY AND OPENNESS TO THE STRANGER

Empathetic self-emptying is particularly appropriate when those in power encounter oppressed or marginalized persons. It involves the active choice of "decentering" and perhaps even becoming a stranger to oneself. There are varying degrees of decentering; it can go so far as to actually view one's own tradition through the lenses of the other who stands outside of that tradition. In his work on "decentered or alienated theology," Darrell Fasching calls for Christian theologians to decenter themselves in relationship to Jews, whom they have for centuries dehumanized. Alienated theology, says Fasching, "is an attempt to critique one's own tradition by imaginatively experiencing it through the eyes of the other who stands outside one's tradition, as if one were the other who has been, or will be, affected by it."[25] In this dual process of opening oneself to the stranger and becoming a stranger to oneself, hospitality to the other is joined with questioning of oneself. In a pluralistic world, this kind of empathy is important for mutual understanding.

It is especially important that those in power develop the capacity for empathy. It is often the case that those who are marginalized have been forced to understand the dominant culture; they have been involuntarily immersed in a world not their own, and they have discerned a good bit about the way it functions. In many cultures, women are the "carriers" of empathetic caring. Woman are socialized for sensitivity, understanding, and the meeting of others' needs, which are all deemed central to being female. Furthermore, girls and women, subordinates to men in our society, develop empathic abilities for the sake of survival. Those who are subordinate to others become "highly attuned" to their superiors, "able to predict their reactions of pleasure and displeasure" in order to protect themselves from abandonment and rejection.[26] Those who are in positions of dominance often have not honed their skills for empathy; because their world is the defining one, they often lack the skills of listening, understanding, and self-emptying.[27]

The fact that women are pressured to specialize in empathy and powerful men are protected from it has some unfortunate consequences. Women may too easily accommodate to the other, losing their own differentness. In fact, for women empathy "can lead to the other always coming first at the expense of valuing one's own experience."[28] *Self-empathy* is very difficult for women because the pull to the other is so strong. This can have negative consequences for the other as well, as the other may become an extension of the female self, diminishing the differentness of the other. This can particularly happen between mothers and daughters.

Men, so concerned about the integrity of self, may have difficulty surrendering to and joining with the other in empathy. They may set up and preserve rigid boundaries between self and other and thus preclude empathy and connection. They close themselves off to influence from the other, or they leave the other alone out of exaggerated respect for their space. As Judith Jordan remarks, raising boys to be good soldiers and effective competitors makes empathy maladaptive. If one has compassion upon one's enemies or understanding of one's rivals, male bravado breaks down. Thus, when measured in terms of one's capacity to care for concrete others, "the dearth of caretaking experiences makes privileged males morally deprived."[29]

Empathy is an extremely important part of learning from others, and when it is exercised, it has an enormous impact on both community life and global justice. When we understand others, we are less inclined to falsely universalize our own experience and we are more likely to have a richer conception of truth.[30] Empathy, however, is both a difficult and a costly process. In order to empathize with another, one must have a well-differentiated sense of self and the capacity to allow for the space and differentness of the other in addition to a capacity for connection with and response to another. Otherwise, the boundary between self and other becomes so blurred that one cannot be fully present to another. If the self vanishes, then the other vanishes as well and becomes an extension of the self. Thus, Alexandra Kaplan refers to the importance of affective bonding and cognitive differentiation in empathetic relationships. Bonding implies intense interconnectedness while differentiation refers to the preservation of each distinct person in the relationship.[31] To establish this connection while maintaining differentiation requires a great deal of investment and skill.

Empathy is neither instinctive nor always energizing. It is hard work, and at its best, it requires a greater sense of self than most women have and a greater openness to others than most men have. The fact that women are expected to carry what Pat Howry Davis calls "the burden of empathy" suggests that we need to do two things in our communities: we need to build up women's sense of self and foster men's openness to the others so that mature empathy and genuine relationality are fostered.[32] We will return to the latter issue when we address women and men caring together. We turn to the first of these issues now.

VOICE AND THE CAPACITY TO CARE

In describing empathy, I reflected on the roles of listening, self-emptying, and understanding. In nurturing the capacity for this kind of empathic caring, we are inclined to preach and teach stories of compassion and neighborly love. We might even offer opportunities for learning with and about "the other" in our midst. These are good approaches to nurturing empathy, and they should be continued. Yet, they do not stand alone; it is important that we also build up the self of the one caring. "In order to empathize, one must have a well-differentiated sense of self in addition to an appreciation of and sensitivity to the differentness as well as the sameness of the other," contends Judith Jordan.[33] The movement toward caring for others is sometimes best promoted by building the self's confidence and not merely teaching the importance of nurture of others and self-sacrificial giving.

Susan Victor, a social worker who was hired to be a "teen parent educator," relates an incident in one of her "teaching" sessions. She was giving a presentation to teen mothers on the social, physical, and cognitive development of children, and she asked the teenagers some questions to assess their learning. It was evident that they were not engaged with the material at hand and that they were bored with her lecture. A spontaneous discussion erupted over a recent episode of the television talk show *Geraldo* dealing with the topic of teenage mothers. Geraldo had presented the lives of teen mothers as dismal and shameful, and the girls minced no words in expressing how "pissed off" they were about that particular show. "They said our lives were over," one girl complained. Smart enough to realize that her intended lesson was derailed, Victor dropped her plans and jumped aboard the discussion that was gaining momentum. The teen mothers expressed dismay over society's stereotypes of their lives, and they named the reality of their own lives, which they felt was different from the stereotypes. The girls came up with the idea that they write a letter of protest to the television station and also to the local paper, which they then did with Victor's full support. Several weeks later, Victor brought them copies of their column in the paper when it appeared. "The pride was in their faces for weeks, and it made me realize how much they had to say about their experience," she observed. Victor reports what they taught her that day. "The transformation of my lesson into an opportunity to have their voices heard promoted their growth and self-esteem (and ultimately awareness of their children's needs) more than the study of a chart of the children's development would have."[34] Paradoxically, their capacity for empathy toward their children came as an outgrowth of the opportunity that was opened to them for self-empathy and voice.

To look at the issue from the other side, Alice Miller's work on narcissism and parenting exposes the way in which parents who have deficient self-knowledge about their own needs may inadvertently neglect their children's needs and work out their own unmet needs through their children.[35] In fact, as Miller argues, one of the primary qualities of bad parenting is that the child is forced to sacrifice her or his genuine self for the sake of parental expectations. In such cases of "narcissistic parenting," the child develops a false-self that reflects the parents' desires, and the child's true sense of self becomes suppressed.[36] This cycle continues as each generation's needs are unmet. Until one generation stops the cycle by honestly attending to and knowing themselves, generation after generation will continue to project their own needs onto their children. Ironically, it is often the most overinvolved, smotheringly "caring" mothers who are the least attuned and empathic toward their children; their care and involvement are often masked narcissism, accompanied by a refusal to let the one they care for differentiate from them.

Self-sacrifice, when it leads to this kind of narcissistic parenting, may look like caring; but it ends up being unempathic overinvolvement completely out of tune to the child's self. "The more women are blocked from proceeding with their own growth and excluded from positions of power and authority outside the home, the more they become excessively child-focused and the more likely they are to thwart the differentiation of their children," contends Harriet Lerner.[37] As Lerner sees it, our culture has perpetuated "the triad" of the overinvolved mother, the distant father, and the smothered child.

In addition to contributing to unempathetic parenting, the expectations for self-denial also play a role in women's depression.

WOMEN AND DEPRESSION: FEMALE CARING AND LOSS OF SELF

In her study of women and depression, Dana Jack found that when women try to fit into the roles of "wife" and "good woman," defined by society as self-sacrificing ("literally putting herself aside to try to live up to the standards of goodness") and oriented to the needs of others, they "run the risk of self-alienation and inauthenticity," precursors to depression.[38] In her tongue-in-cheek but nevertheless profound article, "Why I Want a Wife," Judy Syfers describes a moment of revelation she had one evening while ironing. A friend who was looking for a wife came by, and it suddenly occurred to her that she too "would like to have a wife." Why? A talented woman who had been dissuaded from graduate school by her male teachers, she visioned a wife who would pick up the pieces for her as so many wives did for male professionals. She lists in detail all the caring duties a wife is expected to perform, ranging from good cooking to supporting a husband's career development to nurturing the children to denying her own needs. Her list is striking because it so clearly captures *the ideal.* Whether or not individual women live up to it, it is the standard by which they and others will measure themselves. Syfers ends with the stunning question: "My God, who *wouldn't* want a wife?"[39]

Unfortunately, wives and mothers who are also working outside the home are not spared the ideal; they are often expected to do it all. In a recent book and study guide written for women in the church, *Secret Longings of the Heart*, author Carol Kent includes a session on failure. She begins the discussion with a description of her exhaustion after leading an intense women's retreat. After hours of traveling, she arrives home to discover that her husband has invited friends to dinner the next day after church. Of course, it would be her task to tidy up the house, prepare the dinner, and play hostess (including planning an attractive table arrangement). Having run around "like a maniac" to get everything ready, she discovers that her teenage son is wearing white socks with his dress clothes (an unacceptable ensemble in her eyes). She yells at him for his error, and he responds, "But, Mom, they were the only socks in my drawer," to which she replies, "Son, can you ever forgive me? I've been yelling at you because I'm tired and frustrated—not because you deserve it. The socks are *my* problem, not yours! I'm sorry." She then proceeds to describe her feelings of failure; she had blown it, and she had been transformed into "a monster."[40] Although she does recognize the destructive effects of perfectionist standards for hostessing and mothering, she does not recognize that she had reason to be angry and exhausted, and she had the right (even the responsibility) to hold her family accountable for taking her needs into consideration when making plans, for taking care of their own laundry, and for doing their own entertaining when they arrange for company.

My own experience in an egalitarian marriage tells me that marriage itself is not unhealthy for women; "wifehood," defined as asymmetric self-sacrificial caring, is the problem for women. In a "depressogenic" culture that promotes the de-selfing of women, entering into roles that intensify the loss of self reduces women's resilience. When women submit to a role that denies them selfhood and overemphasizes one-sided caring, then they are prone to depression and poor mental health. Wanting to live up to the ideal of "womanhood," women allow too much of the self to "become negotiable" under pressures from those with whom they are in relation. The loss of self leaves a feeling of emptiness, but neither anger nor assertion is encouraged in women.

This situation worsens when women caught in this paradigm have children. "The group of women most at risk for depression is married women who do not work outside the home and have three or more children under the age of twelve," reports Christie Neuger.[41] Again, it is not having children that is the problem, it is rearing children within a family paradigm of maternal self-sacrifice. Depression that leads to dysfunction is frequently an unconscious protest against a woman's over-functioning and over-responsible position on the domestic scene. Women who reach an incapacity to continue to function are silently going on strike, though they are not able to do so directly and consciously. It is not women's desire for affiliation that predisposes them to depression. "The valuing of marriage, family, intimacy, and attachment is a mental health asset, not a liability," insists Harriet Lerner.[42] It is rather the pressures placed on women to perpetuate false relationships, which entail self-loss, that are the problem.

Empathy is an important part of caring, and we do well to strengthen persons' capacity for self-knowledge and attentiveness to the other. Empathy, even when it is mature, does not stand alone. For genuine relationality to build, one must be capable of naming one's "center" and not merely "decentering" before another. Otherwise there is no dialogue, no conversation, no mutuality to the relationship.

CONVERSATIONAL CARING: CARING THROUGH THE GENEROSITY OF DIALOGUE

In her essay "On Lies, Secrets, and Silence," Adrienne Rich describes the "lies" that patriarchy forces women to tell. Noting that lies can be done with words and also with silence, Rich exposes the way in which women evade painful confrontations. "She is asked, point-blank, a question which may lead into painful talk. 'How do you feel about what is happening between us?' Instead of trying to describe her feelings in their ambiguity and confusion, she asks, 'How do *you* feel?' The other, because she is trying to establish a ground of openness and trust, begins describing her own feelings. Thus, the liar learns more than she tells."[43]

Rich's description of "the liar" who "learns more than she tells" exposes one of the ironic consequences of one-way empathy: in its extravagant listening it can end up becoming stingy about sharing. While empathy is needed, and even demanded, in situations where power abuses need to be redressed, if it does not give way to reciprocity then communication and community do not happen. Communication requires response and not simply listening. Responsible communication depends upon the generosity of offering one's world to others. There is no free exchange if one does not bring something to give. Surely, responsible communication means that even as I give my world to another, I also open my world to the questions and challenges of another. In fact, the act of conversational caring, which I now describe, involves this kind of deep sharing. Conversational caring is extravagant with listening *and* generous with sharing; it is a to-and-fro movement between two others who respect difference while also finding commonality. It is dialogue in depth.

Empathy for the sake of hospitality is valuable and sometimes needed, but the consistent disavowing of the self prevents conversation. In the last chapter I emphasized that social pressures on women to disavow themselves suppress their own development; here I point to the toll this takes on relationships. Recognizing that the self in hiding is often still a self and sometimes there is even a "strong sense of self," Lori Stern argues that "disavowing the self [is] not a problem of the self—for the self can be clearly known and plainly articulated—but a problem of relationship."[44] In many cases, girls and women hide and repress a strong sense of self out of fear that their true self will not be acceptable to those with whom they are in relation. This sense of self can remain very strong (an issue to which we will return in chapter 4), even as they feel they must hide that self from others. This leads to the situation of an "underground self," which is differentiated but hidden from others. Thinking that they are supporting and nurturing their relationships to others, women in hiding actually falsify those relationships along with their selves. This is the unfortunate consequence when empathetic caring absorbs conversational caring.

In chapter 6, I will be developing a "conversational" understanding of education that promotes "hard dialogue" and "deep connections." Conversation, if it is worthy of the name, engages life in hard and deep ways. Paradoxically, while women are often silenced in public discourse, they are the ones who have preserved and honed the art of conversation. In women's circles and quilting bees, they have shared their stories and pooled their wisdom; in feminist consciousness-raising groups, they have named common oppression and pain; in professional networking groups they have encouraged trailblazing and celebrated victories. Sharing stories, naming pain, and celebrating achievements are all part of conversational caring. In sharing stories, women acknowledge and affirm differentness; in naming pain, women foster honesty; in celebrating achievement, women nurture assertiveness.

Conversational caring, as I am using it, is hard and exhilarating work. Those who attempt to care for one another conversationally speak and listen to, question and probe one another. They seek to highlight their particularity while at the same time understand one another; they remain distinctively "other," while being open to being changed by or creating change in the other. They are willing to find commonalities, name disagreements, and even find positions that are syntheses of their differing views. The important thing about conversation is that the conversation partners *mutually* shape the direction and nature of their communication together. Though celebration of difference is a perfectly appropriate part of conversation, authentic conversation is not a "tourists' delight" where surface sharing takes place.[45]

As a vision, conversational caring is appealing. It is a give-and-take, symmetrical concept. It avoids self-abnegation and self-centeredness. As a reality, conversation itself is difficult. Recent studies in communication patterns between men and women raise some difficult issues for conversation. I'd like to turn now to some of those issues, giving some attention to ways that we can facilitate conversations between women and men.

WOMEN, MEN, AND THE PROBLEM OF COMMUNICATION

Gender-based difficulties in informal communication have recently issued in a number of best-selling books ranging from Deborah Tannen's *You Just Don't Understand: Women and Men in Conversation* to John Gray's *Men Are from Mars and Women Are from Venus*. When men engage in conversation, according to both authors, their goals tend to focus on relaying information, solving a problem, or even competing to argue a point; when women engage in conversation, they seek to demonstrate their compassion, offer a listening ear, and deepen their relationship. Men, contends Tannen, approach conversations as negotiations in which people protect themselves from being pushed around; women enter into conversation seeking closeness and connection. Men report, women seek rapport. Referring to the greatest source of frustration between the sexes, Gray humorously writes, "You see the Martian and Venusian languages had the same words, but the way they were used gave different meanings."[46]

In general, I am chary of drawing clear-cut distinctions between men and women. We must be cautious about naming differences that either reinforce existing stereotypes or set a group up for the creation of stereotypes. Gray's depiction of women and men on different planets particularly falls into this trap.[47] "Women" as a group are not all the same, and to describe gender patterns obscures the differences. Cultural differences are sometimes more significant than gender differences in conversational styles; some cultural groups as a whole are more quiet and reserved and others more verbal and expressive. Furthermore, most studies being done on gender patterns, even if somewhat accurate for white middle-class women, may not reflect the situation for women from other cultural or ethnic groups—or what is described as a "female" pattern may describe the situation for subordinate persons of both genders in other groups.

The overlay between culture, region, status, and gender is very complex, and thus anything reported here must be evaluated with caution. Nevertheless, there are some important studies concerning gender and conversational interaction, and we do well to be informed of their findings.

Studies of classroom behavior suggest that men and women exhibit different manners in their speaking, and that (western European) men's style is the valued pattern. Men are more likely to use: highly assertive speech, impersonal and abstract examples, and competitive or adversarial interchanges. The ethos is often "the survival of the fittest"; in more brutal forms of this, there's an "either you make it or you don't." This style and ethos are not only favored, but they are perceived to be more intelligent and authoritative behaviors. Women are more likely to hesitate and qualify their speech ("I'm not sure, but maybe sometimes it is the case that . . ."), end with "tag"questions ("This is really important, don't you think?"), share personal experiences, and belittle their contributions ("This is probably not important, but . . .").[48] The more tentative style of women invites more interruptions from male students and less attention and notice from faculty. Indeed, a point made by a woman in a deferential style may go unnoticed, only to be engaged with and praised when repeated by a man. The fact that teachers may ignore, neglect to call on, expect less of, and forget to credit women for their contributions contributes to discouraging and sometimes to silencing women in discussion settings.[49] On top of all this, a woman may be double bound; if she learns the code of the male, she may be perceived as inappropriately pushy, aggressive, and unfeminine.

These findings about women's silence and deference in classrooms are surprising to many; the prevailing stereotype is that in mixed-gender settings women do all the talking and men patiently listen or tune out. There is some evidence to suggest that the patterns described above are somewhat contextually determined; women are more comfortable in private conversation than in public settings such as the classroom, and they will talk more when they feel that they are experts on a subject. Here is one place, however, where the weight of evidence disconfirms the stereotype.[50] Women are not overall more talkative than men in conversation, according to most research findings. Nor are they more domineering even when they do speak a lot. The stylistic differences, especially the tentative tone, show up even in informal conversation as well as classroom discussion. Even when they are equally talkative, women tend to make more encouraging and supportive comments, thus facilitating and drawing out the contributions of others. Women do engage in conversation for the sheer purpose of developing relationships with others, and thus they may talk at times and for reasons that men may not choose to do so (given that men consider talk to be primarily for informational and competitive purposes). Conjecturing why the stereotype of talkative women is so strong, Dale Spender offers: "The talkativeness of women has been argued in comparison not with men but with *silence*. Women have not been judged on the grounds of whether they talk more than men, but of whether they talk more than silent women."[51] Indeed, one study of male-female discussions found that the contribution of female speakers was perceived to be greater than male speakers if contributions were equal. Another study found that teachers seriously underestimate the amount of attention they give to boys, believing their attention is evenly distributed when girls receive a third of their attention. This is not surprising; if boys and men are used to doing more of the speaking or getting more of the attention, then an equal portion of time or attention given to girls and women will be experienced as favoring women.[52]

WOMEN'S WAYS OF CONVERSING: THE CONTRIBUTIONS

A first look at women's tentative speech patterns may prompt leaders to seek a remedy in the forms of assertiveness and aggressiveness training. The hedges and qualifications strike a confident speaker as remnants of oppression, learned patterns that enable subordinates to survive in a hierarchical context. There is some truth to this view; indeed such patterns are also characteristic of persons, male and female, in lower-status positions. When such speech reflects a person's disregard for themselves, it is troublesome. But, tentative speech is often used by women for positive reasons. And, affirming the positive aspects of this behavior can actually contribute to improving women's regard for themselves. The tag questions and qualifications may promote greater collaboration and cooperation between speakers, and it may enable a more exploratory and creative atmosphere in a classroom community. Competitive styles may work against the communal construction of knowledge. If the learner feels they must bring a polished argument, they are inhibited from testing out new and raw ideas. Furthermore, competitive styles "weed out" vulnerable learners who, with a little encouragement and support, may have a great deal to offer a community of learners.

Julia Wood, in fact, argues that women's provisional speech, rather than being a remnant of oppression that should be eradicated, can be a powerful source of community building. "Rather than reflecting powerlessness, the uses of hedges, qualifiers, and tag questions may express women's desires to keep conversation open and to include others. It is much easier to jump into a conversation that has not been sealed with absolute, firm statements. A tentative style of speaking supports women's general desire to create equality and include others."[53] While Wood acknowledges that such speech can be perceived as weak and lacking in authority and thus should be used judiciously, she opens up the possibility for women reclaiming such speech with intention and purpose. Indeed, the fact that students of both sexes participate more in classes taught by women than by men suggests that the reclaiming process is worth considering.[54]

MOVES FOR EMPOWERMENT

If a leader wishes to create an environment that encourages women as well as men to participate in the conversations of the community, there are a number of small but very significant ways to start. The first step a leader can take is to assess his or her discussion behavior. Leaders can inadvertently reinforce women's invisibility by missing women's cues, following up more fully on men, and using exclusive language. Women, and other participants who are habitually quiet in conversation, can be encouraged to participate if leaders learn their "cues for conversation." A leader can watch for signs (eye movements and slight body gestures indicating interest in joining a discussion, thwarted attempts to enter a fast-moving conversation) and create a space for the person's contribution. A woman's "pause time" may be longer than a man's, and therefore she may wait too long between comments and be unable to insert a comment before another speaker begins. A sensitive leader will watch for this, and will moderate a discussion so that slow pausers who become silenced will have opportunity for gaining the floor. At the least, a leader can watch for inadvertent ways that he or she might ignore a speaker who is visibly trying to enter a conversation.

Similarly, leaders may be prone to follow up more extensively on men's comments than on women's. This can take the form of making more reinforcing statements, referring back to and giving credit for previous statements, or asking more probing questions of men to prolong their speaking. It is important for leaders to be aware that women have to battle status and "performance expectations" that automatically lead others (and even themselves) to assume they are less intellectually competent than men; this means that they will be granted less conversational space, will more likely cede their space to others, and their contributions may be judged less worthy. Leaders may make women feel invisible because they are operating with their own prejudicial "performance expectations" that assume women have nothing important to contribute. The fact that men will be affirmed and given credit for statements previously made by women and ignored by others confirms that expectations for competence often override actual levels of competence.[55] If, in addition, a woman uses the above described tentative language, a leader may tune her out or cut her off prematurely, assuming that she does not understand the topic under discussion. A leader who recognizes that tentative language may have little relation to a person's grasp of the subject matter is better able to support women's contributions.

Exclusive language further contributes to a feeling of invisibility. While using the generic "he" and "mankind" can reduce women's participation, the problem goes beyond that. I have been in countless numbers of lectures where the speaker will say to the audience something like, "suppose your wife says to you . . . ," which makes women (not to mention single persons) feel as if they are not included. Additionally, it is liberating for leaders to provide examples that are not stereotypical or that do not "mark" women as deviant. When I hear someone use wording such as "according to biblical scholar Elisabeth Schüssler Fiorenza," rather than "as female biblical scholar Elisabeth Schüssler Fiorenza," I feel that general humanity includes women.

In addition to avoiding inadvertent discriminatory practices, a leader can empower women by recognizing or developing their expertise, setting up collaborative situations, and encouraging the sharing of personal stories. As noted above, women and others who are reticent to take part in conversations where they have low status, are more inclined to take the risk to contribute if the subject matter involves something for which they have expertise. Leaders who are aware of these areas of expertise, or leaders who encourage women to develop a particular expertise, can promote women's participation in conversation and decision making. Whenever a community discusses an important issue, the possibility for delegating research arises. If women are invited to research particular issues of import, then they will be more likely to take part in discussions.

It is sometimes the case that women have more experience with collaborative explorations than with individual or competitive arguments. While argument and debate should not be avoided, opportunities for cooperative conversational work should be available. In her work on committee meetings, Carole Edelsky looked at the interactional nature of "two kinds of floor." One was the orderly, "one-at-a-time" type of discussion, where a person takes a turn and "holds forth" with a viewpoint; the other was a collaborative form of discussion where two or more people freely and jointly build an idea together. Both kinds can occur in the same meeting. Men are much more likely to take the single floor; both men and women participate equally in the collaborative floor. Edelsky's study suggests that women are not so much reticent to speak as they are uncomfortable with the form of discussion privileged in many public environments. Rather than "hold forth," women may prefer a more "free-for-all" atmosphere in which knowledge is in the process of being constructed as they go along rather than knowledge being chosen from a series of ideas presented from different debaters.[56]

Collaborative forms of knowing can be fostered by the inclusion of story-sharing and personal experience in a discussion or conversation. When stories are shared, the goal is not to convince others to tell their story so it sounds just like ours (or when that is the goal, it is not real storytelling); the goal is to lay stories alongside one another so that the complexity of life is revealed to hearers. Stories, in fact, expose the fallacies of both universalism and objectivism. When we hear of people's life experience, we become aware of how particular and how interested our theological reflection is.

HOSPITALITY AND THE PROBLEM OF POLITENESS

As we work to empower women toward conversational caring, it is important that we not mistake women's inviting and collaborative legacy for conflict avoidance. Conflict avoidance and surface politeness, as I have been arguing, are not empowering for women and not healthy for community life. Sometimes women and men alike expect their female leaders to be maternal and nurturant, and they are thus confused and angry when these teachers challenge or correct them. We will return to this issue again in chapter 6 when we look at education, but here it is important to clarify that conversation is a tough and dynamic process. Collaborative floors are not eviscerated discussions; they are energetic gropings and struggles toward complex truth.

In fact, it is necessary to distinguish between politeness and hospitality in conversation. Politeness, as I am using it, is deference toward another for the purpose of avoiding a deeper and inevitably conflicted conversation. Hospitality is respect for another which empathizes enough with another so as to invite and allow for them to participate equally in a deep and conflicted conversation. Genuine conversations ought to be hospitable but they are not polite.[57]

In a relationship characterized by conversational caring, moments of empathy, where one listens, are joined with moments of prophetic caring, where one confronts.

PROPHETIC CARING: CARING ENOUGH TO CONFRONT

In her novel *The Small Room*, May Sarton tells the story of Lucy Winter, a young English professor. One scene in the middle of the novel is quite compelling. Discouraged by the pile of papers reflecting on *The Iliad* that she has just graded, she faces her class and begins to read from the Bard with great feeling and passion. She follows her reading with selections from three of the worst papers from the pile.

"This was the material before you, and this is how you honored it. . . . Here is one of the great mysterious works of man, as great and mysterious as a cathedral. And what did you do? You gave it so little of your real selves that you actually achieved boredom. You stood in Chartres Cathedral *unmoved,*" she chastises. She assures the class that it isn't grades she is talking about. "You'll slide through all right. It is not bad, it is just flat. It's the sheer poverty of your approach that is horrifying!"

When she finished her passionate outrage, the class applauded her. "That was wonderful," one student remarked, "why didn't you get angry before?"

Winter was passionate about her material, and she cared enough about the students to risk their ire by boldly shaking them out of their slumber into the mystery of literature. Her anger was not provoked by the fact that they failed her by doing mediocre work; it was that they disrespected the material and disadvantaged themselves. She was holding her students accountable to their relationship with her, with the subject matter, and with themselves. To have treated them with kindness and sympathy, to have rationalized and made excuses for their dullness, in Lucy's view, would have been to lack deep care for them. They would have come out of her class in a shallow relationship to her, to *The Iliad*, and to themselves. The dull papers were more than academically disappointing, they were spiritually impoverished. To have let them scrape by without a word would have been to fail as a teacher.

I've shared this illustration with a number of groups, and the response is always mixed. Some folks identify with the applauding students and praise Lucy's prophetic passion. These persons think that kindness in this situation would have been *un*caring. Others, however, are more hesitant. They fear that such behavior can become judgmental and manipulative. The students are vulnerable, and an exhibition of rage risks exploiting that vulnerability, this second group cautions.

Prophetic caring, as I am using it, means caring enough to confront a person or group when they are not holding up their end of a relationship (to other persons, to subject matter, to themselves). Indeed, there is a risk that prophetic caring can become manipulative and judgmental. If Winter does this in each class session, her students will grow weary and discouraged. If she is more worried about how their performance reflects on her reputation as a teacher, her students will feel used. Furthermore, if she always proceeds as if she is the one who knows the truth about something, then she is subject to the temptations of pride and ideological taint. These limitations and temptations, however, ought not to quench prophetic caring when it is appropriate.

As a professor, Winter is in a position of power over her students. This makes their relationship somewhat parental rather than reciprocal. Her word, thus, carries heavy weight. On the one hand, she can push her passion on others inappropriately. On the other hand, however, she is in a position to reveal to them what it takes to become truly literate. If she only pushes her passion, she risks being a zealot; if she withholds herself, she risks closing her students out of the beautiful "mystery" into which she has gained entry.

In more mutual relationships, prophetic caring does not carry the same kind of power imbalance. While the dangers of prophetic caring are still evident (manipulation and judgmentalism), the vulnerability levels are more equal. In communities of faith, we have a responsibility to hold one another accountable and to challenge one another as a part of caring in relation to one another.

It is not always easy for women to express prophetic caring. When women feel mistreated, their image of female goodness often leads them to either blame themselves or suppress their feelings of having been wronged. Clearly, this is neither good for the one mistreated nor for the one mistreating. Those who are not held accountable are not being genuinely cared for, they are being let off the hook inappropriately. While I do not want to blame women and others who avoid prophetic caring out of genuine fear and vulnerability, I do want to expose the unhelpful side of self-sacrifice.

In order to express prophetic caring, a woman needs to recognize and name her own anger. Women may be hesitant to express prophetic caring because our culture puts a barrier between women and their anger and our churches bolster this with a shallow theology of forgiveness. We turn now to consider the problem of anger.

WOMEN AND ANGER

In *The Dance of Anger,* Harriet Goldhor Lerner analyzes the way in which women "have long been discouraged from the awareness and forth-right expression of anger."[58] As nurturers, peacemakers, and soothers, women are not expected to openly express anger. This has unfortunate consequences. Frequently, the "taboos against our feeling and expressing anger are so powerful that even *knowing* when we are angry is not a simple matter." The training starts early. Girls learn that anger is not a safe emotion for them. "You sort of have anger inside but not really," twelve-year-old Jennifer revealed in Gilligan and Brown's study of adolescent girls. "You shouldn't let it out around everyone else. You should just like do it yourself."[59]

Lerner refers to the "nice-lady" syndrome, which leads to the silencing of one's anger to avoid threatening a relationship. Women avoid conflict by defining their own wishes and preferences as being the same as those the one to whom she is in relation wishes or prefers her to be. Depression, which is often masked anger, is a frequent result of having anger inside "but not really."[60] Suppressing anger can alternatively lead to explosive and ineffective displays of pent-up anger. The ineffectiveness of the "blowup" reinforces a woman's fear of anger and prompts her to repress it more fully. Persons must be able to own their feelings, name what it is that is troubling them, and assert their anger with confidence. The person or system that causes the anger must be directly confronted and not simply complained against to another party. Healthy anger, like empathy, emerges when a person is able to differentiate themselves from another enough to own and name the anger appropriately. The "nice-lady syndrome," which prevents any constructive channeling of anger, suggests that women's "sin is not anger but the denial of anger."[61]

The presence of anger indicates that we need to state our feelings, concerns, and opinions about a matter. "If we are chronically angry or bitter in a particular relationship, that may be a message to clarify and strengthen the 'I' a bit more. We must re-examine our own selves with a view toward discovering what we think, feel, and want and what we need to do differently in our lives," Lerner contends.[62] The "selfing" that Lerner promotes is a genuine and honest expression of one's feelings and voice. This does not mean that one must be unswervingly tenacious; expressing one's voice may very well lead to negotiations and compromises. They are, however, mutual negotiations and not compromises by default.

Women need to understand that anger can be a part of genuine caring. Honest and angry assertion is part of communication. One does not bother to get angry if one does not care; it would have been easier for Winter to politely encourage her students to delve more deeply into the material. If they followed her modulated advice, good; if they didn't, well that was their problem. "Anger is a *mode of connectedness* to others and it is always a *vivid form of caring*," contends Beverly Harrison. Surely, expressing one's anger can be risky, particularly if the other partners in relation try to force what Lerner calls "change-back," or return to the way things were. A caring woman will need support to maintain her angry voice. In some cases, the pressure to continue de-selfing may be immense.[63]

Anger is not only important for interpersonal relationships, it is also important in the quest for global justice. "We must never lose touch with the fact that all serious human moral activity, especially action for social change, takes its bearings from the rising power of human anger. Such anger is a signal that change is called for, that *transformation in relation* is required."[64] The repression of genuine anger is tantamount to the repression of justice-seeking. If we are not permitted to feel and express anger, we will be stymied in our fight for justice. One of the ways that our theology contributes to prophetic torpor is by denying women their good and righteous anger. Marge Piercy expresses it well in her poem entitled:

> *A just anger*
> Anger shines through me.
> Anger shines through me.
> I am a burning bush.
> My rage is a cloud of flame.
> My rage is a cloud of flame
> in which I walk
> seeking justice
> like a precipice.
> How the streets
> of the iron city
> flicker, flicker,
> and the dirty air
> fumes.
> Anger storms
> between me and things,
> transfiguring,
> transfiguring.
> A good anger acted upon
> is beautiful as lightening
> and swift with power.
> A good anger swallowed,
> a good anger swallowed
> clots the blood
> to slime.[65]

FORGIVING OUR SELVES AWAY: PROPHETIC CARING AND THE PROBLEM OF FORGIVENESS

Even as avoidance of anger "clots" the artery that leads to prophetic caring, surface understandings of forgiveness block the route to legitimate anger.

Forgiveness is an extremely important Christian concept; an understanding of God's love and forgiveness is at the heart of Christian faith. As Christians we believe that God's forgiveness rains down on us and frees us to forgive others. Rather than living lives of "tit for tat," we aim to live generous, tolerant, and forgiving lives. Knowing that God's graciousness encompasses our failings, we pass that graciousness along to others. Forgiveness is one of the most precious gifts of the Christian community— but it is also one of the most misunderstood and distorted gifts.

Here we must face some of the distortions in our teachings about forgiveness. When forgiveness becomes a means for avoiding genuine conflict and grievances, then it becomes destructive of community life. Once again, the double whammy hits women. Trained to be nice and kind, taught to avoid pride and self-assertion, women may be further encouraged to "forgive themselves away," to repress genuine anger and broken relationships. This has all too often been the case with battered women, many of whom have been pressured by religious leaders to forgive their abusive spouses immediately and repeatedly. We will return to the issue of abuse in chapter 5. But, here I'd like to address the more pervasive problem of "surface forgiveness." The pressure to forgive, forget, and return to destructive patterns of relating contributes to unhealthy dynamics in so-called normal families and communities of faith.

In order for genuine reconciliation to occur in relationships that are broken, confrontation, repentance, and forgiveness are needed. The brokenness must be named, the ones who harmed others must acknowledge the harm, and then the ones who have been harmed can offer forgiveness. Forgiveness, however, cannot be insisted upon too soon. And, most important, forgiving another does not mean returning to the way things were. Forgiveness means that the injured parties are willing to restore the relationship, but full reconciliation only occurs when the injuring parties are willing to redress the situation and change their injuring behavior. If legitimate anger is bypassed, then genuine reconciliation does not occur.

Problematic teachings on forgiveness begin early. Consider with me a session on forgiveness included in a recent curriculum for family education.[66] It is entitled "Learning to Forgive."

Learning to Forgive. Truly one of the gifts of faith we can offer our children is the sure knowledge that forgiveness is a freely given commodity. In biblical terms forgiveness is the act of covering up or sending away the sin in order that the separation caused by that sin may cease. Forgiveness allows us to get right again with each other and our Creator.

Susan is an eight-year-old girl who is learning how to be forgiving. Bobby tormented her in the car pool for days on end: he tore her homework paper, broke her pencil, pulled her hair. Finally, Angela could stand it no longer and cuffed Bobby on the ear. Susan wailed out in unison with the injured party and scolded, "Don't do that, Angela; you'll hurt Bobby." Susan not only had forgiven Bobby and forgotten her anger but she was able even to show concern when he had been wronged.

Inserted as a supplement to the curriculum was a study guide that included the following discussion questions.

Actions for Others. *Relationships with Family and Neighbors: Learning to Forgive.*

1. When someone has treated you very badly, what should you do? a. Do something bad to that person; b. Never speak to the person again; c. Speak to the person but tell your friends how terrible he or she is; d. Forget about it and continue to be nice to the person. Why did you choose the answer you did? Will it make people happier? Will it solve the problem? Talk about this with your family.
2. Read aloud Matt. 18:21-22. Talk together about what this means for you.

The lesson is intended to communicate the importance of forgiveness for restoring relationships. The intended moralism, however, actually promotes *unauthentic* relationships. Rather than "covering up or sending away the sin in order that the separation caused by the sin may cease," the anecdote covers up the sin and *increases* the separation. Rather than genuine caring, which includes honest confrontation, Susan hides herself and silences her prophetic friend. The writer offers a facile understanding of forgiveness and a surface understanding of relationship. Nowhere in the discussion is there mentioned the possibility that Susan would honestly express her anger and discuss it with Bobby; instead the implied proper response is to show concern for Bobby, inhibit concern for self, and "forget about it and continue to be a nice person." While forgiveness is certainly an important ingredient in a deep relationship, a preemptive strike at Susan's legitimate anger dooms the relationship between the two to superficiality. Susan is supposed to be all empathy, and Angela's attempt to insert confrontation into the relationship is stifled.

Aside from the relational distortion, the theological inadequacy of this lesson is glaring. Nowhere are the tensions between forgiveness and accountability, grace and judgment, self-care and care of others brought to the (non-) conversation. The shallow options offered for discussion (under "Actions for Others") thwart any in-depth theological probing. Are these really the only options?! Do the children have any legitimate alternatives from which to choose (who is going to admit to a, b, or c?)? To top it off, genuine communication is decisively thwarted when trump card Matthew 18:21-22 is laid on the table. The final words in this lesson are Jesus' instruction to forgive seventy-seven times.

My major complaint with this lesson, however, has not yet been aired. It is this: the lesson teaches *girls* to silence their own anger and the righteous indignation of other girls. We will look in chapter 4 at the "perilous divide" girls face between grade school and junior high years. The implicit gender themes in this lesson help us to see some of the causes for girls losing a sense of themselves in teenage years when they realize it is time to become a "good woman." Susan is already in training to become a self-sacrificing good woman; girls who read the story are encouraged to do the same. Just in case they have more spunk than is good for them, Angela provides a foil for Susan's goodness. Angela, evidently a bystander to the abusive encounters between Bobby and Susan, can stand by "no longer" and enters the relationship. Susan rebuffs her girlfriend's confrontive behavior; in effect, *Susan cares for Bobby while neglecting Angela*. The lesson writer rewards her behavior, indicating that the best plan is to forget about the abuse, "be nice," and work to "make people [i.e., male people] happier." No thought is given to the fact that Angela is not happier. In this well-intentioned but misguided lesson we have the precursor to the silencing of the female self, relationship inauthenticity, incomplete caring, cheap grace, and the abuse of women by men.

When pondering this lesson on forgiveness, one cannot help asking, "Where was the car-pool *driver* in all this?" Would a mother or father sit by idly while such "tormenting" was going on? Curiously, the lesson writer disempowers the parent. Certainly, parents cannot intervene in all childish squabbles; yet those who care for children sometimes must arbitrate justice and demand mutual consideration. Mothers have a long and noble history of protecting children in their vulnerability, shaping children's moral and social behavior, and tending to their emotional and physical needs.[67] This lesson revokes the power of the mother; or implies that

117

as long as the boy isn't vulnerable, her intervention is unnecessary.[68] In every count, the mother's work has been nullified. The vulnerable ones are left unprotected, the tormenting behavior of Bobby is reinforced rather than reformed, and the physical needs of Susan and the emotional needs of both Bobby and Angela are neglected.[69]

We cannot rebuild our mothers' house if we revoke the role of mothering in the legacy of caring.

ON MOTHERING AND CARING: REBUILDING OUR MOTHERS' HOUSE

If we want to rebuild our mothers' house, and if we want to promote genuine caring, we need to look at the legacy of caretaking that women have carried on, including the history of "mothering."[70] In doing so, we recognize two problems. On the one hand, women's caring and mothering have been sentimentalized and given undue weight in female identity formation; on the other hand, caretaking and mothering have been devalued and neglected both by men who have remained distanced from caretaking and feminists who have refused to be defined by it.

Both the privileges and the burdens of caring for the next generation have fallen on women, and this has deprived women of self-development and men of empathetic competence. While mothering is female caring, the acts of nurture that constitute maternal practice can, and in my view should, be done by male as well as female caregivers. We must affirm that caring for one another, especially for vulnerable ones such as children, is an important endeavor, perhaps the most important aspect of life. But, it is everyone's responsibility, not simply women's. Conservative critics often charge that feminism is harmful to families and children; they have resisted naming the ways in which "traditional" paradigms for family life are harmful to women and children. The clarion call for "family values" has become a "distorted and sometimes politically dangerous code word for reinstating male dominance and female self-sacrifice."[71] Yet, the call to care for children is an important one; it is possible to be "pro-family" without favoring the so-called traditional family structure.

PRO-FAMILY COMMUNITIES

Pro-family communities recognize the importance for women and men to share a commitment to parenting.[72] Some men have joined women in shaping a vision of shared parenting, and they are taking responsibility with women for the future of families. Jack Nelson-Pallmeyer identifies how men have contributed to the so-called "breakdown of the family" by shirking parenting responsibilities in a variety of ways. He particularly exposes the way in which men occasionally "baby-sit," but rarely parent. A father's time with children, Nelson-Pallmeyer has discovered, is often looked upon as the burden "baby-sitting" and the mother's time with children as the privilege of "child rearing."[73] Men take care of their children on the side; women do it as a central task.[74] The "attentive father" is assessed somewhat like the "talkative woman" described earlier in this chapter by Dale Spender. A father is judged as good if he is attentive to his children at all; he is not compared to a woman's parenting, he is being compared to the absent father.

Shared parenting, however, is only the beginning for a new pro-family orientation. A full affirmation of family involves the ability for a community to collectively care for one another and for those beyond its borders.

BROADENING OUR CIRCLES OF CARING

Mothering and fathering, which point us to caring for "our" vulnerable, contain the temptation to disregard the needs of others outside our own family or group. A central issue in any ethic of care is making sure "that the web of relationships is spun widely enough so that some are not beyond its reach" insists Joan Tronto.[75] Even as we nurture a vision of shared parenting, it is important to have a rich enough vision of caretaking that nurtures those near and cares about those far.[76] Genuine caring can do this. Empathetic mothers and fathers, who learn to deal with the differences between themselves and their children and between their different children, teach their children to attend to and understand the differences of those outside their family. Prophetic fathers and mothers, who teach their own children to use their voices and to point out injustices within their families, raise their children to notice injustice in the world. Conversationally generous mothers and fathers, who share their own stories and listen to the stories of their children, equip them for genuine relationships of give-and-take. These parenting practices, which begin in the home, can be shared by all people in communities of faith so that we collectively care for our children. Families and communities of faith can be the "first schools" for genuine relationality and mature caring; they can prepare their children to care for the world beyond their bounds.

CARETAKING IN TRUTH: WITH EMPATHY, CONVERSATION, AND PROPHETIC VOICE

Studies on women's capacity for caring have made an important contribution to our understanding both of human development and moral theory. By placing positive value on women's desire for affiliation and capacity for empathy, such studies have awakened women and men to the fact that women have valuable resources to tap for the future of our world. In rebuilding our mothers' house, we recover the "injunction to care" and the responsibility to discern and alleviate the "real and recognizable" hurts in our communities and world.[77]

I have argued that this rebuilding has been tricky business. The texture of female caring has been woven by a variety of fibers, many of which originate in and continue to perpetuate cultural expectations for femininity. A vision for caretaking must not reinforce rather than overturn the problem "that women care and men take."[78] In the process of recovering caring, insufficient attention has been paid to developing a comprehensive definition of caring that overcomes the close association between caring and self-abnegation. While reclaiming caring, we must be *care-ful* not to hoist the banner of affiliation and connection above individuality and differentiation. I have highlighted those aspects of Gilligan's work that move us toward a more comprehensive understanding of caring, and I have offered a threefold description of caring as empathetic, conversational, and prophetic.

In the next chapter we will examine how an overemphasis on empathetic caring (discerning and responding to the needs and desires of others) has impacted the lives of girls in a destructive manner. Many acutely empathetic girls are caught in the cross fire of a fierce battle between others' expectations for their femininity and their own psychic need for voice and self-authority. These girls are trying to call communities to task, but they are doing it very indirectly. Raised not to name, or even recognize, their own needs, girls and women are struggling to articulate an urgent need: for legitimate voice and genuine relationality. Let us listen for this prophetic word as it comes to us, a word God is sending both in a whirlwind, splitting mountains and breaking rocks, and in sheer silence, barely audible and prone to be ignored.[79]

Chapter Four

Your Daughters Shall Prophesy

"SAFE-HOUSES" FOR RAISING GIRLS IN FAMILIES AND COMMUNITIES OF FAITH

"Once there [in the psychological underground], in the absence of safe-houses where girls can say what they feel and think . . . girls become reluctant to know that they know and fear that their experience if spoken will endanger their relationships and threaten their survival."
—Carol Gilligan and Lyn Mikel Brown[1]

"What gets me into trouble is—chewing gum and not having my shirt tucked in (but it's usually worth it)."
—Twelve-year-old girl, on this side of the "perilous divide"[2]

"You can't, you just can't do whatever you want, you have to do what you should do. . . ."
—Twelve-year-old girl, on the other side of the "perilous divide"[3]

ON NOT INDUCTING OUR GIRLS INTO THE HAREM OF SEXISM

Recall that after Vashti was dethroned a pageant was held in which all the young girls of the kingdom were expected to participate. Like soldiers drafted into an army, the girls were conscripted into Ahasuerus's service without their choice. All the girls were painted and perfumed until they were walking icons of femininity; all would be deflowered to determine who was the most feminine of all. One lucky girl would win, the others would be used and turned out.

In a brilliantly evil scheme, the king not only entrenched a submissive and objectified femininity, but he also pitted girls against girls so that solidarity would be avoided. Only one girl had a future; they were in a vicious competition to be the most beautiful and the most feminine, the lives of those who lost were imperiled. The conscription of these young girls into his harem was the king's insurance that sexism would endure.

In varying forms, this induction still takes place. We do not force girls physically, but we shape them psychically to believe that they should mold, shape, and paint their bodies and spirits according to expected patterns of femininity. Billions are spent each year on products and services to feminize girls' and women's bodies and minds. While I am not opposed to people having choices about their bodies and minds, I am concerned about the kinds of choices we promote. From corsets to silicone implants to spike heels, we constrict their lives rather than open possibilities for women. We in communities of faith need to exercise a collective "no" to the dehumanization of girls and women.

I do not want to prescribe how girls should look or which definitions of femininity are wrong and which ones are right. I do want to prompt us to raise our consciousness about what kinds of images we most frequently offer—and what kinds of images we carefully select out. Without insisting on one definition of what it means to be a woman, I want to assert that telling our daughters that they are inferior to men and expected to alter their looks simply to please men is, in my view, simply wrong, unjust—out of the bounds of alternatives. We need not denigrate particular choices, but we do need to broaden the images and characterizations of women we bequeath to our daughters. We may need to teach our daughters how to negotiate sexism wisely and even craftily, but with an awareness that it is wrong rather than a submission to it. In this way, we must together remember Queen Vashti. For that which she negates—the degradation of women—needs to be negated. Those who are forced to say no alone are rendered extraordinarily vulnerable; if we can create a "panoply" of ways to refuse dehumanization, then drastic reactions to resistance will be less effective. Esther, along with all the Persian maidens, was "inducted" into the harem of Ahasuerus and forced to compete for the role of beauty queen—neither she nor her guardian having a choice in the matter. We must work against this "intolerance of female freedom and choice."[4] Though we cannot and must not demand a particular trajectory for the lives of our girls and women, we can and must demand that they not be similarly inducted into a girl-destroying culture that strips them of their choice.

In this chapter, I will look at the culture into which our girls are being inducted (drawing on my own life, the life of my daughter, and current research), and I suggest ways in which I think we can thwart their conscription into the harem of sexism.

OF DIRTY DRESSES AND GIRLS WHO ARE MUCH

When one of my sons, Paul, was a toddler, he was stocky, assertive, and invariably disheveled from hard play. I wish I had a dollar for every time someone said to me with admiration, "He's a real boy," or, even more poignantly, "He's *all* boy." Emblazoned in my memory is a day when my daughter, too, was a toddler. A group of children was playing on a playground, their parents chatting on the side. Marie, my daughter, was frolicking about in a blue smocked dress. Her cheeks were smudged with dirt, her knees and bare toes were stained green with grass, and her dress was a glorious and dirty collage of all the places she had been; the sheer joy of unself-conscious play emanated from her. I recall that I was beaming, both in vicarious enjoyment and in quiet pride; my daughter was engaging this world with confidence—getting dirty with great dignity! My contentment was disrupted as another mother commented disapprovingly, "She's not much of a girl, is she?"

My response, "It depends on what you mean by girl," was an important step in the development of my parenting. When we raise children, we explicitly and implicitly shape their gender identities. The prevailing pattern is clear: boys are supposed to engage the world with aggression and transform the dirt into dream worlds; girls who do so are scorned. Recent studies indicate that by adolescence, if not before, girls get the message: only boys inherit the earth.[5] That day on the playground flashed in my mind on another occasion, when after preaching, I was handed a small slip of paper. On one side were two verse citations: I Corinthians 14:34 and I Timothy 2:11-15, which prohibit women from teaching and command their silence in church and their subordination to men; on the other side were the words of Proverbs 3:5 printed in bold: "TRUST IN THE *LORD* WITH ALL THINE HEART; AND LEAN NOT UNTO THINE OWN UNDERSTANDING" (KJV). A double whammy: I was not supposed to teach in church, and I was not to have confidence in my own understandings. The message I understood was: "You're not much of a woman, are you?" Men can engage the world and transform it; women who do so will be scorned.

Gender training begins early and it is pervasive. As Susan Bordo notes, "We are creatures swaddled in culture from the moment we are designated one sex or the other";[6] studies show that gender coding has a significant influence on how parents treat their children, beginning in early infancy.[7] The explicit instances of selective gender socialization are only the tip of the iceberg; I shudder to think of the subtle looks and implicit body language that have unconsciously shaped my children's understanding of themselves as "real boy" or "real girl." While I think the consequences for girls are more oppressive than the consequences for boys, I am quite sure that both boys and girls are harmed by gender training. Boys are reared to be autonomous, controlling, and assertive; girls are reared to be connected, submissive, and caring. The fact that women most often do the primary caretaking and men are often distant fathers intensifies boys' growth in separateness (and loss of connection) and girls' growth in connection (and avoidance of separation). Transgressing these expected patterns of behavior will cause difficulties for either gender. In fact, it may be the case that those who exhibit a combination of traits have the most difficulty. Think about it—to say admiringly that Paul is "all boy" is to say that he is no part girl. Had he toted a doll with him in his exploits, he no doubt would not have earned his "all boy" accolades. On the other hand, if my daughter were dressed like a boy and acted like a boy, perhaps she would have been dismissed as a "tomboy" without further thought. But, she was a dirty girl in a pretty dress. She wasn't "much of a girl" because she was a girl who, *as a girl*, grasped much from life. As Beverly Harrison states, the "spooking, sparking power of *real* women who do not need to stand around waiting for male approval" sets fear in the hearts of those committed to a patriarchal world.[8]

Dirty Marie in her pretty blue dress is a symbol for balanced gender nurturing: with autonomy *and* connectedness, with control *and* flexibility,[9] with assertiveness *and* care. For girls, this means that we critique the social restrictions that have been placed on girls (allow them to get dirty with "boys'" activities) while at the same time recover and appreciate those ways of knowing and doing that have been preserved by girls and women (not insist that they have to act or look just like what we would expect boys to act and look like in order to get dirty in the boys' arena). Accomplishing this balance will not be easy. According to the American Psychological Association, social norms are still conventional: "Females who display 'womanly' traits and males who display 'manly' traits are more favorably evaluated and judged more psychologically healthy than those who do not. Conversely, those who engage in what is perceived to be cross-sex behavior can be the victim of social sanctions."[10] In general, male traits are more valued than female traits—except when exhibited by women.[11] For girls and women this creates an intractable "double-bind"; wombs and brains, competency and femininity are perceived to be incompatible. If women are successful, they are unfeminine. If they are feminine, they are perceived incompetent. My words to the woman who betrayed my daughter were more true than I realized; for a lot, indeed, depends on what we mean by girl.

In this chapter I want to consider how we can raise girls who are not afraid to inherit the earth. Picking up on Bordo's metaphor, I believe that we can weave our daughters' (and sons') swaddling clothes in a way that is girl-affirming. I want to begin this weaving by considering the way in which we harmfully confine our daughters by raising them to be "the perfect, nice girl." Culture-wide our girls are trying to tell us that they do not want to be fit into this mold. The question is, Are we listening? It's not easy to hear. Though many are shouting loudly, they are not always using words—they are using the indirect communication of eating disorders. I will explore the "gendering rules and rites" of femininity, I will look at girls' resistance, and I will probe into the way in which family structures pick up where swaddling clothes leave off. Then, I will suggest how we can promote the growth of female persons in communities of faith. This chapter will focus on family and community life dynamics; in chapter 6 we will attend to educational structures and processes.

THE PERFECT GIRL: GENDERING RULES AND RITES

A couple of years ago there was a short article in the *Wall Street Journal* on awards given at a graduation ceremony for kindergartners.[12] A New Jersey father was chagrined to discover that his daughter's school, nestled in a progressive suburb of New York City, had created strikingly gender-stereotyped awards. The boys' awards were: Very Best Thinker, Most Eager Learner, Most Imaginative, Most Enthusiastic, Most Scientific, Best Friend, Mr. Personality, Hardest Worker, Best Sense of Humor. The girls' awards were: All-Around Sweetheart, Sweetest Personality, Cutest Personality, Best Sharer, Best Artist, Biggest Heart, Best Manners, Best Helper, Most Creative. Boys were praised for their intellectual abilities; girls were acknowledged for their sweetness! When I think of Robert Fulghum's claim that "all I really need to know I learned in kindergarten," I shudder.[13] If these are the awards with which the year is supposed to culminate, the boys will have been shaped all year long into hardworking, enthusiastic, and imaginative learners, while the girls will have been molded into sweet, well-mannered, cute, and helpful young ladies.[14]

Unfortunately, the behaviors for which we reward girls—being sweet, well-mannered, and compliant—are the kind of behaviors that drop them out of the competitive workforce later in life.

In their middle years of childhood, many girls are able to shirk off gender expectations. These girls are generally vocal, confident, and determined to voice their opinions. They often know what's expected of them, but they flout expectations boldly. They can say with glee, "What gets me into trouble is—chewing gum and not having my shirt tucked in (but it's usually worth it)." By the time these same girls reach adolescence, however, it's as if their dormant kindergarten training springs back to life. Their conversations become a litany of I don't know's; they no longer know themselves. *Why* does this happen?

THE PERILOUS DIVIDE

In her analysis of Jesse, a girl she studies from preadolescence to teenage years, Lyn Mikel Brown describes the way in which the model of the perfect girl begins to cause Jesse to abandon herself in order to comply with the demands of being "a nice girl."[15] At nine Jesse is not afraid to confront others with "childhood clarity," which lets her feelings be known. But her transformation at adolescence into a nice girl changes this. Nice girls are calm, controlled, quiet, and above all cooperative. If they have an opinion that is opposite from the general consensus, they keep it to themselves because, as Jesse realizes, "they won't want me to do this, or they won't want me in the club because I don't have good ideas," and so, "you sort of get afraid to say it." As we read, we see Jesse become more cautious and "more willing to silence herself" rather than risk conflict and the loss of relationship. Brown notes that Jesse is uncomfortable with anger, noise, bossiness in herself, and disagreements with others; she expresses the importance of speaking quietly, remaining calm, and not getting "nervous and all riled up because it will just start more trouble." Jesse "shows an emerging propensity to separate what she knows and loves from what she believes she ought to do in order to be seen as cooperative, kind, and good—the kind of girls others, she thinks, want to be with." She is finding her role, suggests Brown, in "the established story of the good woman," into which girls are subtly initiated in adolescence.

When girls realize they have crossed the threshold—or perilous divide—from girlhood to womanhood, they take on the role expected of them. Carol Gilligan and Lyn Mikel Brown's recent work on patterns of relationship in an all-girls school (*Meeting at the Crossroads*) examines how the troubling loss of voice that occurs for girls is abetted by educational practices that discourage conflict and foster an oversensitivity to feelings.[16] At an almost unconscious level, girls are trained to keep harmony, avoid hurting others' feelings, and maintain connectedness—at the cost of their own voice and authentic relationality. Overattention to the avoidance of hurting another's feelings inevitably leads to the "tyranny of nice and kind" replete with "a pressure that threatens to silence their realistic and forthright descriptions of the social world."[17] Such an environment, no doubt aided and abetted by congruous parenting practices, takes spunky, even dauntless girls and transforms them into confused and silent young women.[18] While certainly some constraints on speaking one's mind are appropriate, the binding on young women is rather tight. The move toward womanhood becomes a move away from self, fraught with expectations of pious goodness and exaggerated caring. High-spirited girls must become young ladies. Gilligan and Brown describe the struggle that ensues:

> Girls at the edge of adolescence face a central relational crisis: to speak what they know through experience of themselves and of relationships creates political problems—disagreements with authorities, disrupting relationships—while not to speak leaves a residue of psychological problems: false relationships and confusion as to what they feel and think.[19]

The dilemma appears to be a no-win situation, a choice between staying with one's voice and risking alienation or preserving connections (being a nice girl) and losing oneself. In reading *Meeting at the Crossroads*, one is haunted by Adrienne Rich's description of women in college classrooms. "Listen to the women's voices. . . . Listen to the small, soft voices, often courageously trying to speak up, *voices of women taught early that tones of confidence, challenge, anger, or assertiveness, are strident and unfeminine.*"[20]

I wish I could simply note this reality and then celebrate the fact that many of us who are enlightened are sparing our daughters Jesse's fate. To a certain extent we may vaunt significant victories; enough change has come about that some critics charge that the clarion call for concern about girls is making much ado about nothing.[21] I think it is premature to announce female equality; let us not let down our guard. My daughter recently related to me how her brother and an extended family member were constantly at loggerheads during a recent visit. She noted that her brother seemed a bit out of line, but she felt that he was also somewhat justified. Then she surprised me with her wistful musing: "I wish I could be like him sometimes and just say how I feel when I'm mad when we're with Charlotte. He can be so honest; I'm just cooperative. I can't be myself." I was alarmed and saddened. My first thought was "Oh, my God, she's crossed the perilous divide, and I didn't even see it coming. My little girl in her dirty blue dress has cleaned up and shut up."

As I talked to my daughter and son about this, it struck me that Marie and Paul were probably unconsciously compensating for one another—in gender typical ways. Marie sees that her brother's assertiveness breaks the relation, and she compensates with untruth; Paul sees that his sister is being manipulated, and he compensates with imperial assertiveness. My son's brutal honesty was threatening his relationship with his relative; but my daughter's dishonest communication rendered her "preserved" relationship a false one. My son didn't want a false relationship; my daughter didn't want a broken one. There was a kind of systemic equilibrium. I am reminded of Carol Gilligan's description of the "truth teller," who exposes hypocrisy and reveals truths about human relationships. In one way, my son played this role, exposing the "silencing" aspects of this particular relationship.[22] And yet, my daughter is also groping toward a truth, the importance of relationship. Sadly, they are each losing out. My son, by fiercely protecting his autonomy, is breaking a relationship with a basically caring adult relative. My daughter, by cautiously protecting the relationship, is disavowing the parts of herself that would enrich Charlotte. The continuation of a genuine relationship requires the expanded truth of their combined efforts rather than the compensating efforts each puts forth to balance the untruth of the other.

In my daughter's case, continual conversations about this state of affairs has enabled her to name what is going on and to find support for bringing her true self openly to her relationships. This kind of open reflection is important. When there is a genderized equilibrium set up, such as with my son and daughter, where each gender compensates for a lack in the other, these patterns can be unconsciously perpetuated. When girls take the role that my daughter has taken, a role that they imbibe with the culture, they can become habituated to a conflict-avoiding selfhood.

The silenced "good girl" is not the only female strategy for survival. There is another alternative to the disavowing self. Girls can present a false public self while secretly trying to preserve a true inner self—they can go underground. I would like to look at the underground girl in depth, for I think she is trying hard to get our attention.

128

Wild Women Resisters and Underground Girls

Some girls, either because of or in spite of their role models, do manage to "get underneath this patina of niceness and piety" and stay with their own voice. Like blues singer Ida Cox, they realize that: "You never got nothing by being an angel child. . . . Wild women are the only kind that ever get by."[23] Such wild women, public "resisters," break from the conspiracy of silence. Resisting, however, is often either empowered by or results in withdrawing from others. Outspoken Anna, a young teenager interviewed by Gilligan and Brown, was rebuffed by social clubs and popular cliques, but she was confident in her own voice. She projects, however, that she'll end up living in relative solitude "at the bottom of a mountain in Montana" writing books.[24]

If history is a predictor, Anna may very well follow this trajectory, for many women resisters have been writers. It has not been an easy road, and it is not without its costs to the resister. Jennifer Uglow's portrayal of nineteenth-century author George Eliot (Mary Ann Evans) is that of an outwardly strong, intellectual, assertive, and autonomous woman who defies convention repeatedly. Her "inner story" however reveals that her achievements, particularly inimical to her Victorian society, took a toll in "physical ailments, devastating headaches, and feelings of lassitude and depression." The words of Daniel's mother, in Eliot's work *Daniel Deronda*, come straight from Eliot's heart: "You can never imagine what it is to have a man's genius in you, and yet to suffer the slavery of being a girl."[25]

Not all "wild women" are able to exercise their genius to the extent that Mary Ann Evans, despite ailments, did. In fact, society often loses its bright girls, "culture's sharpest critics," who exit from the public sphere when support for flouting cultural conventions is lacking.[26] Linda Kreger Silverman chronicles the long-standing social and political pressures against bright girls. She argues that "the effects of sex-bias are far-reaching, with restrictions on independence playing the heaviest role." Cataloging the importance of independence for achievement, for creativity, for autonomous moral development, for mental health, and for giftedness, Silverman contends that "the major factor impeding the full development of girls is the unspoken decree in our society against female independence." She in fact argues, with compelling supporting evidence, that "to the extent that independence is drummed out of little girls, these girls lose their giftedness."[27]

Some resisters become "underground women," who lead a double life; although they are aware of their feelings and opinions, they keep them hidden—fearing that their voices will jeopardize their relationships.

These girls and women are able to recognize a strong sense of self but are afraid to make that self known. They move their strong feelings and thoughts underground because there is no safe place for them to offer their voice. I'd like to look into one culturally significant manifestation of the underground self—one that I myself have expressed. Let me begin by noting the event that prompted me to articulate what I had known for quite some time.

One evening, several years ago, I was leading a discussion on Queen Vashti, and I asked the group of women: Can you think of a time when you said "no"? What was the response you received? Many interesting examples were given: some women described heroic occasions where they refused to give in to improper demands, others named situations where they simply drew appropriate limits on their willingness to give of themselves (a revealing number of these comments were strewn with guilt, for women shouldn't say no!), and a significant number of women could not think of a time when they said no.

The group then asked me to answer my question.

Although I hadn't planned this particular response, spontaneously I began to speak about my experience of the eating disorder named anorexia nervosa. With caution, but also with conviction, I stated how refusing to eat became my way of silently protesting against a life that I felt was being determined by expectations I wished to resist—expectations for femininity. Since that discussion, I have continued to reflect consciously on my personal experience and to research into the wider phenomena of female eating disorders.

ANOREXIA AND THE UNDERGROUND PROPHETS IN OUR MIDST

The "unrelenting pursuit of thinness" has been identified as the hallmark of anorexia.[28] Technically, anorexia nervosa "is defined as voluntary starvation resulting in a minimum loss of 15% of body weight." In as many as half the cases, anorexia leads into or is accompanied by bulimia, "periodic binge eating followed by some form of purging, such as self-induced vomiting, use of laxatives or diuretics, strict dieting or fasting, or vigorous exercise." Approximately 1 percent of women between the ages of twelve and eighteen will develop anorexia; the figures for bulimia are about half that.[29] Of persons with anorexia 90 to 95 percent are women; however, the number of men seems to be increasing. Theories as to why these eating disorders occur and why they are on the rise now are legion. Below, I will offer my own interpretation.

There were three major episodes of anorexia (and, in the latter two episodes, bulimia) in my life, and all three followed periods of time when I tried to conform to cultural norms of feminine behavior. First around age fourteen, when I knew it was time to enter the "cult of femininity," then in my early years of college, when I realized I was now an adult woman, and finally in the early years of my marriage, when I tried to become a "wife." Though there are girls who reach far more dangerous levels than I did, my first wave was heading into serious physical damage; I diminished to eighty-four pounds, ceased menstruating, had low blood pressure, was perpetually cold, and my skin and hair showed signs of mal-nourishment. My already fragile family structure was completely disrupted. My achievements, however, began to soar. In fact, looking back, I have traced that in each instance, the onset of anorexia was *preceded* by a retreat from achievement (which I equate with adaptation to femininity) and *accompanied* by high achievement and success (which I equate with resistance to femininity). It was as if I heard the "call to femininity" as a call away from public achievement and my starvation was a resistance against that call, which either was precipitated by or allowed for a return to achievement.

Fortunately for me, the third episode occurred just prior to my taking a course by Sandra Bem at Stanford University on "The Psychology of Sex Roles" and in the company of a caring and enlightened husband who had no allegiance to normative definitions of femininity. Within these intellectual and emotional "safe-houses," I could bring what was underground above the surface and forge a conscious and liberating definition of womanhood. It has not been an easy road; the public sphere into which I had entered, with its reigning male paradigms for achievement and success, is not particularly life-giving either.

Of course, I didn't realize at the time that there was any pattern or meaning to what was going on in my bizarre behavior. This was the early 1970s, no one had written about eating disorders; no one had yet given "anorexia nervosa" a name. In those early years, I literally felt I was the only one in the world that had this strange relationship to food and eating. When a friend of mine found an article about what was beginning to be a phenomenon, she gave it to me and said, "This sounds like you." I was amazed that there were others like me. I now believe that I was making a political statement, but it was not a conscious one. At the time I felt shame more than agency. Several years after coming through anorexia, I named it silently as one of the most dangerous and yet also most significant experiences for my growth into adult womanhood. It was a time I refused to be controlled by others, and a time that I went to great lengths to avoid being controlled. Though personally meaningful, for years I was reluctant to articulate any positive significance to such a deadly disorder. I was afraid to provide validation for something that could have killed me and has killed up to one thousand girls a year in our society.[30] And yet, I have come to realize that if I do not talk about what I perceive was happening in me (and I think in many other girls), more rather than fewer lives will be lost. I do not want to valorize what was confusing and hardly exemplary behavior, but I do want to put into words what I was unable to say at that time. I want to do this because I think pastors, communities, and caring families can do a lot to prevent themselves from becoming part of the problem.

ON BEING "TOO MUCH GIRL"

Girls who are much, who want more than the conventional feminine paradigms permit, run the risk of being chided as my daughter was—diminished as girl ("not much of a girl") because they want too much out of life. This sanctioning will not only come from the outside, but by the time a girl reaches adolescence, she will have internal sex-role stereotypes firmly established.[31] One compulsive dieter reflected: "I've often felt that I was *too much*—too much emotion, too much need, too loud and demanding, too much *there*, if you know what I mean."[32] I know exactly what she means: the culture doesn't like girls who are "too much there." And yet, I also know that at a deeper level, this girl means "much" more than she states. She is correct in perceiving that this culture does not support women who are "much"—loud, demanding, assertive of their needs. She doesn't fully recognize, however, that her response is not actually in compliance with, but is rather resistant to, the cultural constraints. As I shall argue, this compulsively thin girl is paradoxically making herself as much, or more, *there* than she was before. She diets to reduce her "muchness," but in her compulsion to control her weight and in her resistance to eating, she also protests stubbornly against a culture that tries to control and "reduce" her. She is subconsciously dieting, not to diminish herself, but rather to go on strike against her "sacred calling" as a girl. When our emaciated girls see their bodies as "too fat" (a common characteristic of anorexics), they are not suffering from a vision impairment or distorted body image, they are displacing onto their bodies the truth of their existence—they are too much in a society that cannot handle female power.[33] In fact, our anorexic daughters are sign-bearers: like the prophet who wears sackcloth and ashes, they are calling our culture to repentance.

This claim may sound jarring to the reader. Anorexia has variously been attributed to infantile regression to dependence, fear of sexual maturation, deficiency in self-regulation, failure to separate and individuate, or victimization to cultural standards of thinness and beauty.[34] How can a regressed, scared, deficient, victimized failure be a prophet?

I do not deny that there are psychological crises going on in girls with eating disorders, and I do believe that family dynamics are a large factor in these crises. In general, however, the attribution of eating disorders to the above-named pathologies is misleading. These are dissatisfying "pathology" models that ignore the cultural protest against sex-role expectations underlying eating disorders. It is my contention that protest is one of the cultural factors in the recent surge in anorexia and bulimia among adolescent girls. If it is the case that girls are socialized to rely heavily on external acceptance and feedback to inform their identity, the anorexic protests by her refusal to please those who cajole and coerce her into eating (hardly a regressive move); if it is the case that girls are raised to be peacekeepers in the family, the anorexic resists that role when she creates havoc with her will (pretty self-regulative, if you ask me); if it is the case that girls are taught to be compliant and sensitive to others' expectations, the anorexic "will" flouts these expectations with a vengeance (this victim fights back); if it is the case that girls are defined by their connection to others, the anorexic rebels by placing her relationships in jeopardy by fiercely guarding her autonomy.[35] Regression, fear, deficiency, and victimization are perhaps operative at one level. There is a regression back from the perilous divide between voice and no voice, a partial recovery of the spunk of preadolescence; there is a legitimate fear of the culturally prescribed functions of a woman; there is seriously deficient cultural support for self-regulation; and there is victimization in the form of gender subordination. Rather than a "failure to separate and individuate," however, anorexia is a desperate attempt to accomplish those very moves.[36]

The protest is both visible and yet underground. I think anorexia is a paradoxical combination of girls "giving themselves away" and "taking themselves back." They give their bodies away by starving them (which has a great deal of social approval in the beginning stages) and eventually losing control to the illness; but they also take them back by asserting amazing amounts of *self*-control and resistance to parental and societal pressures to eat. Having given up on trying to communicate with words, they speak with their bodies instead—and it is a word of resistance.[37]

Eating disorders are, no doubt about it, a complex and overdetermined phenomenon.[38] Eating disorders, particularly anorexia, do, however, reflect the particular stresses that girls in our society are under, and they are a courageous but very dangerous endeavor on the part of girls to be "masters of their own house." While in the end, the "fantasy of self-mastery" proves to be an illusion;[39] families and communities ought not to ignore the desperate *self-preserving* motivations that ultimately lead to this self-destructive behavior. *Anorexia, rather than being a death wish, is a desperate attempt to grasp and take hold of one's life.* The fact that it occurs frequently in "good girls" who accept stereotyped views of sex roles and play by the rules in every other way, suggests that the anorexic has hit upon a means to say no to social conformity (starvation) through the medium of a socially acceptable, indeed—for women—socially proscribed, behavior (dieting for thinness).[40] The anorexic takes a socially sanctioned good (thinness; ability to control one's appetite), turns it into an absolute good (becomes obsessed with controlling oneself), and thereby satisfies her unconscious need to rebel and assert control through a process that is acceptable to her consciousness.[41] Like Mrs. Pontellier, whose story is told in chapter 2, the outward and the inward existence are in contradiction. The outward girl conforms to societal expectations, but the inward girl may want to break out of those expectations. Anorexia is the process of bringing the inward existence to the outside, via an external expression that is initially rewarded (thinness) but eventually disapproved (emaciation). According to Alice Miller, anorexia nervosa is the recourse of a girl who "is no longer able to function like an automaton, but . . . has no chance to express the feelings that are now erupting in her."[42]

Certainly, family dynamics are important to consider. Judith Salzman contends that there are two critical functions of attachment that assume special importance in adolescence: "the recognition of the adolescent as a 'new voice' within the family; and the subsequent recalibration of family decision-making processes based on this recognition." The presence or absence of these changes seems "to mark the difference between attachments in which the developing self may thrive and those in which it may be constrained."[43] Families that are very controlling leave a girl feeling that her only choices are to exert voice at the risk of being "bad" or remain a silent and compliant "good girl," leading to an inability to deal with conflict. This context, it seems to me, is a prime breeding ground for anorexia, with its paradoxical bad girl/good girl blend. Indeed, the families of girls with eating disorders are often intolerant of conflict and they resist autonomy in their children.[44] The anorexic girl uses a silent means of expressing voice; she cries out without directly confronting anyone. Interestingly, the anorexic girl exerts "unprecedented stubborn and oppositional attitudes and behavior" with regards to eating,[45] and becomes controlling and demanding when it comes to others' preparation of food and quite deceiving in convincing concerned parents that she has indeed eaten. This assertive behavior remains localized to food, but I believe her demands are a sublimated and displaced (to use helpful Freudian concepts) desire for genuine voice in her life. In a world where her demands are unheeded, she convinces herself that *these* demands are legitimate; the emaciated anorexic often feels exalted self-esteem from control over her body[46] (in a world where she has little control over anything else). Liza, a twelve-year-old girl in Brown and Gilligan's study who became anorexic, related to her interviewers a time when she and some friends cut a class. "It felt good. . . . It felt like we were heroes for a while. . . . Sometimes it feels really nice to rebel, because I don't do it often."[47] In fact, there is an unconscious Esther-esque quality to anorexia. The girl seems to say, "I'll give you what you think you want, but in doing so I really hope to subvert the structure."

While family dynamics are important, they are an extension of the larger cultural arena in which girls' lives take place. Deeper than rebellion against parents, anorexia is, I believe, a girl's mixed desire to be a woman (thus accepting the cultural definition of femininity as childlikeness and female beauty as thinness) and refusal to be a woman as proscribed (eventually becoming androgynous by obstructing normal female development).[48] Anorexia is a complicated interaction between girls seeking to "transcend" cultural gender restraints while preserving a coded understanding of femininity.[49] "In this illness [is] a dimension of protest against the limitations of the ideal of female domesticity."[50] It's as if the girl is saying, "I am about to become a woman, which is what I've wanted all along. And yet, if this is what it means to be a woman—passivity, dependence, restriction to private sphere—then I'm not sure that I want it. How can I become a woman and yet not become a woman at the same time?"

By effacing female indicators (breasts, hips, menstruation, soft bodies) and constructing an androgynous body, and by developing the will and a transcendence over body, the anorexic girl is tapping into her "male side."[51] In fact, anorexia is often the gifted girl's solution to the dilemma of "having a man's genius while suffering the slavery of being a girl" expressed by George Eliot.[52] Curves, roundedness, and breasts all seem to announce: I am woman, subordinate me![53] This is not, however, confusion over sexual identity; it is resistance to the culturally prescribed role for women and the cultural (and familial and communal) denial of independent voice in girls.

The ambivalence many women feel between the two paths of the masculine and the feminine is expressed in the ups and downs of bulimia, feeding the woman and purging the self of womanhood in a cyclical manner. As mentioned earlier, the woman "purged" of femininity faces the alternative male paradigm, which leaves her equally dissatisfied. Thus, she cycles back and forth, finding no support for a healthy understanding of self in relation to others. The bulimic appears "normal" physically, and thus her underground struggle is often more hidden than the anorexic's. If we listen, however, it exposes the same cultural oppression. Certainly some girls find creative and productive ways to solve this culturally determined dilemma; the girls who resort to starvation or the bingeing/purging cycle probably lacked the relational environment for healthy self-development.

Clearly, it is important to avoid reducing anorexia to an exaggerated expression of female slenderness. The solution is not simply to celebrate rounder bodies and provide healthier images for our girls to imitate (though this is certainly a good idea); it is to stay in relation to girls who assert dissonant opinions and seek to thwart gender stereotypes in a variety of ways. While the prevailing view is that the anorexic is afraid that if she eats a little she will eat a lot, the real fear is that if she gives in to the pressure to eat a little she will give in to the pressure to conform to others' expectations a lot. In many cases, this fear is real. When an anorexic is "healed" by being cajoled into gaining weight to alleviate her family's fears and resume a "normal" life, she may be on the road to passive acceptance of coded femininity. This is, in fact, the tactic taken after my own first bout with anorexia. "You're hurting your mother, you have to start eating," began to gnaw at me. While caring about others' feelings is not a bad thing, motivating me to eat by tending to others was catapulting me back into the very thing I was resisting. The "good girl" conquered the "bad girl" resister, and I began to eat again for the sake of others. My recovery was short-lived, however, as the motivating factor was dissatisfying, and it is no surprise that I experienced a recurrence of the disorder.

Physicians can, unfortunately, contribute to this regressive or transient healing. In her examination of the relation between adolescent female patients and male adult doctors in the nineteenth century, Joan Jacobs Brumberg found that physicians often dismissed and silenced anorexic girls. Conversing *about* the girl with her mother, a doctor's only communication with the anorectic tended to be an order to eat. A recovered anorectic reflected to her doctor: "I saw that you wished to shut me up."[54] By further silencing the girl, the doctor intensified the very sickness he was supposed to heal.

Our discussions on human development are instructive here. Anorexia often occurs at the brink of the movement from girlhood to womanhood. This may correspond with the transition from the "interpersonal" to the "institutional" orientation (Kegan) or the movement from "goodness" to "truth" (Gilligan). Trying to solve the problem by cajoling the girl to meet the needs of others encourages developmental regression. It is important that the solution take into account the growth needs and not simply entrench the girl in a less-mature stage. Indeed, I have been saddened to read that long-term recoveries are not always victories for the self; sometimes they are at the expense of the self. Although the evidence is still being gathered, studies suggest that recovered anorexics are prone to display overly compliant behavior and a limited capacity for social spontaneity.[55]

Clearly, there are dangerous consequences to anorexia: loss of health and life and near inevitable evolution into bulimia—bingeing and fasting, as the struggle takes place between the body's need for food and the psyche's need to control. What begins in unconscious protest ends up being counterproductive.[56] Indeed, the irony is that anorexia may actually function in collusion with the cultural conditions it resists.[57] The feeling of control that satisfies the need to protest becomes an obsession that begins to destroy. As one former anorexic puts it, "I felt all inner development was ceasing, that all becoming and growing were being choked, because a single idea was filling my entire soul."[58] Concludes Susan Bordo, "As a feminist protest, the obsession with slenderness is hopelessly counterproductive." This is because, in desperation and with no sense of alternative, the girl, like Mrs. Pontellier in chapter 2, is willing to give her life but is not willing to give herself. Rather than being "great at self-denial," the self is precisely what the anorexic cannot deny, even if it costs her life.[59] Thus, unlike Bordo, I do not believe anorexia's "most outstanding feature is powerlessness."[60] One of the reasons that anorexia is so frightening is that it is a fierce expression of female assertion; there is hardly a stronger will to break than an anorexic's refusal to eat. Fear of women's power has been widely recognized; if anorexic willpower is able to be redirected, a powerful force is unleashed.[61] Though it may appear that the anorexic women signal with their bodies, "I will take up only a small amount of space. I won't get in the way. . . . I won't be intimidating or threatening,"[62] in actuality they *do* get in the way, and their will *is* extremely intimidating and threatening. What we need to do is help anorexic girls recognize that their disorder will eventually become out of control and positively work to channel their power and assertion in health-giving ways. My own turning point, in fact, came when I realized one day: "My eating disorder is out of

137

control. It now is running my life. I don't have to let this happen. I can regain control." This cannot happen, however, if the girl does not have a caring community where she can be a genuine self-in-relation to others who do not try to control her.

In sum, I believe that anorexia is neither a crying out to be fed (dependency fantasy) nor a mandate to be left alone (assertion of complete autonomy). It is a need to be a self-in-relation. The anorexic is often unable to assert her voice and needs for fear that the relation will be dissolved. What is sought is a relationship in which assertion and cooperation can be woven together. Thus, if we simply treat the symptoms (get the girl to eat) or ignore the protest (leave the girl alone), we fail the girl. If we get the girl to eat, we have saved her life but at the cost of her self. If we leave the girl alone, we have preserved what is left of the self but endangered her life.[63]

For this reason, I think we need to reframe the way we diagnose eating disorders such as anorexia. Anorexia is not primarily an illness from which girls suffer. It is a symptom of an ill culture. The sickness of a society and culture that deny girls and women their voices and choices needs to be named. The way in which we diagnose an anorexic girl as "ill" invites and substantiates efforts to subdue the girl into conforming once again to the expectations of others through "treatment" of *her* diagnosed disorder. We cannot simply "treat" the girl for anorexia, we must also treat the culture for pernicious "girl-destroying." Without ignoring the ill effects of anorexia on the girl, we must *diagnose the culture as ill* in addition to (or even rather than) the girl.[64]

Anorexia and bulimia are not the only forms of eating disorders in our culture. They have been primarily seen in middle- and upper-middle-class Caucasian girls.[65] As anorexia in particular has moved from a subconscious, unnamed disorder to a widely recognized disorder, it has taken on a "trendy" status in some communities. In fact, there is some evidence that anorexia is now becoming a chosen means by which underclass girls identify with and enter the ranks of the privileged.[66] Yet, I'd like to look at another form of eating disorder that represents an underground protest to femininity.

Overeating: Refusing to Be "Too Little"

Among African American girls, resistance to cultural pressures tends to take a different manifestation. Although some black teenagers want to meet "white" standards of beauty, there has been an alarming increase in obesity among African American female adolescents in the last twenty years. There are many reasons given for this increase, but an important motivation for overeating seems to be an active resistance to Anglo standards for beauty that emphasize thinness.[67] Overeating has become a "survival strategy" that aims to redefine acceptable standards of beauty. To a certain degree, this strategy—along with other forms of resistance—"works"; African American girls are less plagued with self-esteem problems than are Caucasian girls.[68] For those who redefine beauty in terms of larger and rounder body types, this is a healthy response that can be supported.

When the largeness and roundness translate into severe obesity, however, the girl engages in self-defeating resistance. Here I tread uneasily. When sharing this material with African American audiences, I am cautioned not to turn this into the very thing that is being protested: an attempt to press Anglo standards for health and beauty onto others. One young man attending a lecture I gave on the varieties of eating disorders, after expressing appreciation for my comments, revealed some misgivings. "You know, I went home recently and saw my mom's cupboards filled with diet foods. My mom, who has always been confident in her beautiful largeness, is now trying to meet someone else's image of beauty. I'm not sure it's a good thing." Largeness and roundness are to be celebrated; thin, weak images of beauty are legitimately resisted. At the same time, whenever I have spoken simply on the subject of anorexia and bulimia, African American women have raised their hands and noted: "We have a different problem, which warrants as much thought and reflection as does anorexia; our girls are overeating in unhealthy ways." I hope I can tread a path between these two concerns: upholding the beauty of largeness while recognizing the dangers of unhealthy overeating. I bring up overeating because it is a *double* protest; it is a protest against sexism and racism. Black girls want to resist female subjugation, but they do not want to do it in the way prescribed by white culture.

Tracy Robinson and Janie Victoria Ward, researchers in African American psychosocial development, contend that as a survival tactic, defiant obesity is shortsighted.[69] Like teenage pregnancy and dropping out of school, these acts of resistance do give the teen a certain feeling of triumph and satisfaction in the beginning. Long-term consequences are, however, disempowering. Though chosen out of an attempt to counteract the cultural devaluation of women of color, overeating is a "quick fix" survival strategy for resistance, which in the end is unwise, unsafe, and counterproductive. Alarming rates of hypertension and diabetes in adulthood are the untoward consequences of this form of rebellion. Thus, both starving and overeating are courageous attempts to resist that threaten the lives of the girls who choose these tactics.

Once again, it is important to recognize and affirm the strength and power of the resistance while trying to rechannel its form. Resisting cultural expectations is valuable; it would be destructive to break the will in the attempt to heal the obesity. The most helpful way to address overeating, according to Robinson and Ward, is to discover and offer "alternative avenues to personal empowerment and positive change," avenues that promote self-validation, affirmation, and self-care. For these are the goals the girls are groping toward. In their groping, however, they are still allowing dominant racist values to determine their behavior. Self-determination is not actually being achieved when identity is formed in reaction to a dominant value rather than in affirmation of a chosen value. A positive celebration of African American identity is a more constructive response.

In facing the phenomenon of girls going into hiding, girls speaking in indirect ways, girls fighting for survival, we must acknowledge a variety of forces that contribute to the painful loss and recovery of voice in girls. I've explored the cultural forces encouraging girls and women to hide, and I will suggest ways in which a community of faith can provide an environment that resists inducting our girls into sexism. Before drawing practical implications, I'd like to consider the way in which ordinary (not pathological) families can contribute to this. Unfortunately, families do not always provide the kind of support girls need to protest cultural expectations. Sometimes families, including mothers, collude with sexism. While obvious cases, such as those involving physical and emotional abuse, are increasingly raised to consciousness, inadvertent cases are often ignored. There are patterns in the "normal" way of doing family that join the girl-denying ethos of our culture. Mothers can "give their daughters away" by communicating to them that their own needs are bad; fathers can give their daughters away by discouraging or neglecting their aspirations for achievement; family structure can give our daughters away by its inherent injustice.

NIPPING "MUCHNESS" IN THE BUD: GIRLS IN FAMILIES

GIVING OUR DAUGHTERS AWAY: MOTHERS

In her best-selling novel *How to Make an American Quilt*, Whitney Otto tells us the story of Sophie. A girl who in childhood and adolescence has had a free and strong spirit, Sophie is on the edge of marrying age. As we read that she is a diver and swimmer with great strength and agility, we begin to anticipate a heroine who breaks the molds of socially proscribed femininity. Then, we are privy to the advice she is given by her mother as to how to win a husband.

> Listen, sweetheart, let him do all the talking. Men love a good listener; it makes them feel important and smart. Be bright, but not too bright, and let him see that you are a young lady, a girl to be respected. . . . Follow his lead or, at least, give the appearance of following his lead. Just to be on the safe side—men are funny that way.[70]

Please your husband, hide your will, be there for your children. These are the phrases the mother repeats. We cheer silently as we learn that her mother's advice "often left her daughter ill tempered and suspicious and lusting after rebellion. . . . Her mother's words forced Sophia from the house to the quarry reservoir, where she swam with fierce, cutting strokes." For a while she is determined "she would not be a woman of her day,"[71] and she recklessly throws expectations to the wind. Then as we follow her journey into marriage and motherhood, we watch in sorrow as she leaves herself behind. She gives up swimming, which is symbolic of giving up any dreams that are for herself. She accepts that "she is not expected to attend to her own intrepid journeys or follow her own desires." She watches her dream of swimming for the rest of her life fade away as a tide, "never to be retrieved."[72] When her husband builds her a small pond in the backyard, she never uses it. He wonders why, given her love for swimming, she does not go near it. It is as if she has chosen a path of no return; perhaps her stunted self could not be resurrected, or perhaps she could not be satisfied with a domesticated substitute for the freedom she sought.

Sophie's de-selfed life is tragic enough. But then the most shattering blow occurs for the reader—Sophie passes on to her own daughters the same advice that her mother gave her, carrying on the legacy. Dissuading her eldest daughter from going to college because they can only afford to send the son, she also dismisses the young woman's claim that she wants something else besides a life of domesticity with a curt, "There is nothing else." Her quilting matches her journey. "Sophia does not enjoy the freedom of color and pattern in the *Crazy Quilt*. . . . Sophia prefers the challenge of a traditional, established pattern. That is the true challenge, she thinks—to work within a narrow confine. To accept what you cannot have; that from which you cannot deviate."[73]

Sophie's story may seem outdated; mothers may no longer give such advice. Many mothers today warn their daughters not to take physical abuse from their partners, and they are less obsessed with their daughters marrying than they used to be. Yet, advice on "capturing the heart of Mr. Right" is sweeping our nation (we shall return to this in chapter 5), and it retains much of the same tone of de-selfing. Even where the outward situation is genuinely changing, Sophie's worldview still lingers in subtle ways.

According to psychoanalyst Louise Eichenbaum and Susie Orbach, it is not uncommon for mothers to unwittingly communicate to their daughters that female needs are bad and must be contained, for it is the role of the woman to meet the needs of others. In a culture where women are coded to be the caregivers, a mother may be frightened by her daughter's free expression of needs and unconsciously train her daughter to repress those needs. "In some ways the little daughter becomes an external representation of that part of herself which she has come to dislike and deny. The complex emotions that result from her own deprivation through childhood and adult life are both directed inward in the struggle to negate the little-girl part of herself and projected outward onto her daughter."[74] The woman who has learned to "hide her emotional cravings, her disappointments and her angers, her fighting spirit" raises her daughter to do the same. She may also seek in her daughter the source for meeting her own needs, and thus the daughter learns at a very deep and emotionally charged level that her task is to satisfy the emotional demands of others.[75] Eichenbaum and Orbach report the stunning frequency with which their female clinic patients speak of their own needs with contempt and shame. Girls learn to feel unworthy and hesitant about pursuing their own desires, hopes, and dreams for themselves. While girls' needs are being "nipped in the bud," their aspirations are sometimes prevented from budding at all.

GIVING OUR DAUGHTERS AWAY: FATHERS

In her engaging book *Cold Sassy Tree*, Olive Ann Burns allows us to view life in a provincial Southern town through the eyes of a twelve-year-old boy, Will. As he struggles to find his way amid the mores and customs of his kin and community, Will often has moments where he distances himself from and reflects on the assumptions of everyday reality in Cold Sassy. Male and female role types, a subtle concern of the author, are occasionally pondered by this young boy. During one pensive moment, we are privy to his thoughts.

> It occurred to me that mine and Mary Toy's punishments never had been equal. Whenever I misbehaved, Mama told Papa and he wore me out with

the razor strop. But when occasionally Mama said to whip Mary Toy, why that was something else entirely. Taking a rolled-up newspaper, he would jerk her up to her room, and from downstairs we'd hear him speak harsh. "Now, young lady, bend over that bed!" Mama would cringe, hearing the blows fall. What she didn't know was that Papa would whisper to Mary Toy to start hollering, and then commence swatting the mattress instead of her. Mary Toy told me about it one time. If I thought about Mama, that seemed like a good joke, but if I thought about me, it made me mad. I realized Papa was strict and hard on me because a boy had to amount to something, whereas Mary Toy didn't, being a girl. But just the same it made me mad.[76]

Will's assessment of the disparity in the way his family (and larger community) rears its male and female children is striking. Boys have to amount to something, so they are prodded with harshness. Girls have no such purpose, so they are either coddled or (most often) ignored rather than challenged. Both Will *and* Mary Toy have a right to be mad. Neither the strop nor the soft bed approach provides an adequate nurturing environment for development. While many of us immediately recognize the abusive nature of Will's rearing, we might miss the injurious consequences of Mary Toy's training. Though the father's apparent tenderness to his daughter is touching, in the end it is hard to define who the "lucky one" is: Will, whom we assume will be whipped into amounting to something, or Mary Toy, who escapes the abusive path to such amounting?

Clearly the "soft bed" approach does not characterize all girls' relationship to their fathers. Far too many girls are physically and sexually abused, and this is devastating to a girl's self-esteem. Approximately one-third of all girls will experience sexual abuse in childhood, many at the hands of fathers or father figures, and as many as two-thirds will face varying degrees of sexual harassment in high school. We do well to provide "safe places" where girls can escape and say no (see chapter 5) to these situations.[77] Compared to these horrifying realities, the "Soft Bed Approach" as I call it, looks pretty good.

Yet, it is the better of two unfortunate realities, not the best of possibilities. Let us not miss the way in which the other pattern (refusing to challenge girls to "amount to something") undermines girls' confidence. Tenacious and pernicious versions of the "soft bed" approach to raising girls are prevalent.[78] And, like actual soft beds that leave one aching and are detrimental to posture, so also this approach to girls has its painful and injurious side. When money is tight, boys are sent to college while girls help support them; when girls do achieve at high levels, they are often warned that they will never get a husband; "Daddy's little girl" usually gets her position for her cuteness and her attentiveness to Daddy's needs. This is especially prevalent in middle-class families, and it lingers in the male unconscious even when fathers make conscious strides to give them opportunities for achievement.

Family therapist Betty Carter has noticed that even a father who consciously wants his daughter to succeed still sees marriage as her main future goal. Such a father may even spend money on her education, "but still not expect personal achievement of her. . . . He prides himself on his strength and competence, but then rewards compliance and dependency in his relationship with her."[79] This pattern is effective. Studies have shown that a father's encouragement of his daughter toward traditional "feminine" behaviors (masking anger with niceness, compliance, seeking the approval of others, overconcern for appearance) is quite effective, even more effective than having a traditionally feminine mother.[80]

School picks up where father leaves off. Although schools are no longer explicitly training girls in the "feminine attributes" as they used to do, they still implicitly educate boys and girls differently. Teachers more often prod and push boys hard while they more frequently ignore and underestimate girls—except when it comes to politeness and neatness; then girls are held more accountable. Where achievement is equal, boys are more likely to be encouraged toward advanced courses (especially in math and sciences) than girls. Textbooks portray boys and men in more adventuresome and competent activities, and they tell history from the (white) male vantage point and through male heroes.

These parental practices are partly determined by the structure of family life in our society.

JUSTICE, GENDER, AND "FAMILY VALUES": SWADDLING GIRLS IN THE "MOMMY TRACK"

The family is the earliest school of moral development; it is where children develop the capacity for care and a sense of justice. Many children are learning in this early school that injustice is normal. The "gender-structured" marriage, which is based on "socially constructed differentiation between the sexes," creates a cycle of injustice and inequality.[81] While this leads to disadvantages for both men and women, it leads to a "deeply entrenched institutionalization of sexual difference" in the worlds of labor and politics, systematically excluding women. The family is thus "the linchpin of the gender structure," contends Susan Okin. She argues that if we are to have a just society, we must create justice in the sphere that forms our first and deepest sense of ourselves and our relations.

Okin further examines the way in which the gender-structured marriage forces women into a cycle of socially caused "asymmetric vulnerability." The expectation that girls will be primary caretakers of children influences their decisions all through life. In fact, girls choose the "mommy track" in childhood long before women choose it in their career paths.[82] There is evidence to suggest that many gifted high-school and college-age women exhibit a "fear of success," believing (with reason) that whereas "success inhibits social life for the girls, it enhances social life for the boys."[83] Although this is changing, girls historically have not been encouraged to consider career development important to their future. It is no coincidence that the kindergarten awards noted earlier reinforce girls toward the qualities they will need to care for home and family (and away from the public workplace) and reward boys toward the qualities they will need in the public workplace. If they choose professions, girls often choose those compatible with child rearing. If they enter less compatible professions, they follow the official "mommy track," rendering them less apt to receive promotions and secured positions (such as tenure, partnerships, and so forth). "The world of wage work, including the professions, is still largely structured around the assumption that 'workers' have wives at home"; women are therefore either discouraged (as was Judy Syfers) from entering this work world so they can be the wife at home, or they are expected to work as if they had such a person at home (thus Syfers's wishful musing).[84]

Those wives who stay at home are very dependent upon their husbands to provide for their children. This renders them less inclined to voice their needs or make demands; threats to the marriage are far too costly. Deciding to end such an asymmetrical marriage often plunges the woman and her children into poverty. If a woman has chosen to suspend her education and professional development in order to care for her family, she may not have the skills needed for well-paying jobs; thus, she is often faced with dismal options if her marriage ends.

FAMILIES AND COMMUNITIES AS SAFE-HOUSES FOR GIRLS' VOICES

Families and communities can respond to the prophetic "word" from girls with eating disorders in a variety of ways. They can provide an environment that allows girls and women to choose more healthy ways to "go on strike against culture." While professional help is needed for those girls who have become clinically anorexic or bulimic, there are a good many things families and communities of faith can do to assuage the need for such desperate measures on the part of girls. Below are several suggestions.

1. Carol Gilligan advises that "[girls] . . . will speak only when they feel that someone will listen and will not leave in the face of conflict or disagreement. Thus the fate of girls' knowledge and girls' education becomes tied to the fate of their relationships."[85] Families and communities of faith can provide the kind of "safe-houses" that allow for voice in girls. They can invite all girls to honestly offer their voices and listen to them, making it clear that assertion will not break the relationship. They can also provide a free enough atmosphere so that girls can be both assertive and flexible; their voices can be respected while allowed to change and grow. If there are girls with eating disorders in our midst, let us make an effort to respond to their audible voices when exercised, seek out their voices, and to listen deeply to them. While self-control is a critical aspect of the protest, I believe that more fundamentally it is refusal to be controlled by others.

One of the opportunities communities of faith can offer to girls is the chance to name their experiences and tell their stories. I do not mean by this the common practice of "testimonial," which often follows a prescribed pattern of "theolingo." I mean rather a time and space for describing one's experience, shaping one's life narrative, and naming one's deepest questions and doubts. People make sense of themselves and their lives by telling their stories; it is a way of exercising voice that crosses all cognitive levels and for which the person herself has automatic expertise. We saw in chapter 3 how empowering it was for teen mothers to describe and name their own experience and to tell their stories to one another. Eliciting their experiences and stories grants girls authority and voice, which increase confidence, selfhood, and the capacity for genuine relationships.

Hearing from girls is not only helpful to them, it is also helpful to others. One of the striking discoveries that those who work with girls make is that girls have an amazing capacity to observe life and relationships. Their perceptions about reality are often more accurate than the adults', although that knowledge is so often kept in the underground. Many girls who fall silent in community settings do have a desire to speak, but they have learned early that they will be ignored or dismissed. When we encourage rather than silence girls' observations, we can surface all that is going on in the underground—for the edification of all. It is therefore important that we listen to girls without trying to repress their negative feelings about situations they find oppressive.

Allowing for voice does not mean that we avoid conflict; I argue in chapter 6 that it means quite the opposite. We should create an environment that is not afraid of disagreement and conflict. It would not help our girls to swing from ignoring their voices to indiscriminately agreeing with everything they say; that is patronizing rather than respecting them. We should foster "hard dialogue and deep connections" that support differences and the pressing of difficult issues. It is in this kind of environment that girls can develop the confidence to assert their voices. It is important that people in communities of faith *stay in genuine relation* to girls who exercise voice, neither demanding submission nor tolerating their opinions condescendingly.

2. It is also important to reconstruct visions of the "feminine," which provide for strength and assertion and do not reduce female identity to the roles of wife and mother. This will involve telling the stories of women of faith who are assertive as well as caring, confident as well as humble. Every religious leader should evaluate the type of stories that she or he tells. Are the biblical stories of assertive women included in the community's teaching ministry? Are the illustrations used in sermons gender-stereotyped? Are the women all nurturing and submissive? Are their roles limited to wife and mother?

One of the purposes of chapter 7 in this book is to revive the "subversive memory" of Deborah. Carol Blessing reveals that despite extensive Bible study at the churches she attended, she was never told the story of Deborah. "Deborah was not reinforced as a role model for girls or women during my Sunday school days." Having discovered Deborah in her adulthood, she has been strengthened as a leader and mentor to others.[86] If we offer girls the stories of women of strength, this will help overcome a feeling of helplessness when they openly name and (when possible) resist sexism; we do not want to convey the idea that girls and women are victims without agency.

Along with reconstructing the feminine, we need to wrestle deeply with the structure of family life. In their support of "family values," communities of faith need to care about girls and the justice of family life. We can promote an understanding of marriage in which partners share equal respect and decision-making power, and we can raise our boys and girls to know they will care for the next generation and they will develop skills and competencies for public life. This does not mean that we should promote the kind of equal opportunity families where both fathers and mothers are workaholics who raise sons and daughters to be workaholics.[87] This solution has become increasingly unappealing to girls and women, who know there is more to life than career and money. Radical rethinking of family life, in middle-class families, includes critical reflection on professionalism, materialism, and consumerism. Men's overworking has been dependent upon women suppressing their own ambitions, and this pattern of male achievement and female support of male achievement still largely prevails. No one has sufficiently challenged the system of professionalism, which refuses to acknowledge that people who work also have children, other family members, friends, and community members in their life.

3. Encourage positive connection between mind and body; affirm the cultivation of bodily strength and fitness; affirm an embodied spirituality that does not denigrate the body. While I think an obsession with thinness is harmful, I do not believe that a concern for physical fitness is girl-destroying. Care for the body is a good thing; the capacity to be attuned to one's physical state contributes to a girl's agency and self-esteem. In fact, even as extreme thinness works against fitness and power so does unhealthy overweightness.[88] Communicating to our girls that their bodies are important can help prevent them from giving their bodies away to boys and men who pressure them into early sexual experiences.

Encouraging girls to take part in sports is one way to promote a positive sense of and control over their bodies. A girl who has disciplined her body in sports is less likely to allow another person to violate her body. Furthermore, sports provide an arena for both cooperation and assertiveness; a good athlete needs to learn both. If we are part of a community that promotes and recognizes athletic accomplishment, we need to make sure that we acknowledge this in both girls and boys.[89]

4. Pastoral persons who are sought out by girls with eating disorders can help these girls understand that they are not childlike victims who are without agency and strength. They may have internalized some of the prevailing cultural attitudes toward anorexia. We can help to name for these girls that anorexia is not simply a private dysfunction, but is rather a desperate move toward healthy expression of a public voice. We can point out the inner strength that is evident, and we can provide a space for the girl to think of alternative ways to channel that strength. In fact, retelling a girl's story in light of the courage her resistance demonstrates rather than simply in terms of its pathology can have healing effects for her. We can as pastoral persons name the authentic valor and courage of her resistance, while at the same time confronting her with the dangerous consequences this form of resistance can have. The first step toward health is to acknowledge the validity of the girl's resistance and anger, and then to move toward an examination of how it can best be expressed.

Interpreting a girl's defiance as healthy and worthy of support is fundamental to recovery and to optimal use of her abilities. Without this affirmation, the voice that is trying to be heard will once again be silenced; the abilities will be suppressed.

5. Educationally, we can nurture the positive resistance of African American girls by working against the cultural devaluation of black women. Robinson and Ward emphasize the importance of recovering the tradition and wisdom of black women and "black women's long history as freedom fighters and social activists."[90] The power of women's history, women's stories, and our foremother's legacies is not to be underestimated. Beverly Jean Smith and Gloria Watkins, among numerous others, report with a fierce pride the stories of resistance of their own mothers, aunts, grandmothers, and great-aunts. Watkins in fact adopted the pen name bell hooks, after being compared to her great-grandmother Bell Hooks, "a sharp-tongued woman, a woman who spoke her mind, a woman who was not afraid to talk back."[91] Claiming "this legacy of defiance, of will, of courage" and affirming her "link to female ancestors who were bold and daring in their speech," Gloria Watkins was empowered by the subversive memory of a strong woman.

This educational implication is just as important for Anglo-American churches as it is for African American churches. In her recent work *Who Stole Feminism?* Christina Sommers takes issue with educational reforms that are pressing multicultural and feminist agenda. She notes with dismay that more children can identify Sojourner Truth than Winston Churchill. I celebrate this statistic, for to lament it is not only culturally nearsighted but also nationally shortsighted. If children in public schools are now being introduced to the story of Sojourner Truth, then not only will African American girls be growing up with role models of resistance but they will be educated in a wider context that publicly recognizes the value of wise and daring African American women who fought against dehumanization on a number of fronts. These girls' self-concepts and the schools' ethos will be working together. Thus, it is important for all communities, not simply African American communities, to know the history of Sojourner Truth. My only concern is that schools still offer a very narrow selection of black heroes; we need a wider, broader range. If we create a wider culture that acknowledges racism and recognizes black heroines, we contribute to long-term solutions toward self-destructive resistance. I don't think it is stretching a point to suggest that this change in education, which Sommers seeks to dismantle, could very well contribute to the reduction of teen pregnancies and hypertension.

The hope is that girls can join with Dorothy Jean Smith and say proudly: "I was raised as a resister. . . . If I believed I was being mistreated or if I had something to say, I was to say it. . . . Surrounded by a large group of women . . . I always felt connected while acting alone."[92] Instead of resisting with their bodies in harmful ways, they can resist with their voices, their minds, and their constructive actions. And surrounded by the stories, the presence, and the will of a large group of women, they will not feel alone.

WHEN THE "OPPOSITE HAPPENS": YOUR DAUGHTERS SHALL PROPHESY

Recall that in the story of Esther, irony abounds. Analogous to the tradition of what German critics call the "Novelle," the development of the narrative "moves unexpectedly in a different direction from that which was anticipated, and arrives at a conclusion which surprises, but at the same time satisfies logically."[93] Those who were slated for annihilation are saved, the one who sought power at the expense of others is punished, and the one who was to be mastered comes out the master. While the story is not completely satisfying—the loss of Vashti at the beginning and the brutal violence at the end do not leave us consoled—the turn of events brings an important reversal. Might we not hope for this surprising reversal in the lives of our girls? Might not the story that begins with the analysis of a "girl-destroying" culture end with a vision of girls and women empowered in the household of God? Might we be able to unleash the fierce will and power expressed in anorexic girls? Our daughters are already prophesying to us, and they are telling us that we have usurped their mastery of themselves. It is now our task to repent and to provide safe-houses for self-development.

In the next three chapters we will look at how communities can do this. In chapter 5, we look at the lives and stories of a number of women who have maintained their sense of self despite the demands of the master. Their stories are told not only to raise up the strength of these women but also to point to their differentness. In weaving the tapestry of women's choices, I specifically do not seek to mold girls and women into one type; I do not pit them against one another. Their stories blend and contrast, show patterns and deviations from patterns.

In chapter 6, we look at the way in which education can foster voice through a process of "hard dialogue and deep connections." Finally, in chapter 7, drawing on the remarkable story of Deborah, we consider how caretaking leadership that is passionate, empathetic, and wise can be empowering.

Chapter Five

Wrestling with Our Sisters

TOGETHER BUILDING OUR HOUSEHOLDS OF FAITH

"Then Rachel said, 'With mighty wrestlings I have wrestled with my sister, and have prevailed.'"
—Genesis 30:8

"Then all the people who were at the gate, along with the elders, said, 'We are witnesses. May the LORD make the woman who is coming into your house like Rachel and Leah, who together built up the house of Israel.'"
—Ruth 4:11

I n the previous chapters of this book, we have considered some general issues in women's development while acknowledging the differentness of particular women. There are some common themes in women's lives, and it has been helpful to consider in broad strokes the social and cultural pressures influencing women's development in North American culture. Yet, we have had to recognize that different women face different personal opportunities, community situations, and cultural expectations. These differences between women can be a wonderful gift to women in community, but they can also be a source of tension and tremendous pain. It is tempting for some women to assume that the choices they make in their lives and in their households of faith are the best choices for other women as well. Surely, some choices are more healthy than others, but this judgment cannot be made superficially. It is only when we examine the complicated texture of the lives of women that we can wrestle more deeply with the varieties of women's choices. In this chapter we will look both appreciatively and critically into a variety of women's choices as we envision the rebuilding of households of faith.

The importance of women's differences is underscored by the cover art selected for this book. The Rossetti watercolor depicts Dante's vision of the famous biblical sisters, Rachel and Leah. Capturing the sisters' portrayal in the *Purgatorio,* the painter shows Leah at the right occupying herself with a bouquet of flowers and Rachel at the left lost in thought, symbolizing the active and contemplative lives. "Her joy is in reflection, mine in act," sings Leah in Canto XXVII.[1] The painter conveys a multitude of impressions; the differences suggest both a workable complementarity and a painful disparity. Even though both sisters earned the artist's admiration, Leah's green gown is the color of fertility and life while Rachel's red gown bespeaks barrenness and an early death. Though I will argue that rivalry is not the lasting impression that we should have of these women, the way in which their different lots in life contributed to rivalry is undeniable.

RIVALS IN OUR COMMON HOUSE

The first thing that we learn about Rachel and Leah's relationship in Genesis 29 is that they are compared to one another. When the sisters are first introduced to us in the biblical story, we are told that Leah's eyes were notable (variously translated "tender," "lovely," or earlier "weak"), while Rachel's beauty was striking. "Leah looks; Rachel is looked at" suggests a modern interpreter.[2] The next thing we learn is that the women's father, Laban, uses the women as pawns to get Jacob to work for him; he sets them up to be rivals for Jacob's love, which sets in motion a tortuous love triangle. The one sister is fertile and the other barren; the one favored by God but rejected by her husband, the other seemingly forgotten by God but loved by her husband; the one living a long life and the other dying young. When Laban disposes of them by referring to "this one" and "the other" (Genesis 29:27), the reader's sense of their opposition is heightened. It is no wonder that in the history of interpretation, alienation between Rachel and Leah is the predominant theme. Although the tale of these two sisters includes moments of collaboration between the women (30:14-22; 31:15-17), there is no sign of the kind of elaborate reconciliation that takes place between the estranged brothers Jacob and Esau (chapter 33). Many commentators assume that the sisters, who wrestled "with mighty wrestlings," at best resigned themselves to a shared fate.[3]

Today, too, women wrestle mightily with one another in communities of faith. Some are more beloved by the systems they are in than others; some are more favored with tangible "blessings" than others; some enjoy long prosperous lives and others face hardship and illness early in life. These differences create great tensions among women. Sadly, these tensions are sometimes nurtured so as to keep women at enmity with one another. Today, too, women are used as pawns and pitted against one another. To shift back to the story of Esther, it sometimes seems as if Ahasuerus's pageant is being revisited. As mentioned in the introduction to this book, there are "heroine wars" going on, and women vie with one another for favor and compete with one another for survival. Some exalt the purity and maturity of Rachel's contemplative spirituality; others promote the earthiness and realism of Leah's activism. Some hold up either Vashti, who refused to accommodate to the master, or Esther, who chose to negotiate within the system, as the paradigm role models for today's girls. William E. Phipps contrasts the "feminist" and "feminine" queens, with a clear partiality to the former, Vashti.[4] Along with Phipps, many view "refusal" as the more righteous strategy for coping in a woman-demeaning system. Lewis Paton rather unkindly remarks that Esther simply "takes her place in the herd of maidens who became concubines of the king. She wins her victories not by skill or by character, but by her beauty."[5] On the other hand, Michael Fox, who clearly admires Vashti, points out that her approach "simply does not work," and he holds up a more temperate means of fighting sexism.[6] Sidnie Ann White, too, is more of a realist, and she is critical of rebels; she recognizes that revolutionary strategies can be impractical and inflexible, and she commends Esther for providing a practical and workable model for living a productive life in exile.[7]

In order for co-building to be in our future, we must avoid pitting women against one another. Sisters do indeed need to struggle together and wrestle with one another and with society. But sisters do not need to prevail against sisters; they need to prevail against the girl- and woman-denying aspects of society and culture.

CO-BUILDERS OF OUR COMMON HOUSE

The Rossetti painting, while underscoring difference, leaves us with some hope that rivalry isn't the only outcome of difference. The painter positions the sisters toward one another; "this one" and "the other one" both lead the viewer to look at them together. The two are not simply rivals or incomplete complements to one another who are "two sides of one being, symbols of our multifaceted natures"; each one, though different from the other, is in her own right a multifaceted being.[8] It is not so surprising that, in the reweaving of the sisters' story that takes place in the book of Ruth (quoted above), Rachel and Leah are remembered not as rivals who coexist but rather as co-builders of the house of Israel. In fact, whereas Jacob and Esau, after reconciling, cannot abide together "for their possessions were too great . . . and the land where they were staying could not support them because of their livestock" (Genesis 36:7), Rachel and Leah find a way to live and work together in the same space. This was not lost on Jewish interpreters; significant midrashic traditions weave tales of the sisters' compassion on one another.[9] Read through the lenses of Ruth 4, the Genesis tales do, I believe, permit a hopeful interpretation. Let's return to the story.

THE WOMEN COMING INTO OUR HOUSE: ON THE JOURNEY WITH RACHEL AND LEAH

Although many threads are either frayed or left dangling, the texture of the sisters' co-building is, I think, evident in the Genesis tapestry of these matriarchs. Their joint work begins in Genesis 30 when the sisters, in dual bids for survival, make an exchange of goods that leaves Rachel supplied with a plant (mandrakes) that aids in fertility and Leah with a promised night in bed with Jacob. Although the deal is crude, it is at least fair; unlike Jacob's exacting Esau's birthright for a bowl of lentils (Genesis 25), the sisters both benefit from the exchange. Their survival tactics pay off, and they are both blessed with sons. Significantly, after the sisters' awkward collaboration, the story of their lives with Jacob is no longer told in terms of their rivalry, but rather in terms of their connection. Jacob asks Laban if he can take his wives (i.e., the two of them) and leave, and he then calls "Rachel and Leah into the field" to reveal to them together that God is calling him home. Most significantly, chapter 31 (v. 14) reports that the sisters choose and announce a common destiny. Rachel and Leah, we are told, in unison agree to leave behind their father's house to build a new life for their children, for there is no inheritance left for them in their father's house. They both realize they have been treated as "foreigners" rather than family and refuse to collude with such treatment any longer (vv. 14, 15). Leaving behind what was home, they stay with Jacob to join forces in building a future household. Although their agency is limited by their social and cultural constraints, the sisters seem confident in their forward look. Their joint decision seems to empower Rachel, who shows additional agency by making a surprising assertive move. She takes control of Laban's household gods, and she brings them with her (vv. 19-35), not to cling to her father but rather to use his means of power for her own future. The family group, after conflict and resolution with Laban, travels on and Jacob receives God's blessing. These two sisters, who together bore the sons and daughters of Israel and secured a future household for their descendants, continue to experience tragedy as well as triumph. Leah's daughter Dinah is raped and Rachel dies in childbirth with her second son, never making it to her final destiny. No longer, however, is the tragedy of one the triumph of the other.[10] We dare imagine that Rachel, legendary for her weeping over lost children (Jeremiah 31), wept with Leah over her daughter's rape; and that Leah, canonized as the active one, ministered to Rachel as she lay dying in childbirth.

In reading the sisters' story in light of the Ruthan revision, I do not want to flatten out the richness of the conflict. That Rachel and Leah "wrestled" is not to be disregarded; genuine bonding requires such intense and serious wrestling. Women *need to* wrestle with one another today. The wrestling between women today may not be based on rivalry for a man's devotion (as in the case of Rachel and Leah); rather, much of the wrestling between women in our communities today comes from trying to sort out the varieties of choices women make. In exploring the wrestling of women in this chapter, I will use the events in Rachel and Leah's joint journey as metaphors for women's travels. Some women must *leave their households* because they are treated as strangers rather than household members. Some women choose to *stay with a household* that promises a future in which they and their children will have a part. Some women must choose hard, and even crude, strategies in order to *survive* in a world that bestows them little power. Some women courageously *take control of the household gods*, bringing them with them into new places. Some women take *creative and even tricky risks* that open possibilities for them. Some women face *tragedy and despair* and appear to have little choice and control over their lives. Based on Rachel and Leah's journey, we will look at these varieties of strategies in women's lives, taking care not to exalt some choices and vilify others without struggling to understand the complexity of each one. The purpose of our struggle to understand women's choices is not to quench conflict but to avoid women's alienation from one another so they can jointly build the common house.

It is important for women to think deeply about strategies for surviving or even flourishing in a sexist culture, and I hope that deep conversations about the stories in this chapter will take place. These conversations do not, however, need to reenact the win-lose dynamics of male-organized female competition. We should not press ourselves, or allow ourselves to be pressed, into a particular mold for womanhood or female identity. "As we reframe, recover, recount, and shatter stereotypes," writes Kathleen Hall Jamieson, "it is important that we not do unto others what has been done unto us. Thou Shalt Not Bind Thine Own Kind—Or Anybody Else," she commands.[11] Different women negotiate their life paths in different ways. While we can attend to the advantages and disadvantages of particular paths, we need to recognize a variety of faithful and respectable ways that women can function in their communities. This does not mean that all women's choices are life-giving and worthy of affirmation; women may be hoisted into or even choose paths that are destructive to themselves and to others. Thus, as we look at women's choices, we will critically assess those choices. Our sisters Vashti, Esther, Rachel, and Leah have woven for us a colorful and very rich tapestry of women's choices, and women have continued to add to its texture through the centuries. As multitudes of gifts and experiences and varieties of choices are threaded in, the history of women's co-building of the household of faith is woven and rewoven. Join me in an attempt to admire, critically evaluate, and contribute to the tapestry.

Leaving Home: When There Is No Inheritance for Us in Our Fathers' House

Leah and Rachel willingly joined Jacob on his journey away from their homeland because they realized there was nothing for them in their father's house. Their father had used them as pawns and attempted to cheat them out of what was theirs; the family covenant was repeatedly broken, and they were no longer willing to accept the injustice meted out to them.

In Christian history, there is a rich (and frequently untapped) store of legends and tales of women who chose to leave behind not only homes but the usual course for women's lives. The legendary Thecla, who repudiated the system of the Roman family structure, is one such woman. According to the second- or third-century account, Thecla was a girl of marriageable age living in Iconium. Betrothed to the young man Thamyris, she was headed for the typical life of a matron within the conventional Roman *paterfamilias* structure. The apostle Paul, however, preached in Iconium and transformed her imagination. "Seized by a new desire and an awesome passion" upon hearing Paul's teaching on the virgin life, she renounced her betrothal to follow the apostle. Other women too were converted, and the citizens of the city were up in arms over Paul's revolutionary teaching. Paul was driven from Iconium, and Thecla was given the choice of marriage or execution. Both her bethrothed Thamyris and the girl's mother, upon her refusal of marriage, urged her execution. It is as if Xerxes' ghost breathed in their ears as their anger burned within, leading them to cry out: "Burn the lawless one! Burn her that is no bride . . . that all the women who have been taught by this man may be afraid!"[12] Charged with committing sacrilege, Thecla was sentenced to death. In a show of solidarity, many of the women bystanders repeatedly protested the sentence and shouted: "An evil judgment, an unholy judgment."[13] Though the patriarchal outrage against Thecla rivals that against Vashti, Thecla was reported to have been miraculously delivered first from fire and then beasts. Moreover, she was then commissioned by Paul to teach the gospel. Her body and soul remained her own, and her choice was vindicated. "Empowered by the gospel," writes Rebecca Weaver, Thecla "possessed the fortitude to resist the social and civic expectations placed on her by family, townspeople, and even the Roman government."[14] For rather obscure reasons, Paul resists baptizing Thecla, and she ends up baptizing herself with water from a large pit while fending off the beasts in the arena.

Thecla's story, unlike Vashti's, leaves no question as to authorial intent; Thecla is a heroine. The account of her life ends with the benediction, "When she had enlightened many people with the word of God, she slept with a good sleep." Thecla's is a story about one who left a confining system, faced a great deal of tribulation in her attempt to leave, but was so confident of her call that she baptized herself! In all this, she came out vindicated. Unfortunately, although the figure of Thecla enjoyed great appeal among Christian women of the time, her story has also "slept with a good sleep." The legend of Thecla lies forgotten and subdued. Unless . . . it was from Thecla that Sheila derived the courage to flout convention and "baptize" herself.

While Thecla and Vashti are not the only role models for women, their stories are important ones for women (and especially young girls) to know. They are stories of resistance. Girls and women should know Thecla's and Vashti's courage, even as they know the stories of others who chose differently. Although we must not make bold resistance the only model for girls' and women's lives, we must recover these stories as important threads in the overall tapestry of our tradition.

Thecla's story, like Rachel's and Leah's, underscores one of the most important Jewish and Christian themes for women: no earthly person or system is a viable lord or master; all other commitments were, as Weaver names it, "subordinate loyalties." One of the reasons the early church was accused of breaking up the Roman paterfamilias was that wives, daughters, and slaves who followed Christ did not recognize emperor and father as their highest loyalty and did not feel constrained to family roles. Ambrose exhorted young women to resist the entreaties of their parents and lead a celibate life devoted to God, announcing that "if you conquer your home, you conquer the world."[15] Early church history contains heartrending accounts of women who left husbands and children upon their conversion to Christianity, refusing to comply with the Roman paterfamilias, which demanded loyalty to the father.

The courage to leave home is particularly needed for those who are in the broken covenant situation of abusive relationships. In situations of abuse, girls and women need to be empowered to name their pain, lament its presence, and to refuse to comply with abuse when possible. Most important, they need to know that God is with them in this *struggle of resistance.*[16] God's will is not for abused persons to endure but to protest. In many cases, safety, and thus leaving (even if the separation is not permanent), is needed for victims to begin the process of resisting and healing.[17]

We in communities of faith need to do all we can to make "leaving" a possible, even if a not lightly chosen option. Otherwise, we inadvertently perpetuate the "battered woman syndrome," a pattern of compulsive loyalty that binds a woman to a hurtful spouse because she feels it is morally wrong to abandon him and she believes that if she is loving and self-sacrificing enough she might save him.[18] This not only has consequences for the abused woman herself, but it trains her daughters to equate "goodness" with silence in the face of abuse. Susan, a woman physically and emotionally abused by her husband, recounts how she learned this response from her own mother's submission to abuse.

> [My mother] never, never dared rock the boat or express needs or say, "I want this." You never say, "I want," you always find out what the other person wants and . . . You don't desert somebody just because they have a weakness or sickness. There again, you be the servant or the keeper of the brother as we must be serving of one another. That was the constant thought that came through everything she taught. *Always serve and be for the guy. Never ever dare think of yourself.*[19]

We need to preach and teach on Vashti's wisdom and integrity. We need to let mothers know that the "goodness" that is theirs must include their needs and those of their daughters. In addition, we need to provide places of refuge for victims of abuse, letting abused persons know that they have a voice and their voice will be respected. By withholding (or corrupting) the story of Vashti and ignoring the problem of abuse, we are leaving women without refuge and without voice, and with self-destructive loyalty. If the only images that come to a woman's mind as she seeks to deal with her abusive situation are of compliant and submissive women, she is more likely to succumb to the battered woman's syndrome and to teach her daughters to do likewise.[20] If, in the richness of her traditioning, she has a variety of foremothers—including resisters—to shape her self-understanding, she is less likely to see compliance as her only alternative.[21]

In abusive situations the choice to "stay with their household" may be untenable, for the survival of the abused (and the accountability of the abuser) is at stake. In the above case, Susan comes to realize that the silenced, self-sacrificing vision she had of "being good" is failure rather than virtue. "I don't believe in that anymore. Just like I don't believe in fairy tales. I don't believe that being good means you allow yourself to be walked on and manipulated, put down, victimized, that is not being good. I feel it's being weak, and I see that I am weak in some areas like that."[22] Susan is in transition, however, and she is not sure where to go from here. Wanting to be "good" without becoming a victim, she does not yet know how she can act in her own best interests without being selfish and hurtful like her husband and father. In terms of Gilligan's scheme of moral development, Susan is ready to move from goodness to truth, and yet she is constricted by having only seen models for selfishness (from the men in her life) and submissive goodness (from her mother). With no other forerunners to guide her, she may easily slip back into submission.

It is not only abused women, but abused children in general who need to know about Vashti's courage. Warning that the Christian "virtues" of forgiveness and obedience can get in the way of recovery from abuse, Sheila Redmond notes that this is problematic for children. "Children must be taught that they have *the right to say no*, the right to question authority, and the right to disobey."[23] While this does not mean that we train children to be disrespectful of parents, it does mean that we make it very clear that parents (and other authority figures) are not God—and that sometimes we must say no to their inappropriate demands. A proper understanding of loyalty to God should make this self-evident. Rabbinic teachers, who were great believers in parental authority, regularly taught that parental authority was provisionalized by loyalty to Torah. "R. Eleazar b. Mattai said: If my father were to say to me, 'Give me some water to drink,' and I had at that moment a command [of the Law] to fulfil, then I should omit the honor due a father, and fulfil the command."[24] In fact, loyalty to God provides a court of appeal if the child perceives the parent to be wrong. Sadly, in many cases, loyalty to parents is conflated with loyalty to God. Children's natural inclination to see their parents as godlike, when combined with religious beliefs that exalt parental authority, can debilitate a child's agency.

It is important to recognize here that the choice for resistance will have consequences. Conflict and disruption may result, and some people might take this as proof that the child or woman should not have caused trouble. In fact, it is a little facile of Michael Fox to contend that "the Vashti episode is prefixed to the story to demonstrate that humility and indirection were necessary to Esther's success. Vashti's fate showed that the king may react badly to strong willed women who do not temper their strength with subtlety."[25] While subtlety may indeed be more effective and more wise, the fact that others "react badly to strong willed women" is not cause enough to temper our strong personalities. Furthermore, just because life gets to be more complicated as a result of our resistance to dehumanization does not mean that it was a mistake to resist. There is a kind of shallow "peace" that prevails in a tyranny; if no one questions the oppressor, then conflict is eliminated. This is not, however, a legitimate understanding of peace. Peace includes justice; thus, we must sometimes disrupt the illusion of peace on the road to genuine peace.

Leaving an oppressive system sometimes preserves more persons than the one doing the leaving; one person's leaving can sometimes be a catalyst to change an oppressive system. Unforeseen others, or even the oppressing persons themselves, can benefit from one person's bravery. The catalyst herself may not be a beneficiary; like Vashti, who is deposed, or Rachel, who dies before she enters the royal city (Genesis 35:19), women on the frontier may not live to see their courage come to fruition. Perhaps, however, their daughters will. In fact, leaving ought not to be seen as simply a last resort; it can be a stand that shakes a system into consciousness. Sometimes, the courageous woman *is* there to see this happen.

In her recent novel *Ladder of Years*, Anne Tyler tells the story of Delia, a woman who, at the age of forty, begins to question her life. We might say, looking back to chapter 2, that Delia faces the developmental transition from an interpersonally oriented self to an inner-directed self. After years of being dependent upon and submissive to a benevolent but rather controlling husband, she grows restless. Seeing no support from those around her, she simply takes off one day during the family vacation. She exits the system, and leaves her family behind. After her exodus, she begins to reflect critically on her life, surfacing from years of immersion. "She had always been such a *false* child, so eager to conform to the grown-ups' views of her," she realizes.[26]

With only a few hundred dollars and the clothes on her back, she begins her adulthood all over, finding a job and a place to live on her own. The stark, empty room she rents is symbolic of this new beginning; each item she adds to her room represents her chosen selfhood. Her family eventually finds her, and they ask her to return, incredulous that she chooses not to resume her former way of life. But she knows that what they want is what she can no longer give them, the person she used to be but no longer is. When her daughter plans to get married, Delia does return for a visit.

After interacting with various family members, she realizes that in her absence they have had to grow in numerous ways, including their capacity to care for themselves and one another now that she is no longer doing all of it. She eventually decides to return to her family, but it is a decision on the other side of selfhood. She now knows herself, and she knows how to express her own needs; her husband now knows how to be accountable to others and not simply himself. Surely, she is still interpersonally skilled, but she is not interpersonally determined; her husband is still very self-directed, but he is no longer able to run full speed ahead without a thought to those in his path. Delia's growth into selfhood strengthened the lives of those around her. She ended up back where she'd started, but she wasn't the same person as before, and neither were her family members. Those she had left behind had "actually traveled further." She realized that she had needed to let go of them so that they could grow apart from her just as much as they needed to let go of her and support her movement into selfhood. Though on the surface it may not appear as if much had changed, Delia remained a wife and mother; but the dynamics of the family were permanently altered.

Leaving, clearly, is not always to the detriment of the system one is exiting, though it may seem so at the beginning. Delia's decision to leave and her insistence on speaking her own voice turned out to be the most important loyalty she could show; it forced the family system to face itself and change. One person's leaving is sometimes the catalyst a system needs for facing itself.

In her pain-filled biography *Lakota Woman*, Mary Crow Dog describes the cruel Catholic boarding school to which she and many other American Indian children were sent to learn to assimilate to Euro-American culture.[27] One day the school got a new English teacher, a young priest. This priest, trying to correct an Indian boy's pronunciation of English, used harassing tactics. Mary (née Brave Bird), then a teenager, stood up for the boy and chastised the priest's insensitivity. The priest made her stay after school, and he treated her in the same rough manner. "Why are you always mocking us? You have no reason to do this," he challenged her. "Sure I do," she replied, many years of pent-up anger being channeled into her response. "You were making fun of him. You embarrassed him. He needs strengthening, not weakening. You hurt him. I did not hurt you." He then twisted her arm and pushed her, and she hit him in the face. Going with him to the principal's office, she announced, "Today I quit school. I'm not taking any more of this, none of this shit anymore. None of this treatment. Better give me my diploma. I can't waste any more time on you people."[28]

In this case, Mary Brave Bird's stand and exit led to the growth of her teacher. Previously seeing the world through the lenses of the establishment that sought to break the Native American spirit and destroy the indigenous language, he was forced to shift his framework and see these children as cultured human beings. "Oddly enough, that priest turned out okay. . . . Later he became a good friend of the Indians, a personal friend of myself and my husband. He stood up for us during Wounded Knee and after. He stood up to his superiors, stuck his neck way out, became a real people's priest." Mary's growth depended on her exiting this highly repressive and imperialistic institution, and her exit included exertion of her voice. Her voice also contributed to the growth of others. In response to the famous statement Colonel Chivington said to his soldiers regarding Indians—"Kill 'em all, big and small, nits make lice!"—Mary Brave Bird retorts: "I don't know whether I am a louse under the white man's skin. I hope I am." Exercising prophetic voice, this creative "louse," in getting under the white man's skin, set redemption in motion.[29]

In the stories above, Delia and Mary Crow Dog were largely on their own. They had only the strength of their spirits to prompt their exits. Critiquing or leaving a system that is constraining can be a difficult choice for one person to make alone; when a group gathers together in solidarity, the capacity for both voice and exit increases. Leah and Rachel joined as one to leave their father's house; women today sometimes gather in solidarity to resist the rules and definitions of reality that are imposed by patriarchy. Sometimes those on the margins can join together and build one another up in a community of resistance. Even brief moments of communal "exodus" from oppressive structures can start the process of awakening and self-discovery.

WOMEN-CHURCH AND SOLIDARITY: SEPARATION FOR A WHILE

In her 1985 book *Women-Church*, Rosemary Radford Reuther suggests that women may need a period of withdrawal from men and from patriarchal culture in order to gather together and define their own experience. This enables women to affirm their own humanity, exercise their thinking and judgment, and reflect critically on the woman-denying culture of church and society. In the company of women, away from the cultural definitions of "femininity," woman can question prevailing structures and reshape their sense of themselves—and ultimately reshape society and culture. Reuther, however, distinguishes this separatist stage from "ideological separatism," which aims at total and permanent separation. Women-church, for most "means, at best, a few hours a week taken out of lives lived in the presence of males." The goal for women-church is "neither leaving the church as a sectarian group, nor continuing to fit into it on its terms," but rather establishing a critique of patriarchy and imagining an alternative religious culture that will eventually lead to a "cohuman church" of women and men.[30] When Alice Walker describes what it means to be a womanist, she names similar goals. A womanist is one who is "committed to survival and wholeness of entire people, male and female. Not a separatist, except periodically for health."[31]

Rather than absolutize itself, women-church acknowledges its fallibility, aims toward mutuality with men, and is critically concerned about its own participation in oppression. Women-church is what I call a "community of solidarity," gathered for the purpose of the full humanity of the Christian church. A "community of solidarity" is not a "lifestyle enclave." "Lifestyle enclaves" were highly criticized by Robert Bellah and his associates in *Habits of the Heart* for being "segmental" groupings that celebrate the "narcissism of similarity." Such enclaves, argue the team of sociologists, "involve only a segment of each individual, for they concern only private life, especially leisure and consumption. And they are segmental socially in that they include only those with a common lifestyle."[32] As opposed to genuine "community," which attempts "to be an inclusive whole" celebrating a variety of lifestyles, enclaves are comfortable and protected gatherings of the like-minded who prefer not to be in the company of those who do not share the same lifestyle. Communities of solidarity, a term that I am using in relation to women-church, are gatherings of persons who share a common oppression, who protest against that oppression, and who attempt to construct alternative understandings of themselves as human beings.[33] "Oppressed groups need to have separate spaces in which to gain their self-respect, name themselves, and discover their own history," argues Davida Alperin.[34] Rather than an escape into private leisure, the goal of these communities is the empowering of oppressed persons for life in a public sphere that discriminates against them. As I will argue in the next chapter, just as solidarity groups nurture the voices of those who speak out against domination, so too must they invite different voices within their own solidarity grouping. It is important that prophetic communities not become ideological strongholds, or else they become increasingly more like lifestyle enclaves.[35]

Leaving, whether temporarily or permanently, is a needed and viable option for some. For others, it is either impossible or undesirable. Leah and Rachel left their father's land, but they stayed with Jacob's household. Many women choose to stay where they are, hoping to build a future for themselves and for others.

Staying to Build a Future Within Our Households: When Home *Is* the Journey

Many women struggling to gain voice and identity wish to do so within the communities of which they are part because they value their history with their communities, and they wish to take part in the creation of the future of these communities. Although not the only viable choice for women, this can be a theologically and culturally valuable choice. North American culture tends to overemphasize the life of independence, journey, and adventure, especially in the lives of men. Those who affirm the wisdom gained from staying put provide an important corrective to the prevailing value system. Woman have (primarily out of necessity), learned that abiding and staying put can be sources for spiritual growth, and they have something to teach those who are always on the move.[36] Although some women have developed the capacity to grow by staying put through full-time "homemaking" in their families, I am using the metaphor of "staying home" more broadly. Staying within one's household, so to speak, involves accepting the challenge and adventure to grow within a familiar context. There is a particular kind of growth that only comes when we know others and are known ourselves through our gropings, changes, mistakes, celebrations, losses, gains, and milestones.[37] Staying put does not mean staying the same; it merely means staying committed to a consistent group of people through the changes.

The willingness to abide in a familiar place with familiar people teaches one to be content and to learn from what is there before one; it wards off the compulsion to always seek something or someone new. In a culture flooded with disposable goods and relationships, this corrective is needed. In this way, staying put with one's community satisfies certain aspects of the Benedictine disciplines of contentment and endurance assessed in chapter 1. And yet, recalling the concerns raised in chapter 1, we cannot promote a superficial understanding of staying put that encourages the passive "enduring with patience the injuries and afflictions we face."

One form of staying put is to choose an identity and future that accept traditional understandings of femininity. Some forms of this choice are life-giving. Women who value homemaking, child rearing, and volunteer work in schools and churches deserve support and respect. Although forcing these choices on women is oppressive, condemning women who make these choices is equally oppressive. My daughter was right to accuse me of narrowing her life options when, in response to her question, "Mom, how many grandchildren should I give you?" I quickly snapped, "I'll answer that question after you finish your Ph.D."[38] Still, we must deal critically with movements that want to recover the way things were, diminish the options open to women, and stave off progress in gender equity. When Marabel Morgan in the 1970s advised the "Total Woman" to worship and obey her husband in order to get what she wants, when Ellen Fein and Sherrie Schneider in 1996 prescribed that "The Rules Girls" capture the heart of a man by manipulating his inescapable need to be the hunter-aggressor, then a viable option for girls and women has been stripped of genuine relationality.[39] Not only are women advised against being themselves (*The Rules Girls* has a long list of Dos and Don'ts, such as "Let Him Take the Lead"; "Don't Accept a Date for Saturday after Wednesday," aimed to quench women's tendency to show their feelings too strongly and too soon in a relationship), but they are encouraged toward "a stunningly low opinion of men."[40] While "womanipulation," the term Ellen Goodman uses to describe such rules, may be effective for a while, in the end it only breeds mistrust between the sexes. While both mystery and playfulness are important to community life, these are not playful games that enrich the participants. These are rules for false relationality.

Staying put requires genuine relationality, including the empathetic, prophetic, and conversational components of caring. It is not only "traditional" women who make a choice to stay put. Many feminists feel as if they are making a similar choice when they stay with traditions and communities that have been historically male-dominated and still reflect a sexist legacy. Letty Russell has stated in many places that she has "always found it difficult to walk away from the church, but [has also] found it difficult to walk with it!"[41] If feminists walk away, they not only give up something that was important to many of our foremothers but also hand over the future of the church to others. Many are claiming their responsibility to add their voice to the ongoing argument over the tradition, a tradition deemed to have a "liberating core." They remain in the household not to passively endure the status quo but rather to actively contribute to the future. One woman, who both loves the church and fears that it will one day reject her, does not leave it. She knows it is "not a friendly place for women," but she also wonders, "Wouldn't the world be different if it was women's visions that shaped it?"[42]

Frequently women who stay within their surroundings to build for the future take control of the household gods as did Rachel; that is to say, they learn to use the master's tools and establish themselves in the household.

Taking Control of the Household Gods: Using the Master's Tools

In ancient times, the possession of the household gods served "as the symbolic token of leadership in a given estate."[43] By stealing the gods, Rachel was perhaps claiming authority over her life, even if a great deal of that authority remained as hidden as the gods under her skirts. Here Rachel's active and assertive side flourishes. Strikingly, it is shortly after Jacob demands from his household that all foreign gods be turned over that Rachel dies in childbirth (Genesis 35). We do not know for sure whether Rachel turned over her gods—or whether Jacob ever knew she had stolen them. If she did turn over these symbols of self-assertion, we might read in the gaps that she turned over the vital part of her self. If taking control of the gods is linked with Rachel's breaking with the patrilocal tradition (which ordered women to stay in their fathers' households); perhaps giving up the gods is tantamount to giving up her assertive self, symbolized by her death.[44]

Women today have increasing opportunities to take the household gods, or to use another metaphor, to equip themselves with the "tools of the master" and to compete with him in his game. In many ways, gaining the tools of the master—access to equitable education and the public life,[45] and freedom to choose their destiny—was the battle of early feminism, and it has enjoyed significant victories. Although it is by no means won, women are gaining entry to male-dominated spheres, and many are competing well. Early feminists fought by insisting on women's similarities to men; their heirs continue to minimize male/female differences, urging women (in the words of Naomi Wolf) to fight "fire with fire" by grasping and responsibly using the kinds of power and opportunities that have been open to men.[46] Wolf argues that women must learn how to "steal one's own female power from under the gaze of the monsters of femininity," monsters that make women "power averse and power illiterate."[47]

Using the master's tools and playing the master's game are often difficult for women to do. Despite genuine advances, women still face setbacks and backlashes. The game is not always played fairly. A woman trying to prove herself in a male-dominated arena may be judged far more stringently than her male peers. Much like the conversational dynamics described in chapter 3, a woman's good ideas are susceptible to be ignored and then picked up by a man, her accomplishments may be noticed less frequently—her mistakes more frequently, and any of her ways of doing things that are different from the prevailing patterns run the risk of being judged inadequate. If women are "viewed 'as women'" they are "frequently denied access to high-powered positions because their presumed attributes cause them to appear incapable"; yet if they engage in the kind of male-associated behaviors expected in demanding jobs, "they are considered to be abrasive, or maladjusted."[48]

Additionally, being "like the boys" sometimes involves tools and practices that are harmful to the well-being of others. In her work *Talking Back*, bell hooks warns African American women that "one of the clear and present dangers" when one enters "hierarchical institutions which daily reinforce domination by race, sex and class, is that we gradually assume a mind-set similar to those who dominate and oppress, that we lose critical consciousness because it is not reinforced or affirmed by the environment."[49] While some household gods should be taken and used, others are better shattered and destroyed.

Susan Bordo describes her own strategy to first "transcend gender" (make it in male spheres) and then "transform through the resource of gender" (to change male spheres). "When I was a graduate student," she muses, "it was necessary to my professional survival that I demonstrate that I could argue 'like the boys.'" She assimilated well and established herself professionally. Having established herself as a legitimate player, she now wishes to make an impact on the way the game is played. "Now that I am a tenured professor, the 'female' aspects of my identity, I hope, can operate transformatively, disturbing received notions of professorial and philosophical expertise and authority." The process of bringing one's marginalized qualities into the central arenas of culture is not an easy one. "Deciding how much one may 'bloom' and how much one has to 'transcend' in any given context is tricky," says Bordo.[50] One not only runs the risk of losing respect when one tries to change the culture by introducing those marginalized qualities, but one also runs the risk of having suppressed the qualities for so long that they are no longer recoverable. This is a dilemma that any marginalized person who has opportunities opened to them faces. Not entering such systems allows them to thrive unchallenged; progression through such systems "threatens to make one a carrier" of its deep-seated practices and values.[51]

For many women, the household gods are out of reach. Privileged women may have the opportunity to learn the "Way of the Master," but impoverished women are often faced with "making a way out of no way." They face basic issues in survival of self and family. They must make difficult choices and decisions in the midst of oppressive constraints. Rachel, faced with barrenness in a culture that prized women for their childbearing capacities, bargained with her sister for a fertility plant. Leah, faced with loneliness and rejection from the man she married, trades the plant for a night in bed with her husband. These were crude choices made for the sake of survival in a limiting situation. We cannot idealize life and pretend that all women are free to choose to do whatever they want to do—or even whatever they think is right to do. Many women are in the position of these sisters: they must find a way to survive when there seems to be no way.

Survival and Hard Choices: Making a Way out of No Way

In her poignant article on "Women and the Burden of Empathy," Pat Howrey Davis describes Anne, the single mother of three children. Having been abandoned by her alcoholic and abusive husband some years ago, Anne seeks counseling from Youth and Family Services when her oldest daughter becomes a truant at school. Barely existing on her scant earnings as a stock person in a local discount store, Anne "seemed frozen, hopeless, drained, depressed—unable to cope with another chronic problem in her life."[52] Seemingly at wit's end, she wondered out loud about the possibility of splitting the family. Her youngest child, Robbie, began sobbing at the end of the counseling session, and Anne made no attempt to comfort him. He whispered, "I don't think anyone loves me," to which Anne replied hopelessly, "Don't expect me to tell him I love him. I can't love anybody. I'm just surviving."

When evaluating the choices of women, we do well to have Anne's situation in mind. It is easy to spin visions of liberation, achievement, and revolution. For some women, however, it is all that they can do to survive; when they reach their wit's end, as Anne seems to have done, even survival is too difficult.

Delores Williams has raised similar issues in *Sisters in the Wilderness*. Williams contends that there is not only one answer to the question: "What can we say about God's relation to the oppressed in history?" She suggests that *survival*, rather than liberation, is often the mode of a faithful life lived in the midst of desperation. She admits that this "is not always compatible with what feminist and womanist liberationists might want to hear,"[53] but it is more often the only future open to oppressed people. Like the Jews instructed how to live in Babylonian captivity, adaptation may be a faithful alternative to liberation (Jeremiah 29:4-7). Williams finds hope for survival in the narrative of Hagar.

> I believe the hope oppressed black women get from the Hagar-Sarah texts has more to do with survival and less to do with liberation. When they and their families get into serious social and economic straits, black Christian women have believed that God helps them *make a way out of no way*. This is precisely what God did for Hagar and Ishmael when they were expelled from Abraham's house and were wandering in the desert without food and water. God opened Hagar's eyes and she saw a well of water that she had not seen before.[54]

Rather than liberate Hagar from her oppressive conditions, God enables her to see resources "where she saw none before." In fact, at certain points, Hagar's own attempts at liberation lead to precarious circumstances. While it is important to struggle deeply with Hagar's story, and that includes questioning the choices of the characters involved, it is equally important that we not too quickly slap a particular agenda onto our struggle. To judge Hagar for returning to her mistress, and thus preserving her own life and the life of her child, is to impose a narrow framework on faithfulness.[55] "The truth of the matter may well be that the Bible gives license for us to have it both ways: God liberates and God does not always liberate all the oppressed. God speaks comforting words to the survival and quality-of-life struggle of many families."[56]

Women faced with survival issues can be under great stress. Not only is their energy, like Anne's, likely limited by lack of support, but the choices open to them may be dispiriting. Emancipated slave Louisa Picquet, when reflecting back on her days as a young slave woman, recalled the struggle in her soul. Compelled by her master to have sex with him, guided by her religious faith to maintain sexual purity, she painfully recalled that she "had trouble with him and my soul the whole time."[57] Sometimes communities of faith make the troubling in the soul even more painful by expecting women to be saintly and pure in all circumstances.

Maria Goretti was a twelve-year-old girl canonized by the Roman Catholic church for protecting her purity. Maria, who subjected herself to repeated stabs in order to fend off the sexual advances of a young man, was willing to die rather than be defiled. She died of stab wounds several days after the attack, but she managed to forgive her assailant and affect his conversion in prison before she died.[58] Maria was indeed a brave and remarkable girl, but her elevation to sainthood is something with which feminists wrestle. In evaluating women's strategies in life, we need to be careful that we not divide the world into the "pure," who resist and exit oppressive systems, and the "defiled," who remain and survive. This can, ironically, be an inadvertent recovery of a centuries-old form of misogyny. Maria's story is complex, and I do not wish to either exalt or renounce her choice. To suggest that it would have been better to submit to her rapist than to resist is not very satisfying either.[59] Yet, to preclude a girl's choice by exalting sexual purity over survival is oppressive. To make sexual purity the ultimate source of feminine goodness is problematic. It not only leads women to repress sexuality, but it also contributes to women refusing to report rape.[60]

We can support women who have faced difficult survival situations by letting them know that tough circumstances and choices within oppressive systems do not mean commitment or loyalty to the system. We can acknowledge with them that survival issues from loyalty or responsibility to dependent others. We can even enable them to see that the difficult choice for survival need not be seen as the quenching of voice or agency. While in some cases it may be passive resignation, in others it is active and willful strategizing.[61] Thus, women caught in desperate circumstances can be encouraged to keep their awareness sharp and their hope for a more ideal future alive, even as they are supported in the hard decisions they make in the present.[62]

When women of privilege set the agenda for feminism and insist on liberation tactics, the possibilities and circumstances of less-fortunate women can be ignored. For instance, a woman with the means to pay a housekeeper can free up time for activism in a way that a poor woman cannot. A highly trained and widely employable woman has more freedom to "say no" to an exploitative supervisor than does a less-skilled worker. A mother whose children are provided for can speak for women's rights in her workplace in a way that a mother whose children depend fully on her paycheck cannot. In fact, though all feats of courage can have untoward consequences for others and this cannot paralyze us from acting, we cannot protect ourselves from the fact that all the ordinary wives of the kingdom suffered the consequences of Vashti's stance. Privileged women must be aware of the situations of their sisters. At the very least, they must not expect their concerns to be the burning issues for others; and, more responsibly, they must proceed cautiously in order not to exact the cost of their activism from those less secure.

Furthermore, we must name the sins against Hagar, and her counterpart in Rachel and Leah's story, Bilhah. Bilhah is the maid whom Rachel offers to Jacob that "through her I too may build up a family" (Genesis 30:3, NEB). In her desperation to assure her place in a society that considered the bearing of children essential, Rachel, as did Sarah before her, decides that her maid will become a surrogate for her. When Bilhah succeeds, it is Rachel who names and claims the sons that the slave woman bore. Rachel attempts to secure her own future at the expense of another woman. This is not simply the case of fighting a battle that leaves unanticipated consequences for more vulnerable women, this is the case of using another woman as an instrument in one's fight for survival. By virtue of living in the midst of systemic oppression, none of us can ever be innocent of harming one another; still, it is needful for us to name and protest ways in which less-powerful women are exploited by more-powerful ones. Thus, Delores Williams argues that feminists cannot simply name and fight the evils of patriarchy, but they must also name and fight racism and classism. The term "patriarchy" "leaves too much out." It is silent about "the positive boons patriarchy has bestowed upon many white women," including "in some cases the *choice* to stay home and raise children and/or develop a career—*and* to hire another woman (usually a black one) to 'help out' in either case."[63] It is for this reason that Elisabeth Schüssler Fiorenza now terms "kyriarchy" (the rule of the elite, propertied, educated, freeborn men) the reigning structure.[64]

In reflecting on survival tactics, here we must remember our girls from the previous chapter, those with eating disorders. Sometimes eating disorders are dismissed as an elitist disease, a spoiled girl's attention-grabbing tactics. I have argued that eating disorders emerge out of the fierce attempt for the self to survive in an identity-repressing environment. Eating disorders are coping mechanisms in response to oppression, and the suffering the girls experience is very real.

Women struggling to survive do so in the best way they can, often with only scraps with which to work. Sometimes, creativity triumphs and women make something beautiful out of "the good for nothing" life has dealt them.

THE WAY OF WOMEN: MAKING SOMETHING OUT OF THE GOOD FOR NOTHING

Drawing upon the following beautiful poem (which I have quoted only in part) by Kathleen O'Keefe Reed, Elizabeth Bettenhausen has linked women's capacity for making something out of nothing with divine creation.

> She is the ragrug woman
> Gatherer of good for nothing
> Weaver of worth
> Expert in creatio ex nihilo
> Her joy any ball of cloth not fit for dust
> Whatever is worn out she receives
> Just dump it right here on the kitchen table
> Where her hands hover over the chaos
> Where fingers dance with scissors, thread and needle
> Making strands of life emerge.
>
> From rags she weaves
> Works of art you can walk on

Rather than following the traditional stream of interpretation, which understands creatio ex nihilo as a pure, uncontaminated act of creating something new out of absolutely nothing, Bettenhausen imagines a messier, dirtier, much more difficult creative act. It is the creation of "life out of what's at hand, out of the worn-outness of our lives, the good for nothing rags of injustice and threadbare hope."[65] In her view, God is present when women sit around the kitchen table and, like ragrug women, weave pieces of nothingness into works of art. Those who are privileged shred their comfort and braid their strips together with the worn and battered lives of those who suffer, for it is "in the good for nothing" that God is found.

Rachel was like the ragrug woman. Hemmed in on one side by a father who treats her as property to pawn and on the other side by a social order that declares her unclean and unfit for public life during her womanly cycles, Rachel weaves the rags she is given into something. After her father has repeatedly cheated her out of her rights, she takes property back from him. She claims the household gods, most likely to bring her children and her new household protection and blessing, and she avoids apprehension by using in her own favor the very thing that men have used against her. "Let not my lord be angry that I cannot rise before you, for the way of women is upon me" (31:35), she utters, using ostensible uncleanness as a ruse to stave off her father's search for his lost property. She has taken the good for nothing rule of women's seclusion during "the way of women" and woven it into a garment of love and protection for her children and household. Rachel, who was looked at by men, now makes sure that she is *only* looked at. Laban, ironically, cannot *see* what is happening because the male fear of woman's uncleanness blinds his sight.[66] But, the reader with tender eyes can see. Like Leah, we look closely, and we see that indeed the way of women is upon this brave sister, and it is a way of creative resistance.[67]

CREATIVE RESISTANCE

While sometimes we are caught in an either/or situation that forces us to choose between survival and transformation, at other times it may be possible to negotiate between the pragmatism of survival and the potential martyrdom of transformation. In her compelling children's novel, *Roll of Thunder, Hear My Cry*, Mildred Taylor describes how a depression-era black family finds ways to creatively resist the racism around them. In one poignant scene, the father tells his daughter (Cassie) that "ther'll be a whole lot of things you ain't gonna wanna do but you'll have to do in this life just so you can survive." He then goes on to qualify this, "But there are other things, Cassie, that if I'd let be, they'd eat away at me and destroy me in the end. And it's the same with you baby. There are things you can't back down on, things you gotta take a stand on. But it's up to you to decide what them things are."[68] This family, better off than their neighbors because they own their land, recognize that they are in a position to take risks that those who are sharecroppers cannot afford to take. When Cassie's brother expresses indignation over the fact that the sharecroppers had to pull out of a boycott to protect themselves from being thrown into the chain gang, the father rebukes the boy. The men had already risked a great deal by participating in the boycott, and were they to go all the way and be thrown into the chain gang, their families would be left to starve. "It's hard on a man to give up, but sometimes it seems there just ain't nothing else he can do," the father concludes.[69]

In a remarkably sensitive and creative insight, the mother in the story helps Cassie deal with the racism that threatens to destroy her self-respect. Forced by a white man to defer to his daughter (Lillian Jean, who is near in age to Cassie) and call her "Miss," she is counseled by her mother to express what Sharon Welch calls "creative defiance." This is subtle defiance that preserves her self-respect but also sets up future possibilities for resistance. "White people may demand our respect, but what we give them is not respect but fear. What we give to our own people is far more important because it's given freely. Now you may have to call Lillian Jean 'Miss' because the white people say so, but you'll also call our own young ladies at church 'Miss' because you really do respect them."[70] The wise parents enable their children to shrewdly understand racism while not accepting it as inevitable. They negotiate a path between yielding to the evil and setting themselves up for martyrdom. While continually remarking that things are not the way they should be, they seek to find realistic and constructive possibilities for resistance and empowerment. Thus, the mother counsels her daughter to submit to the rule to call white girls "miss," but she enables her to resist psychological subordination by extending the deference to her own community. Looking for possibilities for creative resistance does not preclude choosing brazen defiance. As Cassie's father advised, sometimes there are things that "you gotta take a stand on." The girl's mother, a schoolteacher, cannot back down from teaching her black students about the evils of slavery and the dignity of their ancestors. She puts her job at risk, and indeed loses her teaching position. But at other times, as when the lynching of a black man is at stake, she tempers her boldness and proceeds with caution.

Fannie Flagg in *Fried Green Tomatoes at the Whistle Stop Cafe*, a folksy and profound tale about a small town in Alabama in the first half of this century, provides similar tales of creative resistance. Flagg describes how one renegade Southern woman, Idgie Threadgoode, time and time again creatively defied the racism and sexism of her day. In one scene Idgie and Ruth, co-owners of the Whistle Stop Cafe, face a moral dilemma. Some hungry black men working nearby ask if they can buy some of their barbecue sandwiches. Idgie and Ruth, trying to raise a child on their business, are vulnerable. The KKK has been parading a good deal, and Idgie knows this is a tricky situation. She offers a creatively defiant solution. "You know that if it was up to me, I'd have you come on in the front door and sit at the table," she explains to the men. "But you know I cain't do that. . . . There's a bunch in town that would burn me down in a minute, and I've got to make a living. . . . But I want you to go back over to the yard and tell your friends, anytime they want anything, just to come on around to the kitchen door." The sheriff, also a closet member of the Klan, comes by a couple of days later. "Now, Idgie, you ought not to be selling those niggers food. . . . Nobody wants to eat in the same place that niggers come, it's not right and you just ought not to be doin' it."

Idgie, though vulnerable, is not without any resources. She manages to make something out of the scraps before her. Because the sheriff is also her friend, and because she knows a secret or two about him, Idgie convinces him to let her continue to serve "colored people" out the back door. Knowing this was something of a compromise, but not wanting to lose their business by inviting the black men to sit inside, Idgie and Ruth manage to add an additional defiant detail to their resolution. "They both knew they had to make a decision about what to do. And they did. After that day, the only thing that changed was on the menu that hung on the back door; everything was a nickel or a dime cheaper. They figured fair was fair."[71]

A couple in Springfield, Illinois, a few years ago also exercised a creative ethic of risk. When the KKK marched in their town to protest the celebration of Martin Luther King Jr.'s Birthday, Lindy and Bill Seltzer decided to turn "lemons into lemonade." Dubbing their efforts Project Lemonade, they urged citizens to pledge money to civil rights organizations for each minute the Klan members spoke on the capitol steps. Not only did they raise $10,000 for civil rights, but they also put this hate group in the double bind of increasing the cause for civil rights even as they added to their rhetoric of racism.[72]

Raising girls to be cautious but creatively defiant is a way to preserve self-esteem in dehumanizing situations where it is too risky to directly confront the social order. Having a community of imagination and support is important here; one needs the ideas and encouragement of others to keep going. When raised with a creative ethic of risk, a girl realizes that even if there are "a whole lot of things you ain't gonna wanna do but you'll have to do in this life just so you can survive," she has an imagination to help her resist in subtle ways. An African American student describes how culture and gender keep her outwardly enslaved even as she desperately holds on to her inner self.

> Another way to survive is as an assimilated slave these days and that while I may have begun to adopt certain characteristics that the master was going to beat the shit out of me if I didn't [do those things] . . . I became accustomed to them, but *deep down inside, in my baby toe, or in my soul, I still remember and I still know.* I just don't have those opportunities to express it, and if I do express it I'll be penalized.[73]

Even if all we can do is help keep that "deep down inside knowledge" alive, that is something. Perhaps someday this woman will have the opportunity to express herself honestly; on that day it will be important that she still remembers and still knows. In his foreword to *In Memory's Kitchen*, the recently published recipes copied down on scraps of paper by women in the Theresienstadt concentration camp, Michael Berenbaum suggests that this creative act by starving women was something akin to what I am naming creative resistance. The hunger, named and kept alive, was imaginatively sated, while the cultural recipes were preserved in hope that they would one day be prepared in freedom.

> For some, the way to deal with this hunger was to repress the past, to live only in the present, to think only of today, neither of yesterday nor of tomorrow. Not so the women who compiled this cookbook. They talked of the past; they dared to think of food, to dwell on what they were missing—pots and pans, a kitchen, home, family, guests, meals, entertainment. Therefore, this cookbook compiled by women in Theresienstadt, by starving women in Theresienstadt, must be seen as yet another manifestation of defiance, of a spiritual revolt against the harshness of given conditions. It is a flight of the imagination back to an earlier time when food was available, when women had homes and kitchens and could provide a meal for their children. The fantasy must have been painful for the authors. Recalling recipes was an act of discipline that required them to suppress their current hunger and to think of the ordinary world before the camps—and perhaps to dare to dream of a world after the camps.[74]

It is interesting that in her introduction, Cara De Silva includes a poem written by Gertrud Salomon after liberation that celebrates the "after Haman, hamantaschen" (a Jewish pastry).[75]

BOLD RESISTANCE

When we do help keep resistance alive, we will need to be there for those who, like Cassie, come "face to face with the things you can't back down on, things you gotta take a stand on." Like Rosa Parks, who faced grave penalization, a time comes when one has had enough adapting to the master. Rosa Parks refused to sit in the back of the bus because she remembered, she knew in her soul, that she was a person equal to a white person—despite the claim to the contrary in a racist and segregated society. "People always say that I didn't give up my seat because I was tired, but that isn't true," she recently wrote. "I was not tired physically, or no more tired than I usually was at the end of a working day. I was not old, although some people have the image of me as being old then. I was 42. No, the only tired I was, was tired of giving in."[76]

Though the burden for resistance often falls to vulnerable women, secure women may have a special calling to bold risk-taking. Carolyn Heilbrun has noticed that women in the last third of life are "likely to acquire new attitudes and new courage." She asserts that these elders can finally "stop being female impersonators" who live according the expectations of society.[77] Based on our study of girls, we might call it the surfacing of the underground women. The spunky girl who went into hiding at adolescence sometimes returns with vim and vigor to speak her mind again in later years. Recovering in herself the twelve-year-old who chews gum and lets her shirt hang out, the older woman "wears purple" and throws convention to the wind.[78]

In fact, Heilbrun, after writing about the prophetic potential of the later stages in life, at the age of sixty-six decided to retire earlier than she had to from her tenured position at Columbia University, noisily announcing that she was fed up with what she perceived to be the school's lack of attention to women's issues.[79] Heilbrun realizes that secure women in the later stages of life may be in the best position to take the kinds of risks that bring about liberation and transformation. She even recommends risk-taking in later life to avoid stagnation. "It occurs to me now that as we age many of us who are privileged . . . those with some assured place and pattern in their lives, with some financial security—are in danger of choosing to stay right where we are, to undertake each day's routine, and to listen to our arteries hardening," she warns. "I do not believe that death should be allowed to find us seated comfortably in our tenured positions. . . . Instead, we should make use of our security, our seniority, to take risks, to make noises, to be courageous, to become unpopular."[80]

Women who join together in communities of faith have much with which to wrestle: with a girl- and woman-denying culture, with disparities in the way that culture impacts different women, with varying opportunities for liberation and survival. We sometimes cause one another pain, and we sometimes view one another as rivals. As we imagine what it might be like to co-build our common house, a house that takes the messiness of life into consideration, it is important to name what it is that binds us together.

OUR HOUSEHOLD GOD: JESUS CHRIST, BORN OF MARY

In Christian communities it is commitment to Jesus the Christ, born of Mary, which bonds Christian women. This commitment, however, is a complicated one; we must strive with humans and with God to understand what it means to ground both our personal identity and community life in the God become incarnate. In the history of our churches, religious authorities have confused commitment to Christ with commitment to certain interpretations of Jesus Christ. The 'lordship' of Jesus Christ, an early Christian affirmation, has been translated into obedience to religious authorities who claim to be human representations of Christ. Thus, the source of our unity has been used to subjugate and control us. As Christian women co-build communities of faith, we must answer for ourselves the question Jesus put to his disciples, "*But* who do *you* say that I am?"

JESUS: SON OF WOMAN

In the Nicene Creed, Christians profess to believe in Jesus Christ, God's Son, "born of the virgin Mary." Christian history has often emphasized the fact that Mary was pure, but the real impact of this statement is that the One who is God incarnate was born to us through the body of a woman and formed in life through a woman's maternal care. As one theologian put it, God came to dwell with humanity, having a first home in a woman's womb.[81] Though the science of the time believed that the essential personhood of a child was contained in the sperm (the womb providing only nourishment and incubation), the Gospels turn this belief upside down by recounting a story that implies that it was the woman who provided the essential genetic matter of the incarnate God. Furthermore, in the eternal wisdom of God, Jesus did not spring forth fully mature, but rather grew through the ministrations and teaching of women. In addition to his mother who reared him, a Syro-Phonecian woman brought him to self-understanding (Mark 7). The patristics who spoke of Mary as "theotokos," God bearer, underscored one of the most profound traits of the One who is God in the flesh. God in our midst came from the flesh and blood of a young woman. Jesus, the One known as Son of Man, was profoundly Son of Woman.

JESUS: MALE LORD AND SAVIOR?

Because the historic maleness of Jesus Christ has been used to keep women out of leadership in the church, and because of their difficulty identifying with a male Savior figure, some women wonder if Christianity inherently excludes women from the fullness of participation in the tradition. If we claim Jesus the Christ as Lord and Savior, do we inevitably diminish women?

Although Jesus' maleness has been used to exalt men and to keep women out of positions of leadership in the church, the incarnation of God in the male person of Jesus of Nazareth actually represents divine rejection of male privilege. Drawing on his Jewish prophetic tradition, Jesus flouted many of the cultural expectations for male-hood, most significantly by using the power that was his as a means for empowering others. Rather than associate with those who would increase his stature, he was often found in the company of those with low status. He encouraged both men and women to break out of culturally prescribed expectations. Implicitly, he turned patriarchy—and its consequences for men and women—upside down. But, like a spring that maintains its shape no matter how hard you try to straighten it, the church turned it back around. Most perversely, rather than see Jesus as the reinterpretation of what it means to be male and powerful, the church has often interpreted his maleness as the seal of male aggrandizement while promoting his servanthood as exemplary for female self-sacrifice.

Not only did Jesus redefine manhood and womanhood, but he also provisionalized human authority. Even as faith in the God of Israel displaced fathers, lords, and kings, faith in Jesus Christ as Lord provisionalized all other male authorities (Matthew 23:1-12).[82] We can, in faithfulness to the rebellious impulse of our tradition, nurture women who will call no person father, lord, or king. We do this when we take care in using the imagery of lordship, and its corresponding notion of obedience.[83] When offering interpretations of who God in Christ is and what God calls us to do, we can avoid absolutizing these understandings.

Here it is crucial that we *never succumb to the temptation to take the rebellious bite out of the affirmation of Jesus Christ as Lord*. It has been very easy for the church's leaders to evacuate this affirmation of its meaning by identifying their own interpretations and doctrines concerning Christ with the truth. This not only turns obedience to Christ into obedience to an interpretation of Christ, it also translates the confession of divine lordship into a sanction for human lordship. It took no special pervertedness for Nazi leader Herman Goering to make the move from "it is no longer I who live, but it is Christ who lives in me" to "It is not I who live, but the Führer who lives in me."[84] Let us raise women, as well as men, who will not confuse Christ's lordship with the authority of leaders and rulers. Along with confessing Jesus Christ as lord, we can affirm what Rita Nakashima Brock calls "Christa community," where women are equal members of the body of Christ.[85] Even as Jesus liberates women from sexism, women must "liberate Jesus" from a long history of being coopted into reigning ideologies.[86]

As did the God of Israel, the Jesus of the Gospels associated with all kinds of women: women who broke with tradition and studied with him, women who stayed with tradition and served him, rough women who learned from the school of hard knocks, daring women who refused to be excluded from the master's house, creative women who subtly resisted, and broken women who had little resistance left in them. Their stories are recorded in fragments, often their names are not even remembered. When we piece together the scraps of their stories, we celebrate the fact that they participated in the building of the house we have inherited and they, along with Leah and Rachel, inspire us to build for the future.

As we close this exploration of different women's lives and choices, we recognize that gains are to be celebrated and costs are to be named. Vashti spoke her mind and lost her position; Thecla escaped domestic duties but she paid the price of her sexuality; Maria preserved her virginity but lost her life; Hagar survived the wilderness but she remained a slave; Anne hung on to the barest shred of life but was in danger of losing her family. There are varieties of oppressions, coping mechanisms (choices), and prices to pay for resistance; there are many faces of courage, ingenuity, and breakthrough. There are many foremothers in our history, some of whom were pioneers who did not see the fruits of their labors in their day. There are diversities of tradition for women to draw upon when coping and flourishing in their lives. No single situation and no particular response can be made normative.

Rachel is remembered in Jeremiah 31, weeping for her children when Israel is in despair. The final word of that memory is a hopeful one: "Keep your voice from weeping, and your eyes from tears; / for there is a reward for your work," proclaims the prophet. "They shall come back from the land of the enemy; / there is hope for your future, says the LORD: our children shall come back to their own country" (vv. 16-17). Then he magnificently states, *"The LORD has created a new thing on the earth; / a woman encompasses a man"* (v. 22, italics added). No longer in need of protection from a man, a woman in the new order is safe and equally strong.

Women in communities of faith can take part in creating this "new thing." They can even help turn stories of despair into hope for the future. In memory of Maria, they can become safe-houses for victims of abuse; in hope for Anne, they can teach others, especially boys and men, to share the burden of caring. Maria's story moves us to imagine: What "could have happened had this church been Maria's church?"[87] What if Maria knew her life would be valued even if she had been raped? What if Maria had a place of safety where she could have retreated after Allesandro's first

180

unwanted advances? What if the church regularly preached sermons against the abuse of girls and women, which had shaped Allesandro's definition of manhood? What if Maria had known about Vashti? Anne's story moves us to imagine: What if both Anne and her husband had been raised to give and receive caring? What if Anne had been part of a church that considered all children as part of our caring network so that stressed single parents do not have to go it alone? What if Anne had a safe place to cry out to God? What if Anne knew that she was supported by women and by God in her search for survival and quality of living?

Building our common house is a process of supporting one another and wrestling with one another, with tradition, and with God. This kind of supportive wrestling is where our hope lies; and it is at the heart of the educational ministry of the church. We turn to this in the next chapter. Women will wrestle together to prevail against those things that deprive women of well-being. Dare we hope for the day when God creates this "new thing"? When women encompass men and women for the flourishing of all? We dare. We dare. Let all the people who are at the gate, along with the elders, be witnesses. The Lord is making the women coming into our house like Rachel and Leah, who together built up the house of Israel.

Chapter Six

Women and Conversational Education

HARD DIALOGUE AND DEEP CONNECTIONS IN COMMUNITIES OF FAITH

". . . friends sometimes say, 'do we have to go that deep?'"
—bell hooks[1]

HARD DIALOGUE AND DEEP CONNECTIONS

Going deep, where we probe beneath the surface, where we question the way things are, and where it sometimes gets uncomfortable, is crucial for genuine relationality and mature caring. Communities of faith can be places where deep conversation happens, but too often they are not. I propose in this chapter that the educational ministry of the church provide the kind of holding environment where women and men can speak their voices and stay connected to one another. In this chapter we will explore *conversational education*, which is characterized by *hard dialogue and deep connections* in a community of diverse participants with a rich tradition.

In arguing for conversational education, I wrestle with two tensive strands in the fiber of feminist thought: (1) the thread of recovering women's experience of caring and connection and (2) the thread of promoting women's capacity for voice and differentiation. Women's ways of caring for and connecting with others have a lot to contribute to community life, and I will boldly build on this important legacy. Yet, I am concerned that the strength of feminist fiber not be weakened by an overemphasis on *recovery* of caring and connection, especially when the thread of caring has largely been spun for women by the hands of others. In chapters 1 and 2, we looked at the way in which a theological censure on self-assertion and promotion of self-sacrificial caring inhibits the development of voice in women; in three and four, we examined the importance of both separation and connection, prophetic voice and empathetic voice, for genuine relationality between persons. Here I wish to develop more fully the kind of educational ethos that promotes genuine relationality. In such an educational environment, girls, as well as boys, will be encouraged to "be much."

Education involves handing over to our daughters and sons the forbidden fruits of curiosity, inquiry, critical thinking, and voice. Rather than obedience and submission to the status quo, education is an invitation to "hard dialogue and deep connections": (a) with one another, (b) with Scripture and tradition, and (c) with God. In this chapter, we will look at these three aspects of conversational education. We begin by considering the importance of hard dialogue and deep connections with one another.

HARD DIALOGUE AND DEEP CONNECTIONS WITH ONE ANOTHER

The first aspect of conversational education, hard dialogue and deep connections with one another, names the crucial role that education plays in getting people to engage one another in honest and deep ways. Honest and deep conversation is easily thwarted in communities of faith, sometimes by harsh adversarial argumentation that silences some voices, other times by polite affirming discussion that keeps conversation on a surface level. Both inhibit "real-talk" in community life. The influential study *Women's Ways of Knowing* is a helpful starting point for identifying the nature of genuine conversation and the types of interaction that get in the way of such conversation.

The collaborative authors of *Women's Ways of Knowing* interviewed over a hundred women in order to understand women's cognitive styles. Like Carol Gilligan, these researchers were chagrined that early studies of knowing were done using male populations. From their empirical data, the authors described five styles of knowing characteristic of women.

The authors distinguish between "separate" and "connected" knowing. In separate knowing, the goal of learning is to be as objective and critical as possible. The learning is dispassionate and analytical; the learner tries to remove his or her subjective feelings and experiences from the process. The learner comes to another work or person as a critic who finds weaknesses in the object of criticism. In separate education, the learner is treated as one who comes in without knowledge and, through the process of education, ends up a "knower." In contrast, in connected knowing, the personal and subjective are valued. While critique and analysis are not avoided, the learning stance is more empathetic than critical. The learner not only seeks to understand the subject matter, but she or he seeks to relate it to concrete life situations. In connected education, the learner is already a "knower" and ends up building upon and reconstructing what is there.

A mature connected knower evidences a style of knowing that the authors name "constructed." Constructed knowledge begins with an awareness that the knower is an intimate part of the known. Women constructivists "show a high tolerance for internal contradiction and ambiguity. . . . They recognize the inevitability of conflict and stress and, although they may hope to achieve some respite, they also, as one woman explained, 'learn to live with conflict rather than talking or acting it away.' They no longer want to suppress or deny aspects of the self in order to avoid conflict or simplify their lives."[2] Significantly, constructed knowing involves "real-talk," a type of conversation that "includes discourse and exploration, talking and listening, questions, argument, speculation, and sharing."[3] The authors oppose this to "didactic talk," prevalent in separate knowers, where the speaker's intention is to argue for his or her position rather than share ideas, and where there is no attempt for those talking together to collaborate to arrive at a new understanding. Real talk is collaborative, mutual, and deeply inter- and intrapersonal. In such conversations, speaking with and listening to others include speaking with and listening to oneself. Real talk is empathetic, nonjudgmental, and receptive; and yet it is also passionate, honest, and self-disclosing.

According to the authors, the two styles of knowing, while not gender-specific, are gender-related. Men lean toward separate knowing, and women toward connected knowing. Furthermore, Western higher education is generally aimed at separate knowers. Many women struggle in the highly competitive, objectivist, individualistic, and adversarial "majority culture" of college classrooms. Based on the "doubting game," which finds weaknesses in the self, the subject matter, and one's fellow students, this environment, contend the authors, "separates" learners from their inner selves, from personal engagement with the subject matter, and from connections with one another. Such a milieu is frequently "debilitating rather than energizing" to women.

> Women students are reluctant to engage in critical debate with peers in
> class, even when explicitly encouraged to do so. Women find it hard to see

doubting as a "game"; they tend to take it personally. Teachers and fathers and boyfriends assure them that arguments are not between *persons* but between *positions*, but the women continue to fear that someone may get hurt.[4]

Though a good number of women learn the game and play it well, even many of these high-achieving women do not feel that the environment has been conducive to their creativity and growth. And thus, the collaborative authors propose an alternative "believing game," which is based on confirmation of each learner, connection between learners, and personal engagement with the subject matter. Given confirmation, the authors found, the women "felt they could 'just do anything.' Lacking it, as one woman said, they were 'crippled' and 'just can't function.' "[5]

The goal of "connected teaching" is to enable learners to integrate the knowledge they feel intuitively with knowledge they learn from others. While "doubting" may still be employed in real-talk, the authors contend that "believing" is preferred; thus a constructive knower would rather empathize with a new idea first, and she would rather build on her own fledgling ideas in a confirming rather than adversarial environment.

Real-talk as the authors conceive it is similar to what I am aiming for when I speak of hard dialogue and deep connections. When fully developed, this kind of conversation will enable communities to "go deep." Inviting all to participate as knowers, integrating personal feelings and life experience into abstract reflection, and calling for the discipline of listening to and understanding one another—-real-talk is both hard and deep.

KEEPING REAL-TALK "REAL"

It is not easy to keep a conversation real; there are many pressures to avoid the hardness and depth of real-talk. Both "separate" and "connected" forms of education can avoid "real-talk." Recall the story of Mary Toy recounted by her brother Will Tweedy, cited in chapter 4. Will, disciplined by the "razor strop" in order to amount to something, is chagrined that his sister is spared the strop. Raised in the "soft bed" approach because she doesn't need to amount to anything, the girl receives only sham discipline. Will is mad and Mama—who apparently does want her girl to amount to something—is fooled. What nobody seems to realize is that Papa is misguided on both counts. Neither the razor strop nor the soft bed is educationally sound. We can compare the razor strop to the negative side of separate education and the soft bed to the negative side of connected education. Both the razor strop and the soft bed get in the way of real-talk.

"SEPARATE" WAYS OF AVOIDING REAL-TALK: EDUCATION WITH THE RAZOR STROP

One of the greatest temptations for the separate knower is to take an adversarial stance and knock down another person's idea before he or she even has a chance to fully express it. This is especially true when the idea being offered is from a woman. Ideas that are not part of the dominant culture cause discomfort. Separate knowers, unused to ideas from women's spheres, may immediately wish to dismiss them or poke holes in them. In chapter 3, when we examined conversational caring, we considered ways in which male-biased ("separate") classrooms marginalize women. I will not repeat that discussion, but it is important to reiterate that silencing the ideas of women compromises real-talk, for the experiences and perspectives of women are essential for a deep, moral conversation.

Those who are most comfortable with separate forms of knowing and learning may fear the kind of connections that real-talk makes. Used to abstracting ideas from concrete situations, separate knowers will be uncomfortable with conversation that touches the messiness of life. They will gravitate toward theories and ideas, and they will want to work those theories through without bringing their own subjective experience and stories into the theorizing. Bringing in experience, especially women's experience of ordinary reality, is deemed an outside resource that contaminates pure reason—or pure revelation.

All theological reflection is influenced by experience; what is often considered to be "pure reason" or "pure revelation" is simply reason and revelation through the experience of those in the seat of intellectual or religious power. This doesn't make the reason or the revelation false, they may be valid—but only for those in similar contexts. The unfortunate correlate to pure reason is universal applicability. When we think we can receive revelation untainted by our experience, we think that revelation is applicable to all persons equally. Thus, ignoring the role of experience in reason and revelation can lead separate knowers to disregard difference by false universalizing.

False universalizing creates a pernicious false consciousness. Works that come from the dominant perspective (unmarked as having a perspective), because they are deemed universal, are considered to address the needs of

all. Works that come from a marked location (a perspective that is identified) are considered to be special interest. Although the issues raised by
women and others on the margins need to be considered by all persons,
they are often neglected by those who feel that such issues are not relevant
to them. Further resistance comes when any significant attention given to
women's experience is perceived as "that's all we talk about."

Hard dialogue does not mean that we argue until one side wins an argument or demolishes another's viewpoint. It aims to probe the depths of an
issue, to confront the complexities, and to consider other sides of the
issue. There are no winners and losers in genuine conversation; there are
participants who are together seeking and constructing truth.

Those who lean toward separate ways of knowing are not the only ones
who can avoid real-talk with one another. Those who favor connected
knowing face corresponding temptations.

"CONNECTED" WAYS OF AVOIDING REAL-TALK: EDUCATION AND THE SOFT BED

It can sometimes happen that education that takes "connected knowing" and "connected teaching" seriously may avoid the kinds of processes
that are associated with "separate knowing," especially distanced reflection and adversarial debate. Indeed, sometimes the collaborative authors
of *Women's Ways of Knowing* scorn such concepts as contention, judgment
and impartiality, favoring empathy, nonjudgment, acceptance, reception,
and feeling. It is important to correct the traditional overemphasis on
separate forms of knowing and teaching; but in appropriating connected
forms of education, we need to be careful we do not promote false connections by thwarting conflict. In their study of feminist classrooms,
Frances Maher and Mary Kay Thompson Tetreault were heartened by
the empowerment of women's voices, but they did raise some critical
issues. In particular, they observed that in many all-female classes taught
by feminist teachers, "students tended to support each other's contributions and to minimize their disagreement. This pattern of individual support and respect sometimes led to the repression of unresolved conflicts
among participants representing widely different social positions."[6] One
teacher self-critically reported that she had, in coming to the aid of
minority students trying to raise the issue of race, found herself "violat-
ing the cardinal rules of feminist pedagogy. I got angry and argued with
the class."[7] This is, I think, a misunderstanding of the "cardinal rules of
feminist pedagogy." Connectedness in the classroom does not mean that

we do not get angry and we do not argue; deep connections, in fact, require both.[8]

In a similar vein, Iris Young offers a general critique of the "ideal of community." Although community is a worthy goal for a group, it can lead to an avoidance of real-talk by defining its membership too tightly. Any group that desires community may privilege unity over difference, fusion over separation, homogeneity over tension. With sympathy, Young cautions that feminists have sometimes "looked for mutual identification and mutual affirmation in our feminist groups, finding conflict or respectful distance suspect." Impelled by common alienation from patriarchal society as well as by traces of their social grooming, feminists may re-create the kind of harmony-through-tyranny-of-the-nice-and-kind environments they sought to escape. Disagreement, difference, and deviation are interpreted as a "breech of sisterhood, the destruction of personal relatedness and community"[9] and thus are suppressed. Those who identify with the same ends, vocabulary, and practices will join together comfortably; those who are "other" will feel pressed either to assimilate to the group or to remain outside its bounds.

Surely, all communities have identity boundaries, and we must recognize that groups must define themselves and draw some lines of demarcation. Furthermore, relatively homogeneous groups of women do not always represent a setback on the journey toward female autonomy. Indeed, sometimes "safe" and comfortable places must be sought by marginal groups if they are to critique the dominant system they have internalized and gain some control over their construction of knowledge. Grassroots solidarity groups are particularly important for those who have little access to power. Minority groups, in particular, need to be wary of members of the dominant group who wish to "join in solidarity" with them; such "partners" often end up being paternalistic and even domineering. However, solidarity groups are transitional measures, and for women they are increasingly complicated as the unity of the category "women" disperses into many rays and as difference becomes a central concern for feminists. Solidarity that relies too heavily on sameness eventually breaks down as the particular identities of the group members increasingly differentiate. In fact, in recent years feminist groups, instructed by their womanist and lesbian sisters, have led the way in moving toward heterogeneity and the recognition of difference. As noted in chapter 4, it is particularly important that girls have "safe-houses" to explore their voices, not another narrow definition of what is permissible.

On the other side of things, real-talk that confronts the reality of women's pain can be hampered in mixed-sex discussion by women taking a protective posture on behalf of men. Magda Lewis has noticed that women will verbalize their concern over "how the men are feeling right now" in the middle of a discussion in which she raises critical issues about patriarchy in her college classroom. She attributes this to the "woman-as-caretaker ideology," which makes women feel that they must interpret everything through the lens of how it will serve the emotional well-being of men.[10] Although this kind of empathic caring can open a space for men to see that women are seriously struggling to both confront and empathize with men, it can also turn the floor over to men and away from the issues at hand. Lewis has found that if she takes the opportunity to name the caretaking stance of women toward men, she can then ask men how they might also show caretaking toward women in the uncomfortable contexts they might face (e.g., misogynous jokes, stereotyped stories, etc.). Thus, conversational caretaking, which here means gestures made to watch out for the well-being of another in a discussion, could be extended rather than discouraged.

In addition, we can help women learn to identify when difficult moments of consciousness-raising are acts of prophetic caring aimed toward restoring genuine relationality between women and men. Such care, as I have argued, does more than worry about one's comfort level in conversation, it also worries about the depth and competence of the relationship of caring. Sometimes we will make each other uncomfortable, but we will "stay put" for the one whom we have made uncomfortable so that we struggle through the discomfort together. Caring cannot result in bypassing difficult topics or avoiding criticism; then it is reduced to coddling. "Good criticism is an act of love, concern, and appreciation. It means an effort to continue the relationship, not . . . to cut it off."[11]

In contrast to over-connected education, Gloria Watkins (bell hooks) describes a very different pedagogy in her feminist classroom. It is worth quoting at length:

> My classroom style is very confrontational. It is a model of pedagogy that is based on the assumption that many students will take courses from me who are afraid to assert themselves as critical thinkers . . . (especially students from oppressed and exploited groups). The revolutionary hope that I bring to the classroom is that it will become a space where they can come to voice. Unlike the stereotypical feminist model that suggests

women best come to voice in an atmosphere of safety (one in which we are all going to be kind and nurturing), I encourage students to work at coming to voice in an atmosphere where they may be afraid or see themselves at risk. The goal is to enable all students, not just an assertive few, to feel empowered in a rigorous, critical discussion. Many students find this pedagogy difficult, frightening, and very demanding. They do not usually come away from my class talking about how much they enjoyed the experience.[12]

This is not a call to revive the "razor strop" of adversarial education, for the "believing game" is still a fundamental part of a confrontational classroom. It is a recognition, however, that both separation and connection are important to conversation. Adrienne Rich, in her influential essay "Taking Women Students Seriously," sums up very well how we best avoid the pitfalls of both connected and separate styles of knowing. For our women, she says, "we can refuse to accept passive, obedient learning. . . . We need to keep our standards very high, not accept a woman's preconceived sense of her limitations; we need to be hard to please, while supportive of risk-taking, because self-respect often comes only when exacting standards have been met." She goes on to clarify that this does not mean we should be training women to "think like men." "Men in general think badly: in disjuncture from their personal lives, claiming objectivity where the most irrational passions seethe."[13]

Thus, to ensure real-talk in communities of faith, we can aim to be affirming and critical, a "community of support" and a "community of inquiry."[14] A community of support provides a safe-house where people can come in honesty, voice, and freedom for difference—expecting to be listened to and (to the best of others' abilities) understood. The safe-house of support is to be distinguished from the basement, which suppresses honesty and struggle. A safe-house is affirming and tolerant of a variety of perspectives, but it contains within it the doors and windows of inquiry; the basement affirms only the status quo and closes off inquiry. To be a community of inquiry means that in conversation people seek truth together, question unexamined assumptions, and challenge one another to go deeply into the search.

For conversation to occur at the deepest levels, the boundaries can be stretched to include those who are strangers and outsiders to a community. This is particularly important for moral deliberations. Ethical thought and behavior require conversation not only between different individuals within one community but between different communities.

"All perspectives are partial and the creation of a moral vision and a strategy of moral action requires by definition the counterbalance of other groups and individuals," argues Sharon Welch.[15] Welch goes so far as to claim *a single actor cannot be moral* and that an isolated community cannot be faithful. The discernment of truth and true practice requires the interaction among those whose experiences, interests, and perspectives are different. Because all of our views are partial, and because our social locations influence our theologies, we cannot be moral unless we are in engagement with those who are different from us. Pluralism, the bringing together of those who are different, is required "not for its own sake, but for the sake of enlarging our moral vision."[16] Faithful moral and ethical deliberation requires the voices of many.

Stretching the conversational canopy begins when we provide spaces in our own communities for dissenting, prophetic, and unconventional voices. Stretching goes even farther when communities regularly listen to and engage with those who are different from them. In a recent study that brought representatives of diverse congregations together to discuss education, the researchers found that the participants greatly valued opportunities for congregation-to-congregation interaction. These experiences of "grassroots ecumenicity" were very difficult but proved to be transformative for those involved.[17]

In communities of faith, conversation with one another is joined by conversation with tradition and with God. We turn now to the former: hard dialogue and deep connections with tradition.

HARD DIALOGUE AND DEEP CONNECTIONS WITH TRADITION

Another scene from Olive Ann Burns's *Cold Sassy Tree* gives us a glimpse into what hard dialogue with subject matter might look like. Through her characters' rebellious wonderings, Burns repeatedly offers opportunities for the Cold Sassy community to scratch beneath the hard veneer of its religious dogma. Generally, such openings were sealed over before any depth probing was possible. However, in one poignant scene Will Tweedy, the fourteen-year-old hero of the tale, questioned the fundamentalist faith he inherited and found a coconspirator in his grandpa. The following conversation occurred after the death of Will's beloved grandmother. Will, through a freak accident, narrowly escaped death himself, and he realized that others were not so fortunate. He had trouble making sense of the inequality of suffering and hardship around him.

"Grandpa, uh, why you think Jesus said ast the Lord for anything you want and you'll get it? 'Ast and it shall be given,' the Bible says. But it ain't so." I felt blasphemous even to think it, much less say it out loud.

Grandpa was silent a long time. "Maybe Jesus was talkin' in His sleep, son, or folks heard Him wrong. Or maybe them disciples trying' to start a church thought everbody would join up if'n they said Jesus Christ would give the Garden a-Eden to anybody believed He was the son a-God and like thet." Grandpa laughed. Gosh, I'd get a whipping if Papa knew what was going on with the Word in his kitchen. "All I know," he added, "is thet folks pray for food and still go hungry, and Adam and Eve ain't in thet garden a-theirs no more, and yore granny ain't in hers, and I ain't got no son a-my own to carry on the name and hep me run the store when I'm old. Like you say, you don't git thangs jest by astin'. Well, I'm a-go'n study on this some more. Jesus must a-meant something else, not what it sounds like."[18]

In this conversation, Will presses deep and his grandfather plunges in with him. Such a discussion could not go on with most other folks in his community; it was deemed blasphemous. Fatalism was the accepted theology; one who questioned this fundamental premise would normally be told to "shet up," for "hit ain't for us to ast sech questions."[19] Grandpa listens and reflects "a long time" before offering his honest thoughts. Though his theological ramblings seem a bit crude, Grandpa permits real-talk, a conversation with depth. A conversation that not only allows for risky exploration, but one that opens up to future possibilities. Grandpa does not know all the answers, and the most important questions cannot be resolved with pat replies. Studying "on this some more" is not only an affirmation of Will's question, it is an invitation to go even deeper. Rather than being whipped for wrestling with the Word, Will was joined on the mat.

Here I'd like to explore what it means to wrestle with difficult texts, particularly looking at difficult texts dealing with women.

CONVERSATIONS WITH THE BIBLE

The relationship between women and the Bible can be a problematic one. Probably all of the biblical texts were written by men, most—though perhaps not all—of the texts reflect a patriarchal worldview, and most of the texts have either ignored or suppressed the history of women's participation in salvation history. Many women approach the Bible with a legitimate, and necessary, hermeneutics of suspicion toward the authors, and many also bring a hermeneutics of recovery, seeking to reconstruct what has been suppressed. A critical awareness of the realities embedded in biblical texts, however, does not necessarily lead to rejection of the texts.

In this section I will suggest that: affirming the Bible as "the word of God" implies engaging the Bible in conversation; such a conversation requires a community of interpreters and the voice of outsiders; the conversation of Bible study requires hard dialogue with difficult texts and deep connections to God's abiding presence.

Along with Sandra Schneiders, I understand the affirmation that the Bible is "the word of God" to be metaphorical. "Thus, when we call the Bible the word of God, we are not speaking literally but using a metaphor. For some people this immediately evacuates the faith affirmation, suggesting that the expression is either meaningless or radically untrue. Such is emphatically not the case because metaphor is perhaps our most powerful use of language and it always intends the truth."[20] It is in conversation that humans reveal themselves to one another, and thus to call the Bible the word of God is to affirm that we engage in conversation with the Bible for the purpose of understanding who God is. Even as human language only points to the person who is speaking, biblical testimony only points to God. And it comes by way of human witnesses, which is not spared human limitation.

To understand the Bible as the word of God means that we converse with it. We listen to it, we try to understand it, we allow ourselves to be challenged; and also we talk back to it, we argue with it, we critique it. In the conversation, we hope for mutual transformation, and we open ourselves to new truth emerging from the interaction of conversation partners. This means that we avoid two common pitfalls: submitting compliantly to the biblical witness or attempting to dominate the biblical witness. The former occurs when we uncritically accept all that we encounter in the biblical texts; the latter happens when we force the text to submit to our methods and theories about the Bible. We are subjects who bring ourselves to a critical conversation with the Bible, and the Bible is a subject that brings a rich and complex witness to the conversation.

We might look at the Bible itself as a conversation. The biblical texts as we have them record a history of conversation between the people of God, God's Spirit, and their life situation. The situation of the people has always influenced their understanding of God's activity. More than that, the texts invite conversation today as well. Something important is taking place between the conversants in Bible study in the present. When we read the Bible, we are not just overhearing a conversation between people and God back then, we are expecting God to speak to us anew, in our present situation.

Because I hold a conversational understanding of our relationship to the Bible, I do not propose a feminist selective reading of the Bible, one that holds as canonical only the "usable tradition" of liberating texts. This is problematic to me not for dogmatic reasons but because it inadvertently promotes a monological understanding of biblical authority. By only turning toward texts that liberate, we still imply that the Bible only speaks to us, we do not speak back to it (except to say that we will allow only certain of its words into the conversation). When we retain communion with the whole of Scripture, including questioning or even judging it, then we engage it conversationally. It is in the wrestling, rather than merely in the words of the text, that God and the good news of the gospel are revealed. Biblical scholar Katheryn Pfisterer Darr makes a point to "dissuade students who are tempted to ignore [difficult] texts from setting them outside the perimeters of their 'canon within a canon.'" "One may, after wrestling with a text, conclude that its content is not persuasive or acceptable, but that does not mean that the struggle should have been avoided, or that it was unimportant."[21]

Conversing with the Bible is an act of caring for the Bible; it is a desire to be in genuine relationship to its witness. Traditionally, we have been taught to bring empathy to our engagement with the texts, we have been instructed to listen to and receive the words we read. This is certainly an important part of serious conversation with God through the Bible. While empathy is one appropriate response to our conversation with the Bible, it is not all that we do. At the very least, the interests we bring to our listening already influence how and when we listen, it is impossible to be purely empathetic and receptive in our listening. I, however, propose that we acknowledge our side of the conversation with the Bible, and not only that, but we name the appropriateness of our "talking back" to the biblical material. Passionate, prophetic caring is also an aspect of our conversation with the Bible. We listen to, we speak to, and we converse with the Bible in a relationship characterized by hard dialogue and deep connections. In line with Abraham who argued with God, Jacob who wrestled the angel, and the Syro-Phoenician woman who rebuked Jesus, we do not simply receive our tradition as empty vessels but rather we take part in the traditioning process as genuine agents.

When women's voices are brought to the conversation a community has with the biblical tradition, a community is forced to wrestle with some very difficult stories and texts.

STRATEGIES FOR DEALING WITH DIFFICULT TEXTS

1. Correcting distortions in interpretation

The most obvious strategy when dealing with texts that are oppressive to women is to question the history of interpretation. For instance, a revisiting of the Genesis accounts of Eve exposes the way in which the assumptions of commentators influenced the history of interpretation. Because she took the forbidden fruit first and then gave it to Adam, Eve was dubbed the tempter by church fathers and frequently equated with evil itself. "Of all the stories of women in the Hebrew Bible, the story of Eve has been used more than any other as a theological base for sexism," notes Alice Ogden Bellis.[22] Tertullian considered all women to be of Eve, "the devil's gateway . . . the first deserter of the divine law" and thus the reason that the Son of God was compelled to die for human redemption.[23]

Looking with new eyes, with feminist eyes, we notice aspects of the story that were neglected and distorted by interpreters. The Eden tale itself, viewed with distance from the woman/sin-obsessed direction taken in the history of interpretation, portrays Eve as the primary agent and procurer of wisdom—and perhaps even the culmination of creation.[24] Indeed, the text "describes the first woman as an intelligent, perceptive, informed theologian or exegete who, unlike her passive partner, is familiar with the divine command and doesn't hesitate to reflect on it."

The problem leading to the break between humanity and God is not that Eve wanted knowledge, it is that Eve and Adam hid their desire from God and broke their relationship to God in order to attain it. The sin of Eve in this story, contrary to the history of interpretations, is not disobedience, pride, or the refusal to accept necessary boundaries. Unlike Abraham, who questioned God, and the Syro-Phonecian woman, who took Jesus to task for his narrow vision,[25] Eve along with Adam cowed before God. Perhaps like the Syro-Phoenician woman, Eve's assertion to God rather than clandestine disobedience would have changed the outcome. It is not the fruit tree from which Eve and Adam ate that should be associated with sin, but rather those other "trees of the garden," behind which Eve and Adam hid from God that should be the symbol of sin in the garden (Genesis 3:8). *The sin in this story is the sin of hiding.* Thus, the text beckons us to honestly and openly wrestle with our companions, with the rules and traditions we have received, and indeed with the One who created us.

Another text that I believe has been misinterpreted by many is Judges 11, the story of Jephthah's terrible vow. (Please read the story before proceeding if you do not know it.) Interestingly, Jewish tradition severely chided this leader who ends up sacrificing his daughter in his quest for glory. Though the biblical narrative is painfully silent, Josephus wrote that "it was a sacrifice neither conformable to the Torah nor acceptable to God."

Jephthah is, however, canonized in Christian tradition in the line of those who demonstrated great faith (Hebrews 11:32-40). Some call attention to the costliness of Jephthah's faithfulness, suggesting that he was a hero who paid a great price. Others, who stumble over the story, try to draw a more general point and indicate that the sacrifice of the daughter is only incidental to the story and it is not what we should take as the main point of the story. Both of these strategies are misinterpretations. The former justifies Jephthah's actions, suggesting the end justifies the means; the latter fails to notice the power of a text's implicit teachings. The story, when read without struggle, leaves us with a dead girl and the implicit message that the sacrifice of a girl is acceptable. Whenever we interpret texts, we need to look at the "implicit" stories that are being told in the background of our "explicit" stories. The silences and "insignificant" details of a story convey meaning to readers and hearers; it is our task as preachers and teachers to notice these teachings going on in the background. Their consequences are far from incidental to women's lives.

Some may include Judges 11 in the category below of an oppressive memory of suffering that needs to be named and resisted but cannot be redeemed. I categorize this as a text that has been misinterpreted, because Phyllis Tribe's literary analysis in *Texts of Terror* invites us into a closer reading, which reveals that Jephthah's vow and subsequent sacrifice of his daughter did not issue from faith but rather lack of faith. Jephthah calls upon God to give him victory in a battle against Israel's oppressors; the Lord sends the Spirit upon Jephthah; *then* Jephthah makes the vow that he will sacrifice to God whatever comes to greet him after his victory if God will bring him the coveted conquest. The story reaches its climax when his daughter, his only child, is the one who comes to meet him, dancing and playing the tambourine in celebration of his victory. Jephthah, clearly distraught that his vow forces him to sacrifice his daughter, seemingly chastizes the girl for causing him pain but stresses that he cannot break his promise to God. The unnamed girl asks only for some time away for mourning, and she then submits to death. According to the narrative, this became the occasion for the Israelite women to grieve the memory of the daughter of Jephthah annually.

Trible notes that the presence of God's Spirit ought to have been enough for Jephthah. Why would he press for more assurance? Was his faith so weak? Why also did he blame his daughter for breaking his heart when it was the foolish vow that was the cause for his loss? *Someone's* heart was going to be broken, even if not his. Perhaps, the daughter knew this and deliberately came first in order to spare potential victims the pain her father's rash oath would inflict on them.[26] The tenor of the tale is more likely the leader's foolishness rather than faithfulness. Indeed, in chapter 12, when this leader recounts his exploits as "I took my life in my hand," the narrator subtly reveals to us that this scenario indeed was the hand of Jephthah rather than the hand of God at work.

We do well to correct distortions by returning to the text and reading with new eyes, and consulting feminist literary critics can aid us in doing so. This strategy cannot redeem all difficult texts; not all texts are difficult because of faulty commentators. Some are difficult because the texts themselves are steeped in patriarchy and sexism. And yet, even some of these texts may have become distorted by literalism that adheres to the letter of the text and fails to see the movement of the Spirit that was operating behind the text. We turn now to the second strategy, which looks for and follows the movement of the Spirit.

2. Celebrating visions, following trajectories, and naming regressions

Good historical critical methods of biblical exegesis have always looked at the cultural and literary contexts of a text. When dealing with difficult texts concerning women, it is important to ask: Where does the text reflect or accommodate to the cultural assumptions about women? Where does it push the edges of the cultural assumptions in a way that we can follow a trajectory toward liberation?

There are at least four levels of texts concerning women in the biblical witness: (1) those that mirror and assume the patriarchal culture; (2) those that throw a partnership trajectory; (3) those that present a vision of male/female partnership; (4) those that have pulled back from a vision of partnership.

Texts that assume the subordination of women reflect the prevailing cultural ethos. We need not interpret these texts as signs that God approves or commands the subordination of women; we must use these to recognize that the biblical writers were human persons immersed in— though not limited to—the language, mores, customs, and assumptions of their day. The biblical witness mirrors human fallenness even as it reflects human inspiration.

Some texts both reflect and challenge the cultural assumptions toward men and women. By looking at what is new, rather than what is the same, sometimes we can see a trajectory toward greater liberation. What does the text set in motion? Where does it point? For instance, both the letters to the Colossians and to the Ephesians reflect cultural attitudes toward household order. Though reinstating the rule of lord, father, and husband, these texts also call for responsibility on the part of the lord, father, and husband to be caring. In a world when the submission of slaves, wives, and children was a given, the new word in some of these codes is the responsibility of the powerful not the obedience of the less powerful. This does not automatically "redeem" these texts for our guidance; for those who have a literal understanding of Scripture, the bald statement rather than the trajectory of the text is heeded. To follow a trajectory, we must look beyond the specific statements and imagine where the gropings toward liberation would lead. For those who are taught the practice of conversing with Scripture, however, looking for the trajectory of a text is indeed redemptive.

There are some texts that boldly announce God's intention for creation to be the equal partnership of women and men and free status for all people. Many feminists use Galatians 3:28 ("There is no longer Jew or Greek, there is no longer slave or free, there is no longer male and female; for all of you are one in Christ Jesus") as the hermeneutical key for interpreting other texts.

Finally there are those texts that reflect a "regression" based on pressure from the culture. In the epistle to Titus, for instance, the author bends over backward to order Christians not to cause offense to rulers, authorities, or anyone; in I Peter, the writer beseeches Christians to "maintain good conduct among the Gentiles [Romans]." The household codes repeated in various pastoral epistles are directly taken from Roman sources of the day. The fledgling church faced grave persecution, and the writers of these epistles wanted to quell suspicions that the church was destructive to family order. Indeed, the vision of human liberation was subversive to the patriarchal Roman family; that is why it attracted so many women and slaves. The self-understanding of the church as a new family based on faith rather than blood and the vision of equality and mutual respect were revolutionary. It is a great historic irony that the survival-driven compromise of the liberating vision gained the upper hand in the canonization of tradition. Once again, this strategy is not always appropriate. There are texts that seem to be "bad news" for women with no trajectory toward the good. In some of these cases, we turn to the biblical witness as a whole in order to interpret the part.

3. Identify overarching theological criteria

Whether or not it is acknowledged, every biblical reader/interpreter brings an overarching pre-understanding of the gospel to her or his encounter with the biblical texts. This pre-understanding is our dominant sense of the center of the Christian faith. Every part of the Christian canon is thus interpreted in light of the coherence of the whole. Some feminists claim that the liberating, prophetic tradition of the Christian canon is the overarching criterion by which all texts are judged. Just as Martin Luther used the gospel of Jesus Christ as the criterion by which he assessed the books of Esther and James as nonauthoritative, feminists use the liberating acts of God as a critical norm. How the critical norm functions can vary. Some speak of a "usable past," which suggests that there are portions of the tradition that are not usable. Or, some may still engage the whole of the tradition but approach the tradition with new questions in order to prevent texts that deny the humanity of others from being read and used as instruments for oppression.

When one acknowledges and names one overarching theological criterion, one opens up the Lutheran move of allowing the center to speak *to* and sometimes even *against* parts of the canon that obstruct the gospel. Sometimes, when preaching or teaching a text, one brings the gospel to bear on a text that does not contain the gospel.

Even when this strategy is used, the interpreter must be continually open to revising her or his overarching criterion. While Luther's privileging of the gospel of faith (over against a religion of works) was an important move, it sometimes led to the collapsing of an important biblical tension, that between judgment and grace. Luther's context made him sensitive to the destructiveness of judgment; some contexts may lean in the other direction. It may be that instead of a streamlined overarching criteria, we need to uphold tensions in biblical texts. For instance, an overemphasis on grace and forgiveness (as already noted in earlier chapters) can silence women's voices. Thus, we may need to preach and teach in such a way that we bring out the paradoxical, even kaleidoscopic nature of biblical reflection.

4. Conversations *between* texts

In additional to being a conversation between the people of God and God, the biblical texts converse with one another. The Bible is a conversation between diverse and sometimes tensive traditions and emphases. It argues with itself, corrects itself, interprets itself.

When considering the story of Jephthah's vow, it is helpful to compare it to the tale of Saul's "rash" oath. In I Samuel 14, Saul makes an oath very similar to that of Jephthah, and it places his own son Jonathan in peril of death. The parallels are striking. In both stories: the oath is related to battle victory; it is spoken unbeknownst to the child; the child unwittingly places itself in the situation of which the oath demands sacrifice; the child is willing to die when it finds out that the oath demands it. There is one crucial difference: the ending. In the Jonathan narrative, the people rebel against Saul's rigid adherence to the oath. To their own query, "shall Jonathan die," the people respond, "Far from it! As the Lord lives, not one hair of his head shall fall to the ground." The narrator completes the story: "so the people ransomed Jonathan, and he did not die."

Why is the child killed in the one and ransomed in the other? There are answers that can be given (such as Jonathan's value as a warrior, which the people used in his defense); but they only expose the cultural assumptions, they do not theologically justify the disparate conclusions. To bring these two tales together is to let the biblical stories converse with one another. We can deepen our dialogue with Scripture by introducing a number of different voices within Scripture.

Similarly, when women have texts commanding their obedience to lords and husbands hurled at them, they can recall Hebrew midwives Puah and Shiphrah, the initiators of the Exodus, who disobeyed and lied to Pharaoh because they served God not human beings (Exodus 1). They can summon the memory of Abigail, wife of Nabal, who corrected her husband's foolish behavior because she trusted her own wisdom in discerning God's work (I Samuel 25). Indeed, we are to call no man father, master, or lord (Matthew 23:8, 9), for "all who exalt themselves will be humbled, and all who humble themselves will be exalted" (Matthew 23:12).

When engaging two or more voices from Scripture, we may very well decide that one voice corrects and has priority over another. Thus, we may decide that the rebuke of Saul by the people exposes the sin of Jephthah as well. This does not mean that we eliminate from consideration those texts that have been subordinated. They carry important memories of suffering; for the sakes of the victims we cannot repress these memories.

5. Reading an oppressive text as a memory of suffering and a mirror of sin

Some of the most difficult texts to deal with are those that portray, and do not seem to condemn, violence against women. For a number of these texts, no reinterpretation is possible, and the trajectory, were we to follow it, is a trajectory of bondage and suffering. Such is the case of the story of the Levite's concubine in Judges 19. That story is fraught with misogyny. A father offers his virgin daughter and a Levite tosses his concubine to a band of rapists in order to save their own lives. "Ravish them [the women] and do whatever you want to them; but against this man do not do such a vile thing," pleads the father. The concubine is "wantonly raped . . . and abused . . . all through the night," and the men appear to have slept peacefully for the duration. The Levite is angry when he finds his concubine dead, and he provokes his compatriots to join him in retaliation. He craftily omits his role in her murder when he recites the events that took place. The story ends with a show of anger over the destruction of a Levite's "property," but no sign of condemnation toward the Levite's cowardly misogyny.

According to Irmgard Fischer, texts that do not explicitly condemn violence done against women cannot claim the authority of divine revelation but are to be "read as a memory of suffering in order to open up the perspective of hope for liberation as a dangerous, subversive recollection."[27] Thus, it is important, when we encounter texts that include memories of suffering, that we not gloss over the story. This is frequently done, with good intentions. Not knowing what to do with these stories, we either ignore them or we rush to find "the main point" and label the troublesome part only "incidental" to the story. While this is certainly better than claiming God's purposes to be revealed in the violence, it is necessary that we name the violence as sin, mourn for the victims, and identify where the same terror is brought upon women today. In our preaching, we can query, as one preacher did regarding Laban's atrocious treatment of his daughters, "Why is this story in Holy Scripture? Is it not more appropriate as a tale told around a campfire to entertain shepherds than as a message in the sanctuary for the edification of the saints?" And we can also, as did that preacher, "catalogue the embarrassments that throng the text," leading us to suggest: "though this is not an edifying story about God, it is certainly a masterful story about perversity in human nature."[28] When we ignore difficult texts, or when we read them and let them sit before the people without comment, we implicitly communicate that we comply with the (oppressive) situation in the text or that the gospel has nothing to say about the situation.

When remembering women's history of suffering, we need to watch the tendency to hold up the victims of violence as exemplars of faithfulness who were obedient till death. It may be appropriate to note the courage of Jephthah's daughter in accepting her fate, but resistance would have been courageous also. Whatever qualities in the daughter we wish to remember, our admiration of the girl cannot let us forget that she was a victim of an act that we justifiably resist.

6. Naming the sin in the text and resisting oppression

All too often we equate piety and devotion with passive obedience to the biblical texts. Resistance, however, can be a sign of a deep piety. While devout people do certainly listen to and read the Bible, they also actively engage it. Howard Thurman's grandmother is a wonderful rolemodel for the kind of deep connection to the Bible that includes hard dialogue. Thurman, who frequently read the Bible to his grandmother, noted that she was "most particular about the choice of Scripture." She was resistant to most of the Pauline Epistles, and when he asked her why, she replied: "During the days of slavery, the master's minister would occasionally hold services for the slaves. Old man McGhee was so mean that he would not let a Negro minister preach to his slaves. Always the white minister used as his text something from Paul. At least three or four times a year he used as a text: 'Slaves, be obedient to them that are your master . . . , as unto Christ.' Then he would go on to show how it was God's will that we were slaves and how, if we were good and happy slaves, God would bless us. I promised my Maker that if I ever learned to read and if freedom ever came, I would not read that part of the Bible." [29]

This pious woman, out of devotion to a Maker who transcended the pages of her cherished Bible, resisted oppressive teachings. While I stated above that I do not wish for communities to abandon difficult and even oppressive portions of the Bible, sometimes it is necessary for people who have been victimized by those portions to resist them completely—at least for a while. Even when individuals and communities keep the conversation with difficult texts going, they express their faithfulness to their Maker by resisting that which works against God's creating, sustaining, and redeeming purposes.

7. Giving voice to the silenced conversation partners

One form of resistance that is particularly creative is to rewrite or interact with a text or narrative to give voice to silenced players. As noted in the introduction to this book, that is often the purpose of feminist midrash, and that is what I did with Vashti. This can be done in many ways. We can simply bring attention to the silenced persons who are in the story but have no voice, as we did with the Levite's concubine. We can bring in the perspective of background players who are left out of a narrative, as we might bring in Sarah's perspective if we were studying Abraham's near-sacrifice of Isaac. We can do this abstractly or by setting up a dialogue between players; we might imagine what Sarah would say to Abraham if she found out about his planned journey to Moriah. Or, we can offer a reconstruction of the story that grants the silenced players a voice, and perhaps even changes the plot and outcome. This would not be done to replace the scriptural text; it would be done as the act of engaging with the text.

Sometimes, we do not have to create a voice for the silent women, we can recover a voice that was exercised but left out of recorded history. Elisabeth Schüssler Fiorenza has done important work on recovering such repressed voices. By looking back over the Christian tradition with an eye to women's participation, she has carefully reconstructed the active role of women in the early days of the Christian movement. The harshness of the Epistles toward women and the regression of the church toward the household codes expose the fact that, for a while at least, the church had taken seriously that "in Christ there is no male and female" and unleashed female power. The canonized edicts demanding women's submission reveal that both church and culture were uncomfortable with a "discipleship of equals" and worked to overturn that reality. When the epistle orders: women be silent in church, we can read in the gap: women have been talking in church; when the epistle commands: slaves submit to your masters, we can read in the silence: slaves have questioned the legitimacy of their masters. Sometimes when we converse with the Bible, we have to listen for the voice behind the written word.

8. Focus on the questions the text asks rather than the answers it gives

In her essay on troubling texts in Ezekiel—texts that blame the people for their suffering, claim that God brought evil upon them, and justify the abuse of women by analogy—Katheryn Pfisterer Darr advises us to ask such questions as: Why did Ezekiel construct such stories? What were the problems that led him to speak as he did? Looking behind the authors' offensive answers to the questions concerning human responsibility and divine response enables us to see a groping "refusal to abandon faith in God in the midst of crippling tragedy." Though the horrendous answers the authors give may lead us to neglect the book, the questions it raises are important. "Sometimes we continue to embrace hurtful texts not because we affirm their answers, but rather because they force us to confront the important questions," concludes Darr.[30]

One of the most compelling features of the biblical witness is that it deals with hard, deep, and timeless questions. Questions such as, "Where is God in this?" "Why do people suffer?" "What kind of response does a just God make to human irresponsibility?" and "Will our faith sustain the tests that have come along?" the questions at the heart of Ezekiel's justifications of God, are perennial concerns. Other biblical writers address them, and in a kaleidoscope of ways. The answers did not become fixed; indeed, some texts were written specifically to complement or correct others. Many commentators contend that the book of Ruth, striking for its openness to a foreign heroine, is a corrective to Ezra and Nehemiah, equally striking for their closed-minded fear of foreigners.

When affirming the questions of a troubling text, it is important that we still expose the implicit messages that are being communicated. Just as disliking the answers does not excuse us from conversing with the questions, neither does identifying the questions as good ones excuse us from critiquing the answers. Comparing Israel to a harlot who deserves to be humiliated and abused will have harmful consequences for women. Indeed, even though Ezekiel uses the imagery inclusively (that is to say, both women and men are compared with harlots), the inclusivity breaks down; by Ezekiel 23, putting an end to lewdness in the land has been telescoped into putting an end to the lewdness of women (v. 48).

9. Discernment concerning texts that express raw feelings

The various genres of biblical narrative were written for a variety of reasons—and are appropriate for different settings. There are some texts that express the deep, raw human emotions of bitterness, vengeance, and hatred. These texts can be helpful if we use them in contexts where we interpret them, but they can be harmful if we read them to a community without any interaction with them. Psalm 137, that beautiful lament that ends with a vivid image of bashing the babies of one's enemy against a rock, is one such text. We are appalled when we read it, and we are likely to skip over the troubling section when we read it. Excising the offensive text is, however, unnecessary and undesirable.

Here we must distinguish between using texts for "passive formation" and using texts for "engaged (conversational) formation." Passive formation refers to the reading or reciting of tradition without conversation with it. While there may be conversation going on silently in the mind of the hearer, and thus "passive" may be a bit of a misnomer, there is no space provided in the traditioning event for conversation. There are many texts and liturgical pieces that provide passive formation; they are repeated in worship contexts, and they shape our faith identities in subtle ways. The shaping power of texts used in this manner may be beneficial—or it may inadvertently be destructive. Were a community to use Psalm 137 frequently in a passive manner, the hearers might subtly be encouraged toward bitter vengeance on their enemies. Texts such as Psalm 137, in my view, should not be read as a liturgical piece that is left before the hearer without any discussion or interpretation.

Using this text for engaged formation, in a setting where people are free to name the raw feelings as their own and then seek constructive ways to deal with the anger, pain, and hurt is helpful. As noted in chapter 3, women often have a hard time expressing their anger; anger is considered to be both unfeminine and unchristian. If women are introduced to texts such as Psalm 137, then they will know that the pious sometimes feel bitter and vengeant, and that there are sometimes good reasons for those feelings. Reading these texts can be especially cathartic for those who have been victimized or abused. As leaders, we will need to take care to provide the resources for joining the process of catharsis with constructive response.

10. Recognize new ways for texts to function; God is still conversing with us

One of the subtle messages in the book of Esther seems to be the ludicrousness of the law that cannot change. Ahasuerus treats his own word as fixed, even when it is a foolish word; the author seems to say that this absurd obsession with stability creates massive instability. Could this be "a veiled reference to Torah"?[31] Could the author be stating that stagnant texts, even sacred ones, bring death to a community?

Drawing on rabbinic practice, Alicia Ostriker bids women to celebrate and take part in the lively conversation that biblical interpretation has always generated:

> The rabbis have long told us, "there is always another interpretation."
> If biblical interpretation until the present moment has been virtually
> exclusively the prerogative of males, so much the more reason for women
> to make a beginning. "Turn it and turn it," the rabbis say of Torah,
> "for everything is in it." As the poet Adrienne Rich long ago asserted,
> "Re-vision—the act of looking back, of seeing with fresh eyes, of entering
> an old text from a new critical direction—is for women more than a
> chapter in critical history; it is an act of survival." The truths of women,
> then, along with the truths of men.[32]

Even though the words of the biblical witness are fixed, the meanings and functions of the texts are open. New meanings can emerge with new interpreters. To borrow imagery from the book of Ruth, we need not behave like poor relatives, reduced to following behind the interpretive reapers, gathering whatever usable grain falls to the ground from their sheaves (Ruth 2). We ourselves are reapers, harvesting fresh grain from the field of our kinsmen, shaping our own sheaves. Where the biblical writers and interpreters bundle Eve's actions into a sheaf of sin, we come through and bundle a sheaf of courage; where the biblical interpreters bundle the tale of Esther into a sheaf while carelessly letting Vashti's character fall to the ground, we come through and not only glean these fallen grains of Vashti's courage but we wrap them around the entire bundle; where the biblical writers and interpreters leave the tightly wrapped sheaves of violence against women standing undisturbed in the storehouse, we come through and open up the bundle, exposing the putrefied grain that lies inside.

New and different truths are revealed when new and different conversation partners are welcomed. This is what makes a conversational model of small group Bible study so valuable.

THE CONVERSATIONAL WORD: BIBLE STUDY THAT IS MORAL

Stanley Hauerwas, in his characteristically provocative manner, recently wrote: "No task is more important than for the church to take the Bible out of the hands of individual Christians."[33] Hauerwas brings judgment upon the way in which many contemporary Christians read Scripture privately, without knowledge of the tradition, and separated from ethical practice. To a certain extent, I agree with this judgment. Although I do not wish to overturn the gains of the Reformation, which put the Bible precisely into the hands of common people, I do wish to correct an immoral outcome from those gains. When individual persons and communities read the Bible from only one perspective and apart from practice in the world, they engage in a conversation that is too narrow. Returning to Sharon Welch's statement that a single actor cannot be moral, I contend that Bible study done from a single viewpoint cannot be moral. All engagements with and interpretations of the biblical witness are biased (in both helpful and not so helpful ways) and partial. Certainly individual voices—including dissenting voices, minority opinions, and prophetic challenges—are essential to Bible study. Furthermore, individual persons who are in oppressive contexts may find much-needed solace in their private devotional lives. Nevertheless, conversational wrestling with the Bible requires a community of diverse interpreters *and* the voices of outsiders to be faithful.

Small group Bible study can help build a community's ethical and moral life together, but it is subject to the immorality of narrowness. Sociologist Robert Wuthnow, leading expert on small group life in North America, tells us in his book *Sharing the Journey* that 40 percent of North Americans are in small groups, and two-thirds of those groups are Bible studies or adult prayer groups. Although Wuthnow is heartened that so many Americans have found some form of community life, he is troubled by the character of many of these groups. Based on his empirical research, he offers the following portrait of contemporary small groups: they are self-chosen, and they are generally homogeneous. Harmony and comfort are more important than grappling with hard issues, which gives many groups a sentimental quality. There is a tendency to domesticate the Bible to the needs of the individuals in the group, and God is generally experienced as friend or comforter. Commitment to these groups is often light, and the scope of the group's involvement in everyday life beyond its meeting is limited.

Small groups are not inherently provincial and shallow. Small group Bible study in particular can expand and enrich people's consciousness. It is beyond the scope of this book to give a method for Bible study; in a book that builds on this one, I will offer "a conversational model for Bible study."[34] Here, let me state that in my view Bible study that is moral involves a community of interpreters in serious conversation and practice with the Bible, and it actively seeks the interpretive voices of those who bring an outside perspective.

Several years ago, I served for a few years as a minister of education in a fairly affluent and well-educated congregation located in a secluded suburb. Though the town was bordered by a large, crime-ridden city on one side and several small, industrial working class communities on the other sides, it had the feel of being a haven in a troubled world. Many of the young families who moved there chose this borough for its safe ambience. One of my most important responsibilities was pastoring church school teachers. In response to one woman's request, I began a Bible study/prayer group for the teachers. Although there was a handful of male teachers, those who attended this group were all women.

Jane was a participant in this weekly group. In addition to the Bible study group, Jane was also involved in a prison ministry. Every week she joined a small cadre of folk who visited a women's prison. Although a big part of the prison visitation group's mission was to bring craft projects for the women prisoners, they also brought conversation, Bible study, and prayer.

Jane's involvement with the prison ministry became part of the Bible study. At first she "brought the prison" (so to speak) to the Bible study group by asking for help with donations, bringing Christmas packages to wrap, and sharing general concerns in prayer. Then she "brought the prisoners" to the group by way of narrative; she would tell their stories and express her personal involvement with their lives. She also began to struggle openly with both her fear and even her repulsion toward these "criminals" and her simultaneous sympathy and even sense of common humanity toward these women. She brought Angie, her favorite, a surprisingly gentle soul who in desperation and drunkenness had killed her abusive husband. She brought Suzanne, Corinne, and Donna who were transformed from inmates in cells to persons with stories and even faces. We heard about poverty, racism, helplessness, violence, abuse, prostitution, homelessness, and abandonment. We saw glimmers of strength, determination, faith, hope, and love in the midst of hopelessness and recidivism.

Finally, Jane "brought the group" to the prison. I began visiting the prison, and the lives of the women prisoners became an integral part of the Bible study group's life. People didn't just add Angie to their prayer list, they also asked about her regularly. They didn't just think about Corinne at prayer time, they thought about her when they were interpreting the Bible passage. The lives of the women in prison became "voices," strikingly "other" voices, as these women gathered to hear and study the Scripture together. The context for interpreting the Bible was changed; the word of God to be heard had to make sense for and of Angie's life as well as for Jane's life.

To varying degrees, this began a process of enlarging the group's notion of both Christian community and humanity. In the walls of the haven, windows and even doors to the outside were being constructed. Most group members were able to make the transition from thinking of the women as "inmates" to be ignored to considering them "sisters in God's love" with whom to minister. The ministry *to* this prison group became a ministry *from* the group as well. The prayer group started to reflect on the way in which both privilege and deprivation chart the course of lives; we started to hear the hopelessness and helplessness of those whose destiny was wrought by the latter. We tried to hold in tension our awareness of "sin" and seeming bad choices with compassion for the "sinner" and understanding of the origin of those choices, and we made strides toward recognizing our own need of the grace that became more tangible and central in their lives. We cried to God for the pain experienced and caused by these women, and we cried to God for the pain we felt as their voices intruded upon our quiet world.

Certainly there were vestiges of an "us-they" dichotomy between the two worlds, and the windows and doors never brought the walls tumbling down. But the group's world had been irrevocably enlarged beyond its original, somewhat provincial family centeredness. And, most strikingly, the group moved toward embracing its own marginalized members and its own hidden brokenness. A schizophrenic member whose disruptiveness bothered the group was perceived with new eyes; and not only as one to whom to minister but also as one who brought gifts. The sharing of mutual concerns and need became ritualized. Group members were repeatedly mobilized both to seek care from one another and to offer care to one another. Facades of perfection began to be lifted as honest sharing took place. In opening to these "strangers" in prison, members in the group also recognized the strangers within the group itself as well *as the strangeness within each member.*

I use this illustration because it describes a very ordinary way in which a small group Bible study, nudged by one of its members (Jane), made itself moral. By "sharing the journey" with those who were different, even though it did so in a rather modest way, this group ventured into places it would not ordinarily have gone. To be sure, the Bible was not unleashed in revolutionary ways, but neither was it domesticated. The dialogue was harder and the connections deeper when the prison came to the Bible study.

A community of faith where people wrestle with one another and with tradition must not be afraid to wrestle with God. Although this is already implicit in the discussion on wrestling with the Bible, now we name it directly. Hard dialogue and deep connections also characterize our conversations with God.

Hard Dialogue and Deep Connections with God

One evening several years ago, after reading the story of Abraham's near-sacrifice of Isaac, our family wrestled with what the story might mean. We listened to the story, questioned the story, put ourselves in the story, and even attempted midrashes on the story (wondering if Sarah intervened on behalf of Isaac to God, and thus the ram). My son Paul eagerly participated in the discussion but remained dissatisfied with our gropings. Finally, we decided to pray, and this (then) five-year-old ardently addressed God, no holds barred. "God, why in the world did you tell Abraham to do that to Isaac? I don't think it was such a good idea. Don't do that again, God."[35] After praying, Paul looked as if a load had been lifted from him. He announced with confidence, "God heard my prayer. God hears everything because he is here with us."[36] Paul was not about to let this story slip by without calling God to task. He was no doubt spurred by knowing of Abraham's tussling with God over the destruction of Sodom (Genesis 18). The tradition of Jewish *chutzpah*, the questioning of earthly and divine authority, which began with Abraham and continued through the prophets found an exemplar in my house.[37]

Churches, according to Annie Dillard, could use a little more of this kind of questioning. She asked, "Why do people in churches seem like cheerful, brainless tourists on a packaged tour of the Absolute?"[38] On one occasion, when Dillard was in church, a minister broke through the facade, and she was impressed:

> Once, in the middle of the long pastoral prayer of intercession for the whole world—for the gift of wisdom and its leaders, for hope and mercy to the grieving and pained, succor to the oppressed, and God's grace to all—in the middle of this he stopped, and burst out, 'Lord, we bring you these same petitions every week.' After a shocked pause, he continued reading the prayer. Because of this, I like him very much.[39]

Pauses for honest outbursts have no place in a "packaged tour of the Absolute," but they are needed for real-talk with God and for authentic relationships in communities of faith. Our talk with God and about God requires "diving deep" into the realities of life and "surfacing" only when we have wrestled with our God.[40] We worship and trust in a God whom we believe brings life and redemption; we can hold that God accountable to divine promises. It is our privilege, our right, even our responsibility as the people of God to lament and question when the fullness of life is denied to some persons. We do bad theology when we justify suffering or find only redemptive elements in suffering and thus refrain from questioning God and ourselves.

"What God do for me? . . . He give me a lynched daddy, a crazy mama, a lowdown dog of a step pa and a sister I probably won't ever see again," wrote Celie in Alice Walker's *The Color Purple*.[41] When we experience times "when there are no angels present" to redeem us from tragedy,[42] the one thing we do have is the right to summon those angels to wrestle us. Franklin Littell, noting that Christians can learn a lot from Jewish chutzpah, which encourages wrestling with God, remarked that Christians "have not usually been trained to wrestle with the angel, to question what happens under God's sovereignty." Instead, many of our theologians have "raised obedience, submission, and acceptance of one's fate . . . to religious virtues."[43] Similarly, Shawn Copeland, writing on the suffering of black women, warns against an "impoverished idealism" that inculcates "the cardinal virtues of patience, long-suffering, forbearance, love, faith, and hope," in such a way as to forestall resistance and bind sufferers to their condition.[44] This returns us to issues raised in chapter 1 of this book; our theologies are taming, even breaking our spirits, and we hold ourselves back from a genuine relationship to God.

It is commonplace for communities to espouse theologies that link faithfulness with prosperity and well-being, but this is not the experience of many people, especially girls and women.[45] As we have seen, girls are all too often the victims of discrimination, physical and emotional abuse, and rape. Not knowing where else to take their anger, some will turn it on themselves in self-destructive behavior or inflict it on their own children. We need to give girls and women, along with boys and men, the knowledge that they can cry out to God, lament God's seeming absence, and demand God's presence in the wrestling. We cannot promise anyone that a ram will be provided by divine intervention; but we can assure them that God is present with them when they resist suffering and hold accountable those who cause suffering. The forbidden fruit of theodicy, when partaken in a supportive community, can be nourishing to the soul.

Here I come to another marvelous "turning" of the Torah.

JOB'S WIFE: THE HELPMEET OF THE ANGELS

In the prologue to the story of Job, when our hero has lost children and cattle and is inflicted with an agonizing disease, Job's wife takes God to task. Scorning her husband's pious resignation to his fate, she challenges: "Do you still persist in your integrity? Curse God, and die" (2:9). Job rebukes her challenge as the speech of a "foolish woman," and he counters that they must receive the bad as well as the good from the hand of God. Augustine was incensed at the wife's provocation of her husband, and he dubbed her "the helpmeet of the devil." And yet, interestingly enough, the unfolding story of Job suggests the opposite. Her words are followed by the lengthy dialogues between Job and his pious friends, and it is clear by the end that God disapproves of the empty platitudes the friends offer in the face of Job's suffering. In fact, God's "wrath is kindled against" them for their shallow attempts to justify God and blame Job for his plight. Although the tale ends cryptically, it seems clear that God prefers Job's protest against divine injustice to the dogmatic, thoughtless faith of his friends.

By setting the comment of Job's wife just before Job's own wrestling with God, the redactor of the story hints that it is her impatience with God that ushered in Job's development. "Much like Eve, the well-known 'helpmeet' to whom Augustine alludes, Job's wife spurs her husband to doubt God's use of His powers, but in doing so she does him much good, for this turns out to be the royal road to deepen one's knowledge, to open one's eyes."[46] Having questioned God (42:4), Job is both humbled and enlightened.

As it turns out, Job not only engages in deep dialogue with God but also enters more fully into human community. In contrast to the lonely, rather controlling figure (obsessed by whether or not his children have sinned in their hearts, 1:5) in the beginning, we are met with a host who welcomes and entertains visitors by the end. Formerly complacent in his theology, now his own grappling with suffering has enabled him to see things from the perspective of others who suffer. In his "powerful speech in 24:1-17 Job describes the desperate condition of the very poor . . . [drawing] particular attention to the plight of the widow and the orphan. . . . Here Job stands in solidarity with all the wretched of the earth."[47]

Official theological reflection is often done by privileged people who, relative to the rest of the world, enjoy a fair amount of power, influence, comfort, and control. This can issue in optimistic, triumphal, and conquest-oriented theologies that suppress the realities of failure, oppression, and defeat. The cries of women and others who suffer are not only permissible threads but also needed strands in the cloth of our theologies so that they are not woven from an inadequate fiber.

Communities of faith that welcome real-talk with God give permission for people to grapple privately with God and also provide opportunities for people to lament in the midst of others. A leader can make this possible by promoting a vision of God's justice that cares for the vulnerable, by creating an environment that shares the burden of empathy, and by guiding people to make decisions to act on behalf of others. We now turn to a discussion of the role of leadership in communities of faith that seek to promote hard dialogue and deep connections.

Chapter Seven

Caretaking Leadership

WOMEN OF FIRE AND MOTHERS OF ISRAEL

"At that time Deborah, a prophetess, woman of fire, was judging Israel. She used to sit under the palm of Deborah . . . and the Israelites came to her to dispense justice."
—Judges 4:4, 5[1]

"Are you kidding me; Deborah is really in the Bible? How come no one ever told me before?"
—Susan, twenty-year-old churchgoing college student

"Reading the story of Deborah is what prompted me to go into pastoral ministry. Until I read that story (in college) I had no real sense that women really could be leaders in the church."
—Dolores, twenty-one-year-old college student

Keeping in mind the vision of "hard dialogue and deep connections" from chapter 6, we come to the question in this chapter: What kind of leadership promotes such conversation in community life? As we probe this question, let me begin with two case studies that demonstrate leadership decisions that can inhibit conversation in a community.

Consider the following classroom scenario:

I watched a bright colleague of mine teach a small and enthusiastic group of advanced Women's Studies students. Discussion went very well, up to a point, on a number of tough theoretical issues about female imagery in women's art. Although I knew my colleague knew perfectly well how to synthesize the disparate issues the students brought up, I watched her suppress her own capacity to conceptualize what the students had discussed.[2]

For the purposes of discussion, let's call this professor Dr. Bright. Dr. Bright, a caring teacher who sought to encourage and empower her students, withheld a great deal that she had to offer them. Why did this professor hide her viewpoint and skill and recoil from using her authority? What did the students lose by her restraint?

Consider now the case of Heritage United Methodist Church, reported in *Handbook for Congregational Studies*. Located in an ethnically changing community, this congregation, which began as a community of struggling European immigrants, received the Reverend Deborah Jones as its pastor. After launching a study of the area, which revealed that the church was surrounded by aging persons living in deteriorating housing, Rev. Jones convinced the administrative board to convene a meeting to consider sponsoring a housing project for the elderly. She had the encouragement of the bishop and the backing of a local bank, and she thought the congregation would move ahead on this project for which she had great passion. Indeed, there were congregational members who lived in the substandard housing.

At the board meeting, however, Rev. Jones discovered that the people were not behind the project. One board member argued that, in view of the decline in church membership and budget, they should begin to upgrade the church school and hold off on the housing project. "Too many of the church's resources are already going outside the church, and not enough is available to nourish the congregation's faith and worship," seemed to be the majority view. Though Rev. Jones then pointed to the church's own history as a mission for immigrants and the United Methodist tradition of caring and service, she did not persuade the board. The project was vetoed. "The pastor was perplexed. It seemed to her that Heritage had just passed up its first opportunity in a long time for new purpose and renewal."[3] Why did Rev. Jones fail in her bid to mobilize her church for service to the community? Her vision was a good one; what went wrong?

Dr. Bright demonstrated a great capacity for *power-sharing* in her leadership. Drawing on the understanding of caring presented in chapter 3, we can say that she cared empathetically for the group. She, however, demurred both from offering her own critical analysis and from developing the group's capacity for drawing conversation toward closure; thus, the group was empowered to share but uninformed by the teacher's view and undisciplined in bringing their insights together into any kind of summary or application. Rev. Jones, in comparison, offered very clearly her own *prophetic vision* for compassionate community life. She, however, shortchanged two other aspects of caring leadership, *empathy* for the people and *wise conversation* with the people. She didn't seem to be in touch with or take time to mobilize the people's viewpoints and needs. Leadership involves the kind of caring that both of these women have to offer, but with a tempering by the other aspects of caring; it is a complex blend of prophetic (visional), empathetic, and conversational caring.

In this chapter we will examine what I call "caretaking leadership," leadership that manifests the fullness of genuine caring as described in chapter 3. To begin our discussion of leadership, we will engage a particularly relevant biblical narrative: Judges 4 and 5, the story of a leader named Deborah. Our conversation with this text will be in light of the above case studies and our ongoing concern for girls' development. As with the other tusslings with biblical texts in this book, I am also engaging this one to recover it for our corporate memory and vision. The statements above, made by Susan and Dolores, have been made in various forms by other college women during workshops I have led. Sadly, Susan is more representative than Dolores; our girls' psychological and religious imaginations aren't being shaped by this story. My hope is that there will not be one single girl in Jewish and Christian communities who will have the same experience as Susan. My dream is that our girls will (and earlier in life than Dolores) have their imaginations shaped by the story of Deborah so that they see themselves as legitimate agents and potential leaders as they grow in communities of faith.

DEBORAH: WOMAN OF FIRE AND MOTHER OF ISRAEL

Reading the story of Deborah feels more like a jump into the future than a peek into the (quite distant) past. In 1898, Clara B. Neyman asked:

> If Deborah, way back in ancient Judaism, was considered wise enough to advise her people in time of need and distress, why is it that at the end of the nineteenth century, woman has to contend for equal rights and fight to regain every inch of ground she has lost since then?[4]

Indeed, the story of Deborah seems to suggest the opposite of the Virginia Slims ad, for we have gone a long way back, baby. Various Christian commentators and preachers throughout history, afraid that Deborah would set a precedent, warned that Paul *overturned* Judges 4 and 5 in 1 Timothy 2:12 ("I permit no woman to teach or to have authority over a man; she is to keep silent").[5] Tragically, far more people (including women) know the Timothy passage than the Judges story.

Deborah is first introduced to the reader as a leader who displays authority over all men in the narrative and speaks for God to the people. Apparently she rose to power by common consent of the people, who recognized her wisdom and sought her counsel and guidance in important matters. Though the narrative speaks from a patriarchal milieu in which women are presumed subordinate to and owned by men, there is a surprising suspension of some key aspects of patriarchy in Deborah's case. A significant handful of women emerge as heroines in biblical narrative, but they are usually in stereotypic female roles: either as faithful mothers, wives, daughters, or sisters—or seductive tricksters.[6] Biblical women are rarely independent agents. Most surprisingly, though Deborah's husband may be alluded to (it is unclear whether she is "wife of Lapidoth," or "woman of fire"—Hebrew could go either way), and though she is given the title "mother of Israel," she functions in the story apart from any role as wife to a husband, mother to a son, or sister to a brother. To top it off, in contrast to other biblical war finales, Deborah sings to celebrate her own victory; she doesn't come out to revere the returning male heroes. Cheryl Ann Brown catalogs her astounding resume: "Deborah stands out as a unique figure in the Hebrew Bible. . . . She is at once a prophetess; a poetess; a great military leader on a par with male military leaders; and even a judge, not simply like others, but a judge to whom Israelites turned for legal counseling and settling of court cases (Judg. 4:5)."

Deborah's exceptional nature has always been a problem for interpreters. First-century historian Josephus, famous for his voluminous *Jewish Antiquities* with its retelling of biblical stories, edited the story line to diminish Deborah's stature, and a later legendary rendition of the tale censures Deborah for behaving in an unseemly way. Some rabbis nicknamed her "the hornet" or "buzzing bee" because they thought she was arrogant. Presbyterian theologian John Knox admitted to Deborah's prowess and wisdom, but claimed that as a woman she was an aberration. In his diatribe against the English Catholic queen Mary, he puzzles over why God "did so mightily assist women, against nature and against his ordinary course," and he conjectures that God, "exempted Deborah from the common malediction given to women . . . and made her prudent in counsel, strong in courage, happy in regiment, and blessed mother and deliverer to his people."[7] More modern interpreters are equally uncomfortable; some project that Deborah's success in the public arena was at the cost of her private life. As if in warning to women who aspired to be leaders, Clovis Chappell commented:

> I have an idea that [Deborah] was not highly successful as a homemaker. Perhaps in spite of her greatness she was not quite great enough to succeed fully in two careers. Few women are. Of course there are exceptions to the rule. . . . But such are rare indeed. It is my conviction that the career of wifehood and motherhood is big enough for any woman in the world. If she undertakes to run a home and to run her nation as well *she is mighty apt to make a mess out of one or the other.*[8]

Sara Buswell, believing women should never take a leadership position over a man, allegorizes the story, transforming the public battle into a private spiritual warfare. With literary dexterity Buswell domesticates this tale of a woman's public authority:

> Deborah challenges us to accomplish the routing of foreign armies (personal sins in our lives) by becoming more deeply rooted in God's Word. Personal growth may be a less glamorous task than public government, but it is an equally crucial endeavor.[9]

Even those who accept Deborah's public persona find a means of explaining it away. Some modern commentators have obscured Deborah's preeminence and attributed her rise to the fact that Israel was "hard up" for leaders. However, because the military leader Barak takes a strong role in the narrative, we can assume that Deborah is not judge because there was no one else available. Furthermore, other brave men are vaunted in Deborah's song for their readiness to protect Israel.

Interpretive stutterings notwithstanding, the narrative eloquently portrays this woman as a leader *extraordinaire.*

Deborah emerges as judge during a time when the people of Israel have fallen into idolatry and suffered decades of cruel oppression from the hands of the Canaanites—"in [those days], caravans ceased and travelers kept to the byways" (5:6). The rustic Hebrews were a loose federation at that time, and they rejected Canaan's absolutism of the city-states and the extreme hierarchy that created sharp divisions between the privileged elite and the subjected others. In contrast to the later days of monarchy, social organization was based on family households. Military engagements "tended to be defensive rather than offensive in character," protecting the interests of the household against outside aggressors.[10] Considered intruders and revolutionaries from the perspective of the indigenous Canaanites, the alien Israelites were continually in conflict with the inhabitants of the land. Because warfare was the universal paradigm for handling territorial disputes, battles figure prominently in the sagas of the Judges. The dynamics of this political strife were complicated by religious overtones; in the ancient world religious fervor and national allegiance were linked. In Israel's understanding, God was on the side of the suffering minority people, and interaction with the other nations (who "followed other gods") was believed a key source of religious apostasy. The identity of this Iron Age woman-of-fire is forged within this paradigm, and she emerges as one who has credibility and prowess in this setting.

The battle for which Deborah is remembered took place around 1125 B.C.E. The technologically advanced Canaanites, boasting an army of nearly a thousand chariots of iron, controlled a strategically located stronghold that threatened to strangle the main route of Israelite trade. Deborah follows three earlier leaders, referred to as judges, who functioned primarily as warrior-liberators for victims of military aggression; Deborah alone fulfills the additional roles of prophet and judicial arbitrator. It was Deborah's habit to sit under a particular palm tree (the "palm of Deborah") and counsel the people in dispensing justice. As tribal judge, her task was to rally the people together to defend their customs and territory. As a prophetess, her call was to speak God's word and bring the wayward people back to faithfulness in God.

In her capacity as God's messenger, Deborah beckons Barak, Israel's general, and conveys to him God's command that he mobilize the troops to confront the Canaanite troops in battle. Her oracle contains a strategic plan and the promise of divinely accomplished victory. Barak entreats Deborah to go with him into battle ("If you will go with me, I will go; but if you will not go with me, I will not go" [4:8]). Deborah chides his hesitance, but complies:[11] against overwhelming odds, God delivers the enemy into Israel's hands by means of a torrential downpour that creates a mud trap for the chariots. The enemy troops are routed; however, Sisera, the Canaanite general, escapes on foot. The story reaches its denouement when the desperate general finds apparent refuge in the tent of Jael, the wife of a man whose clan is at peace with Sisera's. Evidently Jael, in a surprising display of independence from her husband and clan, makes her own decision as to whose side she is going to be on (emphasized in the phrasing "the tent of Jael" rather than, as would be expected, the tent of Heber, her husband). She entices Sisera into her tent in feigned hospitality; adept at the women's work of staking tents to the ground, she uses her skill to kill this general by hammering a tent peg through his skull. Taking her place in a long line of underdogs who use "guerrilla war tactics" against oppressors, Jael outsmarts her victim.[12] In pursuit of Sisera, Barak reaches Jael's tent and learns of her exploit. Victory over Canaan complete, Deborah and Barak sing a gloating and celebratory ballad that congratulates the brave warriors who offered themselves, chastises the tribes who did not come to Israel's aid, extols the bravery and wiles of Jael, and praises the God who crushed the enemy.

The story of Deborah offers three images for leadership: Deborah as warrior-woman-of-fire who projects a vision of justice; Deborah as mother-of-Israel who knows the needs of her people and cares for the vulnerable; Deborah as wise-woman-judge who adjudicates problems and decisions. We will first look at the way in which Deborah embodied these three themes in her own day and context. Later in this chapter we will build on these images and reinterpret them for our own context.

WOMAN OF FIRE: WARRIOR FOR THE VULNERABLE

Nineteenth-century preacher George Matheson, who was blind, remarks that "many are the daughters" who are "endowed with the spirit of meekness" and some, such as Deborah, "are daughters" endowed "with the spirit of indignation." Deborah's leadership is marked by a fiery indignation at the oppression of her people; she leads them in a fight for their just rights. Most strikingly, she works to protect the least vulnerable of her people, the young girls.

It has frequently been noted that Deborah's song brings in aspects of a woman's perspective on battle. In the last stanzas of the poem, the singer paints a poignant verbal picture of the scene on the home front of Sisera's family. Deborah imagines the noble women waiting, peering out their windows, wondering what is taking so long; Sisera's mother and her ladies presume that Sisera and his men, victorious, are dividing spoil, including the customary booty of the women ("Are they not finding and dividing the spoil?—A girl or two for every man" [5:30]).

Why does the composer of this song include this voyeuristiclike scene? Those who decry the violence of the passage (an issue to which we will return) project that the stanzas are taunting, insinuating that the proud will soon fall, and the plunder will go in the other direction. Surely, Deborah's song gloats over the poetic justice rendered when a band of ill-prepared peasants bests a rich and powerful army and a lone woman fells its general with her crude hammer and peg (5:24-27). But, rather than taunting, I think these stanzas represent a brief but significant suspension of the us/they perspective so pervasive in the ancient world. For a moment, these mothers share a common experience. Though the dichotomy returns and the two companies of mothers separate into the winners and the losers, the commonality is etched in our minds. Hearers and readers of Deborah's song are lured into this scene, and traces of its empathy linger even as the singer's journey takes us to another scene.[13]

Deborah's war-victory song ends with the poignant awareness that women suffer the long-term consequences of war defeat. That awareness includes a fleeting empathy for "the other" mother. However, the sustained empathy is for Israel's daughters. Sisera's victory would give every male victor an Israelite "woman or two" (literally, a *womb* or two); Sisera's defeat protects Israel's daughters from this sexual slavery. There is an implicit but profound celebration for the women and girls who were spared from Canaan's ravishment. Jael is "most blessed of women," not because she was so bravely violent, but rather because she has redeemed the Israelite wombs. We are brought to eavesdrop on the Canaanite hearth so that we do not miss the often hidden story of equal opportunity of suffering during war—sons *and* daughters are lost, and sons *and* daughters are spared.

More than mere celebration for the lucky daughters, there is a hint of protest in these odd stanzas. The recitation of the Canaanite despoiling of women forces the hearer of the song to face the brutality of war. Interestingly (although it very well may have taken place), Israel's counter-plundering is neither celebrated nor even mentioned. In a culture where bragging over booty was a familiar theme in war epics, the silence here may be poignant. Though one might argue that the reserve in detailing Israel's booty-taking reflects an unwillingness to admit to reciprocal brutality, it is still a move beyond the kind of bravado that vaunts such machismo. The war whoop of Deborah's harsh song contains a subtle counterpoint to the melody.

This woman of fire who named herself Mother of Israel is perhaps "a bellicose mother who pushes her 'children' to victory" and reprimands those who demur.[14] Her heart goes out to her willing military commanders who risked their lives, but curses are pronounced on those tribes who did not come to their nation's aid. However, her fire was fueled by a vision of the aftermath of war that includes the brutal ravishing of her daughters. Just as Deborah celebrated that the common people prospered (5:7), so too does she rejoice in her daughters' well-being. Deborah's fiery indignation not only protected her people and saved her daughters from sexual slavery and her sisters from widowhood, it also exposed the cruel (and misogynist) realities of war.

Indignant, even bellicose, though she was, the name for which she is most often remembered (when she is remembered, that is) points to another side of her leadership.

MOTHER OF ISRAEL: PARTNERSHIP AND THE SHARING OF POWER

Deborah is generally associated with the accolade she is reported to have given herself: Mother in Israel (5:7). In what may be the oldest part of the Hebrew Bible, the song of Deborah retells the story of Israel's victory over Sisera. As "mother," Deborah knew the values and needs of her people, understood the dangers and opportunities of their context, and rallied them to come together as a community to fight their oppressors. When Canaanite cruelties forced Israelite caravans off the main roads and onto the treacherous byways, this mother gathered her brood together and fought for their safety.

Beyond these capacities, the song makes clear that one of the most important characteristics of Deborah's "mothering" was to create a system of partnership.[15] The song commends the people who "offer[ed] them-selves willingly" (5:2) and the variety of leaders who "offered themselves willingly among the people" (5:9). Though in some ways Deborah may seem larger than life, her story is as striking for the number of players that she brings onto center stage with her as it is for the number of laurels that she accumulates. The three-part cooperation between Deborah, Barak, and Jael (an Israelite woman, an Israelite man, and a Kenite—a people aligned with the Canaanites—woman) is an interesting study in partner-ship. Typically in the judge stories, a single man is identified as the mili-tary deliverer. In this story, three characters together weave the tapestry of the nation's deliverance. Each of the three is indispensable for the deliv-ery of the suffering nation, and all three share the glory of Israel's victory. Though Deborah is remembered as the judge, Barak and Jael are equally likely to take center stage in communal and scholarly reflection on this story.[16] Deborah's unique role as leader does not seem to be at the expense of or in exclusion of other heroes. The song on her lips specifically praises God for partnership, and yet it does not diminish her own role ("The peasantry prospered, they prospered in Israel, because I, Deborah, arose, arose, a mother in Israel" [5:7, NEB]). Authority and empowerment seem to go together in Deborah's leadership.

Interestingly, the first-century writer of *Biblical Antiquities*, known as

Pseudo-Philo (his work was erroneously attributed to Philo), compares Deborah's leadership to that of the usually incomparable Moses. Moses and Deborah, in the range and significance of their calling and competencies, seem to stand apart from all other leaders. There is, however, a twist in the parallelism. While, according to the Moses narratives, a similar triad formed between Moses, his brother Aaron, and his sister Miriam, God jealously protected Moses' preeminence—to the near-demise of Miriam (Numbers 12). In the Deborah narrative, sustained partnership, including perhaps mutual correction, is the trajectory. It has even been suggested that in Judges 4, Deborah and Jael are described in such a way as to evoke recollection of Canaanite partner goddesses whose joint efforts eventually became inseparable.

While Deborah's concern and capacity to share power were within the confines of her own community, we can recall here that her fiery indignation and her compassionate commitment to the powerless included the brief moment of empathy with other mothers. Perhaps this mother of Israel, though limited by the desperate circumstances of her people, was straining to widen her embrace and take into account the children outside of her hearth. First introduced to us as an arbiter of justice, a wise-woman judge, we can imagine that Deborah was accustomed to taking a wide variety of concerns and viewpoints into consideration.

WISE-WOMAN JUDGE: GROPING TOWARD FAIRNESS AND PEACE

After describing the plight and the cries of the people, the first image the storyteller gives us is of the leader Deborah sitting under the palm tree helping people sort out their differences and working to preserve peace and justice in her community (Judges 4:4-5).

The pastoral scene of Deborah adjudicating justice beneath a palm tree signals that neither holy war nor treachery was Deborah's chief modus operandi. Margaret Wold muses "Would Deborah rather have accomplished the deliverance of the people by peaceful means?"[17] In fact, Deborah's oracle itself represents a movement beyond the traditional glorification of human might and control. Deborah's battle-call (4:6, 7), though it still ensues in brutal consequences for the enemy, is framed in what Susan Niditch calls "an ideology of non-participation." The task of Israel is not to muster its power and vanquish its enemy; it is rather to relinquish control and trust in God, who "loves the weak and controls the war." When it comes down to it, this is the story of a man deferring to and following a woman who is leaving it up to God. Yairah Amit comments that the hero of the story is neither Deborah, nor Barak, nor even Jael, but rather God.[18] Certainly, we could critique this ideology for its apparent lack of realism and responsibility (which is one interpretation given for Barak's hesitance). But, it is groping toward an alternative understanding of war; perhaps it even portrays, as Niditch sees it, a "breakthrough toward an ideology of peace."[19]

LEADERSHIP AND BOUNDARIES: REFLECTIONS ON HAMMERS, CARAVANS, AND MIRED CHARIOTS

Within the book of Judges, Deborah stands out as one leader whose character does not get sullied by some moral lapse. The next judge, Gideon, requested that the gold the people had taken as booty from war be fashioned into an idol of sorts. Jephthah ended up sacrificing his own daughter in his bid for power. And Samson depended on his physical prowess to the exclusion of wisdom and responsibility, brandishing that power in personal vendettas and foolish escapades. Modern critics, however, find Deborah and her collaborators to be morally wanting. Although Deborah seems not to be confined by the power structures and expectations of patriarchy, neither does she stand over against some of its questionable assumptions. In song, Deborah glorifies the protective aggression of her army, celebrates the violent demise of Sisera and his people, and singles out Jael for special adulation. Elizabeth Cady Stanton, in *The Woman's Bible*, severely condemns Jael's "revolting" behavior as that "more like the work of a fiend than a woman." In the end, it seems to be the case that "the authority of violence is justified. And in the face of that authority, the woman, Deborah, has offered no real alternative."[20]

There is justification for this social critique. Audre Lorde has warned that "the master's tools will never dismantle the master's house," and control, violence, and exclusiveness are the master's tools.[21] Surely we yearn for something other than the order-as-it-is obsessed leadership exhibited by Ahasuerus, but as we build our common house we do not want to use the master's tools and simply force a new order. The ultimate test of faithfulness to Israel's God is just and merciful treatment of those on the margins (widows, orphans, strangers, and poor). Indeed, as one progresses through the book of Judges, the tactics of oppressors and oppressed are sometimes indistinguishable; trust in God's compassionate presence becomes commandeered by national fervor. God's enemies and God's friends are rigidly delineated. The narrative depicts an us/they, win/lose worldview—Israel's victory is celebrated and Canaan's demise is legitimated.

The narrative gives both a compelling image of legitimate leadership and a realistic picture of leadership dangers. For those of us with a passion for our vision and an outrage at injustice, the hammer and the tent peg are always a temptation; passion for justice can issue in either authoritarianism or violence. For those of us with great empathy toward our people and compassion on our vulnerable ones, we will want to pull our caravans in a circle to protect against outside dangers; such empathy can lead to nationalism, parochialism, and exclusivism. These are real dangers, and we must name them and remain aware that they lurk in the background of any community. We need more than a moment of empathy for others, we need sustained attention to those who are outside of our bounds. The dangers of exclusivism and violence are boundaries we will have to work hard not to cross.

There is another danger, however, that we also must name. A groping toward peace, which includes lengthy processes of decision making and arbitration, can become, like the Canaanite chariots, mired in the mud and result in the spinning of our wheels. Egalitarian and inclusive processes can be slow and limited when confronting ideologies, structures, and systems of injustice—and thus they may themselves extend the forms of injustice and violence already present.[22] Even in "fair" processes, not all players come with equal personal or political power; processes of arbitration favor those who are skilled at the privileged type of discourse. While those who enjoy power and safety are especially called upon to listen to outsiders and others, those who are powerless and vulnerable are at greater risk. A let's-all-sit-down-and-talk-about-it vision of achieving justice may inadvertently flout the suffering of the oppressed. Leadership is thus complicated and contextual; metaphorically speaking, leaders must adjudicate between protecting their own daughters' wombs and caring about the wombs of the other mothers' daughters. A passionate, empathetic, and wise leader watches out for violence, exclusivism, and inertia.

Pseudo-Philo portrayed Deborah as a visionary leader and enlightener whose impending death threatens to leave a great void in her community. "To whom do you commend your sons whom you are leaving? Pray therefore for us, and after your departure your soul will be mindful of us forever," the people implore. In Pseudo-Philo's retelling, Deborah exhorts the people to live as she has taught them. What would it mean to live as Deborah has taught us? Ancient biblical narratives are often interpreted in light of the trajectories they throw. Where do they point? What new reality do they usher in? Let's follow a possible trajectory thrown by the story of Deborah and envision leadership in our common house.

Deborah—woman of fire, mother of Israel, judge. What might we learn from her today? This Mother of Israel shows her empathy and shares her power: she calls us to participation and partnership in community; this Woman of Fire speaks her passion for justice: she calls us to battle on behalf of the ravished and oppressed ones; this Wise Woman exercises judgment: she calls us to deliberate fairly and carefully as we make decisions in our life together.

Passion, empathy, and judgment are all present in caretaking leadership; the temptation to control, protect only one's own, or become mired in process are the boundaries we hope not to cross. At any one time, passion or empathy or judgment may be emphasized. When one of these aspects of leadership is emphasized, it is important to temper that emphasis by still taking the other two aspects of leadership into account. We will consider what benefits a community (including the girls) will receive and what concerns a leader will wrestle with when the leader opts to focus on the different aspects of leadership (passion, empathy, judgment). Then, using the opening case of Rev. Jones as an example, we will examine what leadership choices Rev. Jones might have made from the vantage point of each leadership emphasis. We begin by examining caretaking leadership from the perspective of an emphasis on passion.[23]

WOMEN OF FIRE: NAMING OUR PASSION FOR JUSTICE

WOMEN OF FIRE AND "COMMUNICATED JUSTICE"

In articulating Deborah's call to justice, I have interpreted her story in conversation with feminist theologian Carol Christ. When I first read Christ's proposal for feminist scholarship, which follows what she calls an "ethos of Eros and empathy," I immediately thought of Deborah's leadership.[24] Drawing on women's interest in connection, Christ poses three "moments" in the course of research: (1) naming the passion; (2) enlarging the perspective; (3) exercising judgment. The first moment involves an awareness and articulation of one's position as a scholar, particularly the passion for transformation that drives the scholar's work. The second moment opens and enlarges the passion by listening, studying, and conversing with enriching sources. This second move is both self-preserving and self-expanding, for as we saw in chapter 3, empathy and self-knowledge grow together. The third moment involves a return to the now-expanded standpoint, incorporating the insights gained based on one's careful judgment concerning the contributions of the sources one has consulted. A researcher who works in this manner is confident in her voice but also aware of her finitude and the partiality of her passion. The ethos Carol Christ describes illumines the important role that empathy and judgment play when one pursues one's passion. Caretaking leadership also involves naming our passion for justice, enlarging our understanding through empathy, and reshaping our passion through wisdom and judgment.

A leader should always be aware of the passion and a vision for transformation that guide her leadership. While it is not *always* appropriate to lead by presenting one's vision to a people (as we shall discuss below), *sometimes* it is appropriate for a leader to communicate the vision of justice and community life that impassions her ministry. Furthermore, there will be occasions when a leader is impelled to put forth a difficult and controversial stance to the community of which she is a part.

When a leader offers her vision, it is in a sense an "imposition." She is telling people where she is coming from, and she offers her own position as a preferred choice of options. Furthermore, she hopes for change and transformation; she aims to inspire and incite action that we see is for the bettering of humanity. Yet, even when a caretaking leader presents a vision, the invitation to change that she offers is not based on tyranny. Thus, it is very important that such communication of vision be a teaching process, and not simply an authoritarian assertion of truth. The leader should describe why she has this vision or takes this stand, and she should make very clear the struggle that has preceded her hard-won position. Furthermore, the passionate leader should stress that her vision is provisional, on-the-way, and open to renewal. She might even acknowledge that other visions may also be legitimate, but she has constructed hers for good reasons that she will share. In naming our passion for justice, we must recognize that passion can always lead to an overzealous imposition of our vision. This is why openness, empathy, and a public acknowledgment of the provisional nature of our passion are needed.

Even when sharing one's vision, empathy is needed. The "just" leader will invite questions, consider alternative positions, welcome "back talk," allow for argument, and set up further study opportunities. This empathy is not only for the purpose of helping to clarify the issues to others, but it is also for the purpose of expanding and enlarging the leader's vision. Compassion toward those who cannot see her vision is necessary, particularly if her vision is shattering comfortable frameworks. It can be especially helpful for a leader to share her own struggle with a particular issue rather than frontally attack those who are not practicing the vision. For instance, if one wishes to present one's views (passion) on the importance of inclusive language, it would be helpful to share one's personal journey from assumed generic language to necessary inclusive language. Similarly, if one chooses to argue for community affirmation of gay and lesbian persons, it would be helpful to share one's personal journey and struggle in coming to this position. In this way, one both identifies with the hearer and avoids launching an attack.[25] This doesn't guarantee that the hearers will value the vision, but it does place the hearers on a more level playing field with the vision.

The leader sharing her vision also exercises judgment if she allows her vision to be stretched and reformulated through conversation with others. Liberation educators Paulo Freire and Ira Shor recognize that this kind of judgment—which Freire calls *reknowing* of subject matter—is essential for dialogical teaching. In this kind of educational situation the teacher [leader] "enters knowing a great deal but leaves the course 'relearned' because of the dialogue-inquiry, the rediscovery of the material *with* the students."[26] Sometimes the community promotes the kind of reknowing that, in the judgment of the leader, alters the original vision quite significantly.

Allowing one's passion to be tempered by empathy does not mean that the leader capitulates her vision at the first sign of critique or resistance. A leader, when questioned, should offer a reasonable defense of her position. To put it another way, it can be helpful to defend one's position without being defensive. This is educationally very valuable. Rather than communicating "you should believe this because I believe it—period" (the authoritarian posture) or "I will feel betrayed if you don't think as I do" (the defensive posture) or "my way or the highway" (the exclusivist posture) the leader can present her position in a manner that says "here are the good reasons why I believe this and maybe they will be convincing to you as well" (an authoritative posture). Questions, challenges, and alternative positions should be tolerated and given serious respect, even as the leader gives a defense for her own position.

Women leaders in particular, who are often reluctant to claim their authority, need to recognize that there are positive uses of authority and power. "In our eagerness to be non-hierarchical and supportive instead of tyrannical and ruthlessly critical, we have sometimes participated in the patriarchal denial of the mind to women," argues Susan Friedman. "In our sensitivity to the psychology of oppression in our students' lives, we have often denied ourselves the authority we seek to nurture in our students," Friedman continues.[27] And thus, although we may nurture the voices of girls and women in our classrooms for a while, if we demur from our own authority, we will implicitly pass on to girls a fear of assertiveness when they go outside the classroom. If we seek to nurture a sense of personal authority in girls and women, we do well to claim our own right to "authorship," understood as the power to describe reality as one perceives it and the right to have one's description taken seriously by others.[28]

While a self-critical leader may shy away from presenting her passion, sometimes a group really needs to know the mind of the leader before they feel free to dialogue with her or him. Paulo Freire, in his collaborative dialogue with Ira Shor, relays a criticism one student offered of his dialogical style of teaching.

> Paulo, today after our experience this semester I have something to tell you which is a criticism. But for me it is a necessary criticism and I hope I can help you. . . . Look, Paulo, you committed just one mistake but it is a serious mistake in working with us. When you arrived here in the beginning of the semester, you thought we were ready to assume the responsibility of shaping ourselves with you, but you had no right to think like this. You assumed something that was not tested. . . . And what did you do? *You committed suicide* as the teacher. Instead of that, you should have exposed yourself to our assassination! . . . We would have to kill you as the only professor in the seminar for you to be re-born as a student who is also a professor. Instead of that, you committed suicide in our presence and it created in us a feeling of being orphans.[29]

Although the imagery is brutal, the illustration is extremely helpful. A liberating teacher or leader does not need to withdraw her leadership. It not only makes the community of learners feel bereft, it also makes them anxious if they have to be continually guessing where their leader is coming from. This does not mean that the leader, at the other extreme, always creates the vision for the group. It means that the leader makes her passions known but provides an atmosphere where her passions can be stretched, challenged, and reworked. Clearly, for this student to express his sentiments so boldly, Freire had created such an atmosphere. It preserves the leader as both leader and learner, and it empowers the learners as both learners and leaders. It is neither repression of self, based on a faulty notion of "goodness" nor repression of others, based on an ideological rigidity. It is leadership that models and fosters selves in relation with one another and with God.

In fact, it is self-deceiving and "voyeuristic" to think that our task is to elicit the voices of others without identifying—and opening to examination—our own; we cannot function without agendas and biases. If we want others to take the "risk to be known," then we must also take that risk. By naming our passion, we offer it so that people do not have to anxiously guess "where we are coming from"; by knowing our agendas and biases, and knowing we are open to revising them, participants in a community can be invited to examine and help shape—not simply accept as completed—the ongoing formulation of these passions.

There are two very specific ways in which leading by presenting one's passion can also embrace empathy: by fanning into flames the embers already burning in a community, by sparking "back talk" from other persons. We might say that these are "connected" forms of passionate assertion.

CONNECTED PASSION: FANNING EMBERS INTO FLAMES AND SPARKING BACK TALK

A pastor who has an ardent passion for justice (her vision) need not presume that she has to light a fire underneath the people. Very often there are embers already burning, even if slowly and tentatively. A leader can observe and study her community so that she can identify these embers. Then, she can intentionally affirm and seek to extend those practices that support her vision until they grow stronger and spread; or she can recover and reinterpret for a community their theological and historical roots in light of a new potential direction they can take. Thus, rather than point out what's wrong or present something that's missing, she can fan into flames what is already there. For instance, when theologian Elisabeth Johnson presented a new way to speak of God, she invoked the Roman Catholic heritage of mystery, which forbids any one image from capturing the imagination.[30]

Alternatively, if a leader feels that she needs to "present something missing," one way to do this while remaining open to the views of others is to encourage "back talk." She can lay out her vision before her community, and then she can directly invite folks to talk back to her about it.

She can even appoint a "catalyst" or "devil's advocate" who sparks it all off by posing challenging questions to her views. She can, in the way she responds to the catalyst, model what it looks like to be passionate about one's views while open and responsive to questions. When responding to back talk, a leader can affirm where she is in agreement with her challenger, state honestly when a challenge prompts her to enlarge her vision, state clearly where she disagrees with her challenger, and give good reasons for her position. Back-talk sessions are especially helpful in freeing people to think. *Rather than train devotees, the passionate leader nurtures thinkers.* If she communicates to the community that they are all in the process of learning together, then the leader will provide an atmosphere that generates "back talk," for the benefit of all.

Back talk is an important process for girls to observe and take part in; it lets them know that conflict and challenge are not to be avoided. The leader who is able to meet challenges to her position with both respect and voice unravels the "patina of niceness and kindness" binding our girls. More than that, passion combined with back talk teaches girls to think. Those who are in psychological transition from the interpersonal orientation to the institutional orientation can be helped by a leader who shares her passion in a confident but open manner. Sharing one's passion without forcing it can enable interpersonally oriented people to view and learn from a self-authored perspective without being forced to comply with it. It thus models selfhood while permitting the development of other selves.

A VISIONING STRATEGY

Rev. Jones's leadership in the case above was passionate; she wanted her congregation to express the vision of justice that energized her. It was a good vision, but it was clear that the congregation did not own it. While it is possible that they never would have owned it, she didn't really give them a chance to take part in the creating of the vision. In many ways, Rev. Jones erred on the side of the master. She allied herself with the opinions at the top (the bishop and banker), and she had little sense for the grassroots viewpoint. The plan was conceived of unilaterally, presented too quickly, and decisions were made without full community input.

It is not necessarily the case, however, that Rev. Jones's task was to table her vision and take a more empathetic approach (see below). While this may have been a better alternative, she could have stayed with her passion but educated the community more fully before seeking to enact it. Even when choosing the passion strategy, a caretaking leader uses education and persuasion rather than command. As noted above, each leadership strategy is influenced by the others; passion without empathy and judgment is unacceptable.

A leadership strategy that promotes a passion for justice best begins by educating a community toward the vision. Were she to do it over again, before bringing the proposal to a vote, Pastor Jones could educate her congregation on the issue by engaging the congregation's history of outreach to immigrants. Rather than bringing this information in at the end of the process to defend the doomed proposal—when it was too late—she could begin the campaign by recovering the community's history. She could remember and describe for Heritage the plight of the first immigrants who came and worshiped there, and she could affirm and celebrate the congregation's compassionate response. Additionally, she could research old bulletins and other memory-laden material to recover and retell the formative themes and practices that would contribute to the vision she wishes to promote. Though not always effective, in this case a "fan into flames" approach, which began with the sparks of justice already present, would have been valuable. Even if the community did not catch her particular form of the vision, they would benefit from the retelling of their history and story.

In addition to tracing the history and theological sparks of justice in this congregation, Rev. Jones could offer a study of Scripture and tradition that supports her vision. Such a study should be presented with hermeneutical honesty; she names her findings as her particular (rather than "the only") theological interpretation. This theological and scriptural background helps those in the community to understand how this vision is in continuity with the tradition at large as well as with their own particular history.

The study of the neighborhood and its needs could be done with the full involvement of the people. Rev. Jones could then spend a congregational meeting interpreting the results of the neighborhood study with the people. It would be important during this process and at this meeting for Rev. Jones to be aware of internal needs that are expressed; it might very well be that at this point she revises her vision and attends to the neediness of the congregation first.

The final step for this first option would be preparing and presenting in fullness her vision for the housing project. Then Rev. Jones would create a space for questioning, responding, and refining her vision. At this point, if the congregation wasn't willing to follow the vision, good judgment would require that Rev. Jones modify her plans for this congregation, taking into consideration their viewpoints. Clearly, this strategy emphasizes her vision all the way along, but it is educationally sensitive.

Sometimes the most helpful strategy is presenting one's vision; at other times it is more helpful to mobilize others toward jointly shaping a vision. Now we turn to an examination of a leadership strategy that emphasizes empathy and the sharing of power.

MOTHERS OF ISRAEL: PARTNERSHIP AND THE SHARING OF POWER

MOTHERS OF ISRAEL AND "COMMUNICATIVE JUSTICE"

Deborah arose as one in Israel who had authority. Authority is legitimated power that is bestowed on persons who are acknowledged by the community. People grant a leader authority because they believe she or he will "protect, interpret, and represent the group's core values and beliefs and contribute to their realization." People follow an authoritative person because "they believe the directives to be consistent with the core values, beliefs, and purposes of the group."[31]

A leader who does not discern a congregation's "taken-for-granted patterns of conduct, outlook, and story" will not establish legitimate authority.[32] In our opening case study, Rev. Jones did not have authority because she was not in touch with the core values and needs of the people. She had a wonderful vision, but she created it apart from a deep engagement with the values of those in her community. She presented her vision of justice, but she did not listen to the people and share her power in shaping the vision. She wanted to spread the goods of the community around, but she did not involve the community in deciding what that would look like and how it should be done.

There are two major aspects of the empathetic task of leadership: understanding and empowering. Understanding requires the capacity to observe, listen to, and learn about a particular community. New pastors can too easily go into a congregation with the assumption that they will bring an identity and vision to the people; changing the congregation is their first order of business. When the history and current identity of the people are ignored like this, the pastor is likely to inadvertently trample on values and beliefs that she or he hadn't taken the time to discern. Pastor Jones was so energized by her concern for the aged that she seems not to have understood Heritage's concern for youth and their need for self-care.

Empowering involves the sharing of power and the mobilizing of differences within a community. This is more complicated than understanding, because the central values of a community may be shaped by particular persons and groups. Those outside of the central power positions may have less impact on the direction of the congregation. The more levels that a leader takes empathy to, and the more voices that are brought into a community's life, the more difficult the process becomes. Dr. Bright, the professor in our opening example, was a master at empowering her students; they were active participants, deeply engaged in the classroom process. Perhaps she took a cue from Susan B. Anthony, who argued vigorously that the National American Woman Suffrage Association should be distinguished by its tolerance for and engagement with difference; she thus opposed a resolution put before the Association by an assigned committee to distance itself from Elizabeth Cady Stanton's controversial *Women's Bible*.

> The one distinct feature of our Association has been the right of individual opinion of every member. We have been beset at every step with the cry that somebody was injuring the cause by the expression of some sentiments that differed with those held by the majority of mankind. The religious persecution of the ages has been done under what was claimed to be the command of God. I distrust those people who know so well what God wants them to do to their fellows, because it always coincides with their own desires. . . . *What you should do is to say to outsiders that a Christian has neither more nor less rights in our Association than an atheist. When our platform becomes too narrow for people of all creeds and of no creeds, I myself shall not stand upon it.* Many things have been said and done by our orthodox friends that I have felt to be extremely harmful to our cause; but I should no more consent to a resolution denouncing them than I shall consent to this. *Who is to draw the line? . . . This year it is Mrs. Stanton; next year it may be me or one of yourselves who will be the victim.*[33]

In contrast to Dr. Bright, however, Susan B. Anthony was not chary of including herself in the circle of empathetic caring. She clearly understood that she had no more, but also no less, right than any other person; thus, she brought a clearly focused statement before the group that reminded them of their distinctive vision and way of being. She exercised her authority to keep the inclusive process intact. She did not remove herself from the process, but she worked hard to keep others in as well.

The commitment to empowering the diversity of viewpoints in community is a difficult one, but it has important implications for a community's well-being. So often when leaders care for people in their communities, they look to see that their physical needs are met. Thus, caring involves bringing food when people are sick, providing money when people are strapped, and even building shelters when people are homeless. Rev. Jones was particularly attentive to this kind of caring. The empathetic impulse of leadership goes beyond distributing tangible goods to needy persons, however. Iris Marion Young, in her important book *Justice and the Politics of Difference*, contrasts a paradigm of "distributive justice" with one of "communicative justice." "The distributive paradigm defines social justice as the morally proper distribution of social benefits and burdens among society's members."[34] Some groups have social goods that others lack, distributive justice works out the best way to allocate goods more equitably. There is much merit in this view, and I will affirm appropriate uses of a modified version of distributive justice below, but as a paradigm for justice it is incomplete. The distributive paradigm often fails to take into account the "justice of decision-making power and procedures." Sharing goods is benevolent, but sharing the power for making decisions, defining culture, and shaping procedures is much more important. For example, we can make sure that every person in our community is served supper every night, given adequate clothing to wear, and supplied with a house to keep them warm. This is distributive justice. Benevolent and charitable though it is, it generally falls short of full justice. If only one group determines the menu, selects the fashion styles, and draws up the blueprints for the house, then communicative justice, the "justice of decision-making power and procedures," is lacking for the other groups.

Self-respect, a good that cannot be allocated, is highly dependent on cultural definitions of what is worthy. If persons feel that they are validated by and able to shape the direction of the wider culture, they are more likely to have self-respect. If, however, decisions are being made and culture is being defined apart from their contributions, then they have little social/cultural power and are marginated. The caring leader who only communicates her vision of justice or only distributes the goods already prescribed is still missing the communicative dimension of justice. Communicative justice would aim toward processes and procedures that disperse social/cultural power among all groups of persons. The scope of justice, then, is wider than distribution of goods. Communicative justice requires a fair discussion of and argument over the future of a social group.[35] Communicative justice demands that we not simply distribute food, clothing, and shelter but we empower many groups to take part in the discussion over menu, clothing styles, and architecture.

Thus, empathy at its deepest level requires more than knowing the pulse of a community; it engages the varieties of difference within the community. An empathic emphasis in leadership recognizes that difference is not merely something to tolerate; the interplay of differentness foments creativity and vitality. So often we are taught either to ignore difference (and thus maintain a shallow relationship) or to change those who are different (and thus create an oppressive relationship). To dismantle "the master's house," which fears differentness, we must be willing to encounter and take seriously those who are "other" to us. "Difference must be not merely tolerated, but seen as a fund of necessary polarities between which our creativity can spark like dialectic," asserts Audre Lorde. This courageous encounter with difference fosters an understanding of interdependence that is nonthreatening. "Only within that interdependency of different strengths, acknowledged and equal, can the power to seek new ways of being in the world generate, as well as the courage and sustenance to act where there are no charters," remarks Lorde.[36]

I will argue below that distributive justice entails teaching people how to get along in present power structures; it is passing on "street smarts" for democratic living. Communicative justice is not simply teaching people to adapt (play the master's game); it is also building on the skills, powers, experience, knowledge, and talents people have that are unacknowledged in the power structures (so they can reshape the master's game). It is inviting people to shape a community's life not simply by rational discourse, but also by storytelling, spiritual expression and "God-talk,"[37] dance, song and music of all kinds, drama, folk and classic art, poetry, meditation, prayer, encounters with nature, anger, defiant speech, wrenching lament, mourning, weeping, silence, and more. It is acknowledging that women's ways of communicating have something to contribute to community life. Therefore, when a leader emphasizes empathy, she attends to the fact that people who use nonmainstream forms of communication do not have equal power and thus do not always feel safe expressing these forms of communication in community. She responds to alternative communication styles when they emerge, goes seeking for them when they are underground, and utilizes them herself to encourage their expression.

One style of communication that is particularly empowering for women who struggle to gain voice is storytelling. "The new stories that women tell each other in conversations with each other, in consciousness raising, and in fiction, poetry, and other literary forms are key sources for discovering the shape of women's spiritual quest," reports Carol Christ.[38] Story sharing fosters the emergence of tensive themes that are necessary for dynamic community life. No two stories are the same, and different stories describe God's activity differently. God's grace is evident in one; God's absence in another; God's judgment in another; God's comforting presence in still another. When storytelling occurs, a rich and multidimensional culture is formed. Furthermore, story sharing has been an important mainstay of oral cultures, which are generally marginated in our society.[39]

This educational emphasis on empathetic leadership is particularly important for communities that wish to be inclusive rather than homogeneous. White middle-class churches are often bewildered when their inclusive rhetoric is ineffective in diversifying their demographics. While there are many reasons that churches are one of the most segregated institutions, it is largely because they really do not invite participants to share in shaping the worship culture. Different folks can come in if they want to assimilate, but they are not given the voice and the power to contribute to the future of the community. Churches can easily become the kind of lifestyle enclaves exposed by Bellah and associates.[40]

It is the case that when a leader chooses to emphasize empathy, she actually brings about a process that *shares* the "burden of empathy." She is not the only one in a listening and empowering posture, the rest of the community is also. By creating situations to foster voice and participation, by letting it be known that differentness is valued, she readies people for listening to and hearing one another. As skills for listening and sharing power develop more fully, women will no longer carry the greater share of the burden. A community with a developed capacity for corporate empathy will raise girls who are capable of empathy but also aware of the community's responsibility to share in it.

How might Rev. Jones have engaged an empathetic strategy when she started her new pastorate?

AN EMPATHETIC STRATEGY

To fully understand a community, a leader needs to have a sense of its identity, its internal workings, its social context, and the programs that are at its heart.[41] Rev. Jones began the process of listening to her community, but she only went partway. She undertook a study of the social context, which uncovered the needs of the aged, but she neglected to discern the identity and pulse of the congregation itself. Had she opted for a more empathetic strategy, she would have taken more time to understand the congregation and its life before initiating new programs.

After getting a good sense for the identity and workings of the congregation, she could have worked to mobilize their energies. She could have planned a variety of open processes that invited the people to come and brainstorm ideas about the future of the church. She could have held forums that she announced ahead of time, encouraged people to reflect on their ideas, and then moderated in a manner that welcomed a diversity of ideas. She could have made it clear that there was of yet no agenda, and perhaps many of the concerns of the people about their own needs would have come out at such a gathering. She still could have offered her idea for a housing project as one idea in the mix during this forum (thus not hiding her own vision), and then she could have assessed the people's interest or disinterest in it. Furthermore, it would be her task as leader to do what Dr. Bright was loathe to: at some point she would need to exercise judgment and bring this kind of brainstorming to a focus point so that the community could move forward. By stopping short of offering her expertise in her classroom, Dr. Bright allowed her empathy to skew the educational process.

Here it must be noted that an emphasis on empathy and diversity can be in tension with a commitment to change and transformation. This leadership emphasis can become inward-looking and mired in brainstorming kinds of processes; while it could be argued that this itself is a contribution to justice, it is also the case that it is sometimes simply the spinning of wheels. People can be so committed to diversity that they lose passion for anything, and then the listening itself loses meaning. This, however, is mitigated if a leader encourages and supports "decentralized" forms of ministry; ministries initiated and led by people who have a particular passion and purpose (such as the prison ministry described in chapter 6). In fact, it is important for leaders, especially those with a passion for a large project, to consider the importance of vital grassroots ministries. It is not always a good idea to consolidate, organize, or manage ministries that seem fragmented.

In evaluating the limits and possibilities of empathetic strategies for education and leadership, a leader must be prepared for outcomes or decisions different from the one to which she would come. I know of one pastor who deeply believed in empowering the congregation to make their decisions. He had led them through many decision-making processes, and he felt that he was quite able to give up control. When the congregation received a donation to replace their tattered pew Bibles, he led them through a long process of studying their options. He moderated numerous forums and study groups, where he worked hard to elicit thoughts and opinions, and he formed a representative committee that studied the issue further. When asked, he demurred from offering his own opinion. Various translations were considered, and the decision was made to go with a beautiful edition of the old King James Version, in large part due to widespread attachment to KJV translation of the Psalms. When the committee made their choice, he respected it, but he secretly nursed heavy disappointment. Since the church had previously used the Revised Standard Version, the move to the KJV felt like a huge step backward to him. He made an effort to support the choice, but he found himself resenting it when he had to read from it in worship. He ended up leaving the congregation soon after, although he never told the congregation why he wished to move on.

A leader's own views and skills cannot be suppressed even in empathetic strategies of leadership. When using an empowering process, a leader needs to name—at least to herself or himself—what views and feelings she or he has about an issue. No one is ever completely open-minded; it is therefore important to know our view even if we don't present it. Then a leader must ask herself or himself if she or he can genuinely accept decisions that differ from her preference or passion. In the case of the leader above, this particular decision turned out to be more personally problematic than the many others he had withstood. If a leader deep down knows that she cannot abide certain decisions, then strategy one, educating toward one's vision, is the most honest choice.[42] Sometimes, it is not only the most honest but also the most faithful. A leader who is *only* empathetic and empowering may find that her or his community is stagnating in their "taken for granted patterns of conduct, outlook, and story."[43] This is when a prophetic vision may be needed to prod the community into new areas of growth. This, however, is not generally helpful at the beginning of one's leadership. Furthermore, prophetic impulses can come from any person in a community; it may as often be the case that the leader *responds* to prophets in the midst rather than takes on the role herself.

Although empathic strategies aim to include the widest number of persons, we delude ourselves if we think we can ever create a fully open and fully inclusive interaction. Any community and leader is limited by a number of factors. Time limits, if we set them, establish fairness but limit freedom; power dynamics, which are unavoidable, constrain some persons and not others; varying degrees of commitment to diversity affect the dynamics of the process. This should be acknowledged. It is also crucial for a leader to acknowledge her or his own limitations; it is very damaging for a leader to profess complete openness and then to contradict that openness along the way. It is more helpful for a leader to name the parameters up front and acknowledge the boundaries of the process. The third leadership strategy, which emphasizes arbitration and reasoning, names the process very clearly, and in many ways bridges sharing one's vision and sharing the power to envision.

WISE-WOMEN JUDGES: GROPING TOWARD FAIRNESS AND PEACE

WISE-WOMEN JUDGES AND "DISTRIBUTIVE JUSTICE"

Feminist and liberational educators tend to discuss education in an "empathetic" manner; they aim to listen, understand, empower, and mobilize students in their classrooms. In an interesting article on the strengths and liabilities of liberational approaches to education, Lauren Smith suggests that a teacher must "coach" two types of games going on. She coaches the transformational game that she is playing—encouraging students to find their own voice and reflect on their own experience. She must also, however, coach the game going on outside her playing field. The transformational classroom is not the only court in which the student plays. To ignore the skills for survival needed in the larger world is to disadvantage the learner. "To expect students to negotiate power structures and inequities we do not admit exist is to ask them to play what I call Secret Basketball: the hoops are out there somewhere, but nobody's going to say where they are."[44] The wise leader must also empower her community toward recognized processes of decision making. Feminist teachers are increasingly aware that "in spite of positive motivation, students lack the experience or skills to participate actively and equally in a democratic classroom."[45] I consider democratic process to be in Iris Young's category of "distributive" (doling out the goods of society) rather than "communicative" justice (taking part in the constructing of society) because it is bringing people into a process already designed.

Coaching people in the process of rendering reasoned judgment is coaching people to participate in the best of the dominant Western tradition. Critical theorist Jürgen Habermas contends that "ideal" conditions for speech are possible. Recognizing the problems of conflicting interests and ideological taint in communication, Habermas offers a complex theory of "undistorted communication," which supplies norms for reasonable and valid discourse among different parties. The competencies required for undistorted communication are: to make factual claims about things in the world that can be tested by experience, to say things that will help regulate our interpersonal relations, and to express oneself and one's intentions authentically. His basic assumption is that communication inherently requires the capacity to give good reasons for our actions and beliefs, reasons that make sense even to those who do not share our presuppositions. Furthermore, Habermas believes that if all persons seeking truth engage in genuine communication, they can reach consensus concerning what is right. The "core idea" behind this theory of "communicative ethics" is: "namely the processual generation of reasonable agreement about moral principles via an open-ended moral conversation."[46]

I believe that this strategy for empowerment is a useful one, and I employ it frequently. The limitations, however, need to be named. The intention for fairness and justice is genuine, but the reality is being questioned by many educators and social critics. Though meant to "level the playing field" and give an equal voice to all players, democratic processes privilege those who are articulate in rhetoric, linear in their thinking, immersed in and committed to the Western tradition and its classics, and comfortable with direct speech and open conflict.[47] While many persons assume that the "rules" of argument and reasoning are universally (objectively) valid, this is a modern bias based on Enlightenment assumptions. Those who speak indirectly (for instance, through story rather than linear explanation), nonverbally (including through art, dance, silence, and music), in religious or metaphorical language (invoking spiritual and transcendent speech), or paradoxically (holding contradictory truths in tension) are disadvantaged or excluded from the communicative process. Lofty though its goals are, it marginalizes those who speak in other ways, know a different tradition, and are uncomfortable in argumentative settings. This doesn't mean we disregard such processes, it means rather that we recognize the bias and use other processes along with democratic ones.

If a leader works to develop the skills for this kind of process, marginalization can be minimized.[48] When leaders provide ground rules and guidelines that describe the procedures for fair conversation, all participants begin with a level of know-how and continue with limits and parameters. The "code for communication" is not a hidden secret that "outsiders" are left to crack; it is made explicit *and it holds all people accountable.* Sometimes women and other subordinate persons are empowered by being given the "street smarts" for conversational competence; men and others in power are checked by being held accountable to rules they might easily disregard in an open forum or laissez-faire conversation. Ground rules not only pass on the code to the uninitiated, but they also remind those who take their position of dominance for granted what the rules of the game really are. Those who have enjoyed power and have not had to name their reasons for their viewpoints and actions are restrained by democratic practices. In this way, there *is* a kind of leveling; the rules of democracy discipline those within its tradition even as the rules impose upon those outside that tradition. Even when clearly defining the procedure, a leader need not hold it rigidly. At its best, democracy contains within it the seeds of its own reform; a successful dialogue is judged by the capacity for those taking part in it to clarify and enlarge their standpoints.

Girls who participate in this kind of process in a community of faith may be helped to argue and converse more confidently in other contexts. If the procedure is clearly explained, then girls and women will not have to guess what the secret code for participation is. They will know the code, and this may help them feel more empowered. While this leadership emphasis does not unleash all forms of communication as does the empathetic emphasis, it may be less stressful in that it is more predictable. Even if a leader makes it clear that a wide variety of expression is permissible, no one really knows how others will respond to their style. With a procedure such as conversational theological reflection, the guesswork is removed.

CONVERSATIONAL THEOLOGICAL REFLECTION

In this section, we will consider how leaders can employ a democratic process of theological reflection and decision making. This kind of process is based on a linear style of reasoning and the principles of good argument, and thus it reflects a Western, male-derived framework. Yet, the framework is stretched so that conversation rather than adversarial debate, the construction of truth rather than the promotion of a truth characterizes the process.

Various educators and practical theologians have offered models for "practical theological reflection," which provide a structured procedure for leading communities through reflection on theology, cultural wisdom, and life practice. Thomas Groome's pioneering proposal for a Shared Praxis Approach remains helpful.[49] Drawing on classic sources in theology and philosophy, Groome outlined five movements for an active/reflective educational process: Naming Present Action (which asks participants to describe current practice); Critical Reflection on Present Action (which asks participants to describe why they do what they do); Making Accessible the Christian Story and Vision (which draws on Scripture and Tradition in order to evaluate present practice and guide future action); Dialogue to Appropriate Story/Vision to Participants' Stories and Vision (which nudges participants to converse with their tradition); Decision/Response for Lived Christian Faith (which moves participants to decide on future action in response to their study). Groome also suggests a "focusing activity" at the beginning to center the group before it engages in the process.

Looking back to the case of Heritage Church, Rev. Jones could have led the community through a Shared Praxis process that posed the question in their pastor's heart: How can we minister to our neighbors? Who is our neighbor and what do they need? Let's examine, modifying the Shared Praxis Approach, what this might have looked like.

Deep Centering: Although Groome suggests that educators prepare a "focusing activity" that turns participants' attention to a "generative theme" related to the present practice they will evaluate,[50] I propose a somewhat different starting place. Before engaging in a reflective process, communities of faith can remind themselves of what it is that centers and grounds their life together. This centering activity is paradoxically both deeply affirming and highly iconoclastic. They affirm their identity in a God who grants them worth; and they confess that this God alone is sacred—traditions and practices can be affirmed and revised but never absolutized. Rev. Jones could begin the study with a prayer, meditation, reading, or piece of artwork that focuses the common attention on the God who both unites them and frees them for serious debate. I frequently use for "deep centering" a litany based on Acts 15, which recalls the presence of the Spirit of God *within the process* of debate and dissention.

Naming Present Practice: In naming their practice, they could examine what existing ministries they are carrying out to their neighbors. They could address such questions as: What are our existing programs? What are we doing in them? Are we doing them well? Are these sufficient?

Critical Reflection on Present Practice: They could then move into a critical probing. Why do they focus on these particular programs? Is this where they want to place their energy and priorities? Here is where Pastor Jones might involve them in the kind of contextual study she did by herself; she could give them the tools for canvasing their neighborhood and calling or writing the appropriate places to obtain information on demographics in order to answer the question: Who are our neighbors and what do they need?

Making Accessible the Christian Tradition: When leading a group through an educational process, a leader makes a number of decisions that impact the educational outcome. One of the most important "political decisions" a leader makes is at this stage of making the Christian tradition accessible.[51] Groome understands this step in the process to be akin to a "catechetical process" of handing down the "revelational heritage." It is not, however, a dogmatic procedure, but rather one that invites participants to "reflect upon, grapple with, question, and personally encounter what is being presented." Thus, Groome stresses how important it is for an educator or educating group to present the story and vision of tradition in a way that is "disclosure rather than closure." "The presenter must never make his or her version of the community Story/Vision sound like the fullness and final statement of the 'truth.'" A presenter or presenting group would make their dialogical posture evident by ending their presentation, says Groome, with something like: "And that is my understanding of the tradition on this topic. What do you think?"[52]

Although Groome doesn't make this distinction, it is helpful here to note that there are at least two political options open to a leader at this step. I call these the "authoritative democratic" option and the "collaborative democratic" option. The "authoritative option," which is probably the one Groome had in mind when articulating the approach, is where the leader makes the decision to guide the group according to specific themes in Scripture and tradition she has selected. She still engages the community, as Groome suggested, but she presents a particular interpretation of the selected themes. For example, Rev. Jones could selectively choose to focus on traditions and scripture that promote care of the elderly. She would still invite questions, challenges, and suggestions for alternative traditions and scriptures to be considered, and she would convey to the community an awareness that she is a wise but fallible guide. Yet, the tradition that she made accessible would have a particular bend to it.

Alternatively, she could take the "collaborative democratic" option and structure the study around what I call "tensive texts and traditions" (tensions in our tradition) regarding this issue. With this option, the community would be instructed to wrestle with the conflicting sides of the tradition (for instance, the importance of ministering to the young and the old; to ourselves and to others). In collaboration, they would have to work out which aspect of the tradition to follow or how to hold the sides of the tension together in a constructive manner. They may decide to pursue one side of the tension, but by wrestling with tensive strands the participants are taught to acknowledge the complexities in the tradition and to be open to the possibility that the unchosen side of the tension may need to be recovered at some point in the life of the community.

Dialogue to Appropriate Tradition to Participants' Lives: Rev. Jones, having either presented an interpreted theme or tensive traditions, then would instruct the community to bring the tradition in dialogue with their situation. They would consider the question: How does the tradition inform what we do? They would also consider: How does our experience illumine the tradition? What insights have emerged from carrying on a conversation between our situation and the words in Scripture?

Although Groome doesn't address this, we do well, as argued in chapter 6, to invite the voices of those who interpret Scripture and think through things differently from us. The categories of "other" that a community should keep in mind are: those on the margins of one's own community (children, women, specially challenged persons); those from a different socioeconomic class; those outside Euro-American mainstream; gay and lesbian persons; those from a different faith. These others need not come in person; a leader can bring their voices through commentaries, other books and stories, films, and even music. The idea is to expand the number of voices contributing to the eventual judgment and decision that will be made.[53]

Decision/Response for Lived Christian Life: Finally, Rev. Jones guides toward practice. She focuses the community on answering the question: What do we do now? She can begin with brainstorming possibilities, having the community name the value and limitation of each suggestion. If there are basically two different views, the leader can bring the group through a "controversy exercise." The general idea here is to get each group to name the reasons for their view, to get each group to listen to and fairly reflect the viewpoint of the other group, to provide time for mutual questioning, and to brainstorm possible "third options."[54] Even if one group "wins," the concerns raised by the other group should be incorporated into the plan of action. Thus, if in the process of this study, the majority of the people want to put their energies into a youth program rather than a housing complex for the elderly, perhaps the youth leaders could involve young people in ministering to the elderly through friendship and service (including house repairs). While Rev. Jones might not see the housing complex built, she might see greater interaction between people in the congregation and the elderly people about whom she cares.

A process such as Shared Praxis works well when one's leadership strategy emphasizes reasoning and judgment; it calls on the best of our critical thinking abilities. Like the other strategies, it does not stand alone. A leader with passion, empathy, and judgment will weave and be woven into a community life that calls for her to share her vision, to empower others to shape the common life, and to foster and moderate democratic processes.

SHE WHO TEACHES HER FRIEND'S DAUGHTER TORAH

I began this book with the question: *Can caring families and communities of faith, specifically the church, make a difference in the outcome of my daughter's development and in the development of other girls and women?*

Deborah's memory was recently evoked for me when I read an article about a modern-day woman also deemed a mother of Israel. Anne Scheiber, who lived a modest life, recently left millions to Yeshiva University to provide scholarship aid for needy women. Through good judgment during her life she turned a $5,000 investment into $23 million. Her vision was to spare the daughters of Israel from having their minds ravished. Having experienced painful sexism in her own career, she wanted to make sure that other women wouldn't be shortchanged in the ways that she was. When she died at 101 years of age, she clearly had hope that the world might be different for the "daughters" who came after her. "The Torah says that he who teaches his friend's son Torah, it is as if he gave birth to him," recited Dr. Norman Lamm, the president of the university.[55] "Here's a woman who for 101 years was childless and now becomes a mother to a whole community. Not only now, but for generations to come."[56] She was indeed "a mother to a whole community" after the style of Deborah. Her vision of justice embraced a group beyond the bounds of her family, her generation, and even her life.

SHE WHO TEACHES HER TORAH TO BEFRIEND HER DAUGHTERS

Many of the girls and women we know have been shortchanged by our communities of faith. They have suffered under theologies that enervate them, they have been discouraged from developing their own voices, they have carried too heavy a burden of empathy, they have been discouraged from getting dirty in men's business, they have been pitted against one another, they have been silenced or oppressed by biblical teachings, and they have been left out of leadership in their houses of faith. Yet, we also have a cache of resources in our midst. The cache is perhaps, at this time, rather modest. But, we can invest it wisely, and it will bear much fruit.

What is this stockpile? A reclaimed theology promoting prophetic vigor, the God-given capacity for personal strength and voice, caring mothers and fathers and sisters and brothers in our midst, girls with spunk, older women with courage, the stories of women of faith, a tradition with which we can converse and to which we can even talk back, women of fire who have been raised up to lead, and a God whose Spirit both weeps for her ravished daughters and sings songs of celebration for her redeemed daughters.

Let us say no to the dehumanization of girls in theology, the biblical witness, ours and other cultures, communities of faith, and unjust families. When our daughters refuse to be silenced and resist expectations for compliance, let us be there. Let girls everywhere romp around in dirty dresses, delighting in the work and play of inheriting the earth. Let the mothers and fathers beam proudly while the grandmothers call out knowingly and approvingly, "You girls are much, thanks be to God!"[57]

Caring families and communities of faith, specifically churches, can make a difference in the outcome of my daughter's development and in the development of other girls and women.

Notes

Introduction

1. Michael V. Fox, *Character and Ideology in the Book of Esther* (Columbia: University of South Carolina Press, 1991), 164.

2. Letty Russell, *Becoming Human* (Philadelphia: Westminster Press, 1982), 57. Italics added.

3. A letter to the editor, name withheld, *New Woman*, (May 1994): 16.

4. The notion of the "perilous divide" is used by Jane O'Reilly in "The Lost Girls," *Mirabella* (Apr. 1994): 116.

5. Mary Pipher, *Reviving Ophelia: Saving the Selves of Adolescent Girls* (New York: Ballantine Books, 1994), 37-44.

6. Susan Faludi, *Backlash: The Undeclared War Against American Women* (New York: Crown, 1991).

7. While I write this book from the perspective of a Christian and for Christian communities of faith, what I have to say is relevant also for other communities of faith that wish to support girls' development.

8. Paula Gunn Allen refers to the "red roots of white feminism," indicating that power and freedom for women were an inherent part of Native American worldviews. Sadly, forced assimilation to the dominant worldview has compromised this value. See, "Who is Your Mother? Red Roots of White Feminism," in *The Sacred Hoop: Recovering the Feminine in American Indian Traditions* (Boston: Beacon Press, 1986).

9. I am acutely aware of the history of Christian anti-Judaism; correcting this legacy is a recurrent theme in my work. An influential study has been Franklin H. Littell, *The Crucifixion of the Jews: The Failure of Christians to Understand the Jewish Experience* (New York: Harper & Row, 1975).

10. Susan Bordo (*Unbearable Weight: Feminism, Western Culture, and the Body* [Berkeley: University of California Press, 1993], 40) while acknowledging the problematic aspects of making generalizations, also cautions against too severe a "taboo on generalization." Whenever a society has categories, those who are placed in the same category will have some significant experiences in common. This doesn't necessarily mean that they are making claims about what is "essential" to being a woman (though some would do this), it simply means that there are at least some social experiences and forces in common.

11. My particular orientation is akin to what David Tracy calls "mutually critical correlations," the process by which theology correlates "the meaning and truth of an interpretation of the Christian fact and the meaning and truth of an interpretation of the contemporary situation." See "The Foundations of Practical Theology," in Don S. Browning, ed. *Practical Theology: The Emerging Field in Theology, Church, and World* (San Francisco: Harper & Row, Pubs, 1983), 63.

12. Wolfhart Pannenberg, *Anthropology in Theological Perspective* (Philadelphia: Westminster Press, 1985).

13. This portrait of feminist research is indebted to Sandra Harding, "Is There a Feminist Method?," in Sandra Harding, ed., *Feminism and Methodology* (Indianapolis: Indiana University Press, 1987).

14. bell hooks, *Feminist Theory: From Margin to Center* (Boston: South End Press, 1984), Ch. 5.

15. This section is indebted to my entry on "Vashti," in Anne Commire, ed. *Women in World History* (Yorkin Publications, forthcoming). I recommend this forthcoming volume to communities seeking to recover important historical women.

16. Ibid.

17. The story of Esther has traditionally enjoyed historical status. However, modern critics consider the

major plot to be improbable, and many allow for only a kernel of historicity. Numerous features of the novella are collaborated by other historical sources, including the reign and personality of Ahasuerus, identified as Xerxes I, who was renowned for building great palaces, giving lavish parties, and displaying a bellicose temper. However, other details are either incompatible with known facts or considered too fantastical. The fact that Amestris, rather than Vashti, is recorded as Xerxes' queen during the period under study has raised questions about Vashti's historicity. Scholars today find study of the literary themes of the story to reveal important aspects of world history, even if not actual events. In terms of its inclusion in the Hebrew scriptures, the story of Esther provides an explanation for the origins of Purim, a Jewish festival. The core of the book dates to the period of Persian dominance (539-332 B.C.E.), and its final form probably took shape in the second century B.C.E.

18. See for instance, Carey A. Moore, *Esther,* Anchor Bible Series, 7B (Garden City, N.Y.: Doubleday, 1971). For the alternative viewpoint that I am adopting, see Michael V. Fox, *Character and Ideology,* Ch VI.

19. Herodotus, *The History,* trans. David Grene (Chicago: University of Chicago Press, 1987).

20. According to David J. A. Clines (*The Esther Scroll: The Story of the Story* [Sheffield: JSOT Press, 1984], 30), the setting of this story has a "satirical tone," which grants us permission to bring a hermeneutics of suspicion toward this exhibitionist king.

21. Though the evidence is scanty and contradictory, it may have been the custom for wives to leave the banquet before heavy drinking began, at which point concubines would provide entertainment and company to the drunken men. The king, in asking Vashti to enter at the point he did, would be treating her as a courtesan. See Andre LaCocque, *The Feminine Unconventional: Four Subversive Figures in Israel's Tradition* (Minneapolis: Fortress Press, 1990), 55. Whether the degradation is explicit (reducing Vashti to the level of concubine) or implicit (reducing the queen to a sexual object), it seems to be operating—and also seems to call for resistance.

22. One rabbinic opinion held that "the king felt remorse because he remembered (in 2:1) that Vashti had acted properly, and that what was decreed against her was contrary to what was right" (Est. Rab. V 2). The inference of the king's remorse is based on the narrator's description that "when the anger of King Ahasuerus had abated, he remembered Vashti and what she had done and what had been decreed against her." See Fox, 165.

23. Alice Laffey, *An Introduction to the Old Testament: A Feminist Perspective* (Philadelphia: Fortress Press, 1988), 215.

24. See Fox, *Character and Ideology,* 164.

25. Martin Luther, *Table Talks,* Tischreden (Wiemar, 1912), 1:208. William Phipps wryly notes that the "protestant reformer presumably admired only conscientious *males* who protested against the powers that be." It is bitterly ironic, I think, that a woman's "here I stand" was anathema. (Quoted in William E. Phipps, *Assertive Biblical Women* [Westport, Conn.: Greenwood Press, 1992], 96.)

26. The author's mockery of Ahasuerus was noted in 1858 by M. Samuels in his book *Certain People of the Book* (New York: Alfred A. Knopf, 1858), 3-29.

27. Fox, *Character and Ideology,* 168.

28. In fact, this story seems to suggest that Freud got it wrong. Male, not female, hysteria is the problem in this narrative.

29. Michael Fox ventures that, though praiseworthy in the abstract, Vashti's actions were not savvy. The massive and tender egos of the men required more shrewd maneuvering, and thus Esther's manipulative tactics were justified. *Character and Ideology,* p. 170.

30. This view is also held by Mieke Bal, who writes that Vashti "is eliminated only to reemerge in Esther, who takes her place, avenging her punishment by turning disobedience into access to power." "Lots of Writing," *Semeia* 54 (1991):77-102. See especially pp. 92-93.

31. Renita J. Weems, *Just a Sister Away* (San Diego: LuraMedia, 1988), 99.

32. Katheryn Pfisterer Darr, *Far More Precious Than Jewels: Perspectives on Biblical Women* (Louisville: Westminster/ John Knox, 1991), 182.

33. One could just as easily argue that the authorial intention is to warn men that suppressing women will backfire on them as one can argue that the intention is to warn women not to rebel against their men. In fact, I believe the weight of the story supports this interpretation.

34. Interestingly, commentators have celebrated Mordecai's "spirit of independence" while ignoring Vashti's similar spirit (Lewis Bayles Paton, *A Critical and Exegetical Commentary on the Book of Esther,*

International Critical Commentary [New York: Scribner's, 1908], 62). Mordecai's independence had just as dire of consequences as Vashti's; the only reason Mordecai is spared Vashti's fate is that he had a heroine to reverse that fate. Carey Moore's statement that between Mordecai and Esther "the greater hero is Mordecai, who supplied the brains while Esther simply followed his directions" [See Moore, *Esther*, lii] is inaccurate. Mordecai got the Jews into trouble in the first place; Esther came up with the plan to unravel the tangled mess he created. As Sidney Ann White puts it, "having precipitated this crisis, he must rely on Esther to undo the damage" ("Esther: A Feminine Model for Jewish Diaspora" in *Gender and Difference in Ancient Israel*, ed. Peggy Day [Minneapolis: Fortress Press, 1989], 169). Unlike White, I do not condemn Mordecai for "refusing to accept and work with his subordinate position," for I think resistance to subordination—both on the part of Vashti and Mordecai—is courageous and potentially transformative. I do agree with White, as shall become clearer in chapter 5, that survival and adaptation are, however, sometimes wiser than liberation.

35. Herodotus [IX 107] reported that "to call a man 'worse than a woman' is of course, the greatest insult one can offer a Persian."

36. Darr, *Far More Pecious Than Jewels*, 164.

37. The story of Esther, in fact, exists in three versions. In addition to the Hebrew Masoretic text, the version in most of our canons, there are two later Greek texts. It appears that one of the reasons additional versions were written, especially the "B" text, which is part of the Septuagint, is that the writers compensated for the lack of religious piety in the original version. This lack of religiosity (as well as the violence—which is ironic, given the course of Luther's life) offended Martin Luther, who wished the book of Esther, along with the gospel of James, had never been included in the canon. For a discussion of the characterizations of Esther in the three versions, see Linda Day, *Three Faces of a Queen: Characterization in the Books of Esther* (Sheffield, Eng.: Sheffield Academic Press, 1995).

38. Marjory Zoet Bankson, *Braided Streams: Esther and a Woman's Way of Growing* (San Diego: LuraMedia, 1985).

39. Esther was one of the books Martin Luther sought to excise from the canon. The brutality at the end of the story was unbecoming to the people of God in Luther's eyes. I have to agree with this complaint; there is no transformative vision toward violence as the means to achieve liberation. I, however, wonder if the author isn't making a point we ought not to miss. The violence at the end signals to me the fact that violence has come full circle; the opening scene with Vashti is the precursor to the bloodshed at the end. It is almost as if the author is naming the earlier scene for what it is by ending with brutality.

40. Weems, *Just a Sister Away*, 108.

41. Taken from the New International Version. Unless otherwise noted, the translation will be the NRSV. Here I acknowledge feminists who have gone before this work and paved the way for what I am doing in this book. Freda Gardner is a feminist teacher who models caretaking in a common house (see Freda A. Gardner and Herbert Anderson, *Living Alone* [Louisville: John Knox Press, 1997]; see also Carol Lakey Hess, "Freda Gardner: A Master Teacher Whose Faith Has Helped Us Understand," in *Faith of Our Foremothers: Women Changing Religious Education*, ed. Barbara Anne Keely [Louisville: Westminster/John Knox, forthcoming 1997]). Maria Harris (See *Dance of the Spirit: The Seven Steps of Women's Spirituality* [New York: Bantam Books, 1989]) and Mary Elizabeth Mullino Moore (*Teaching from the Heart: Theology and Educational Method* [Minneapolis: Fortress Press, 1989]) are feminist Christian educators whose works have shaped my thinking. Katharine Doob Sakenfeld's work in feminist hermeneutics is both foundational ("Feminist Uses of Biblical Material," in *Feminist Interpretation of the Bible*, ed. Letty Russell) and cutting-edge (especially her understanding of "culturally cued readings" begun in "The Daughters of Zelophehad and Feminist Biblical Interpretation," *Theology Today* [July 1989]: 154-68).

42. Rosemary Catalano Mitchell and Gail Anderson Ricciuti, *Birthings and Blessings: Liberating Worship Services for the Inclusive Church* (New York: The Crossroad Publishing Co., 1991), 71.

43. Mary Gendler, "The Restoration of Vashti," *The Jewish Woman*, ed. E. Koltun (New York: Schocken Books, 1976), 241-47.

44. Alicia Suskin Ostriker, *The Nakedness of the Fathers: Biblical Visions and Revisions* (New Brunswick: Rutgers University Press, 1994), 228.

45. I am not the first to imagine solidarity between Vashti and Esther. At least one early rabbi portrayed Esther as siding with Vashti and accusing Haman of orchestrating her demise out of envy (b. Beg. 16a). See Fox, *Character and Ideology*, 165.

46. See Arthur Waskow, "God's Body, the Midrashic Process, and the Embodiment of Torah," *Body and*

Bible: Interpreting and Experiencing Biblical Narratives, ed. Bjorn Krondorfer (Philadelphia: Trinity Press Int'l., 1992), 133-44.

47. Judith Plaskow, *Standing Again at Sinai: Judaism from a Feminist Perspective* (New York: HarperSanFrancisco, 1990), 53.

48. "The Secret Jew: An Oral Tradition of Women," in *On Being a Jewish Feminist: A Reader*, Susannah Heschel, ed. (New York: Schocken Books, 1983), 273.

49. It would be helpful to read the text of the book of Esther before reading the midrash.

50. Idea posed by women participating in workshop.

1. Theology and Women: Giving Our Selves Away

1. Jean Baker Miller, *Toward a New Psychology of Women*, 2d ed. (Boston: Beacon, 1986), 50.

2. Julia Wood, *Who Cares? Women, Care, and Culture* (Carbondale, Ill.: Southern Illinois University Press, 1994), 33.

3. Søren Kierkegaard, *The Sickness Unto Death* (Princeton: Princeton University Press, 1980), 32.

4. J. Vernon McGee, *Esther: The Romance of Providence* (Nashville: Thomas Nelson, 1982), p. 33. I owe this citation to my colleague Nora Tubbs Tisdale.

5. Wood, *Who Cares?*, 33.

6. Shel Silverstein, *The Giving Tree* (New York: Harper & Row, 1964).

7. Reinhold Niebuhr, *The Nature and Destiny of Man*, vol. 1, *Human Nature* (New York: Scribner's Sons, 1941), 25.

8. Niebuhr, *The Nature and Destiny of Man*, vol. 2, *Human Destiny*, 111.

9. Niebuhr, *The Nature and Destiny of Man*, vol. 1, *Human Nature*, 137-38. Italics added.

10. For example: Valerie Saiving, "The Human Situation: A Feminine View," in *Womanspirit Rising: A Feminist Reader in Religion*, ed. Carol Christ and Judith Plaskow (SanFrancisco: Harper and Row Publishers, 1979); Judith Plaskow, *Sex, Sin, and Grace: Women's Experience and the Theologies of Reinhold Niebuhr and Paul Tillich* (New York: University Press of America, 1980); Daphne Hampson, "Reinhold Niebuhr on Sin: A Critique," *Reinhold Niebuhr and the Issues of our Time*, ed. Richard Harries (Grand Rapids: Eerdmans, 1986).

11. George Eliot, *Daniel Deronda*, ed. Barbara Hardy (1876; reprint, New York: Penguin Books, 1967), 694.

12. Saiving, "The Human Situation," 39.

13. Carmen Braun Williams, "The Psychology of Women," *Women's Studies Thinking Women: Revised Printing*, ed. Jodi Wetzel et al. (Dubuque, Iowa: Kendall/Hunt, 1993), 33.

14. Hampson, "Reinhold Niebuhr on Sin," 47. Emphasis added.

15. In the introduction to his book *Narratives of a Vulnerable God: Christ, Theology, and Scripture* (Louisville: Westminster/John Knox Press, 1994), William Placher locates himself with this remark: "While the world's disadvantaged may often need to reflect first and foremost on how to empower themselves, I find myself thinking more about the dangers and ambiguities of power." This is an appropriate acknowledgment of the need for some to share power and the need for others to assume it. I would not want the former to be neglected, even as the latter is upheld.

16. Daniel Patte is engaged in what he terms "an androcritical perspective," which acknowledges the contextuality of all theology (including that which was once taken for universal), critiques the oppressive nature of Eurocentric thought, and affirms the validity of "male, European-American critical exegesis" when it acknowledges its partial and "interested" nature. It can therefore be said that a theological/ideological perspective doesn't always protect and promote the interests of a group but can sometimes challenge and correct those interests. See "Acknowledging the Contextual Character of Male, European-American Critical Exegeses: An Androcritical Perspective," in Fernando F. Segovia and Mary Ann Tolbert, eds., *Reading From this Place: Social Location and Biblical Interpretation in the United States*, vol. 1 (Minneapolis: Fortress Press, 1995).

17. Niebuhr, *Human Nature*, 194.

18. Niebuhr, *Human Destiny*, 197.

19. Susan Nelson Dunfee, "The Sin of Hiding: A Feminist Critique of Reinhold Niebuhr's Account of the Sin of Pride," *Soundings* (Fall 1982): 317.

20. "The Sin of Servanthood," *A Troubling in My Soul: Womanist Perspectives on Evil and Suffering*, ed. Emilie M. Townes (Maryknoll: Orbis, 1993), 211.

21. Ted Peters, *Sin: Radical Evil in Soul and Society* (Grand Rapids: Eerdmans, 1994), 29.

22. Peters is fond of quoting Proverbs 16:18, "Pride goes before destruction." It is interesting to note that this same theme is evident in 11:2, "When pride comes, then comes disgrace," and yet it is counterbalanced by v. 16, "The timid become destitute, but the aggressive gain riches." Pride is an important theme, but it is not the only sin to which the Bible speaks.

23. "Remarks on the Special Politics of Reason," in *Women and Moral Theory*, Eva Feder Kettay and Diana T. Meyers, eds. (Totowa, N.J.: Rowman & Littlefield, 1987), 246.

24. See Anne Wilson Schaef, *When Society Becomes an Addict* (San Francisco: H&R, 1987).

25. This is a refrain in *The Woman's Bible* (1898; reprint, Salem, N.H.: Ayer Company Publ., 1988).

26. See Bruce Kirmsee, *Kierkegaard in Golden Age Denmark* for a summary. (Indianapolis: Indiana University Press, 1990), 359-78.

27. Niebuhr, *Human Nature*, 3.

28. Kierkegaard, *Sickness*, 34.

29. Ibid., 36.

30. Ibid., 50. Here I am indebted to Hampson, "Reinhold Niebuhr on Sin," cited above.

31. Ibid., 69.

32. This connection was made by John Zizioulas, in *Being as Communion: Studies in Personhood and the Church* (Crestwood, N.Y.: St. Vladimir's Seminary Press, 1985), 42.

33. Kierkegaard, *Sickness*, 43.

34. Kierkegaard, *Sickness*, xi.

35. In his slim volume, *For Self Examination* (translated by Edna and Howard Hong [Minneapolis: Augsburg Publishing House, 1940]), Kierkegaard reinforces female passivity. He extols the woman for her capacity for silence (and reprimands those who do not have it), and chides the man for his noisiness. However, this has the effect of a backhanded compliment. Men are almost excused to go back to being assertive and opinionated, and women are given the honorable duty of representing silence. "Men have so much to hurry through, so much to do with noisy things, all too much. If you do not see to it that all is in order, that silence is there, silence will never come into your house," he warns women (61). "If you want to be a power, woman, let me confide in you how—learn silence!" (58). This quality is essential to the home, just as "it must be the characteristic of man to have a strong personality" (59). Kierkegaard notes with less than enthusiasm the many things "in these times a girl learns" in school. "The question is whether in these times she learns the most important thing of all . . . —the question is whether she learns *silence*, learns to be quiet." Alas, what Kierkegaard gives with the one hand (the clarion call for women to become selves), he takes back with the other.

36. Kierkegaard, *Sickness*, 81.

37. Ibid., 44.

38. Richard J. Foster and James Bryan Smith, eds., *Devotional Classics* (San Francisco: Harper Collins, 1993), 178-83.

39. *The Holy Rule of Our Most Holy Father Benedict*, trans. the Rev. Boniface Verheven, O. S. B. (Benedictine College).

40. See Clement of Alexandria, *Christ the Educator*, trans. Simon P. Wood (New York: Fathers of the Church, Inc.), 1954.

41. I noticed this several years ago when I was invited to speak at a conference. I was slated to room with another woman who was giving several presentations on Benedictine spirituality. I ended up with a room to myself when this presenter insisted that the spartan conditions of the room, and the presence of a roommate, were not conducive to her preparation for a rigorous schedule of lectures. She requested to be put up at a local hotel. I had no problem with her assertion of what I thought were legitimate needs. I did have a problem, however, when the next day she spoke of the Benedictine understanding of contentment as the capacity to remain within the limits of one's situation—with no nuancing. Although she lived a complex understanding of contentment that enabled her to discern when to accept and when to challenge situational limitation, she presented a flattened portrayal of contentment. She was willing to challenge the limits of her world, but she hadn't taken that complexity into her theorizing. Thus, while *she* has the power and wherewithal to assert herself, the spir-

ituality she presented could be dangerous to those who take "contentment" and "limits" at face value.

42. For a critique of the Benedictine emphasis on obedience, see Dorothee Soelle, *Creative Disobedience* (Cleveland: Pilgrim Press, 1995), Ch. 3, "Obedience as Submission to a Person: An Authoritarian Model." For an appreciative account of Benedictine spirituality, see Esther de Waal, *Seeking God: The Way of St. Benedict* (Collegeville, Minn.: Liturgical Press, 1984).

43. Soelle, *Creative Disobedience*, 16.

44. Roberta C. Bondi, *To Pray & To Love: Conversations on Prayer with the Early Church* (Minneapolis: Fortress Press, 1992), 101.

45. Soelle, *Creative Disobedience*, xxi.

46. In early lists, apathy (acedia) and sadness (tristia) are listed as separate sins. The two eventually became merged into one.

47. Dorothy Sayers, quoted in Donald Capps, *Deadly Sins and Saving Virtues* (Philadelphia: Fortress, 1987), 61.

48. I am indebted to Donald Capps's book, *The Depleted Self: Sin in a Narcissistic Age* (Minneapolis: Fortress Press, 1993). Capps argues that shame rather than pride, self-depletion rather than self-centeredness, is the primary condition in our culture. He further contends that the pervasive need is for affirmation ("mirroring") in our culture, and this is often quenched in our guilt-oriented theologies that prohibit pridelike tendencies. Like Kierkegaard, but drawing on Emerson, Capps argues that shame-based societies produce people who are slaves to social conformity and who abandon their central selves.

49. Capps, *Deadly Sins and Saving Virtues*, 108.

50. Carol Gilligan, "In a Different Voice: Women's Conceptions of the Self and of Morality," *Harvard Educational Review* 47 (1977): 486.

51. Indeed, I have had more than one woman tell me that she became a feminist upon reading of Deborah in the book of Judges.

52. Placher, *Narratives of a Vulnerable God*, 151.

53. See my article, "Abomination and Creativity: Shaking the Order of the Cosmos," *The Princeton Seminary Bulletin*, XV (1994): 28-45.

54. This metaphor comes from Robert Kegan, *In Over Our Heads: The Mental Demands of Modern Life* (Cambridge: Harvard University Press, 1994), 206.

55. See Carroll Saussy, *The Gift of Anger: A Call to Faithful Action* (Louisville: Westminster/John Knox, 1995), for a helpful distinction between destructive and healthy expressions of anger.

56. Elisabeth Schüssler Fiorenza, *Discipleship of Equals: A Critical Feminist Ekklesia-logy of Liberation* (New York: Crossroad, 1993), 346.

57. Gabrielle Uhlien ed., *Meditations with Hildegaard of Bingen* (Sante Fe, N.M.: Bear & Co., Inc., 1996). Included in *Cries of the Spirit: A Celebration of Women's Spirituality*, ed. Marilyn Sewell (Boston: Beacon Press, 1991), 253.

58. Alice Walker, *Horses Make a Landscape Look More Beautiful* (London: Harcourt, Brace, Jovanovich, Inc., 1986). Included in *Cries of the Spirit*, 141-42.

59. David F. Swenson and Walter Lowrie, trans., *Concluding Unscientific Postscript* (Princeton: Princeton Univ Press, 1941), 387-88; *Journals and Papers*, ed. and trans. Howard V. Hong and Edna H. Hong (Bloomington, Ind.: Indiana University Press, 1975), 46-82.

60. Soelle, *Suffering* (Philadelphia: Fortress, 1975). The two perspectives on suffering are not necessarily exclusive of one another. As I argued earlier, submission to one's own lot can be a pious adherence to suffering, and yet it also leads to apathy and insensitivity to the suffering of others (prophetic torpor), who are also expected to accept their lot.

61. bell hooks, *Yearning: Race, Gender, and Cultural Politics* (Boston: South End Press, 1990), 153.

62. The distinction between gender-related and gender-specific comes from Belenky et al., *Women's Ways of Knowing: The Development of Self, Voice, and Mind* (New York: Basic Books, 1986), 102.

63. Charles W. Kegley and Robert W. Bretall, eds., *Reinhold Niebuhr: His Religious, Social, and Practical Thought* (New York: The Macmillan Company, 1956), 241.

64. Elisabeth Schüssler Fiorenza more recently speaks of *kyriarchy* to highlight that the power of men rests in "that hand of elite, propertied, educated, freeborn men." Not all men share in kyriarchal

power. See her "Introduction," in Elisabeth Schüssler Fiorenza and Mary Shawn Copeland, eds., *Violence Against Women* (Maryknoll, N.Y.: Orbis Books, 1994), xxi-xxii.

65. There is some evidence that males are more aggressive than females due to testosterone levels, but even this is complicated by the fact that aggression can be demonstrated in a variety of manners, some of which women are more likely to exhibit. For a helpful examination of research on sex differences see Carol Tavris and Carole Wade, *The Longest War: Sex Differences in Perspective*, 2d ed. (Orlando: Harcourt Brace Jovanovich Publishers, 1984). Although I am open to being convinced that some behavioral and psychological traits are sex-linked, I tend to believe that gender differences are socially rather than biologically constructed.

66. Surely, we must note that there is a difference between Abraham's power and the limited and derivative power of Sarah. Though Sarah participates in hierarchy and classism, she does not have the same degree of power as does Abraham.

67. Audre Lorde, *Sister Outsider* (Trumansburg, N.Y.: Crossing Press, 1984), 66.

68. Ibid., 69.

69. Evelyn S. Bassoff, *Between Mothers and Sons* (New York: Penguin Books, 1994), 230.

2. The Dance of Human Development: In Celebration of "Sheila"

1. From Marge Piercy, "Maggid," in *Available Light* (New York: Middlemarsh, Inc., 1988), 124-25.

2. Adrienne Rich, *On Lies, Secrets, and Silence* (New York: W. W. Norton and Co., 1979), 35.

3. Subsequent studies have suggested that when corrected for educational level, men and women are more equal. Lawrence Kohlberg, with Charles Levine and Alexandra Hewer, "Synopses and Detailed Replies to Critics," in Lawrence Kohlberg, *Essays on Moral Development*, vol. 2, *The Psychology of Moral Development: The Nature and Validity of Moral Stages* (San Francisco: Harper & Row, 1984), 340.

4. Carol Gilligan, *In a Different Voice: Psychological Theory and Women's Development* (Cambridge: Harvard University Press, 1982), 5-23.

5. Robert Kegan, *The Evolving Self* (Cambridge: Harvard University Press, 1982), vii.

6. Robert Kegan, *In Over Our Heads: The Mental Demands of Modern Life* (Cambridge: Harvard University Press, 1994), 229.

7. Carol Christ, *Diving Deep and Surfacing: Women Writers on Spiritual Quest*, 2d ed. (Boston: Beacon Press, 1986).

8. See Robert Kegan, "There the Dance Is: Religious Dimensions of a Developmental Framework," in *Toward Moral and Religious Maturity*, James Fowler and Antoine Vergote, eds. (Morristown, N.J.: Silver Burdett Company, 1980).

9. Kegan, *The Evolving Self*, 107.

10. Kegan, *In Over our Heads*, "Dealing with Difference," 198-233.

11. Kegan, *In Over our Heads*, 222. The contrast Kegan draws between "making up" and "being made up" reflects the basic assumption of object-relations theory that the developmental task is the individuation of the self out of a presumed original oneness with the mother. This assumption has been challenged in more recent years by those who emphasize the lifelong relation between the mother and child. Kegan is also informed by the latter group, but perhaps his use of the autonomous notion of "making up" reveals that, in addition to his training, he is somewhat enmeshed in the cultural myth of the "self-made man." Morwenna Griffiths, in *Feminisms and the Self: The Web of Identity* (New York: Routledge, 1995), critiques this formative and pervasive cultural myth. No one can entirely make their relationships; similarly, no one is ever fully made up by them. We are always selves-in-relation, even if the relationship is not a good one.

12. Men who inherit an understanding of masculinity as powerful and controlling but who themselves do not have power can act out in destructive ways toward women. Feeling entitled to but isolated from power, they exercise control over the women in their lives. Bryan Turner, *The Body and Society: Explorations in Social Theory* (Cambridge: Basil Blackwell, 1984), 137ff.

13. Helen Prejean, C.S.J., *Dead Man Walking* (New York: Vintage Books, 1993), 188.

14. Kegan, *Evolving Self*, 97.

15. Ibid., 96-97, 231-32.

16. Sharon Parks, "Faith Development and Imagination in the Context of Higher Education" (Th. D.

diss., Harvard Divinity School, 1980). Cited in James Fowler, *Stages of Faith* (San Francisco: Harper & Row, 1981), 158.

17. Julia T. Wood, *Who Cares? Women, Care, and Culture* (Carbondale, Ill.: Southern Illinois University Press, 1994), 50-56.

18. In Mary Jane Moffat and Charlotte Painter, eds., *Revelations: Diaries of Women* (New York: Vintage Books, 1974), 142-43.

19. See Anne Wilson Schaef, *Escape from Intimacy: Untangling the "Love" Addictions: Sex, Romance, and Relationships* (San Francisco: Harper & Row, 1989), 78, 85. In a popular best-seller, Penelope Russianoff raises the question *Why Do I Think I Am Nothing Without a Man?* Developmentally, we might respond by saying at this stage in the evolution of the self, the self *is* its relationships, and thus feels like nothing without them. And in our culture, the prized relationship for women is attachment to a male. Her proffered solution, becoming "undependent," requires more than just a cognitive reorientation; it requires a renegotiation of life's key tensions in the direction of independence. When promoting such things as self-assertiveness and independence, we need to be aware of the magnitude of the transition that will take place.

20. Niebuhr, *Human Nature*, 234. In my view, it is unfortunate that Niebuhr used the term "sensuality" to describe this form of sin. Sensuality, which I understand to be an appreciation for the senses and the body, is a positive term.

21. See Niebuhr, *Human Nature*, 240.

22. Saiving, "The Human Situation," 36.

23. Ibid. Emphasis added.

24. Paul Ramsey, "Love and Law," in *Reinhold Niebuhr: His Religious, Social and Practical Thought*, ed. Charles Kegley and Robert W. Bretall (New York: The Macmillan Co., 1956), 110.

25. I am indebted to my colleague Dan Migliore for this insight. "Sin and Self-Loss: Karl Barth and the Feminist Critique of Traditional Doctrines of Sin," *Many Voices, One God: Being Faithful in a Pluralistic World*, ed. George Stroup and Walter Brueggemann (Louisville: Westminster/John Knox Press, forthcoming).

26. Virginia Woolf, "Professions for Women," in *The Death of the Mother and Other Essays* (New York: Harcourt, Brace and Jovanovich, 1942), 236-38.

27. Kegan, *Evolving Self*, 222.

28. Ibid., 102.

29. Kegan, *In Over Our Heads*, 133.

30. Shulamit Reinharz, "Toward an Ethnography of 'Voice' and 'Silence,'" in *Human Diversity: Perspectives on People in Context*, ed. Edison J. Trickett, and Roderick J. Watts and Dina Briman (San Francisco: Jossey-Bass, 1994), 183.

31. Christie Cozad Neuger, "Pastoral Counseling as an Art of Personal Political Activism," in Christie Cozad Neuger, *The Arts of Ministry: Feminist and Womanist Approaches* (Louisville: Westminster/John Knox Press, 1996), 100.

32. Dana Jack, "Silencing the Self: The Power of Social Imperatives in Female Depression," in *Women and Depression: A Lifespan Perspective*, ed. Ruth Formanek and Anita Gurian (New York: Springer Publishing Co., 1987), 166.

33. Interviewee quoted in Miriam Therese Winter, Adair Lummis, and Allison Stokes, *Defecting in Place: Women Claiming Responsibility for Their Own Spiritual Lives* (New York: Crossroad, 1994), 157.

34. Robert N. Bellah et al., *Habits of the Heart: Individualism and Commitment in American Life* (Berkeley: University of California Press, 1985), 220-35.

35. William Placher, *Narratives of a Vulnerable God: Christ, Theology, and Scripture* (Louisville: Westminster/John Knox Press, 1994), 138.

36. Kegan, *Evolving Self*, 213. As we will see in the next chapter, a well-differentiated sense of self is crucial for genuine relationships and for deep caring.

37. Teen mothers, who are moving into (rather than out of) the interpersonal orientation, value this kind of informal mentoring over book knowledge and theories. One of the ways that teen mothers have been empowered as mothers is through parenting training that is dispensed in a personal, relational manner. See Susan Victor, "Becoming the Good Mother: The Emergent Curriculum of Adolescent Mothers," in *Repositioning Feminism & Education: Perspectives on Educating for Social Change*, ed. Janice Jipson et al. (Westport, Conn.: Bergin & Garvey, 1995), 50.

38. Kegan, *Evolving Self,* 197.

39. Sharon Conarton and Linda Kregar Silverman, "Feminine Development Through the Life Cycle," in Mary Ann Dutton-Douglas and Lenore E. A. Walker, *Feminist Psychotherapies: Intergration of Therapeutic and Feminist Systems* (Norwood, N.J.: Ablex Publishing Corp., 1988), 55.

40. Kate Chopin, *The Awakening* (1899; New York: Dover Publications, 1993), 13.

41. Ibid., 57.

42. Ibid., 116.

43. Reinhold Niebuhr, *The Nature and Destiny of Man,* 2 vols. (New York: Charles Scribner's Sons, 1941 and 1943), *Destiny,* 206.

44. Kegan, *Evolving Self,* 222-23

45. Ibid., 242.

46. That is *not* to say that content is irrelevant. Structure and content *do interact,* and the content of one's ideology can determine whether or not the ideology permits its own renewal. Furthermore, the nature of the symbols and images available to one's imagination is also influential. Sharon Parks critiques Piagetians and other developmentalists who "have attended to structure to the neglect of content." *The Critical Years: The Young Adult Search for a Faith to Live By* (New York: Harper & Row, 1986) 111.

47. Hannah Arendt, *Eichmann in Jerusalem: A Report on the Banality of Evil* (New York: Viking Press, 1963), 150.

48. Heinrich Himmler, Address at a meeting of SS Group Leaders in Posen, October 4, 1943, cited by Dorothee Soelle in *Suffering,* 28.

49. Erik Erickson, *Gandhi's Truth: On the Origins of Militant Nonviolence,* (New York: W. W. Norton, 1969), 230-31.

50. Here Piaget's conception of "horizontal decalage" is pertinent. Developmentally, it is important that an individual be able to apply the same operation to different content and in different contexts. Rapid movement from one stage to another may hinder the generalization process and result in a lag in a person's ability to apply a specific operation in particular contexts. Kolberg asserts that "premature development to a higher ego stage without a corresponding decalage throughout the child's world and life presents problems," and he cautions that the danger of acceleration at the expense of permeation and integration may lead to regressive behaviors. Lawrence Kohlberg and Rochelle Mayer, "Development as the Aim of Education," in *Curriculum: An Introduction to the Field,* ed. James Gress and David Purpel (Berkeley: McCutchen, 1978), 91.

51. Soelle, *Creative Disobedience,* 39.

52. Bonnie Miller-McLemore, *Also a Mother: Work and Family as Theological Dilemma* (Nashville: Abingdon Press, 1994), 34. It does seem to me that the uproar over individualism and the nostalgia for "family values" has a Johnny-come-lately ring to it. Why weren't family values being heralded when men were abandoning their families to the seventy-hour workweek? While I do not wish to ignore sociological evidence of tendencies toward privatism and away from concern for the common good, these studies do not sufficiently analyze both the contributions made by and the costs incurred by women in working toward the common good.

53. Niebuhr, *Destiny,* 88.

54. Reinhold Niebuhr, *Faith and History: A Comparison of Christian and Modern Views of History* (New York: Charles Scribner's Sons, 1949), 183.

55. Reinhold Niebuhr, *Christianity and Power Politics* (New York: Charles Scribner's Sons, 1940), 30. Niebuhr's work on family life is ambiguous. While he repeatedly named male arrogance as a problem, he also tended to see motherhood as a biological constraint on women's vocation. See Rebekah Miles, "Freeing Bonds and Binding Freedom: Reinhold Niebuhr and Feminist Critics on Paternal Dominion and Maternal Constraint," in *The Annual of the Society of Christian Ethics* (1996): 121-44.

56. Bellah et al., *Habits of the Heart,* 143.

57. Ibid., 221.

58. Ibid., 34.

59. Kegan's thinking on institutionality has evolved toward something like this. In *In Over our Heads,* he recognizes that there are gender-associated differences in the ways of being institutional. The "connected" way "exercises personal authority on behalf of inclusivity, keeping communication open for

maximum participation and input, preserving connections and surfacing threats to colleagues' collaborative capacities"; the "separate" way "exercises personal authority on behalf of advancing or enhancing one's own position, status, advantage, agenda, mission, or profile," 225.

60. Kathleen B. Jones, "On Authority: Or, Why Women Are Not Entitled to Speak," in *Feminism & Foucault: Reflection on Resistance*, ed. Irene Diamond and Lee Quinby (Boston: Northeastern University Press, 1988), 123, 128.

61. In my view, this is the most important factor for ensuring that a woman's transition from higher education to public life goes smoothly. Highly intelligent persons who are interpersonally oriented have usually mastered the skills of understanding what a mentor/professor wants and being able to reflect that to the professor. In educational situations, one can usually meet the demands of one mentor at a time. If persons haven't been encouraged to challenge their mentors and to think for themselves, when they get into settings where they have to meet the challenges and concerns of a variety of viewpoints (including multiple mentor/supervisor figures), they will feel at sea. Thus, higher education can be a significant barrier to a woman's development of voice.

62. Kegan, *In Over Our Heads*, 351.

63. Cited in Mary Field Belenky et al., *Women's Ways of Knowing* (New York: Basic Books, 1986), 117.

64. I am indebted to Leanne Simmons for pressing me to clarify this.

65. Susan Brownmiller analyzes femininity very thoughtfully, exposing that it is a "female aesthetic" aimed at male-pleasing "because it makes them appear more masculine [stronger, wiser, more competent] by contrast." See *Femininity* (New York: Fawcett Columbine, 1984), 16.

3. Rebuilding Our Mothers' House: Caretaking and Being in Genuine Relation

1. Similarly, Morwenna Griffiths describes her theory of "the web of identity" as both "highly individualistic" and "highly communalistic." See *Feminisms and the Self: The Web of Identity* (New York: Routledge, 1995), 93.

2. Ł. Kohlberg, C. Levine, and A. Hewer, *Moral Stages: A Current Formulation and a Response to Critics* (New York: Karger, 1983), 229.

3. Carol Gilligan, "In a Different Voice: Women's Conceptions of the Self and of Morality," *Harvard Educational Review* 47 (1977): 490.

4. Gilligan, "Different Voice," 70-71.

5. Joan C. Tronto, "Beyond Gender Difference to a Theory of Care," in *Signs: Journal of Women in Culture and Society* 12 (1987): 652.

6. Comment made by Gilligan, quoted in "Confident at 11, Confused at 16," by Francine Prose, in *New York Times Magazine*, 23: 1 (Jan. 7, 1990): 22-25, 37-38, 45-46.

7. Bill Puka, "The Liberation of Caring: A Different Voice for Gilligan's 'Different Voice,'" from *Hypatia* 5:58-82.

8. This is a particularly difficult transition for teen mothers. "Vacillat[ing] between the obstinacy of adolescents and the passivity of women forced to assume subservient roles," they find themselves between a rock and a hard place. They are still full of needs themselves, and in many ways their survival is an issue; and yet, they must also care for a new life. If goodness were less oppressively defined for women, then the movement to caring for others would not need to be at the expense of survival. Those who see survival as the only way forward may neglect their children; those who feel self-sacrifice is the ideal will avoid self-development (including job training and further education). See Susan Victor, "Becoming the Good Mother: The Emergent Curriculum of Adolescent Mothers," *Repositioning Feminist & Education: Perspectives on Educating for Social Change*, ed. Janice Jipson et al. (Westport, Conn.: Bergin & Garvey, 1995), 44.

9. Gilligan does not describe these levels in terms of a hard-core structuralism (which presumes an invariant, progressive sequence). Although she does imply a progression, development isn't necessarily linear. One can regress, and she does not describe her participants as necessarily going through all three stages. Bill Puka ("The Liberation of Caring") argues that these are not stages at all, but rather coping strategies for women in a sexist environment. Nevertheless, it is tempting to compare her levels with Kegan. In fact, what may look like a regression to survival, may in fact be something like the institutional stage Kegan describes. This means that the choice for survival, or "deliberate isolation," should be distinguished from the earlier form of survival, which is more preconscious and less deliberate.

10. Gilligan, "Different Voice," 138.

11. Joan Tronto, "Women and Caring," in A. Jagger and S. Bordo, eds., *Gender/Body/Knowledge*, (New Brunswick: Rutgers University Press, 1989), 180.

12. Janet L. Surrey, "The Self-in-Relation: A Theory of Women's Development," in Judith V. Jordan et al., *Women's Growth in Connection* (New York: The Guildford Press, 1991).

13. Carol Gilligan, "Teaching Shakespeare's Sister: Notes from the Underground of Female Adolescence," in Carol Gilligan, Nona P. Lyons, and Trudy J. Hanmer, eds., *Making Connections: The Relational Worlds of Adolescent Girls at Emma Willard School* (Cambridge: Harvard University Press, 1990), 9.

14. "Some Cautionary Words for Historians," in Mary Jane Larrabee, ed., *An Ethic of Care: Feminist and Interdisciplinary Perspectives* (New York: Routledge, 1993), 107.

15. Julia T. Wood also critiques Gilligan for *essentializing* the view of women as caring and thus "reiterating and revalorizing the definition of woman that has been resoundingly oppressive historically." *Who Cares? Women, Care, and Culture* (Carbondale, Ill.: Southern Illinois University Press, 1994), 83. While I agree with the concerns raised, and I highly recommend Wood's book for its analysis of caring, I think Gilligan has been misread.

16. Carol Gilligan and Lyn Mikel Brown, *Meeting at the Crossroads: Women's Psychology and Girls' Development* (Cambridge: Harvard, 1992).

17. Carol Gilligan, Janie Victoria Ward, and Jill McLean Taylor, eds., *Mapping the Moral Domain: A Contribution of Women's Thinking to Psychological Theory and Education* (Cambridge: Harvard, 1988), xxx.

18. Reinhold Niebuhr, *The Nature and Destiny of Man*, vol 2, *Human Nature* (New York: Scribner's, 1943), 69.

19. Ibid., 74.

20. Ibid., 282.

21. Don Browning, *A Fundamental Practical Theology* (Minneapolis: Fortress, 1991), 159. See Louis Janssens, "Norms and Priorities in a Love Ethics," in *Louvain Studies* 6:220.

22. Browning, *Fundamental Practical Theology*, 159.

23. Quoted in Nel Noddings, *Caring: A Feminine Approach to Ethics and Moral Education* (Berkeley: University of California Press, 1984). See also entry *On Caring* in 1965 *International Philosophical Quarterly*.

24. Noddings, *Caring*, 31.

25. Darrell Fasching, *Narrative Theology After Auschwitz* (Minneapolis: Augsburg Press, 1992), 5.

26. Jean Baker Miller, *Toward a New Psychology of Women*, 2d ed. (Boston: Beacon Press, 1987), 10.

27. For a helpful discussion of the varieties of factors that contribute to the cultural link between women and caring, see Julia Wood, *Who Cares?*, 86-130.

28. Judith Jordan, "Empathy and the Mother-Daughter Relationship," in Judith V. Jordan et al., *Women's Growth in Connection* (New York: Guilford Press, 1991), 30.

29. Joan Tronto, "Beyond Gender Difference to a Theory of Care," in Mary Jane Larrabee, *An Ethic of Care* (New York: Routledge, 1993), 245.

30. See Morwenna Griffiths, "Other Lives: Learning from Their Experiences," in *Feminisms and the Self: The Web of Identity* (New York: Routledge, 1995).

31. "Empathic Communication in the Psychotherapy Relationship," in Judith V. Jordan et al., *Women's Growth in Connection* (New York: Guilford Press, 1991), 44-50.

32. See Patricia H. Davis, "Women and the Burden of Empathy," *Journal of Pastoral Theology* 3 (Summer 1993): 29-38.

33. "Empathy and Self Boundaries," in Judith V. Jordan et al., *Women's Growth in Connection* (New York: Guilford Press, 1991), 69.

34. Victor, "Becoming the Good Mother, 39.

35. Alice Miller, *The Drama of the Gifted Child* (New York: Basic Books, 1981).

36. Marcia Westkott, building on the work of Karen Horney, warns that this can particularly happen between girls and mothers. She is thus less appreciative of mother-daughter empathy than Judith Jordan (who identifies this empathy as an origin for visioning relationality), whose work she critiques quite trenchantly. Marcia C. Westkott, "On the New Psychology of Women: A Cautionary View," in *Women, Men, and Gender: Ongoing Debates*, ed. Mary Roth Walsh (New Haven: Yale University Press, 1997), 362-72.

37. Harriet Goldhor Lerner, "Female Depression: Self-Sacrifice and Self-Betrayal in Relationships," in *Women and Depression: A Lifespan Perspective*, ed. Ruth Formanek and Anita Gurian (New York: Springer Publ. Co., 1987), 219.

38. Dana Jack, "Silencing the Self: The Power of Social Imperatives in Female Depression," in *Women and Depression: A Life-Span Perspective*, 164. The link between "elements of the traditional female role" and depression is also made by G. Klerman and M. Weissman in "Depressions Among Women: Their Nature and Causes," in *The Mental Health of Women*, ed. M. Guttentag, S. Salasin, and D. Belle (New York: Academic Press, 1980).

39. In Marcia Stubbs and Sylvan Barnets, eds., *The Little, Brown Reader* (Boston: Little, Brown and Company, 1977). Although it is losing hold, Syfer's description of the prevailing definition of wife was still accurate in the early years of my own marriage. When my husband and I were seminarians, we were both very serious students. Being committed to an egalitarian marriage, we shared all household tasks. We also shared similar priorities; when the going got tough, the household got neglected. During one particularly busy week, one of our friends came to our apartment for a visit. As we ushered him in, he discretely stepped over piles of books and other assorted items strewn here and there. He followed us into the kitchen for a cup of coffee, and plunged in to join us as we excavated for mugs under the pile of dirty dishes in the sink. After a minute of digging, he looked at the two of us and said through a grin: "Carol and Ernie, you guys need a wife!" I both chuckled and winced. It was a funny comment, and it was also a revealing one. Not only was I being told that I wasn't much of a wife, but being a wife was reduced to cleaning up after the rest of the family. Our friend was only joking; his joke, however, is funny because it reflects the prevailing definition of wifehood. When a gay friend of mine commented that he didn't want to call the covenant he and his partner shared a "marriage" because of its association with "wife" and "husband" roles, I nodded knowingly. *My God*, I thought, thinking back to Syfers's exclamation, *who would want to be the wife!* Another friend responded, "Well we don't have a wife or a husband. My wife doesn't clean the house and I don't provide much money!" In anticipation of issues coming in chapter 5, we cannot ignore the fact that white privileged women *have* hired women of color to be something like the cultural definition of a wife.

40. Carol Kent, *Secret Longings of the Heart: Overcoming Deep Disappointment and Unfulfilled Expectations* (Colorado Springs: NavPress, 1992), 147-49.

41. See "Pastoral Counseling as an Art of Personal Activism," in Christie Cozad Neuger, ed., *The Arts of Ministry: Feminist and Womanist Approaches* (Louisville: Westminster Press, 1996), 102.

42. Lerner, "Female Depression," 218.

43. Adrienne Rich, *On Lies, Secrets, and Silence* (New York: W. W. Norton and Co., 1979), 187.

44. Lori Stern, "Disavowing the Self in Female Adolescence," in *Women, Girls & Psychotherapy: Reframing Resistance*, ed. Carol Gilligan, Annie G. Rogers, and Deborah L. Tolman (Binghamton, N.Y.: Harrington Park Press, 1991), 115.

45. Mark Kline Taylor, *Remembering Esperanza: A Cultural-Political Theology for North American Practice* (Maryknoll, N.Y.: Orbis, 1990), 62.

46. John Gray, *Men Are from Mars: Women Are from Venus* (New York: HarperCollins, 1992), 59.

47. A male colleague of mine found Gray's dichotomy between women's need to be cherished and nurtured and men's need to be admired and encouraged particularly troublesome. This split is troublesome on both sides; it leaves the impression that men do not need unconditional love and women do not need to be encouraged to accomplish things.

48. For further dicussion of these issues, see Barry Thorne and Nancy Henley, eds. *Language and Sex: Difference and Dominance* (Boston: Rowley, 1975).

49. An excellent resource, which is helpful for classrooms but also groups other than classrooms, is "The Classroom Climate: A Chilly One for Women?" a pamphlet put out by the Association of American Colleges. The paper can be obtained from the Project on the Status and Education of Women, Association of American Colleges, 1818 R St., NW, Washington, DC 20009.

50. Deborah James and Janice Drakich, "Understanding Gender Differences in Amount of Talk: A Critical Review of Research," in *Gender and Conversational Interaction*, ed. Deborah Tannen (New York: Oxford University Press, 1993), 281-312.

51. Dale Spender, *Man Made Language* (Boston: Routledge and Kegan Paul, 1980), 42.

52. Anne Cutler and Donia R. Scott, "Speaker Sex and Perceived Apportionment of Talk," in *Applied Psycholinguistics* 11 (1990):253-72; Dale Spender, *Invisible Women: The Schooling Scandal* (London: Writers and Readers Publishing Cooperative, 1982). This "perceived apportionment syndrome," as I call

it, is evidenced in a variety of ways. When a college course reading list expands to include two or three works by women, students may feel that "all we read about is women." Similarly, I frequently hear the complaint that "all the jobs are going to women and minorities." Statistics show this is not at all the case; while the white male *advantage* has perhaps diminished, this slight diminishment of favor is perceived as a move to inequality, even when inequality still exists.

53. Julia T. Wood, *Gendered Lives: Communication, Gender, and Culture* (Belmont, Calif.: Wadsworth Publishing Co., 1994). In relation to preaching, see Nora Tubbs Tisdale, "Women's Ways of Communicating: A New Blessing for Preaching," in Jane Demsey Douglass and James F. Kay, eds., *Women, Gender, and Christian Community* (Louisville: Westminster/John Knox Press, 1997).

54. Virginia Brooks, "Sex Differences in Student Dominance Behavior in Female and Male Professors' Classrooms," in *Sex Roles* 8 (1982): 683-90.

55. Deborah James and Janice Drakich, "Understanding Gender Differences in Amount of Talk: A Critical Review of Research," in *Gender and Conversational Interaction*, ed. Deborah Tannen (New York: Oxford University Press, 1993), 286.

56. Carole Edelsky, "Who's Got the Floor?" in *Gender and Conversational Interaction*.

57. One of the most interesting issues in relation to hospitality is that of "interruption." Pioneering studies found that men interrupt women much more frequently than the reverse, and thus the implication was that men should be more careful not to interrupt women in discussion. While interruptions for the sake of dominating another are causes for concern, a recent review of the research sees the process of interruption was much more variegated. Interruptions are not always a form of domination or disrespect but can actually be a sign of deep involvement in the discussion. Women frequently interrupt one another in their engaged conversations. Deborah Tannen contrasts "high considerateness" and "high involvement" conversational styles, noting that the former style is polite and full of pauses while the latter style is enthusiastic and full of overlapping speech. When the two styles come into contact with one another, the high-considerateness speaker will view the involved speaker as rude, while the high-involvement speaker will consider the considerate one as disinterested. Women and men can reflect either style, although men seem to be more prone to interrupt for purposes of gaining dominance and women for purposes of showing solidarity. What Tannen wishes to teach us is that considerateness can take the form of involvement, interruptions can be a form of hospitality, if they emerge from one's serious interest and involvement in the conversation. For an overview of "interruption studies," including Tannen's work on this, see Deborah James and Sandra Clarke, "Women, Men, and Interruptions: A Critical Review," in *Gender and Conversational Interaction*.

58. Harriet Goldhor Lerner, *The Dance of Anger: A Woman's Guide to Changing the Patterns of Intimate Relationships* (New York: Harper & Row, 1985), 1.

59. Lyn Mikel Brown and Carol Gilligan, *Meeting at the Crossroads: Women's Psychology and Girls' Development* (Cambridge: Harvard University Press, 1992), 174.

60. Dana Jack (in "Silencing the Self: The Power of Social Imperatives in Female Depression," 179) contends with the tendency in clinical literature to depict women's depression as a result of lost affiliation. "The women in this [Jack's] study depict their depression as precipitated not by the loss of affiliation, but by the recognition that they have lost themselves in the process of trying to establish an intimacy they never attained." Thus, it is false relationality (absence of genuine intimacy and dialogue with others and with self) that is the prime factor in women's depression.

61. Carroll Saussy, *The Gift of Anger: A Call to Faithful Action* (Louisville: Westminister/John Knox Press, 1995), 112.

62. Lerner, *Dance of Anger*, 31.

63. Although we cannot make women's choices for them and we have to be sensitive to the risks women may be taking, we can at least not perpetuate a theology that turns de-selfing into a virtue. When a degree of de-selfing is chosen as a strategy for survival (see chapter 5), then it is viewed as a necessary tactic rather than an automatic spiritual virtue.

64. "The Power of Anger in the Work of Love: Christian Ethics for Women and Other Strangers," in *Making the Connections: Essays in Feminist Social Ethics*, ed. Carol S. Robb (Boston: Beacon Press, 1985).

65. Marge Piercy, "A just anger," in *Circles on the Water* (New York: Alfred A. Knopf, Inc., 1982).

66. Ann Reed Held, *Faith in Families* (Illinois: National Presbyterian Mariners, 1987).

67. Aspects of mothering indebted to Sara Ruddick, *Mothering: Essays in Feminist Theory* (Totowa, N.J.: Rowman and Allanheld, 1984).

68. For a discussion on fear of the mother's power and its consequences for women, see Dorothy Dinnerstein, *The Mermaid and the Minotaur: Sexual Arrangements and Human Malaise* (New York: Harper & Row, 1976).

69. For a helpful discussion of forgiveness, see Maria Harris, *Proclaim Jubilee: A Spirituality for the Twenty-First Century* (Louisville: Westminster/John Knox Press, 1996), 46-55.

70. Bonnie Miller-McLemore has written a wonderful book entitled *Also a Mother: Work and Family as Theological Dilemma* (Nashville: Abingdon Press, 1995), and I do not need to duplicate her insights on mothering. Revisiting the story of Orpah, Ruth's sister-in-law who chooses to return to her mother's house rather than remain with her dead husband's mother (Naomi), Miller-McLemore writes: "She has her own story to tell. She make a most difficult decision, to reclaim something of her maternal past, returning to 'the mother's house.'" For a political commitment to the "maternal," see Sara Ruddick, *Maternal Thinking: Toward a Politics of Peace* (Boston: Beacon Press, 1989).

71. Miller-McLemore, *Also a Mother*, 84.

72. See Diane Ehrensaft, "When Women and Men Mother," in *Mothering: Essays in Feminist Theory*, ed. Joyce Trebilot (Totowa, N.J.: Rowman & Allanheld, 1983), 43.

73. Jack Nelson-Pallmeyer, *Families Valued: Parenting and Politics for the Good of All Children* (New York: Friendship Press, 1996).

74. According to Nancy Chodorow this is the source of boys' deficiencies in attachment. See *The Reproduction of Mothering* (Berkeley: University of California Press, 1978), 169.

75. Joan Tronto, "Beyond Gender Difference to a Theory of Care," in Larrabee, *An Ethic of Care*, 250.

76. One of the reasons that so many women have been involved in volunteer ministries and services is precisely because they have made this extension of caring from their children to others.

77. Gilligan, *Different Voice*, 100.

78. Marcia C. Westkott, On the New Psychology of Women: A Cautionary View," in Mary Roth Walsh, ed., *Women, Men, and Gender: Ongoing Debates* (New Haven: Yale University Press, 1997), 362-72.

79. Allusion to I Kings 19:11-12.

4. Your Daughters Shall Prophesy:
"Safe-Houses" for Raising Girls in Families and Communities of Faith

1. Lyn Mikel Brown and Carol Gilligan, *Meeting at the Crossroads* (Cambridge: Harvard University Press, 1992), 185.

2. Quoted in Carol Gilligan, "Teaching Shakespeare's Sister: Notes from the Underground of Female Adolescence," in *Women's Study Quarterly* 19, nos. 1 & 2 (Spring/Summer 1991): 36.

3. Brown and Gilligan, *Meeting at the Crossroads*, 203.

4. Michael V. Fox, *Character and Ideology in the Book of Esther* (Columbia: University of South Carolina Press, 1991), 197.

5. Jane O'Reilly, "The Lost Girls," *Mirabella* (Apr. 1994): 116.

6. Susan Bordo, *Unbearable Weight: Feminism, Western Culture, and the Body* (Berkeley: University of California Press, 1993), 36.

7. See James A. Doyle, *Sex and Gender* (Dubuque: Wm. C. Brown, 1985). Adults will interact differently with and even see different qualities in an infant *when the same infant* is designated as either boy or girl.

8. Beverly Harrison, "The Power of Anger in the Work of Love: Christian Ethics for Women and Other Strangers," in *Making the Connections: Essays in Feminist Social Ethics*, ed. Carol S. Robb (Boston: Beacon Press, 1985), 42.

9. Note that I wish to replace the concept of submissiveness, which I think is part of female gender socialization, with flexibility. "Submissiveness" is a term that, for women, needs to be given a moratorium.

10. Kathleen Hall Jamieson, *Beyond the Double Bind: Women and Leadership* (New York: Oxford University Press, 1995), 138. See also *The Bem Sex-role Inventory*, Consulting Psychologists Press, 1974.

11. See Inge K. Broverman and Donald M. Broverman et al., "Sex-Role Stereotypes and Clinical Judgments of Mental Health," *Journal of Consulting and Clinical Psychology* 3 (1970): 1-7. This study found that the "feminine" is linked with childlike qualities.

12. *Wall Street Journal*, (December 5, 1994):B1. I thank my mother-in-law, June Hess, for sending me this startling piece. Knowing the topic of my book, she has kept a steady stream of clippings and articles coming my way.

13. Robert Fulghum, *All I Really Need to Know I Learned in Kindergarten* (New York: Random House, 1988).

14. These awards bear a striking resemblance to the 1974 *Bem Sex-Role Inventory*, which surveyed preferred personality traits for men and women. Desirable traits for men included: acts as a leader, aggressive, ambitious, analytical, assertive, competitive, decisive, strong personality, willing to take risks. Desirable traits for women: affectionate, cheerful, compassionate, gentle, loves children, sensitive to the needs of others, sympathetic, yielding. Published by Consulting Psychologists Press, Inc., Palo Alto, CA 94303.

15. Lyn Mikel Brown, "Telling a Girl's Life: Self-Authorization as a Form of Resistance," in *Reframing Resistance*, 71-86.

16. Brown and Gilligan, *Meeting at the Crossroads*.

17. Lyn Mikel Brown, "A Problem of Vision: The Development of Voice and Relational Knowledge in Girls Ages Seven to Sixteen," *Women's Studies Quarterly*, vol. XIX, nos. 1 & 2 (Spring/Summer 1991): 66.

18. Maria Harris, "Women Teaching Girls: The Power and the Danger," *Religious Education*, vol. 88, no. 1 (Winter 1993).

19. Brown and Gilligan, *Meeting at the Crossroads*, 214.

20. "Taking Women Students Seriously," in *Gendered Subjects* (Boston: Routledge & Kegan Paul, 1985), 27. Italics added.

21. Christina Hoff Sommers, *Who Stole Feminism? How Women Have Betrayed Women* (New York: Simon and Schuster, 1994).

22. Carol Gilligan, "Exit-Voice Dilemmas in Adolescent Development," in *Mapping the Moral Domain*, edited by Carol Gilligan, Janie Ward, and Jill McLean Taylor (Cambridge: Harvard University Press, 1988), 147.

23. Quoted in Frances A. Maher and Mary Kay Thompson Tetreault, *The Feminist Classroom* (New York: Basic Books, 1994), 129. Ida Cox, in reference to Wild Women in Music and Literature course taught by Angela Davis and Chinosole.

24. Brown and Gilligan, *Meeting at the Crossroads*, 194.

25. George Eliot, *Daniel Deronda* (New York: Penguin Books, 1967, orig. 1876), 694.

26. Lyn Mikel Brown, "A Problem of Vision: The Development of Voice and Relational Knowledge in Girls Ages Seven to Sixteen," in *Women's Study Quarterly*, vol. 19, nos. 1 & 2 (Spring/Summer 1991): 36. Brown feels that high-achieving girls who become anorexic and low-income girls who drop out of school have this in common.

27. "What Happens to the Gifted Girl?" in C. June Maker, *Critical Issues in Gifted Education: Defensible Programs for the Gifted* (Rockville, Md.: Aspen Publishers, 1986), 63-67.

28. Hilda Bruch, *The Golden Cage: The Enigma of Anorexia Nervosa* (New York: Vintage, 1979).

29. Information obtained from Robert F. DiCuio and Stefan Greene, "An EAP Guide to Anorexia and Bulimia," Employee Assistance Digest, May/June 1989.

30. Harold Goldstein and Harry Gwirtzman of the National Institute of Mental Health's Eating Disorders Program claim that about one thousand women a year die from anorexia. "Who Stole Feminism," *Book World* (August 28, 1994), 10. Cited in Kathleen Hall Jamieson, *Beyond the Double Bind: Women and Leadership* (New York: Oxford University Press, 1995), 189.

31. Broverman, IP and SR Broverman, "Sex Role Stereotypes: A Current Appraisal," in *Social Issues* 28:59-78.

32. Susan Bordo, "Anorexia Nervosa: Psychopathology as the Crystallization of Culture," in *Feminism & Foucault: Reflections of Resistance*, ed. Irene Diamond and Lee Quinby (Boston: Northeastern University Press, 1988), 106.

33. The frequently reported "distorted body image" in anorexic girls who think they are too fat is not so much, in my view, a vision or perceptual impairment as it is a displaced assessment; indeed, they *are* "too much girl" for a society that wants to keep girls dependent and subordinate.

34. To attribute anorexia and eating disorders to conformity to the ideal of beauty as thinness is to disre-

gard the fact that anorexic bodies are not beautiful in the eyes of the beholder. One male friend of mine summed up the appraisals that most people—male and female—gave to me, "You look like shit." Furthermore, though our society may demand more of women than men in terms of beauty, the overwhelming disproportionate number of eating disorders in women (90 percent) cannot be overlooked. My view that anorexia is a protest against gendered femininity rather than an attempt to meet standards for thinness helps to explain the low prevalence in men. Validation for autonomy is not so urgent an issue in men.

35. See J. Kagan, "Acquisition and Significance of Sex Typing and Sex Role Identity," in *Review of Child Development Research*, vol. 1, ed. M. L. Hoffman and L. W. Hoffman (New York: Russell Sage Foundation), 137-67; Catherine Steiner-Adair, "The Body Politic: Normal Female Adolescent Development and the Development of Eating Disorders," in *The Journal of the American Academy of Psychoanalysis* 14, no. 1: 95-114.

36. This is the thesis of E. Rothchild, "Female Power: Lines to Development of autonomy," in *Female Adolescent Development*, ed. M. Sugar (New York: Brenner-Mazel, 1979), 274-96.

37. Catherine Steiner Adair, "When the Body Speaks: Girls, Eating Disorders and Psychotherapy," in *Women, Girls & Psychotherapy: Reframing Resistance*, ed. Carol Gilligan, Anne C. Rogers, and Deborah L. Tolman (Binghamton, N.Y.: Harrington Park Press, 1991), 255.

38. Eating disorders are a complex and irreducible phenomenon. I certainly do not want to deny the host of factors that contribute to such disorders. (See Paul Garfinkel and David Garner, *Anorexia Nervosa: A Multidimensional Perspective* [New York: Brunner/Mazel, 1982].) I, however, agree with Harriet Lerner when she claims that "individual and family dysfunction are inseparable from the dysfunction of patriarchal culture" ("Self-Sacrifice and Self-Betrayal in Relationships, in *Women and Depression*, 219). The fact that eating disorders are on the rise suggests to me that there is a correlation between women gaining power and cultural prescriptions against this empowerment. While I will engage many thinkers on this issue, I wish to make it clear that these persons would not necessarily agree with the following analysis I offer.

39. Bordo, *Unbearable Weight*, 100.

40. See R. H. Striegel-Moore, L. R. Silberstein, and J. Rodin, "Toward an Understanding of Risk Factors in Bulimia," *American Psychologist*, 41 (1986): 246-64.

41. Frederick Buechner, sharing his pain-filled feelings regarding his daughter's anorexia, surmises that anorexia is a paradoxical combination of desires. "Young people crave to be free and independent. They crave also to be taken care of and safe. The dark magic of anorexia is that it satisfies both of these cravings at once. By not eating, you take your stand against the world that is telling you what to do and who to be. And by not eating you also make your body so much smaller, lighter, weaker that in effect it becomes a child's body again and the world flocks to your rescue." *Telling Secrets* (San Francisco: Harper Books, 1991), 23.

42. Alice Miller, *For Your Own Good: Hidden Cruelty in Childrearing and the Roots of Violence* (New York: Farrar, Straus, and Giroux, 1983), 131.

43. Judith P. Salzman, "Save the World, Save Myself: Responses to Problematic Attachment," in *Making Connections: The Relational World of Adolescent Girls at Emma Willard School*, ed. Carol Gilligan, Nona P. Lyons, and Trudy J. Hanmer (Cambridge: Harvard University Press, 1990), 113. Salzman's statement is a general one; the implications for anorexia are mine, not Salzman's.

44. Sal Minuchin et al., *Psychomatic Families: Anorexia Nervosa in Context* (Cambridge: Harvard University Press, 1978).

45. Suzette Finkelstein, "Eating Disorders: Why Women and Why Now?" in *Women and Depression: A Lifespan Perspective*, ed. Ruth Formanek and Anita Gurian (New York: Springer Publishing Co., 1987), 106.

46. J. A. Sours, "The Anorexic Nervosa Syndrome." *International Journal of PsychoAnalysis*, 55: 567-76. Bingers, however, who do not develop the same kind of control, are likely to feel shame. In fact, it may be the case that anorexics whose starved bodies push them into bingeing end up with the lowest self-esteem. See R. C. Casper et al., "Bulimia: Its Incidence and Clinical Importance in Patients with Anorexia Nervosa." *Archives of General Psychiatry* 37 (1980): 1030-35.

47. Brown and Gilligan, *Meeting at the Crossroads*, 209-10. Liza is dubbed by these researchers a "psychological resister," who struggles to remain in touch with herself in a voice-denying environment. What Liza does not fully realize is that her life is actually permeated with, not simply occasionally spiced by, an underground rebellion.

48. This ambivalence is exploited in the resurgence of the "baby doll" look for women. Ads featuring sexually mature women in baby doll lingerie are prevalent; while their bodies are posed in sexually alluring positions, their faces are composed in looks of vacuous innocence and submissiveness.

49. Bordo, *Unbearable Weight*, 36-37.

50. Ibid., 104.

51. Ibid., 155. Many anorexics, when children, fantasized about growing up to be boys.

52. Sometimes the anorexic is described as feeling her body to be "an alien force," which is to be transcended. Indeed, sometimes they do speak in mind/body dualisms, glorying in their capacity to "control" (a recurrent word and theme) their bodies. I do not think it is the body per se that is alien, but the body as signifier of culturally prescribed female gender. They want control over their "femininity," and they feel that their body automatically assigns them to being controlled. Again, this is not sexual confusion but rather a cry against the codes that are assigned to their sex.

53. In addition to links between parental control and eating disorders, there is growing evidence of some linkage between eating disorders and sexual abuse. Some contend that anorexic behavior is a replaying of the abuse (Dusty Miller, *Women Who Hurt Themselves* [New York: Basic Books, 1994]). While this is plausible, once again we must not miss the protest. Sexually abused women who become anorexic recognize that the female body is slated for abuse in this society. Rather than reducing their behavior to repetition of punishment, we need to see that it is also assertive. Who wants a body that is marked for subordination and abuse?

54. Joan Jacobs Brumberg, *Fasting Girls: The Emergence of Anorexia Nervosa as a Modern Disease* (Cambridge: Harvard University Press, 1988), 167.

55. "Persistent Perfectionism, Symmetry, and Exactness After Long-Term Recovery from Anorexia Nervosa," *American Journal of Psychiatry* 152 (Nov. 1995): 11.

56. Bordo, *Unbearable Weight*, 64-65.

57. Ibid., 159.

58. Ibid., 105.

59. Mary Pipher states that "Anorexic girls are great at self-denial," in *Reviving Ophelia: Saving the Selves of Adolescent Girls* (New York: Ballantine Books, 1994), 174.

60. Bordo, *Unbearable Weight*, 164.

61. Teresa Benardez-Bonesatti, then Associate Professor of Psychiatry at Michigan State University, wrote of "irrational beliefs about women's power, which if unleashed is considered devastating" that are prevalent, even among therapists. See Theresa Bernardez, "Unconscious Beliefs about Women Affecting Psychotherapy," *NCJ Mental Health* 7, no. 5 (Winter, 1976).

62. Pipher, *Reviving Ophelia*, believes anorexia is a metaphor, "a young woman's statement that she will become what the culture asks of its women, which is that they be thin and nonthreatening," 175.

63. If there is a death wish or a regression fantasy operating in anorexia, it is (in the case of the death wish) the desire for the false self to die and (in the case of regression fantasy) a new self to be nurtured. The success of programs that take girls near death and treat them by catering to their needs is, I think, due to the fact that her own needs and desires are precisely the very thing the good girl has been raised to deny. Solicitous care can renurture the true self; recovery and weight gain bring the chance to allow this true self to emerge. It is my belief that if the girl is once again forced into a false self, relapse is likely.

64. Brumberg, *Fasting Girls*. Here let me acknowledge that Joan Brumberg warns against valorizing anorexic girls. She charges feminists who treat anorexia as a protest with venerating and romanticizing very ill girls. Rather than "heroic freedom fighters" who freely choose a hunger strike as a form of intentional political action, anorexics are helpless and desperate girls in need of medical attention, contends Brumberg. She argues that instead of dignifying the disorder, we should name the "infantile" behavior and treat it biomedically. While I share the concern that we not venerate a destructive behavior, I am more than willing to treat these desperate girls as the heroic freedom fighters I think they are, even though I do not believe they are fully conscious of their "political action." Of course, as Susan Bordo notes, to acknowledge this is to recognize that the "patient might have as much to teach the 'experts' as the other way around." Bordo, *Unbearable Weight*, 65.

65. Here, I deviate from the norm, but not completely. Though my family was always beneath the poverty line in terms of income, and though by my junior-high years (we were one of the families helped by government housing aid) we settled into a working-class neighborhood, I attended schools largely composed of white, upwardly mobile middle-class families.

66. Becky W. Thompson, *A Hunger So Wide and So Deep: American Women Speak Out on Eating Problems* (Minneapolis: University Press, 1994). I am indebted to a presentation on eating disorders by Leanne Simmons, doctoral candidate at Princeton Theological Seminary, for this information.

67. I would also venture to guess that overeating in women is a subconscious resistance to cultural proscription against women caring for themselves. In a culture that expects selflessness and caring for others, feeding oneself is an expression of satisfying one's needs. Like anorexia, however, it is counterproductive. When feeding oneself is the only form of self-care that one exercises, overeating is likely to occur in place of more pervasive self-care.

68. See Margaret Anderson, *Thinking About Women* (New York: Macmillan, 1988); See also Joyce A. Ladner, *Tomorrow's Tomorrow* (New York: Anchor, 1972).

69. Tracy Robinson and Janie Victoria Ward, "A Belief in Self Far Greater Than Anyone's Disbelief: Cultivating Resistance Among African American Female Adolescents," in Gilligan, Rogers, and Tolman, eds. *Women, Girls & Psychotherapy*, 87-104.

70. Whitney Otto, *How to Make an American Quilt* (New York: Ballantine, 1991), 60.

71. Ibid., 61.

72. Ibid., 75.

73. Ibid., 82-83.

74. Louise Eichenbaum and Susie Orbach, *Understanding Women: A Feminist Psycho-analytic Approach* (New York: Basic Books, 1983), 44. Quoted in Bordo, *Unbearable Weight*, 326n.109.

75. See Marcia Westkott, *The Feminist Legacy of Karen Horney* (New Haven: Yale University Press, 1986).

76. Olive Ann Burns, *Cold Sassy Tree* (New York: Dell Publishing, 1984), 248-89.

77. See Patricia H. Davis, *Counseling Adolescent Girls* (Minneapolis: Fortress, 1996), for a good overview of girls and violence and for suggestions for pastoral caregivers.

78. This situation may be reversed in some African American families. Jawanza Kunjufu, who has written several books on black youth, worries that in African American families "some mothers raise their daughters and love their sons." *Adam, Where are You?* (Chicago: African American Images, 1994), 16.

79. Betty Carter, "Fathers and Daughters." In *The Women's Project in Family Therapy*, 90-157. Quoted in Patricia H. Davis.

80. Ellen Kaschak, *Endangered Lives: A New Psychology of Women's Experience* (New York: Basic Books, 1992).

81. Susan Okin, *Justice, Gender, and the Family*, 4-5.

82. In 1989, F. N. Schwartz coined "mommy track" to refer to women who were "not serious professionals" because of family commitments and suggested that organizations explicitly track women according to whether or not their career was primary. No suggestion was made that there be a "daddy track." This not only indicated that women should choose, but also that caring for children was only women's concern. Schwartz, "Management Women and the New Facts of Life," in *Harvard Business Review* (Jan./Feb. 1989): 65-76. See Julia Wood, *Who Cares? Women, Care, and Culture* (Carbondale, Ill.: Southern Illinois University Press, 1994), 127-28.

83. See Matina S. Horner, "Fail: Bright Women," in *Psychology Today* 3, no. 6 (Nov. 1969): 62. See also "Toward an Understanding of Achievement Related Conflicts in Women," in *Journal of Social Issues* 28 (1972): 157-75.

84. Okin, *Justice, Gender, and the Family*, 139. Of course, they will be criticized for being incompetent if they allow room for family life and thus produce less; but they will be criticized for neglecting their children if they compete as a man.

85. Gilligan, "Teaching Shakespeare's Sister," 47.

86. Carol Blessing, "Judge, Prophet, Mother: Learning from Deborah," in *Daughters of Sarah* (Winter 1995): 34-37.

87. I was appalled recently when my son Nathan, a sophomore in high school, brought home a booklet on preparing for college. The booklet had a large section on elite colleges, which were listed for the students. In addition to being told how they should spend their next four school years, the students were advised that they better spend all four summers of high school doing something that they can justify academically or the top college admissions boards will frown on them. They were told: family vacations, unless they were structured to be highly educational, were inadvisable! Although my own alma mater, which I value, was on that list, I thought: *What are we raising our kids to think about life?*

For what will amount to one-fourth of their life up to that point, students must avoid taking time out for leisure and family. The pattern will only perpetuate itself after that.

88. When I was in college, I tried my hand at weight training for a while. I remember a male friend was appalled that I chose this form of exercise. "Women should be soft and supple, not hard and muscled," he exclaimed. This celebration of female softness and roundness did not strike me as a liberating affirmation, but rather as a limiting ideal. I don't think women should feel that "hardness" is their goal, but female strength and power should not be censored as unfeminine. Fitness, when chosen as an expression of love and care for one's body, is a form of resistance to feminine selflessness and external control.

89. Here we must caution that there is some evidence of a link between eating disorders and individual sports such as gymnastics and ballet.

90. Robinson and Ward, "A Belief in Self," 97.

91. hooks, *Talking Back*, 9.

92. Dorothy Jean Smith, "Raising a Resister," in Gilligan, Rogers, and Tolman, eds., *Women, Girls & Psychotherapy*, 146.

93. E. K. Bennett, *A History of the German Novelle from Goethe to Thomas Mann* (Cambridge: At the University Press, 1934).

5. Wrestling with Our Sisters: Together Building Our Households of Faith

1. *Dante's Purgatory*, trans. Mark Musa (Bloomington: Indiana University Press, 1981), 293. For Rossetti print and brief interpretation see *Great Women of the Bible in Art and Literature*, commentary by Dorothee Soelle (Macon, Ga.: Mercer University Press, 1994), 76.

2. Danna Nolan Fewell and David M. Gunn, *Gender, Power & Promise: The Subject of the Bible's First Story* (Nashville: Abingdon Press, 1993), 78.

3. Ilana Pardes understands the Ruthan passage to be an idyllic revision of the "limited representation of female bonding in Genesis." See *Countertraditions in the Bible: A Feminist Approach* (Cambridge: Harvard University Press, 1992), 101.

4. William E. Phipps, "Feminist and Feminine Queens," in *Assertive Biblical Women* (Westport, Conn.: Greenwood Press, 1992), 93-103.

5. Lewis Bayles Paton, *A Critical and Exegetical Commentary on the Book of Esther*, ICC (New York: Scribners, 1908), 96. As is often the case with women, you're damned if you do and damned if you don't. Paton later comments on Esther's fierceness in avenging her people: "it must be admitted that her character would have been more attractive if she had shown pity toward a fallen foe," 264. Her female beauty is denigrated as less than fully human; her exercise of the typically male virtue of assertive strength reduces her attractiveness.

6. Michael V. Fox, *Character and Ideology in the Book of Esther* (Columbia, S.C.: University of South Carolina Press, 1991), 207.

7. Sidnie Ann White, "Esther: A Feminine Model for Jewish Diaspora," in *Gender and Difference in Ancient Israel*, ed. Peggy Day (Minneapolis: Fortress Press, 1989).

8. See Norman J. Cohen, "Two That Are One—Sibling Rivalry in Genesis," in *Judaism*, no. 125, 341. It is noteworthy that, while the church fathers and later Christian tradition often equated Leah with the active life and Rachel with the contemplative life, Jewish mystics saw the two in exactly the reverse manner.

9. See Pardes, *Countertraditions in the Bible*, 116.

10. Here I disagree with Pardes, who considers Rachel's burial outside of Jacob's home and her own burial next to Jacob to be "Leah's ultimate triumph." The story ends without a clear sense of triumph on the part of either Rachel or Leah, but rather with a poignant sense of the tragedy of the rivalry. The Joseph cycles reveal that the rivalry between the mothers passed even more bitterly on to the sons; the writer implicitly condemns all those who created and nurtured the rivalry in the first place. Although God wove the entire tragedy into triumph, neither Leah nor Rachel was the victor. *Countertraditions*, 74.

11. Kathleen Hall Jamieson, *Beyond the Double Bind: Women and Leadership* (New York: Oxford University Press, 1995), 189.

12. "Acts of Paul and Thecla," *New Testament Apocrypha*, ed. Wilhelm Schneemelcher, vol. 2 (Philadelphia: Westminster Press, 1964), 358.

13. Elizabeth A. Clark, *Women in the Early Church* (Wilmington, Del.: Michael Glazier, 1983), 83.

14. Rebecca Weaver, "A Subordinate Loyalty," *Affirmation: Union Theological Seminary in Virginia* 5, no.1 (1982), 25.

15. Ambrose, *Concerning Virgins* 1.12.63 (Nicene and Post-Nicene Fathers, second series, vol. 10, 373). Though Christian teachings on marital and familial relations have gone through a tortuous history, the theme of the subordination of loyalties seems to be a persistent and recoverable one. In the latter part of the second century, an avowed critic of Christianity named Celsus charged that Christians persuaded the children of pagans to ignore the instruction of their fathers and schoolmasters and to follow the teachings of Christ instead. Though the Alexandrian theologian Origen refuted other accusations made by Celsus, he seems to have acknowledged and let this one stand uncontested. See Origen, *Contra Celsum* 3:55, trans. and ed. Henry Chadwick (Cambridge: Cambridge University Press, 1980), 165-68.

16. Carroll Saussy, *The Gift of Anger* (Louisville: Westminster/John Knox, 1985), 76.

17. See Marie M. Fortune, *Keeping the Faith: Questions and Answers for the Abused Woman* (San Francisco: HarperCollins, 1987), 30-31, 83.

18. L. Walker, *The Battered Woman* (New York: Harper & Row, 1979).

19. Dana Jack, "Silencing the Self," in *Women and Depression*, ed. Ruth Formanek and Anita Gurian (New York: Springer Publishing Co., 1987), 173.

20. See Sheila Redmond, "Christian 'Virtues' and Child Sexual Abuse," in *Christianity, Patriarchy, and Abuse: A Feminist Critique*, ed. Joanne Carlson Brown and Carole R. Bohn (Cleveland: Pilgrim Press, 1989), 78.

21. Susan Thistletwaite has learned that fundamentalist women who are abused are faced with an impossible choice when they are encouraged to abandon the religious affiliation that promotes their obedience to an abusive husband. They tend to stop attending victims' rights groups that view Christianity as an obstacle to healing. The best strategy is to teach these women that the God of the Bible is on the side of the powerless, and that the Scriptures offer them more support for healing than they have been told. Still bound to the authority of the Bible, they need to know that they "have a right" to both their religious beliefs and their self-esteem. "Every Two Minutes: Battered Women and Feminist Interpretation," in *Feminist Interpretation of the Bible*, ed. Letty Russell (Philadelphia: Westminster Press, 1985).

22. Jack, "Silencing the Self," 174.

23. Redmond, "Christian 'Virtues' and Child Sexual Abuse," 78. Emphasis added.

24. Montefiore, C. G., and H. Loewe, *A Rabbinic Anthology* (Cleveland: World Publishing Co., 1963), 501. Quoted in James Leechan, *Defiant Hope: Spirituality for Survivors of Family Abuse* (Louisville: Westminster /John Knox Press, 1993), 156.

25. Fox, *Character and Ideology*, 205.

26. Anne Tyler, *Ladder of Years* (New York: Fawcett Columbine, 1995), 123.

27. As one with Native ancestry, I prefer to use "Native American" when speaking of those indigenous to North America. However, in this particular narrative, the author, reflecting the name given to her people, uses "Indian."

28. Mary Crow Dog, *Lakota Woman* (New York: Harper Perenial, 1990), 40-41.

29. I want to be cautious here. While exit can sometimes benefit the system one exits, the well-being of the system should not be the first priority. Sometimes one must exit to preserve oneself or others, and the system may remain unchanged.

30. Rosemary Radford Reuther, *Women-Church: Theology and Practice of Feminist Liturgical Communities* (San Francisco: Harper & Row, 1985), 62. This, in fact, is precisely what Marlaine Lockheed, creator of "innoculation groups," advocates at the classroom level. Lockheed recommends that females, often silenced in co-ed classrooms, work in same-sex segregated groups prior to their integration into mixed-sex learning situations. She has discovered that once young women hear their own voices speaking on topics, having opinions, and being heard in an all-female group, they then feel better prepared and worthy of participation in a mixed-sex group. See "Classroom Organization and Climate," in *Achieving Sex Equity Through Education*, ed. S. Klein (Baltimore, Md.: Johns Hopkins University Press, 1986).

31. Alice Walker, *In Search of Our Mothers' Gardens: Womanist Prose* (New York: Harcourt, Brace, Jovanovich, 1983), xi.

32. Robert Bellah et al., *Habits of the Heart* (Berkeley: University of California Press, 1985), 72.

33. I have been greatly helped by Karla Ann Koll, "Theology of Solidarity," in *500 Years, Domination or Liberation? Theological Alternatives for the Americas in the 1990s,* ed. Philip E. Wheaton (Ocean City, Md.: Skipjack Press, 1992).

34. Davida Alperin, "Social Diversity and the Necessity of Alliances: A Feminist Perspective," in Lisa Albreach and Rose M. Brewer, eds., *Bridges of Power: Women's Multicultural Alliances* (Philadelphia: New Society Publishers, 1990), 31.

35. While the distinction between social enclaves and solidarity groups is an important one to make, actual analysis of a group's placement is difficult. There are groups that may claim to be solidarity groups that do not meet the criteria for common oppression. It is thus important that such groups be self-critical about their own status. Furthermore, solidarity groups need to be conscious of the various types and levels of oppression that exist within their constituency. Racism, classism, sexism, and heterosexism often exist inside of groups fighting injustice on one front only. Ethnic solidarity groups must be aware of their own sexism and possibly classism; gender- and sexual-orientation solidarity groups must watch for internal classism and racism; social-class solidarity groups must be on guard against racism and sexism in their midst.

36. Sharon Daloz Parks, "Home and Pilgrimage: Companion Metaphors for Personal and Social Transformation," *Soundings* 72.2-3 (Summer/Fall 1989).

37. According to Robert Kegan *(Evolving Self)*, one of the great losses of contemporary life is having a community that knows us over our life and stays put for us through our changes.

38. In defense of myself, I must say that it was being asked to think of myself as a grandmother as much as the prospect of my daughter following a traditional path that made me so surly.

39. *The Total Woman* (Old Tappan, N.J.: Fleming H. Revell, 1973); *The Rules: Time-Tested Secrets for Capturing the Heart of Mr. Right* (New York: Warner Books, 1996).

40. Ellen Goodman, "Let's Trash 'The Rules,'" printed in *The Courier-Post,* November 1, 1996. Debbie Then, a Los Angeles psychologist, recognizes that "in some ways, the book is encouraging women to stop being doormats and to stick up for themselves," which is laudable. "But what troubles me," she qualifies, "is that the authors encourage women to do that by playing games—which never works in the long run." Cited by Laura Muha, "The New Rules of Love: Some Women Swear It Has Helped Them Find True Romance—Other Women Swear About It," review in *Fitness* (October 1996): 105.

41. Letty M. Russell, *Church in the Round: Feminist Interpretation of the Church* (Louisville: Westminster/John Knox Press, 1993).

42. Miriam Theresa Winter, *Defecting in Place: Women Claiming Responsibility for Their Own Spiritual Lives* (New York: Crossroad, 1994), 40.

43. Ilana Pardes, "Rachel's Dream of Grandeur," in *Out of the Garden: Women Writers on the Bible,* ed. Christina Buchmann and Celina Spiegel (New York: Ballantine books, 1994), 34.

44. It is interesting that Rachel steals the gods while Laban has gone to shear his sheep (Genesis 30:19). Rachel is first introduced as the one who kept her father's sheep (29:9), and Laban deceives Jacob out of sheep that he had promised him (30:35ff.). It is possible that in juxtaposing Rachel's thievery with Laban's having gone to shear the sheep, the narrator implies that Rachel has claimed something due her.

45. Elizabeth A. Say traces the history of attitudes toward women's education in chapter 1 of her book *Evidence on Her Own Behalf: Women's Narrative as Theological Voice* (Rowman & Littlefield, 1990). Say describes the separation between public and private spheres and its attendant dichotomy between masculine (aggressive, competitive, and prone to immodesty) and feminine (passive, deferent, and virginal). Within the feminine ideal, women's education was limited to religion and morals—for "the profoundly educated women rarely make good wives or mothers," as one Victorian moral leader contended (p. 20).

46. An alternative strategy has been to emphasize female differentness, and to work to bring more of that differentness to public life. Rather than being included in a game already being played, some feminists wish to help define and reconstruct the way the game is understood. Labeled cultural feminists or maximalists, these women aim to transform culture by bringing to it female identified qualities such as: valuing subjective feelings and personal experience, working collaboratively with others, trusting intuitive knowledge, and supporting the vulnerable. For instance: Nel Noddings, *Caring: A Feminine Approach to Ethics and Moral Education* (Berkeley: University of California Press, 1984); Sara Ruddick, "Maternal Thinking," *Feminist Studies* 6 (Summer 1980): 342-67.

47. Naomi Wolf, *Fire with Fire: The New Female Power and How It Will Change the 21st Century* (New York: Random House, 1993), 236-37.

48. Kathleen Hall Jamieson, *Beyond the Double Bind: Women and Leadership* (New York: Oxford University Press, 1995), 138-39. Jamieson quotes from a briefing given by the American Psychological Association in a court case dealing with discrimination.

49. bell hooks, *Talking Back: Thinking Feminist, Thinking Black* (Boston: South End Press, 1989), 78.

50. Susan Bordo, *Unbearable Weight: Feminism, Western Culture, and the Body* (Berkeley: University of California Press, 1993), 36-37.

51. For a personal and insightful analysis of these issues, see Rosita deAnn Mathews, "Using Power from the Periphery: An Alternative Theological Model for Survival in Systems," in Emilie M. Townes, ed., *A Troubling in My Soul: Womanist Perspectives on Evil and Suffering* (Maryknoll, N.Y.: Orbis, 1993), 97.

52. Pat Howrey Davis, "Women and the Burden of Empathy," *Journal of Pastoral Theology* (1993): 29-38.

53. Delores Williams, *Sisters in the Wilderness: The Challenge of Womanist God-Talk* (Mary Knoll, N.Y.: Orbis Books, 1993), 194.

54. Ibid., 198, emphasis added.

55. For an alternative reading of Genesis 16 and 21, which interprets it as a story of liberation that was redacted to become a story of oppression, see Irmgard Fischer, "'Go and Suffer Oppression!' Said God's Messenger to Hagar: Repression of Women in Biblical Texts," in Elisabeth Schüssler Fiorenza and Mary Shawn Copeland, *Violence Against Women* (Maryknoll, N.Y.: Orbis Books, 1994). Writes Fischer, "The revision of the texts *turns the liberator God who in the basic narratives in Gen. 16 and 21 supports those who are deprived of their rights*, oppressed and outcast, and who breaks open the structure of a slave-owning society, into one who preserves the system" (italics added). While acknowledging the story's realism, we may still wish to question the portrayal of God (as one who upholds, and perhaps even legitimates, the status quo of slavery) in this passage.

56. Williams, *Sisters*, 199.

57. Quoted in M. Shawn Copeland, "Wading Through Many Sorrows: Toward a Theology of Suffering in Womanist Perspective," in Townes, *A Troubling in My Soul*.

58. Eileen J. Stenzel, "Maria Goretti: Rape and the Politics of Sainthood," in Schüssler Fiorenza and Copeland, *Violence Against Women*, 96. Maria's story is told in the book by A. Butler, ironically—or perhaps revealingly—titled, *The Lives of the Fathers*, vol. 5, ed. B. Kelly (Chicago: 1956), 488-91.

59. Maria was in a tragic double bind. Had she submitted to rape and preserved her life, she would have been condemned by church and society as a defiled woman. "Imagine," writes Stenzel, "the possibility that for Maria, life was worth saving but that what she faced in a society that defined rape as a crime one man [e.g. her assailant] committed against another [e.g., her father whose possession she was] and which rape could be used to force marriage. Imagine a society that renders a child too frightened by social consequences to seek the protection of adults from threatened rape and death. Imagine a child too frightened by possible condemnation by her priest to seek his refuge. The world in which Maria struggled to survive promoted the belief that a woman was better dead than raped, and the church agreed." Stenzel, "Maria Goretti," 96-97.

60. There is a double tragedy in this story: "Allesandro killed her because she refused to submit to him. The Roman Catholic church canonized her because she submitted to the higher authority of the church. Neither her attacker nor the church recognized Maria's right to decide her own fate." Ibid., 97.

61. Survival, which is choosing to make a way in the midst of recognized oppression, must be distinguished from expediency, which is lying to oneself to avoid facing the reality of one's oppression.

62. Such is the case with Esther's survival strategies in the second half of the story. Knowing the Jews were dependent upon her for their life, Esther negotiates the system using all that she has. Sidnie Ann White praises Esther's conduct, which "throughout the story has been a masterpiece of feminine skill. From beginning to end, she does not make a misstep." White goes so far as to claim that she is a model for successful living in "the often uncertain world of the Diaspora." Rather than fighting her place, she accepted the reality of her subordinate position and learned "to gain power by working within the structure rather than against it." Though her tactics, using her "feminine skill," may seem questionable, she ended up saving a lot of lives. (White, "Esther: A Feminine Model for Jewish Diaspora," 173.)

63. Williams, *Sisters*, 185.

64. Elisabeth Schüssler Fiorenza, *Jesus: Miriam's Child, Sophia's Prophet: Critical Issues in Feminist Christology* (New York: Continuum Books, 1995), 12-18.

65. Kathleen O. Reed, "Creatio Ex Nihilo," in Elizabeth Bettenhausen, "Re-Imagining Creation: Gathering at the Table of Necessity," in *Church & Society* 84, no. 5 (May/June 1994): 77.

66. Mieke Bal, "Tricky thematics," in *Reasoning with the Foxes: Female Wit in a World of Male Power,* Cheryl Exum and Johanna W. H. Bos, eds. (Atlanta: Scholars Press, 1988), 151. For the title of this section I am indebted to Danna Nolan Fewell and David M. Gunn, "Chapter Two: The Way of Women," in *Gender, Power and Promise: The Subject of the Bible's First Story* (Nashville: Abingdon Press, 1993).

67. I am arguing that the "way of women" in this story is to make something good out of the good-for-nothing that has been handed to a woman. Perhaps my interpretation itself is an attempt to make something out of the good-for-nothing tale of a woman's deceptivenesss. Esther Fuchs argues that biblical tales regularly imply that deception is the way of women and that this association between women and deception perpetuates the rule of men. See her essay, " 'For I Have the Way of Women': Deception, Gender, and Ideology in Biblical Narrative," in *Reasoning with the Foxes: Female Wit in a World of Male Power,* Cheryl Exum and Johanna W. H. Bos, eds. (Atlanta: Scholars Press, 1988).

68. Mildred Taylor, *Roll of Thunder, Hear My Cry* (New York: Bantam Books 1984), 133-34; Interpretation indebted to Sharon Welch, *A Feminist Ethic of Risk* (Philadelphia: Fortress, 1990), chapter 4, "An Ethic of Risk."

69. Taylor, *Roll of Thunder,* 155-56.

70. Ibid., 97.

71. Fannie Flagg, *Fried Green Tomatoes at the Whistle Stop Cafe* (New York: McGraw-Hill, 1987), 53-55.

72. Cited in *Teaching Tolerance* (Spring 96).

73. Quoted in Frances A. Maher and Mary Kay Thompson Tetreault, *The Feminist Classrooms: An Inside Look at How Professors and Students Are Transforming Higher Education for a Diverse Society* (New York: Basic Books, 1994), 199. Italics added.

74. Cara De Silva, ed., *In Memory's Kitchen: A Legacy from the Women of Terezín* (Northvale, N.J.: Jason Aronson, Inc., 1996), xv-xvi.

75. Ibid., xxxvi.

76. *Rosa Parks: My Story,* with Jim Haskins (New York: Dial Books, 1992).

77. Carolyn Heilbrun, *Writing a Woman's Life* (London: W. W. Norton & Co, 1988), 126.

78. Jenny Joseph, "Warning," in Sandra Halderman Martz, ed., *When I Grow Old I Shall Wear Purple* (Watsonville, Calif.: Papier-Mache Press, 1987), 1.

79. See Carolyn Heilbrun, "Rage in a Tenured Position," *New York Times Magazine* (Nov. 8, 1992).

80. Heilbrun, *Writing a Woman's Life,* 131.

81. Susan A. Ross, "Extravagent Affections: Women's Sexuality and Theological Anthropology," in Ann O' Hara Graf, *In the Embrace of God* (New York: Orbis, 1995), 105.

82. Thomas Ogletree notes that exclusive attachment to Yahweh provided Israel with "resources for resisting any religious sanctification of what might otherwise appear to be 'natural' hierarchies among human beings." *The Use of the Bible in Christian Ethics* (Philadelphia: Fortress Press, 1983), 61.

83. Again, let me reiterate that I think we must be very cautious when using concepts of obedience and submission to lords. I take seriously Dorothee Soelle's warning that education for obedience, a training that played a significant role in Nazi Germany, leaves a legacy that we cannot ignore: "Who forgets this background or conveniently pushes it aside and once more naively attempts to begin with obedience, as if it were merely a matter of obeying the right lord, has not learned a thing from the instruction of God called history." *Creative Disobedience,* 10.

84. Statement by Goering. See Joaquim Fest in *The Face of the Third Reich,* trans. Michael Bullock (New York: Pantheon Books, 1970), 75.

85. Rita Nakashima Brock, *Journeys by Heart: A Christology of Erotic Power* (New York: Crossroad, 1988).

86. Jacquelyn Grant speaks of liberating Jesus from the oppressive theology of the white church, in "The Sin of Servanthood: And the Deliverance of Discipleship," in Townes, *A Troubling in My Soul,* 213.

87. Stenzel, "Maria Goretti," 97.

6. Women and Conversational Education:
Hard Dialogue and Deep Connections in Communities of Faith

1. bell hooks, *Talking Back: Thinking Feminist, Thinking Black* (Boston: South End Press, 1989), 1.

2. Mary Field Belenky et al., *Women's Ways of Knowing* (Boston: Beacon, 1987), 137.

3. Ibid., 144.

4. Ibid., 105.

5. Ibid., 195.

6. Frances A. Maher and Mary Kay Thompson Tetreault, *The Feminist Classroom: An Inside Look at How Professors and Students are Transforming Higher Education for a Diverse Society* (New York: Basic Books, 1994), 82.

7. Ibid., 113.

8. In his book, *Using Discussion in Classrooms* (Philadelphia: Open University Press, 1994), 74, James T. Dillon lists several "enemies of open discussion," the first of which he names "kindliness," or protecting certain members from the truth because it might hurt them or they might not handle it well. While kindness is a good thing, protective kindliness thwarts genuine relationality. It is something like the "patina of niceness and kindness" that Gilligan and Brown named as harmful to girls' development.

9. Iris Young, "The Ideal of Community and the Politics of Difference," in Linda J. Nicholson, ed., *Feminism/Postmodernism* (London: Routledge, 1990), 300.

10. Magda Lewis, "Interrupting Patriarchy: Politics, Resistance, and Transformation in the Feminist Classroom," *Harvard Educational Review* 60, no. 4 (Nov. 1990): 473-76.

11. Maher and Tetreault, *The Feminist Classroom*, 160 .

12. hooks, *Talking Back*, 53.

13. Margo Culley and Catherine Portuges, *Gendered Subjects: The Dynamics of Feminist Teaching* (Boston: Routledge and Kegan Paul, 1985), 27-28.

14. Ann Diller, Barbara Houston, Kathryn Pauly Morgan, and Maryann Ayim, "Is Rapprochement Possible Between Educational Criticism and Nurturance?" in *The Gender Question in Education: Theory, Pedagogy, and Politics* (Boulder, Colo.: Westview Press, 1996), 141.

15. Sharon Welch, *A Feminist Ethic of Risk* (Philadelphia: Fortress, 1990), 38.

16. Ibid., 126.

17. Conference on the findings of: "Education In and Through the Congregation: A Research Project Funded by the Lilly Foundation, Auburn Theological Seminary." Oct. 22-24, 1996.

18. Olive Ann Burns, *Cold Sassy Tree* (New York: Dell Publishing, 1984), 98.

19. Burns, *Cold Sassy*, 89.

20. Sandra Schneiders, "Scripture as the Word of God," *Princeton Theological Seminary Bulletin*, (Feb. 1993): 20.

21. Katheryn Pfisterer Darr, "Ezekiel's Justifications of God: Teaching Troubling Texts," JSOT 55 (1992), 110.

22. Alice Ogden Bellis, *Helpmates, Harlots, Heroes* (Louisville: Westminster/John Knox Press, 1995), 45.

23. Quoted in Vern Bullough, *The Subordinate Sex* (Chicago: University of Illinois Press, 1973), 112.

24. Carol Meyers, *Discovering Eve: Ancient Israelite Women in Context* (New York: Oxford University Press, 1988), 91. Meyers argues that sin is not the paramount theme in Genesis 3 and that "the focus on Eve as the source of sin is not rooted in an intrinsic component of the Eden tale," 86. It is important to note that not all feminist interpreters are comfortable with the alleged rehabilitation of the Adam and Eve story from sexism. Susan Lanser feels that it is important to notice and remember the evidence of patriarchy ["(Feminist) Criticism in the Garden: Inferring Genesis 2-3," *Semeia* 41 (1988): 67-84]. Alice Bellis concludes that "The story does not depict women as inferior or as the origin of evil. Such depictions are the product of the sexism of the commentators. The story is certainly androcentric. Is it intrinsically sexist? That is the question each reader should consider," *Helpmates, Harlots, Heroes* (Louisville: Westminster/John Knox Press, 1995), 63.

25. During a debriefing session after an informal dramatic performance of this text, a student in one of my classes had an interpretive insight. Her reenactment of the passage convinced her that when the woman "bowed down" and "begged him" to heal her daughter, Jesus rebuked her because, rather than beg, he wanted her to assert her voice with agency and strength. When she met his rebuke with one of her own, he praised her and rewarded her by granting her request. Now she was an agent rather than a victim. While I still favor the interpretation that this woman taught Jesus something about his work, this student's reading is also quite plausible.

26. This interpretation is offered by Danna Nolan Fewell in her entry "Judges" in Carol A. Newsom and Sharon H. Ringe, eds., *The Women's Bible Commentary* (Louisville: Westminster/John Knox Press, 1992), 71.

27. "'Go and Suffer Oppression!' said God's Messenger to Hagar: Repression of Women in Biblical Texts," in Elisabeth Schüssler Fiorenza and Mary Shawn Copeland eds., *Violence Against Women* (Maryknoll, N.Y.: Orbis Press, 1994), 76.

28. William E. Hull, "Working for Rachel," a sermon in *The Christian Ministry*, 17, no. 4 (July 1988): 27-29.

29. Howard Thurman, *Jesus and the Disinherited* (Nashville: Abingdon Press, 1949), 30-31.

30. Darr, "Troubling Texts," 117.

31. Danna Nolan Fewell, *Reading Between Texts: Intertextuality and the Hebrew Bible* (Louisville: Westminster/John Knox Press, 1992), 14.

32. Alicia Suskin Ostriker, *Feminist Revision and the Bible* (Cambridge, Mass.: Blackwell, 1993), 31.

33. Stanley Hauerwas, *Unleashing the Scripture: Freeing the Bible from Captivity to America* (Nashville: Abingdon Press, 1993).

34. Tentatively titled, *Constructing our Common House: Practical Strategies*. Indebted to Ernest Hess, "Practical Biblical Interpretation," *Journal Religious Education* 88, no. 2 (1993):190-211.

35. Nel Noddings comments that Søren Kierkegaard's interpretation of this passage, which attributes Abraham's actions to utmost faith, "does not satisfy the mother." Obviously, it does not satisfy the son either! *Caring: A Feminine Approach to Ethics and Moral Education* (Berkeley: University of California Press, 1984), 44.

36. Paul and I, to this day, have an ongoing disagreement about the appropriate pronoun to use for God. If I say "God, She," he will quickly correct me, "No, God, He." Then I'll suggest, "OK, how about She/He," and he'll counter, "No, He/She." Then he'll say, "Mom, you know God isn't a man or a woman, he's a Spirit." I'll reply, "Yes, you're right, she is Spirit." With a devilish grin, he refuses to relent: "He is." So we tussle my son and I, and I think God is amused. In fact, I know She is!

37. Alicia Suskin Ostriker, *Feminist Revision and the Bible* (Cambridge, Mass.: Blackwell, 1993), 57.

38. Annie Dillard, *Teaching a Stone to Talk* (New York: Harper & Row, 1982), 40.

39. Ibid.

40. Language borrowed from Carol Christ, *Diving Deep and Surfacing: Women Writers on Spiritual Quest*, 2d ed. (Boston: Beacon Press, 1986).

41. Alice Walker, *The Color Purple* (New York: Harcourt, Brace, Javanovich, 1982), 164.

42. Alicia Suskin Ostriker, *The Nakedness of the Fathers: Biblical Visions and Revision* (New Brunswick: Rutgers University Press, 1994), 161.

43. Franklin Littel, *The Crucifixion of the Jews* (New York: Harper & Row, 1975), 127.

44. M. Shawn Copeland, "Wading through Many Sorrows: Toward a Theology of Suffering in Womanist Perspective," in Emilie M. Townes, ed., *A Troubling in My Soul: Womanist Perspectives on Evil & Suffering* (Maryknoll, N.Y.: Orbis, 1993), 122.

45. Not too long ago I encountered a woman who adamantly believed that the recent death of a young infant was due to the parent's lack of faith in God's capacity to heal the baby. Lest we write this off as the belief of a marginal sect, let me just say that this was a highly educated woman raised in a privileged suburb.

46. Ilana Pardes, *Countertraditions in the Bible: A Feminist Approach* (Cambridge: Harvard University Press, 1992), 151.

47. Carol A. Newsom, "Job," in *Women's Bible Commentary*, 134.

7. Caretaking Leadership: Women of Fire and Mothers of Israel

1. The translation of the Hebrew phrase *'ēšeth lapidoth* has long been debated; the Hebrew could be translated "fiery woman" or "wife of Lapidoth." For midrashic grappling see Megilla 14a (Yairah Amit, 106, n. 8). Cheryl Anne Brown, *No Longer Be Silent: First Century Portraits of Biblical Women* (Louisville: Westminster/John Knox Press, 1992), argues (drawing on Pseudo-Philo's interpretation) for "woman of fire," 43. See also Danna Nolan Fewell and David M. Gunn, "Controlling Perspectives," *Gender, Power, and Promise: The Subject of the Bible's First Story* (Nashville: Abingdon Press, 1993), 391.

2. Susan S. Friedman, "Authority in the Feminist Classroom: A Contradiction in Terms?" in M. Culley and C. Portuges, eds. *Gendered Subjects: The Dynamics of Feminist Teaching* (Boston and London: Routledge and Kegan Paul, 1985), 206.

3. Jackson W. Carroll, Carl S. Dudley, and William McKinney, *Handbook for Congregational Studies* (Nashville: Abingdon Press, 1986), 10.

4. See Elizabeth Cady Stanton, ed. *The Women's Bible. Part II: Comments on the Old and New Testaments from Joshua to Revelation* (New York: European Publishing Co., 1898).

5. Here we must recognize that claims made by Christians (including feminists) that Christianity is a liberating contrast to Judaism vis-à-vis women are deceived; in some instances Christianity lost ground. See Judith Plaskow, "Christian Feminism and Anti-Judaism," *Cross Currents* (Fall 1978): 306-9.

6. For a helpful treatment of the role of women's mothering in the biblical texts, see Danna Nolan Fewell and David M. Gunn, "The Way of Women," in *Gender, Power, & Promise: The Subject of the Bible's First Story* (Nashville: Abingdon Press, 1993).

7. *The First Blast of the Trumpet Against the MONSTROUS Regiment of Woman*, written in 1558. Quoted in Carol Blessing, "Judge, Prophet, Mother: Learning from Deborah," in *Daughters of Sarah* (Winter 1995): 35.

8. Clovis G. Chappell, *Feminine Faces* (New York: Abingdon Press, 1942), 68-69, italics added.

9. Quoted in Gale A. Yee, "By the Hand of a Woman: The Metaphor of the Woman Warrior in Judges 4," in *Semeia* 61 (1993).

10. Ibid., 111.

11. The presence of Deborah as judge is a striking instance of gender equality. However, her relationship to Barak may reveal more of the texture in which such equality was wrestled. Though many male commentators are embarrassed by Barak's refusal to go into battle without Deborah (one legend called him an ignoramus), his reticence may point to his courage rather than his cowardice. He is not afraid to defer to a woman's authority, and he is not above seeking a woman's wise and comforting counsel in battle. It is a tribute to Deborah's character that Barak seeks her presence, and it is to Barak's credit that he does not denounce or bypass Deborah's judgment. Deborah's plan for battle no doubt seemed unwise in light of Canaan's overwhelming technological advantage. Asking only for her presence alongside, Barak is willing to proceed with her strategy. Deborah apparently upbraids Barak for handing the glory of killing Sisera over to a woman ("I will surely go with you; nevertheless, the road on which you are going will not lead to your glory, for the Lord will sell Sisera into the hand of a woman"). Although her words are more a portent of what is to take place (Jael will come upon the scene) than an attempt to humiliate her general, it is possible that Barak exposed and challenged remnants of patriarchy in Deborah. Why not be joined in the battle front with a woman? Why not share glory with a woman? The upshot of the scenario is that Barak subordinates his own strategic calculation to Deborah's insight and wisdom. Rather than an ignoramus, Barak may be a man of great social courage, a man willing to stand by and even a little bit behind a woman he is not afraid to count as his social equal and political superior. The "road" that he goes on does not lead to *his* personal glory, but Barak surely prepares the way for what turns out to be *their* mutual glory. This leads into the broader theme of partnership that is suggested in the overall narrative.

12. See Susan Niditch, *Underdogs and Tricksters: A Prelude to Biblical Folklore* (New York: Harper & Row, 1987).

13. Katharine Doob Sakenfeld read this text with women in Asia, and she asked them to share any insights they could offer U.S. women. "If you American women would just realize that your place in this story is with Sisera's mother, waiting to collect the spoil of your interventions across the world . . ." was the bold reply from one woman. This prophetic word adds another dimension to this story. See Sakenfeld in "Deborah, Jael, and Sisera's Mother: Reading the Scriptures in Cross-Cultural Context," in Jane Dempsey Douglass and James F. Kay, eds., *Women, Gender, and Christian Community* (Louisville: Westminster/John Knox Press, 1997), 22.

14. Danna Nolan Fewell, "Judges," in Carol A. Newsom and Sharon H. Ringe, eds., *The Women's Bible Commentary* (Louisville: Westminster/John Knox Press, 1992), 70.

15. In her provocative book *The Chalice and the Blade: Our History, Our Future* (San Francisco: HarperCollins, 1987), Riane Eisler distinguishes between the "dominator model" and the "partnership model" of social organization. The former is structured by male-based hierarchy and forced conformity, and it is actually a later arrival in history than the latter, which is characterized by gender equality and the celebration of diversity. Partnership is, in Eisler's view, the original—disrupted—direction

of human civilization. Eisler's thesis is "that the direction of the cultural evolution for dominator and partnership societies is very different" (xxi), and she optimistically promotes a conscious and active transformation toward (return to) partnership. While Eisler's analysis is somewhat simplistic and romanticized, her view that the future lies in a *return* to the partnership of the past is perhaps not so far-fetched. Deborah's story gives us glimpses into the kind of social organization Eisler reports to have uncovered. I charge that Eisler's analysis is simplistic in that any dichotomy between two polarities makes sharp distinctions between realities that are actually much more nuanced and variegated than described. Similarly, I find that her description of partnership societies, generally those that were goddess worshipers, usually glosses over the cruel side of these societies. I think there is much in goddess worship that we can recover, but we need to be honest that such practices as human sacrifice were part of these societies. For a more in-depth exploration of history see Elise Boulding, *The Underside of History*, vols. 1 and 2, Sage Publications.

16. Sadly, Christian tradition reversed the partnership of the passage and remembers only Barak (Hebrews 11:32).

17. Margaret Wold, *Women of Faith and Spirit: Profiles of Fifteen Biblical Witnesses* (Minneapolis: Augsburg Press, 1987), 49.

18. Yairah Amit, "Judges 4: Its Content and Form," *JSOT* 39 (1987), 96.

19. Susan Niditch, *War in the Hebrew Bible* (New York: Oxford University Press, 1993), 288.

20. Quoted in Danna Nolan Fewell and David M. Gunn, "Controlling Perspectives: Women, Men, and the Authority of Violence in Judges 4 and 5," *Journal of the American Academy of Religion* 58 (1990), 389-411.

21. Audre Lorde, *Sister Outsider: Essays and Speeches* (Trumansberg, N.Y.: The Crossing Press, 1984), 53.

22. A point made by Judith Orr, "Administration as an Art of Shared Vision," in Christie C. Neuger, ed., *The Arts of Ministry: Feminist and Womanist Approaches* (Louisville: Westminster/John Knox Press, 1996), 130.

23. I was recently reading a case study on pastoral leadership and, much to my chagrin, was jolted when, five pages into the case I discovered the pastor was a woman. No gender being given, I just assumed it was a man. If I, an ordained clergy person and seminary professor still subconsciously associate pastoral leadership with men, then my guess is it's pretty pervasive. Although this chapter is written using the female imagery for leadership inspired by Deborah, the implications are as valid for men as they are for women. Our imaginations have been primarily shaped by male leaders; perhaps this chapter will help to broaden the images that come to mind when we think of leaders.

24. Carol Christ, "Toward a Paradigm Shift in the Academy and in Religious Studies," in C. Farnham, ed., *The Impact of Feminist Research in the Academy* (Bloomington, Ind.: Indiana University Press, 1987).

25. It may be that there are times a leader feels the need for a passionate prophetic attack. I do not wish to remove this as an occasional possibility. I think it may be justifiable on occasion; I do not think it is a legitimate general style, however. The leader who does use this style should also be willing to receive it from others when it is also deemed appropriate.

26. Paulo Freire and Ira Shor, *A Pedagogy For Liberation: Dialogues on Transforming Education* (New York: Bergin & Garvey, 1987), 101.

27. Friedman, "Authority in Classrooms," 207.

28. See Jo Ann Pagano, *Exiles and Communities: Teaching in the Patriarchal Wilderness* (Albany: State University of New York Press, 1990).

29. Freire and Shor, *Pedagogy for Liberation*, 89.

30. Elisabeth Johnson, *She Who Is: The Mystery of God in Feminist Theological Discourse* (New York: Crossroad, 1992).

31. Jackson W. Carroll, *As One With Authority: Reflective Leadership in Ministry* (Louisville: Westminster/John Knox Press, 1991), 36.

32. Joanna Bowen Gillespie, *Women Speak: Of God, Congregations and Change* (Valley Forge, Penn.: Trinity Press International, 1995), 195.

33. Emphasis added. Quoted in Kathleen Hall Jamieson, *Beyond the Double Bind: Women and Leadership* (New York: Oxford University Press, 1995), 184-85.

34. Iris Young, *Justice and the Politics of Difference* (Princeton: Princeton University Press, 1990), 16.

35. Ibid., 152.

36. Lorde, *Sister Outsider*, 111.

37. Joanna Bowen Gillespie, who interviewed "ordinary women in a mainline denomination," borrows this expression from one of her interviewees who boldly announced what it is she wanted from church: "I want real God-talk." *Women Speak*, 2.

38. Carol Christ, *Diving Deep and Surfacing: Women Writers on Spiritual Questions* (Boston: Beacon Press, 1980), 12.

39. Anne Wimberly's wonderful book *Soul Stories: African American Christian Education* (Nashville: Abingdon Press, 1994) makes "story-linking" between personal stories and biblical stories the basis for education.

40. It is important to reiterate here that groups that are marginated in our culture and that have had their own cultures repressed may find necessary sanctuary and cultural preservation in ethnic churches. As one African American man said to me, "Don't go diversifying your white churches at the expense of the one place black folk can feel worthy." We have to realize that dominant groups that need to diversify must not divide (and thereby conquer) solidarity groups that are needed. It may be that "grass-roots ecumenicity," where different communities interact with one another, are the better alternative. Furthermore, "affinity groups" within a community may need to be formed in order to support those who band together in shared marginality within the community.

41. See Jackson W. Carroll, Carl S. Dudley, and William McKinney, *Handbook for Congregational Studies* (Nashville: Abingdon Press, 1986).

42. If a leader, however, consistently finds that she cannot empower others to make decisions in any area, then she is veering toward a controlling, authoritarian style that is, in my view, unacceptable and harmful to girls especially. As I argued in chapter 2, authoritarian imposition of a viewpoint—whatever the viewpoint may be—works against girls' development of voice.

43. I have been influenced by James Hopewell's book *Congregations: Stories and Structures* (Philadelphia: Fortress Press, 1987), already a classic work in congregational studies. Hopewell is helpful in giving leaders tools for understanding congregational worldviews and overarching idioms or myths. He is less helpful, however, in articulating the role of the leader in challenging, nudging, or transforming a given worldview. Clearly, he was reacting to overzealous and insensitive leaders who lacked empathy and understanding, and he thus tipped the balance far in favor of empathy.

44. Lauren Smith, "Secret Basketball: One Problem with the Student-Centered Classroom," *Feminist Teacher*, 8, no. 1: 16.

45. Nancy Schniedewind, "Teaching Feminist Process in the 1990s," in *Women's Studies Quarterly (Issue on Feminist Pedagogy: An Update)* XXI, nos. 3 & 4 (Fall/Winter 1993): 17. Schniedewind considers democratic processes to be part of feminist pedagogy.

46. Seyla Benhabib, *Situating the Self: Gender, Community and Postmodernism in Contemporary Ethics* (New York: Routledge, 1992), 37. In this section, I am indebted to Seyla Benhabib's understanding of discourse ethics as a "conversational model of enlarged mentality," which builds on the principles of good reasoning, fair procedure, and the capacity to understand another's viewpoint.

47. See Elizabeth Ellsworth, "Why Doesn't This Feel Empowering? Working Through the Repressive Myths of Critical Pedagogy," in Carmen Luke and Jennifer Gore, *Feminisms and Critical Pedagogy* (New York: Routlege, 1992).

48. In her important book *Affirming Diversity: The Sociopolitical Context of Multicultural Education*, 2d ed. (New York and London: Longman Publishers, 1996), Sonia Nieto recognizes that there are certain historically accepted "basics" that need to be part of education, but she argues for a broader understanding of the "basics," which opens up the "canon" of acceptable knowledge and processes.

49. Thomas H. Groome, *Christian Religious Education: Sharing our Story and Vision* (San Francisco: Harper & Row, 1980); *Sharing Faith: A Comprehensive Approach to Religious Education & Pastoral Ministry* (New York: HarperCollins, 1991).

50. Groome, *Sharing Faith*, 155-74.

51. Along with Paulo Freire (*The Politics of Education: Culture, Power, and Liberation* [Massachusetts: Bergin and Garvey, 1985]), I believe it is crucial for us to acknowledge the "political nature" of education; the choices we make as leaders and educators influence and impact the communities we lead in significant ways.

52. Groome, *Christian Religious Education*, 214-17.

53. Ernest Hess names this as a step in his method for Bible study. See "Practical Biblical Interpretation," *Religious Education Journal* 88, no. 2 (Spring 1993): 190-210. In one of my seminary courses, I gave an assignment called "Listening to the Voice of the Other." The participants were instructed to select any person they deemed their other (e.g., theological other, ethnic other) and to informally interview

them. The goal was to understand this person and learn from him or her. It strikes me that a pastoral leader might suggest or even arrange something similar. Of all the assignments I have given, this one seemed to be the most meaningful to students.

54. For a helpful resource, see David W. Johnson and Frank P. Johnson, *Joining Together: Group Therapy and Group Skills* (Needham Heights, Mass.: Allyn and Bacon, 1994), chaps. 6: Decision Making; 7: Controversy and Creativity; 8: Conflicts of Interest; 10: Dealing with Diversity.

55. The irony implicit in this quote is poignant. Even though left out of this Torah teaching, this woman fulfills Torah.

56. *New York Times* (Saturday, Dec. 2, 1995), 23.

57. Allusion to comment made by twelve-year-old girl and quoted by Gilligan in chapter 4.

Selective Bibliography

Albreach, Lisa and Rose M. Brewer, eds. *Bridges of Power: Women's Multicultural Alliances.* Philadelphia: New Society Publishers, 1990.

Allen, Paula Gunn. "Who is Your Mother? Red Roots of White Feminism." *The Sacred Hoop: Recovering the Feminine in American Indian Traditions.* Boston: Beacon Press, 1986.

Anderson, Margaret. *Thinking About Women.* New York: Macmillan, 1988.

Arendt, Hannah. *Eichmann in Jerusalem: A Report on the Banality of Evil.* New York: Viking Press, 1963.

Bal, Mieke. "Lots of Writing." *Semeia* 54 (1991): 77-102.

Bassoff, Evelyn S. *Between Mothers and Sons.* New York: Penguin Books, 1994.

Belenky, Mary Field et al. *Women's Ways of Knowing: The Development of Self, Voice, and Mind.* Boston: Beacon Press, 1987.

Bellah, Robert et al. *Habits of the Heart: Individualism and Commitment in American Life.* Berkeley: University of California Press, 1985.

Bellis, Alice Ogden. *Helpmates, Harlots, Heroes.* Louisville: Westminster/John Knox Press, 1995.

Benhabib, Seyla. *Situating the Self: Gender, Community and Postmodernism in Contemporary Ethics.* New York: Routledge, 1992.

Bennett, E. K. *A History of the German Novelle from Goethe to Thomas Mann.* Cambridge: At the University Press, 1934.

Bondi, Roberta C. *To Pray and to Love: Conversations on Prayer with the Early Church.* Minneapolis: Fortress Press, 1992.

Bordo, Susan. *Unbearable Weight: Feminism, Western Culture, and the Body.* Berkeley: University of California Press, 1993.

Brock, Rita Nakashima. *Journeys by Heart: A Christology of Erotic Power.* New York: Crossroads, 1988.

Brooks, Virginia. "Sex Differences in Student Dominance Behavior in Female and Male Professor's Classrooms." *Sex Roles* 8 (1982): 683-90.

Broverman, Inge K. and Donald M. Broverman et al. "Sex-Role Stereotypes and Clinical Judgments of Mental Health." *Journal of Consulting and Clinical Psychology* 3 (1970): 1-7.

Brown, Joanne Carlson and Carole R. Bohn, eds. *Christianity, Patriarchy and Abuse.* Cleveland: Pilgrim Press, 1989.

Brown, Lyn Mikel. "A Problem of Visions: The Development of Voice and Relational Knowledge in Girls Ages Seven to Sixteen." *Women's Studies Quarterly* XIX: 1 & 2 (Spring/Summer, 1991): 52-71.

Browning, Don. *A Fundamental Practical Theology.* Minneapolis: Fortress, 1991.

Brownmiller, Susan. *Femininity.* New York: Fawcett Columbine, 1984.

Bruch, Hilda. *The Golden Cage: The Enigma of Anorexia Nervosa.* New York: Vintage, 1979.

Brumberg, Joan Jacobs. *Fasting Girls: The Emergence of Anorexia Nervosa as a Modern Disease.* Cambridge: Harvard University Press, 1988.

Buchmann, Christina and Celina Spiegel. *Out of the Garden: Women Writers on the Bible.* New York: Balantine Books, 1994.

Buechner, Frederick. *Telling Secrets.* San Francisco: Harper Books, 1991.

Bullough, Vern. *The Subordinate Sex.* Chicago: University of Illinois Press, 1973.

Burns, Olive Ann. *Cold Sassy Tree.* New York: Dell Publishing, 1984.

Capps, Donald. *Deadly Sins and Saving Virtues.* Philadelphia: Fortress Press, 1987.

_____. *The Depleted Self: Sin in a Narcissistic Age.* Minneapolis, Minn.: Fortress Press, 1993.

Carroll, Jackson W. *As One with Authority: Reflective Leadership in Ministry.* Louisville: Westminster/John Knox Press, 1991.

_____, and Carl S. Dudley and William McKinney. *Handbook for Congregational Studies.* Nashville: Abingdon Press, 1986.

Carter, Betty. "Fathers and Daughters." in *The Women's Project in Family Therapy.* 90-157, 1988.

Casper, R. C. et al. "Bulimia: Its Incidence and Clinical Importance in Patients with Anorexia Nervosa." *Archives of General Psychiatry* 37 (1980): 1030-35.

Chappell, Clovis G. *Feminine Faces.* New York: Abingdon, 1942.

Chodorow, Nancy. *The Reproduction of Mothering.* Berkeley: University of California Press, 1978.

Chopin, Kate. *The Awakening.* 1899. Reprint, New York: Dover Publications, 1993.

Christ, Carol. *Diving Deep and Surfacing: Women Writers on Spiritual Quest.* 2d ed. Boston: Beacon Press, 1986.

Clark, Elizabeth A. *Women in the Early Church.* Wilmington, Del.: Michael Glazier, 1983.

Culley, Margo and Catherine Portuges. *Gendered Subjects: The Dynamics of Feminist Teaching.* Boston: Routledge and Kegan Paul, 1985.

Cutler, Anne and Donia R. Scott. "Speaker, Sex and Perceived Apportionment of Talk." *Applied Psychodynamics* 11 (1990): 253-72.

Darr, Katheryn Pfisterer. "Ezekial's Justifications of God: Teaching Troubling Texts." *JSOT* 55 (1992): 97-117.

_____. *Far More Precious Than Jewels: Perspectives on Biblical Women.* Louisville: Westminster/John Knox Press, 1991.

Davis, Patricia H. *Counseling Adolescent Girls.* Minneapolis: Fortress, 1996.

_____. "Women and the Burden of Empathy." *Journal of Pastoral Theology* 3 (Summer 1993): 29-38.

Day, Linda. *Three Faces of a Queen: Characterization in the Books of Esther.* Sheffield, Eng.: Sheffield Academic Press, 1995.

Day, Peggy, ed. *Gender and Difference in Ancient Israel.* Minneapolis: Fortress Press, 1989.

Diamond, Irene and Lee Quimby, eds. *Feminism and Foucault: Reflection on Resistance.* Boston: Northeastern University Press, 1988.

Dillon, James T. *Using Discussion in Classrooms.* Philadelphia: Open University Press, 1994.

Dinnerstein, Dorothy. *The Mermaid and the Minotaur: Sexual Arrangements and Human Malaise.* New York: Harper and Row, 1976.

Doyle, James A. *Sex and Gender.* Dubuque: Wm. C. Brown, 1985.

Dunfee, Susan Nelson. "The Sin of Hiding: A Feminist Critique of Reinhold Niebuhr's Account of the Sin of Pride." *Soundings* (Fall 1982): 16-27.

Eichenbaum, Louise and Susie Orbach. *Understanding Women: A Feminist Psychoanalytical Approach.* New York: Basic Books, 1983.

Eliot, George. *Daniel Deronda.* New York: Penguin Books, 1967.

Exum, Cheryl and Johanna W. H. Bos. *Reasoning with the Foxes: Female Wit in a World of Male Power.* Atlanta: Scholars Press, 1988.

Faludi, Susan. *Backlash: The Undeclared War Against American Women.* New York: Crown, 1991.

Farnham, C., ed. *The Impact of Feminist Research in the Academy.* Indiana University Press, 1987.

Fasching, Darrell. *Narrative Theology After Auschwitz.* Minneapolis: Augsburg, 1992.

Fest, Joaquim. *The Face of the Third Reich.* Translated by Michael Bullock. New York: Crossroads, 1988.

Fewell, Danna Nolan and David M. Gunn. *Gender, Power, and Promise: The Subject of the Bible's First Story.* Nashville: Abingdon Press, 1993.

Fiorenza, Elisabeth Schüssler. *Discipleship of Equals: A Critical Feminist Ekklesia-logy of Liberation.* New York: Crossroad, 1993.

_____. *Jesus: Miriam's Child, Sophia's Prophet: Critical Issues in Feminist Christology.* New York: Continuum Books, 1995.

_____ and Mary Shawn Copeland. *Violence Against Women*. Maryknoll, N.Y.: Orbis Books, 1994.

Formanek, Ruth and Anita Gurian, eds. *Women and Depression: A Lifespan Perspective*. New York: Springer Publishing Co., 1987.

Fortune, Marie M. *Keeping the Faith: Questions and Answers for the Abused Woman*. San Francisco: Harper Collins, 1987.

Foster, Richard and James Bryan Smith, eds. *Devotional Classics*. San Francisco: Harper Collins, 1993.

Fox, Michael V. *Character and Ideology in the Book of Esther*. Columbia: University of South Carolina Press, 1991.

Freire, Paulo and Ira Shor. *A Pedagogy For Liberation: Dialogues on Transforming Education*. New York: Bergin & Garvey, 1987.

_____. *The Politics of Education: Culture Power and Liberation*. Massachusetts: Bergin and Garvey, 1985.

Gardner, Freda and Herbert Anderson. *Living Alone*. Louisville: John Knox Press Press, 1997.

Gendler, Mary. "The Restoration of Vashti." in *The Jewish Woman*, edited by E. Koltun. New York: Schocken Books, 1976.

Gillespie, Joanna Bowen. *Women Speak: Of God, Congregations and Change*. Valley Forge, Penn.: Trinity Press International, 1995.

Gilligan, Carol. "In a Different Voice: Women's Conceptions of the Self and of Morality." *Harvard Educational Review* 47 (1977): 481-517.

_____. *In a Different Voice: Psychological Theory and Women's Development*. Cambridge: Harvard University Press, 1982.

_____ and Nona P. Lyons and Trudy Hammer, eds. *Making the Connections: The Relational Worlds of Adolescent Girls at Emma Willard School*. Cambridge: Harvard University Press, 1990.

_____ and Janie Victoria Ward and Jill McLean Taylor, eds. *Mapping the Moral Domain: A Contribution of Women's Thinking to Psychological Theory and Education*. Cambridge: Harvard University Press, 1992.

_____ and Lyn Mikel Brown. *Meeting at the Crossroads: Women's Psychology and Girls' Development*. Cambridge: Harvard, 1992.

_____ and Annie Rogers, and Deborah L. Tolman, eds. *Women, Girls & Psychotherapy: Reframing Resistance*. New York: The Haworth Press, 1991.

Goodman, Ellen. "Let's Trash 'The Rules.'" *The Courier-Post* (November 1, 1996).

Graf, Ann O'Hara. *In the Embrace of God*. New York: Orbis Books, 1995.

Gress, James and David Purpel, eds. *Curriculum: An Introduction to the Field*. Berkeley: McCutchen, 1978.

Griffiths, Morwenna. *Feminisms and the Self: The Web of Identity*. New York: Routledge, 1995.

Groome, Thomas H. *Christian Religious Education: Sharing Our Story and Vision.* San Francisco: Harper and Row, 1980.

_____. *Sharing Faith: A Comprehensive Approach to Religious Education and Pastoral Ministry.* New York: Harper Collins, 1991.

Guttentag, M., S. Salasin, and D. Belle, eds. *The Mental Health of Women.* New York: Academic Press, 1980.

Harries, Richard. *Reinhold Niebuhr and the Issues of Our Time.* Grand Rapids, Mich.: Eerdmans, 1986.

Harris, Maria. *Dance of the Spirit: The Seven Steps of Women's Spirituality.* New York: Bantam Books, 1989.

_____. "Women Teaching Girls: The Power and the Danger." *Religious Education* 88:1 (1993).

Harrison, Beverly Wildung. "The Power of Anger in the Work of Love." In *Making the Connections: Essays in Feminist Social Ethics,* edited by Carol S. Robb. Boston: Beacon Press, 1985.

Heilbrun, Carolyn. *Writing a Woman's Life.* London: W. W. Norton & Co., 1988.

Held, Ann Reed. *Faith in Families.* Illinois: National Presbyterian Marinars, 1987.

Herodotus. *The History.* Translated by David Grene. Chicago: University of Chicago Press, 1987.

Heschel, Susannah, ed. *On Being a Jewish Feminist: A Reader.* New York: Schocken Books, 1983.

Hess, Carol Lakey. "Abomination and Creativity: Shaking the Order of the Cosmos." *The Princeton Seminary Bulletin.* XV (1994):28-45.

_____. "Freda Gardner: A Master Teacher Whose Faith Has Helped Us Understand." In *Faith of Our Foremothers: Women Changing Religious Education,* edited by Barbara Anne Keely. Louisville: Westminster/John Knox Press, forthcoming 1997.

Hess, Ernest. "Practical Biblical Interpretation." *Journal of Religious Education.* 88, no. 2 (1993): 190-211.

hooks, bell. *Feminist Theory: From Margin to Center.* Boston: South End Press, 1984.

_____. *Talking Back: Thinking Feminist, Thinking Black.* Boston: South End Press, 1989.

_____. *Yearning: Race, Gender and Cultural Politics.* Boston: South End Press, 1990.

Hopewell, James. *Congregations: Stories and Structures.* Philadelphia: Fortress Press, 1987.

Hull, William E. "Working for Rachel." *The Christian Ministry* 17, no. 4 (July 1988): 27-29.

Jagger, Allison and Susan Bordo. *Gender/Body/Knowledge: Feminist Reconstructions of Being and Knowing.* New Brunswick: Rutgers University Press, 1989.

Jamieson, Kathleen Hall. *Beyond the Doublebind: Women and Leadership.* New York: Oxford University Press, 1995.

Janssens, Louis. "Norms and Priorities in a Love Ethics." *Louvain Studies* 6 (1977): 207-38.

Jipson, Janice et al. *Repositioning Feminism and Education: Perspectives on Educating for Social Change.* Westport, Conn.: Bergin & Garvey, 1995.

Johnson, David W. and Frank Johnson. *Joining Together: Group Therapy and Groups Skills.* Needham Heights, Mass.: Allyn and Bacon, 1994.

Johnson, Elisabeth. *She Who Is: The Mystery of God in Feminist Theological Discourse.* New York: Crossroads, 1992.

Jordan, Judith et al. *Women's Growth in Connection: Writings from the Stone Center.* New York: Guilford Press, 1991.

Kaschak, Ellen. *Endangered Lives: A New Psychology of Women's Experience.* New York: Basic Books, 1992.

Kegan, Robert. *The Evolving Self: Problem and Process in Human Development.* Cambridge, Mass.: Harvard University Press, 1982.

_____. *In Over Our Heads: The Mental Demands of Modern Life.* Cambridge: Harvard University Press, 1994.

Kegley, Charles and Robert W. Bretall, eds. *Reinhold Niebuhr: His Religious, Social and Practical Thought.* New York: The Macmillan Co., 1956.

Kettay, Fred and Diana T. Meyers, eds. *Women and Moral Theory.* Totowa, N.J.: Rowman & Littlefield, 1987.

Kierkegaard, Søren. *Concluding Unscientific Postscript.* Translated by David F. Swenson and Walter Lowrie. Princeton: Princeton University Press, 1941.

_____. *For Self-Examination.* Translated by Edna And Howard Hong. Minneapolis: Fortress Press, 1940.

_____. *The Sickness Unto Death.* Princeton: Princeton University Press, 1980.

Kirmsee, Bruce. *Kierkegaard in Golden Age Denmark.* Indianapolis: Indiana University Press, 1990.

Kohlberg, L., C. Levine, and A. Hewer. *Moral Stages: A Current Formulation and a Response to Critics.* New York: Karger, 1983.

Koll, Karla Ann. "Theology of Solidarity." In *500 Years, Domination or Liberation? Theological Alternatives for the Americas in the 1990's,* edited by Philip E. Wheton. Ocean City, Md..: Skipjack Press, 1992.

Kunjufu, Jawanza. *Adam, Where Are You?* Chicago: African American Images, 1994.

LaCocque, Andre. *The Feminine Unconventional: Four Subversive Figures in Israel's Tradition.* Minneapolis: Fortress Press, 1990.

Ladner, Joyce A. *Tomorrow's Tomorrow.* New York: Anchor, 1972.

Laffey, Alice. *An Introduction to the Old Testament: A Feminist Perspective.* Philadelphia: Fortress Press, 1988.

Lanser, Susan. "Feminist Criticism in the Garden: Inferring Genesis 2-3." *Semeia* 41 (1988): 67-84.

Larrabee, Mary Jane, ed. *An Ethics of Care: Feminist and Interdisciplinary Perspectives.* New York: Routledge, 1993.

Leechan, James. *Defiant Hope: Spirituality for Survivors of Family Abuse.* Louisville: Westminster /John Knox Press, 1993.

Lerner, Harriet Goldhor. *The Dance of Anger: A Woman's Guide to Changing Patterns of Intimate Relationships.* New York: Harper and Row, 1985.

Lewis, Magda. "Interrupting Patriarchy: Politics, Resistance, and Transformation in the Feminist Classroom." *Harvard Educational Review* 60:4 (Nov. 1990): 473-76.

Littel, Franklin. *The Crucifixion of the Jews.* New York: Harper and Row, 1975.

Lorde, Audre. *Sister Outsider.* Trumansburg, N.Y.: Crossing Press, 1984.

Luke, Carmen and Jennifer Core. *Feminisms and Critical Pedagogy.* New York: Routledge, 1992.

Maher, Frances A. and Mary Kay Thompson Tetreault. *The Feminist Classroom: An Inside Look at How Professors and Students Are Transforming Higher Education for a Diverse Society.* New York: Basic Books, 1994.

McGee, J. Vernon. *Esther: The Romance of Providence.* Nashville: Thomas Nelson Publishers, 1982.

Meyers, Carol. *Discovering Eve: Ancient Israelite Women in Context.* New York: Oxford University Press, 1988.

Miles, Rebekah. "Freeing Bonds and Binding Freedom: Reinhold Niebuhr and Feminist Critics on Paternal Dominion and Maternal Constraint." *The Annual of the Society of Christian Ethics* (1996): 121-24.

Miller, Alice. *The Drama of the Gifted Child.* New York: Basic Books, 1981.

_____. *For Your Own Good: Hidden Cruelty in Childrearing and the Roots of Violence.* New York: Farrar, Straus and Giroux, 1983.

Miller, Jean Baker. *Toward a New Psychology of Women.* 2d ed. Boston: Beacon Press, 1987.

Miller-McLemore, Bonnie. *Also a Mother: Work and Family as Theological Dilemma.* Nashville: Abingdon Press, 1994.

Minuchin, Sal et al. *Psychosomatic Families in Context.* Cambridge: Harvard University Press, 1978.

Mitchell, Rosemary Catalano and Gail Anderson Ricciuti. *Birthings and Blessings: Liberating Worship Services for the Inclusive Church.* New York: Crossroad, 1991.

Montefiore, C. G. and H. Loewe. *A Rabbinic Anthology.* Cleveland: World Publishing Co., 1963.

Moore, Carey A. *Esther.* Anchor Bible Series 7B. Garden City, N.Y.: Doubleday, 1971.

Moore, Mary Elizabeth Mullino. *Teaching from the Heart: Theology and Educational Method.* Minneapolis: Fortress Press, 1989.

Musa, Mark, trans. *Dante's Purgatory.* Bloomington: Indiana University Press, 1981.

Neuger, Christie C., ed. *The Arts of Ministry: Feminist and Womanist Approaches.* Louisville: Westminster/John Knox Press, 1996.

Nicholson, Linda, ed. *Feminism/Postmodernism.* London: Routledge, 1990.

Niditch, Susan. *Underdogs and Tricksters: A Prelude to Biblical Folklore.* New York: Harper and Row, 1987.

——————. *War in the Hebrew Bible.* New York: Oxford Press, 1993.

Niebuhr, Reinhold. *Christianity and Power Politics.* New York: Charles Scribner's Sons, 1940.

——————. *Faith and History: A Comparison of Christian and Modern Views of History.* New York: Charles Scribners Sons, 1949.

——————. *The Nature and Destiny of Man.* 2 vols. New York: Scribner's, 1943.

Nieto, Sonia. *Affirming Diversity: The Sociopolitical Context of Multicultural Education.* 2d ed. New York and London: Longmans Publishers, 1996.

Noddings, Nel. *Caring: A Feminine Approach to Ethics and Moral Education.* Berkeley: University of California Press, 1984.

Ogletree, Thomas. *The Use of the Bible in Christian Ethics.* Philadelphia: Fortress Press, 1983.

Okin, Susan. *Justice Gender and the Family.* New York: Basic Books, 1989.

O'Reilly, Jane. "The Lost Girls." *Mirabella* (Apr. 1994): 116-20.

Ostriker, Alicia Suskin. *Feminist Revision and the Bible.* Cambridge, Mass.: Blackwell, 1993.

——————. *The Nakedness of the Fathers: Biblical Visions and Revisions.* New Brunswick: Rutgers University Press, 1994.

Pagano, Jo Ann. *Exiles and Communities: Teaching in the Patriarchal Wilderness.* Albany: State University of New York Press, 1990.

Pardes, Ilana. *Countertraditions in the Bible: A Feminist Approach.* Cambridge: Harvard University Press, 1992.

Parks, Sharon Daloz. "Home and Pilgrimage: Companion Metaphors for Personal and Social Transformation." *Soundings* 72, vols. 2/3 (Summer/Fall 1989): 297-315.

——————. *The Critical Years: The Young Adult Search for a Faith to Live By.* San Francisco: Harper and Row, 1986.

Paton, Lewis Bayles. *A Critical and Exegetical Commentary on the Book of Esther,* International Critical Commentary. New York: Scribner's, 1908.

Peters, Ted. *Sin: Radical Evil in Soul and Society.* Grand Rapids: Eerdmans, 1994.

Phipps, William E. *Assertive Biblical Women.* Westport, Conn.: Greenwood Press, 1992.

Pipher, Mary. *Reviving Ophelia: Saving the Selves of Adolescent Girls.* New York: Ballantine Books, 1994.

Placher, William. *Narratives of a Vulnerable God: Christ, Theology, and Scripture.* Louisville: Westminster/John Knox Press, 1994.

Plaskow, Judith. "Christian Feminism and Anti-Judaism." *Cross Currents* (Fall 1978): 306-9.

_____. *Sex, Sin and Grace: Women's Experience and the Theologies of Reinhold Niebuhr and Paul Tillich.* New York: University Press of America, 1980.

_____. *Standing Against Sinai: Judaism from a Feminist Perspective.* San Francisco: Harper, 1990.

Reuther, Rosemary Radford. *Women-Church: Theology and Practice of Feminist Liturgical Communities.* San Francisco: Harper and Row, 1985.

Rich, Adrienne. *On Lies, Secrets and Silence.* New York: W. W. Norton and Co., 1979.

_____. *Your Native Land, Your Life.* New York: W. W. Norton and Co., 1986.

Ruddick, Sara. *Mothering: Essays in Feminist Theory.* Totowa, N.J.: Rowman and Allanheld, 1984.

Russell, Letty. *Becoming Human.* Philadelphia: Westminster Press, 1982.

_____. *Church in the Round: Feminist Interpretation of the Church.* Louisville: Westminister/ John Knox Press, 1993.

_____, ed. *Feminist Interpretation of the Bible.* Philadelphia: Westminster Press, 1985.

Saiving, Valarie. "The Human Situation: A Feminine View." In *Womanspirit Rising: A Feminist Reader in Religion,* edited by Carol Christ and Judith Plaskow. San Francisco: Harper and Row Publishers, 1979.

Sakenfeld, Katharine Doob. "Feminist Uses of Biblical Material." In Letty M. Russell, ed. *Feminist Interpretation of the Bible.* Philadelphia: Westminster Press, 1985.

_____. "The Daughters of Zelophehad and Feminist Biblical Interpretation." In *The Princeton Seminary Bulletin* (November 1988): 179-86.

Saussy, Carroll. *The Gift of Anger.* Louisville: Westminster/John Knox Press, 1985.

Say, Elizabeth A. *Evidence on Her Own Behalf: Women's Narrative as Theological Voice.* Rowman & Littlefield, 1990.

Schaef, Anne Wilson. *Escape From Intimacy: Untangling "Love" Addictions: Sex, Romance and Relationships.* San Francisco: Harper and Row, 1989.

_____. *When Society Becomes an Addict.* San Francisco: Harper and Row, 1987.

Schneemelcher, Wilhelm, ed. *New Testament Apocrypha.* Philadelphia: Westminster Press, 1964.

Schneiders, Sandra. "Scripture as the Word of God." *Princeton Theological Seminary Bulletin.* (Feb. 1993): 18-35.

Schniedewind, Nancy. "Teaching Feminist Process in the 1990s." *Women's Studies Quarterly (Issue on Feminist Pedagogy: An Update)* XXI, vols. 3 & 4. (Fall/Winter 1993): 17-30.

Segova, Fernando F. and Mary Ann Torbert, eds. *Reading From This Place: Social Location and Biblical Interpretation in the United States.* vol 1. Minneapolis: Fortress Press, 1995.

Sewell, Marilyn. *Cries of the Spirit: A Celebration of Women's Spirituality.* Boston: Beacon Press, 1991.

Soelle, Dorothee. *Creative Disobedience.* Cleveland: The Pilgrim Press, 1995.

_____. *Suffering.* Philadelphia: Fortress Press, 1975.

Spender, Dale. *Invisible Women: The Schooling Scandal.* London: Writers and Readers Publishing Cooperative, 1982.

_____. *Man-Made Language.* Boston: Routledge and Kegan Paul, 1980.

Stanton, Elizabeth Cady, ed. *The Women's Bible.* New York: European Publishing Co., 1898.

Steiner-Adair, Catherine. "The Body Politic: Normal Female Adolescent Development and the Development of Eating Disorders." *The Journal of the American Academy of Psychoanalysis.* 14, vol. 1 (1986): 95-114.

Stoltenberg, John. *Refusing to Be a Man: Essays on Sex and Justice.* New York: Meridian, 1989.

Striegel-Moore, R. H., L. R. Silberstein, and J. Rodin. "Toward an Understanding of Risk Factors in Bulimia," *American Psychologist* 41 (1986): 246-64.

Tannen, Deborah, ed. *Gender and Conversational Interaction.* New York: Oxford University Press, 1993.

Tavris, Carol and Carole Wade. *The Longest War: Sex Difference in Perspective.* 2d ed. Orlando: Harcourt Brace Jovanovich Publishers, 1984.

Taylor, Mark Kline. *Remembering Esperanza: A Cultural-Political Theology for North American Practice.* Maryknoll, N.Y.: Orbis, 1990.

Thompson, Becky W. *A Hunger So Wide and So Deep: American Women Speak Out on Eating Problems.* Minneapolis: University Press, 1994.

Thorne, Barry and Nancy Henley, eds. *Language and Sex: Difference and Dominance.* Boston: Rowley, 1975.

Thurmann, Howard. *Jesus and the Disinherited.* Nashville: Abingdon Press, 1949.

Townes, Emilie M., ed. *A Troubling in My Soul: Womanist Perspectives on Evil and Suffering.* Maryknoll, N.Y.: Orbis, 1993.

Trebilot, Joyce. *Mothering: Essays in Feminist Theory.* Totowa, N.J.: Rowman and Allanheld, 1983.

Trickett, Edison J., Roderick J. Watts, and Dina Briman. *Human Diversity: Perspectives on People in Context.* San Francisco: Jossey-Bass, 1994.

Tronto, Joan C. "Beyond Gender Difference to a Theory of Care." *Signs: Journal of Women in Culture and Society.* 12 (1987): 644-63.

Tyler, Anne. *Ladder of Years.* New York: Fawcett Columbine, 1995.

Walker, Alice. *In Search of Our Mother's Gardens: Womanist Prose.* New York: Harcourt, Brace, Jovanovich, 1983.

Walker, L. *The Battered Woman.* New York: Harper and Row, 1979.

Walsh, Mary Roth, ed. *Women, Men, and Gender: Ongoing Debates.* New Haven: Yale University Press, 1997.

Weaver, Rebecca. "A Subordinate Loyalty." *Affirmation: Union Theological Seminary in Virginia* 5, no. 1 (1982): 21-50.

Welch, Sharon. *A Feminist Ethic of Risk.* Philadelphia: Fortress Press, 1990.

Westkott, Marcia. *The Feminist Legacy of Karen Horney.* New Haven: Yale University Press, 1986.

Williams, Delores. *Sisters in the Wilderness: The Challenge of Womanist God-Talk.* Mary Knoll, N.Y.: Orbis Books, 1993.

Wimberly, Anne. *Soul Stories: African American Christian Education.* Nashville: Abingdon Press, 1994.

Winter, Miriam Theresa. *Defecting in Place: Women Claiming Responsibility for Their Own Spiritual Lives.* New York: Crossroad, 1994.

Wolf, Naomi. *Fire with Fire: The New Female Power and How It Will Change the 21st Century.* New York: Random House, 1993.

Wood, Julia T. *Gendered Lives: Communication, Gender and Culture.* Belmont, Calif.: Wadsworth Publishing Co., 1994.

_____. *Who Cares? Women, Care, and Culture.* Carbondale, Ill.: Southern Illinois University Press, 1994.

Woolf, Virginia. *The Death of the Mother and Other Essays.* New York: Harcourt, Brace and Jovanovich, 1942.

Wuthnow, Robert. *Sharing the Journey: Support Groups for America's New Quest for Community* (New York: Free Press, 1994).

Yee, Gale A. "By the Hand of a Woman: The Metaphor of the Woman Warrior in Judges 4." *Semeia* 61 (1993): 99-131.

Young, Iris. *Justice and the Politics of Difference.* Princeton University Press, 1990.

Index

humility, 42–44
humanworth, as related to, 44
humility based spirituality,
Benedictine, 42
Ladder of Humility, 42–44

identity, defined, 83–84
intuition, 69–70
counter intuitive thinking, 70

Jael, 218–19
Janssens, Louis, 95
Jephthah, 195–97
Jesus, 177–80
male Savior, 178–80
son of woman, 178
justice
communicative, 225–39
distributive, 239–45
and leadership 225–39

Kegan, Robert, 15
evolution of self, 58–60
feminist concerns, 57
separation, connection, and
differentiation, 58–61
Kierkegaard, Søren
feminine and masculine forms of
despair, 40–41
life in the basement, 41
and self-examination, 251 n. 35
and self-loss, 40
suffering, 49
three manifestations of despair, 39
women, 40–41
knowledge, separated and connected,
183–84

constructed, 184
Kohlberg, Lawrence
Gilligan's critique of, 89
justice reasoning, 89
kyriarchy, 171, 252 n. 64

leadership
and boundaries, 223–25
nurturing thinkers, 229–30
and passion, 225
and power-sharing, 221–22
understanding and empowering:
two aspects of leadership, 232–36
Leah, 15, 152–56, 265 n. 10

Mary, 177–78
methodology, 15
midrash, 26
Miller, Alice
on the false self, 100
narcissistic parenting, 100–101
motherhood
and family values, 118
generational conflict, 72–73
and *The Giving Tree*, 53–54
honoring mother's histroy, 85–86
mothers and daughters, 257 n. 36
mothers and sons, 53–54
teen mothers, 100, 254 n. 37, 256 n. 8

Native American females, 161–63, 247
n. 8, 266 n. 27
Niebuhr, Reinhold
critiques of: Plaskow, 34; Saiving,
34; Hampson, 36–37; Wolf,
50–51
justice, 81

Scripture Index